GREECE 1940-41
EYEWITNESSED

GREECE 1940-41 EYEWITNESSED

Costas N. Hadjipateras - Maria S. Fafalios
Introduction by Patrick Leigh Fermor

EFSTATHIADIS GROUP

The book is based on "MARTIRIES 1940-44" by the same authors, published by Kedros, Athens 1988.

Cover by SOFIA ZARAMBOUKA
Index and bibliography by KYRIAKOS DELOPOULOS

Efstathiadis Group S.A.
Agiou Athanasiou Street,
GR - 145 65 Anixi, Attikis

ISBN 960 226 533 7

Printed and bound in Greece by Efstathiadis Group S.A.

**To the Unknown Soldier who
lives among us forever**

BY THE SAME AUTHORS

Costas N. Hadjipateras:
CENDRES, 'A la Baconnière, Neuchâtel, 1944 (in French)
HÉROÏSMES ET DROITS DE LA GRÈCE,
Librairie Générale de Droit et de Jurisprudence,
Paris, 1946 (in French)
L' ÉVOLUTION DE L' ÉTALON MONÉTAIRE,
Librairie générale de droit et de jurisprudence, Paris, 1946 (in French)
LA GRÈCE ET LA MER, Aix en Provence, 1963 (in French)

Maria S. Fafalios:
FORTY OLD STORIES FROM CHIOS,
Athens, 1979, 2nd edition 1985 (in Greek)
TALES AND LEGENDS FROM CHIOS,
Athens, Akritas Publications, 1990 (in English) and 1994 (in Greek)
IERA ODOS 343 - TESTIMONIES FROM DROMOKAïTEION
HOSPITAL FOR MENTAL HEALTH

Joint publications:

TESTIMONIES 40-41, Athens, Kedros, 1982,
Academy of Athens Award, 3rd edition 1988 (in Greek)
TESTIMONIES 40-44. WAR - OCCUPATION,
Athens, Kedros, 1988 2nd edition 1993 (in Greek)
CRETE 1941 EYEWITNESSED,
Athens, Efstathiadis Group, 1989, 3rd edition 1993; and New Zealand,
Random Century, 1991 (in English)
DAYS OF CRETE 1941 - OPERATION MERCURY,
Athens, Efstathiadis Group, 1991 (in Greek)
TESTIMONIES - CRETE 1941, Athens, Kedros, 1993, (in Greek),
Under preparation:
TESTIMONIES FROM THE OCCUPATION 1941 - 1944
Hellenic Society of Christian Literature Award

CONTENTS

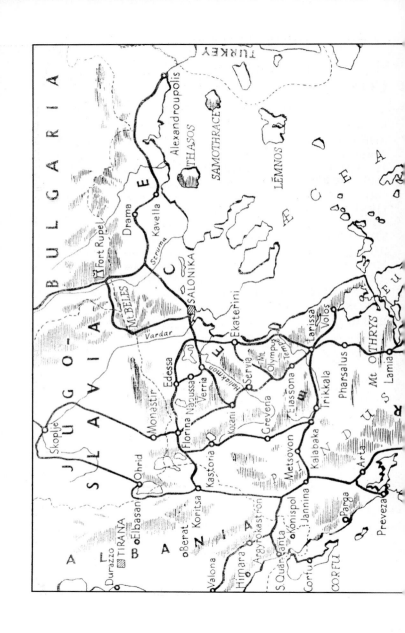

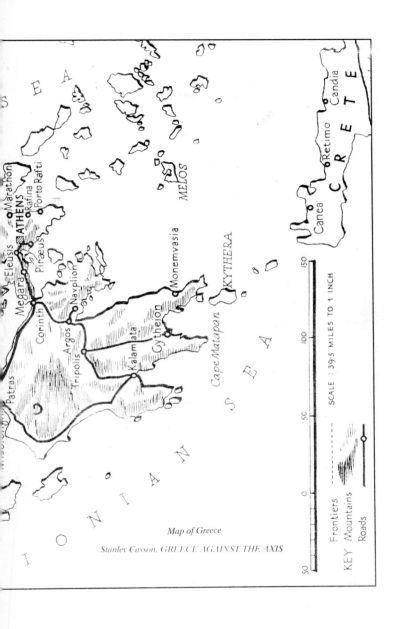

Map of Greece

Stanley Casson, GREECE AGAINST THE AXIS

SCALE : 39.5 MILES TO 1 INCH

KEY
Frontiers ----------
Mountains
Roads

INTRODUCTION

Nobody in the free world who had reached the years of discretion in time for the Second World War can ever forget the impact of the Italian invasion of Greece in 1940, and the Greek reaction to it. The previous year had been a long series of disasters, and after the fall of Belgium, Holland and France, and with the Baltic states torn in two, half of Scandinavia over-run, and with the Soviet Union an eerie and unnatural accomplice of triumphant Germany, most of Europe was now in willing or unwilling partnership with it, or subjugated or threatened, and the United States were still a year short of entering the war. The prospect was dark indeed. For many, perhaps most, in the uninvolved or neutral countries, German victory seemed a foregone conclusion.

Geography had saved England from the grim fate of her allies and this, coupled with the feeling that the fate of the Free World rested, for the time being, with the United Kingdom, had touched the inhabitants with a feeling of destiny, responsibility and hope which must have seemed illogical and surprising to much of the outside world, and a temptation to Nemesis. There had, of course, been some encouraging landmarks: The first of our famous retreats had been dialectically transposed into a "victory"; things seemed to be more or less in hand in the Western Desert, arms and aircraft were being turned out at speed, and soldiers trained; the country had reacted stoically to German bombs, the battle in the air had been won for the moment and the danger of invasion had - or so it seemed - been postponed or even overcome. But there was nothing else to cheer the heart except the words of Churchill and as the autumn days of 1940 shortened, the early dark seemed somehow symbolic of our embattled and precarious isolation.

Suddenly there were sinister portents in South Eastern Europe: in the Aegean, a Greek warship was sunk without warning by an anonymous submarine which was known to be Italian; this was followed by threatening movements in Fascist-occupied Albania on Greece's north-west frontier. There were ominous and growing hints that the pre-War Italian seizure of Abyssinia, the occupation of Albania and, finally, the petty annexations in S.E. France under the lee, as it were, of the German successes earlier in the year were about to be followed by an Italian onslaught on Greece; and, after a midnight ultimatum which the Greek leader Metaxas rejected without a second's hesitation, Italian troops - the columns of tanks which had been massing all through the preceding days - advanced into North West Greece. The result of this sudden confrontation of a heavily-armed Western power with a small and unarmed country, however famous and brave, seemed easy to predict. There would be a brief token resistance, the Italians thought, followed by an unopposed and triumphant descent on Athens.

What happened next seemed a miracle. It still seems one. Metaxas's rejection of the Italian ultimatum was unanimously echoed by the entire population of Greece, as though he had read their thoughts. Unity was complete and the whole country leapt into action with astonishing speed. Field Marshal Papagos, who had avoided precautionary troop movements to banish any semblance of provocation, rushed the dispersed units of the Greek Army to where the railways ended in the mountain ranges of Epirus and Western Macedonia. The invasion routes were blocked, mountain guns were dismembered, manhandled over precipitous cordilleras and reassembled where they could do most damage to the suddenly hesitant Italian armour; fierce bayonet charges routed the advance troops; when the transport-mules were not enough, ammunition and supplies were shouldered by thousands of village women up the winding mountain tracks in unending single file; and, within a matter of days, the invaders were halted and then, after bitter and unflagging counter-attacks, driven back in disorder and with heavy loss until, unbelievably, they were in full retreat over the violated frontiers with the Greeks pursuing them deep into Albania.

The Pindus, Kalpaki, Ivan-Morava, Koritza, Pogradets, Premeti, Ayioi Saranta, Argyrokastro, Cheimarra - these names which have become so famous - were a concatenation of victories which astonished the world. It became still more astonishing when the disparity of the odds was fully realized, and the fact that the advancing Greek soldiers now had not only the enemy to contend with but the cold, the wind, the rain and the snowstorms of a savage Balkan winter. An added stimulus for the Greeks was the fact that the mountain ranges through which they were advancing and the southern Albanian towns they captured belonged to Northern Epirus, Greece's *terra irridenta*. They were greeted by rejoicing inhabitants, and the bells of victory that pealed in Athens were celebrating a two-fold triumph.

Every step of the Greek advance was followed by the rest of the world, and nowhere more so than in the United Kingdom and the Commonwealth, soon to be engaged there themselves. The Blue and White Greek flag and the Union Jack were everywhere hoisted side by side, and a spirit wholly akin to that prevailing in London during the Battle of Britain took hold of the Greeks, a feeling that, though they were fighting and winning quite on their own, they were partners in carrying the destiny of the free world. These feelings were all the deeper for the exhilarating awareness that these battles were the first victories in Europe since the beginning of the War.

Nothing can convey the atmosphere and the mood of these extraordinary months more convincingly than "MARTIRIES 40-41". Costas Hadjipateras and Maria Fafalios have discovered a perfect formula for capturing history. They set about it by unearthing and collecting contemporary evidence - the letters of Greeks at home and in foreign countries, the accounts of observers from abroad, the headlines of newspapers, notes scribbled by soldiers on the sides of mountains sheltering from the wind, the poems which sprang up in sudden abundance, the newspaper caricatures, the satirical revues on the vaudeville stage, the songs which swept through Athens and soon along scores of snowy Albanian gorges and round a thousand campfires. These, and especially the thrillingly hair-raising songs of Sophia Vembo, seemed the very spirit of that northward and westward thrust through the Albanian crags.

Reading this brilliant selection, and the accompanying comments, nobody who had anything to do with these events, however remotely, can fail to recapture the drama and the exhilaration. In a minor way, I can join a testimony to theirs. I remember with great vividness the tonic excitement and stimulus that affected the allies of the Greeks at the other end of Europe. For someone like me who had walked all over Greece three years before and picked up an idea of her inhabitants, these events seemed a confirmation of every notion I had formed about them both; and when I got to Athens not much more than a month after the beginning of the counter-attack, I - indeed all of us on the British Military Mission - felt caught up in the astonishing mood of the capital and of the whole country. The air seemed to be alive with a kind of infectious controlled ecstasy. When I managed to get sent as a liaison officer to the Greek Third Army Corps, based on recently captured Koritza, I began to get a clear and devastating vision of the extreme toughness of the campaign and the merciless mountain theatre where it was being fought. Everything was deep in snow, the forward posts and the machine gun nests were open to every wind that blew and the wards and corridors of the field hospitals were packed with men wounded by every kind of weapon, but chiefly by trench mortars and frostbite. Travelling to and from Pogradets in the North, close to Serbia on the shores of Lake Ochrid, to Kleissoura and Argyrokastro and Tepeleni and Cheimarra in the west, hundreds of conversations in camps and billets built up a sort of insight into the vigour, the courage, the stoicism and the humour that had inspired and buoyed them up: the few army vehicles that pitched about the mud and the rocks, which were the only roads, were all labelled "TO ROME". All these soldiers were convinced that they would drive the whole Italian army into the Adriatic Sea. So they would have done if the Germans had not been compelled to come to their rescue...

This fine book, then, is a reminder and a chronicle with a special relevance for Greece's allies. It calls to mind and celebrates those perilous months when final victory and the survival of the free world hung in the balance, and Greece and Great Britain were their solitary guardians.

Patrick Leigh Fermor

AUTHORS' PREFACE

Among the many fiftieth anniversaries commemorated in recent years the Greek defiance of the Axis powers in 1940-41 has sadly been completely overlooked. Not a word was said about the six-month uneven struggle of the Greeks against Mussolini's crack divisions in Albania's rough mountains. Not a word was written about the valour and sacrifices of the Greek army and the entire Greek nation during the sombre 1940-41 period which was characterised by Winston Churchill as "their greatest hour." Not a single mention of that gallant stand of Homeric proportions against all odds and the harshest of winters. It fell to C.M. Woodhouse to remind us that "between the fall of France in 1940 and the invasion of Russia in 1941 it is false to say that we stood alone. We did not. Even if the already existing resistance movements are discounted, the cliché is still false; for on 28th October 1940 the Greeks voluntarily entered the war and became part of us. The Greeks won the first victories of the Allies anywhere on land, ahead of the British in North Africa."

It is a historical fact that there was a time when Greece, during the darkest phases of World War II, was an inspiration to all nations. That small country aroused everywhere the spirit of freedom and won the admiration of the whole world. A breath of hope suddenly blew into the heart of a Europe wrapped in a shroud of despair and fear. Without exaggeration Greece was then the centre of the world's attention; it stood on a pedestal. Marshal Jan Smuts did not hesitate to say that the Greeks, by their heroic resistance, "changed the flaw of the war."

15

When Churchill on 15th September 1940, the day that the valiant pilots of the RAF finally won the Battle of Britain, immortalised them by expressing the nation's gratitude to "the few", who could imagine that nearly a month after the RAF's victory the famous words of the British leader would have fitted the other "few", that handful of Greek soldiers who dared defy the mighty Axis by opposing Mussolini.

The aim of this book is to recall Greece's battle in World War II, a battle which lasted six full months to the day, i.e. from the 28th of October 1940 to the 27th of April 1941. The conflict is presented here almost exclusively through the eyes of the soldiers and civilians who lived and witnessed those stirring times; that is, oral and written testimonies of survivors, Greek, British, men of the Commonwealth, Italians and Germans, supported by diaries, letters, poems, photographs, sketches, also by authentic documents, mostly unpublished in English before. This book is the result of thorough research. It is not a work of military and political history. It is a human document shedding brilliant light on that forgotten epic which, in the opinion of most military commentators, contributed considerably to the fateful postponement of Hitler's attack on Russia, thus turning the tide of World War II in favour of the Allies.

We are aware of the fact that we have omitted many persons and events either unintentionally or because of lack of space, but this does not minimise the merits of their military and human contribution. The highest tribute should especially be paid to the British Expeditionary Force and the men of the British Empire who went to the assistance of Greece and fought with bravery and tenacity hand in hand with the Greek army to defend mainland Greece when Hitler's Wehrmacht invaded it. As for the thousands of British and Allied soldiers who were left behind after the Allies' evacuation, they were taken into hiding by the Greek people who became their everlasting friends. In the words of Michael Chapman these "were cared for and fed in towns, villages and mountains by ordinary brave civilians, themselves short of food and risking death if discovered." (The Times, 14. 1. 1994).

The method for the presentation of our material, obviously in an edited form, is the following. Verbal testimonies are reported as "oral accounts." Testimonies written exclusively for the book bear simply the signature of the writer. Next to the signature of the person testifying, his or her nationality is indicated. No titles of contributors are mentioned, except when necessary for identification purposes. As for the names and geographic places, we left the spelling as it appears on each individual testimony. We also use the term "contributed by" for any text, material or document reported to us. Extracts of already published books refer to their author and title.

We wish to express our grateful thanks to Patrick Leigh Fermor, that fervent philhellene, for honouring us with his introduction, a gem of its kind. Also our warmest thanks go to George Angeloglou for his painstaking translation assistance and his moving piece of writing.

In recording the spontaneous and often candid testimonies of the Battle of Greece, the book aims not only to keep alive the memory and high significance of the Greek prowess but also to stress the spirit of unity and ultimate quest for peace. Beyond the horror of the war, beyond even national pride, there is human compassion. The Italian soldier, when taken prisoner of war, ceases to be the enemy; he becomes a friend in need. The soldier, deep in his heart, longs for reconciliation. May these testimonies remind us not only of the laurels of victory, but also of the heavy penalty of freedom, of the high price of peace.

C.N.H.   M.S.F.

Acknowledgements

Together with all those who willingly and unobtrusively gave us permission to use material from their private collections, we would especially like to thank the following foundations which gave us permission to reproduce material from their archives and libraries and who brought us into contact with veterans of the 1940-41 period:

The Greek Parliament Library, Gennadius Library, The Army's Department of History, The Jewish Museum of Greece, The Department of Greek Archives for History and Literature (E.L.I.A.), The Greek Theatre Museum of Athens, The Alexander Turnbull Library New Zealand, Biblioteca dell'Archiginnasio Bologna, Bibliotek für Zeitgeschichte Stuttgart, British Museum Library London, Bund Deutscher Fallschirmjäger Munich, Bundesarchiv Militärarchiv Freiburg, 'Crete News' New Zealand newspaper, Crete Veteran Association of England and the United Kingdom, Hellenic Philatelic Society of Great Britain, Imperial War Museum London, The Trustees and Director of the B.B.C. Film Archives, Institut für Zeitgeschichte Munich, 'Legs Eleven Minor' Australian Newspaper, The Mitchell Library Australia, The National Archives Wellington New Zealand, New Zealand House London, The University of Copenhagen Department of Modern Greek and Balkan Studies, 'Reveille' Australian Newspaper.

It would be an oversight on our part to conclude without one more grateful acknowledgement. We would like to thank all those who were not acquainted with us or who are no longer with us, but who entrusted their memories, manuscripts, sketches, photographs and letters and made this book possible.

THE SACRILEGE:
SOMBRE PRESAGE OF WAR

15th August 1940. Torpedoing of the cruiser ELLI at Tinos, by an "unknown" submarine. And other enemy acts, a warning that the clouds are gathering. Any moment now, the Greeks are waiting for Italian attack.

Standing by for orders...

We were standing by for orders. On the eve of the Virgin's Assumption, August 15, we received orders from the leader of the fleet to set sail for the harbour of Tinos to attend the litany and doxology of the Virgin Mary of Tinos. Shortly after midnight we sailed out of the harbour of Adamantos in Milos on a course for open sea, at a slow speed in order to reach Tinos at dawn.

Oral account of N. Lalaounis, Petty Officer on the ELLI

The cruiser ELLI anchored at Tinos
15 August 1940

Sketch by Manuel E. Kulukundis

Rocks from above and fire too

As I was sitting in the Kafenion I heard a loud noise. I turned to see what it was. It was raining. Was it rain, thunder, what was it? I didn't see anything. Just then, at that moment, in front of the harbour's bay, I saw a volcano which had thrown a huge piece of rock two or three meters in the air. There were rocks from above and fire too.

Oral account of G. Vidalis, Tinos

Ο ΤΟΡΠΙΛΙΣΜΟΣ ΤΗΣ ΕΛΛΗΣ:

Torpedoing of the cruiser ELLI.
From a series of wartime posters

The lady didn't leave, she was crying

During those truly tragic moments we also tried, children   though we were, to do whatever we could. At one time a fire   broke out. It was exceedingly dangerous as we had supplies of ammunition. The loudspeaker gave directions that everyone was to leave the area because the ship might explode at any moment. The area was evacuated save for a woman who stood alone and people were telling her 'Madam leave, it can explode at any moment!'   The lady didn't leave, she was crying. She was my mother who had come to wish me a happy name day as my saint's feast day was being celebrated that day, and who replied, 'How can I leave now that my son is in there.'

Oral account of Marios G. Hors, midshipman on the ELLI

Of course I remember the DELFINO

In Leros we repaired the diesel engines of submarines. They would come there after their missions and we carried out lengthy mechanical repairs. I was an employee of Fiat at that time... Of course I remember the submarine DELFINO. There were four of the same type; the DELFINO, the KOALO, the NARVALO and I can't remember the fourth one. At that time, just before the Feast of the Assumption, a submarine had arrived from a mission, but which wasn't exactly a regular mission since all the other missions lasted for fifteen days and this one returned only after two or three days with a damaged hatch. We removed the engine's hatch to repair it. As a matter of fact we were all asking ourselves why it had returned from its mission only after two or three days. Why did it return so soon? We asked several sailors who told us:

'We are here in Grecia, in Greece on a mission'.

Of course we didn't know what mission they had. Later we found out that it had torpedoed the ELLI.

Oral account of an Italian mechanic from the dockyard of Leros

An Italian torpedo officer remembers

I was a torpedo officer aboard the submarine DELFINO. I was on duty in the torpedo chamber on the stern side... We fired three torpedoes. One was fired from the prow and two from the stern against the cruiser and two steamships. I don't know anything else. Afterwards we returned to our base. We thought that all three ships had sunk, but in fact only the cruiser had sunk... I couldn't say if the ship was English or Greek. We had put to sea as usual. Suddenly, the alarm sounded and a little later I heard 'fire'. We fired a small 450 kilo torpedo and a few moments later from the prow's side, from where I was, I fired two more torpedoes of 500 kilos each. They appeared to hit the quay side... The orders were the same as those we had received on many previous occasions. This is all I can tell you. Afterwards we heard the explosion. If the torpedoes had not struck their target we wouldn't have heard anything. At first I didn't understand why they ordered us to return to base. We had only been two or three days on this mission and our usual patrols lasted twenty days. Orders were given to return. Why? We were like the blind men who are guided by others. After our mission at Tinos we went to Leros.

Oral account of Antonio Geneloni. Extract from an ERT documentary on the torpedoing of the ELLI, October 1985

Letter to the Editor of TA NEA

Dear Director,

.... He who writes you these few lines, is an Italian citizen who was a member of the 11th regiment during the years 1940-1943. A soldier who lived year by year, month by month and day by day, the entire war period, a soldier who, even though he loves his country (the main duty of every citizen) and with no Fascist tendencies or boastfulness, knew how to distinguish the just from the unjust and to condemn from 28 October 1940 the unjust Fascist war against the brave Greek people who showed and taught not only us but the whole world how one should defend one's country. I was prompted to write this letter by an article which appeared in the Italian newspaper 'The Dawn of Central Italy'. The article stated among other things, the following:

"We all unanimously condemn the sinking of the Greek cruiser ELLI which was attacked by one of our own submarines even before our declaration of war on Greece. On that day the Greek ship was bound for the island of Tinos. A stately religious procession was passing through the streets of the small town. The commander of our submarine executed the orders of his superiors. Perhaps he carried them out against his will. In any case, this does not prevent the Italian sailors, who are honourable fighters, condemning this pirate act and to reach the conclusion that blind and total obedience does not always enhance the prestige and interests of a fleet."

Silvano Guerri
Athens, 27 October 1947

Declarations and Violations

London, 27 November.

On September 26th, namely a few months ago, the 'London Times' published a list of Hitler's guarantees, all of which have been violated for the sake of Blitzkrieg. But Mussolini has betrayed Hitler with false promises; and with the difference that instead of bringing about Blitzkrieg he brought about Blitzgreek... But Mussolini's worst violation occurred 5 or 6 months ago when Italy, without any reason, attacked France and Mussolini announced from the Palazzo Venezia on the 10th June 1940:

'I formally proclaim that Italy is not prepared to bring other countries into the battle, irrespective of whether these countries are Italy's neighbours by sea or by land. Let Switzerland, Southern Slavia, Egypt and Greece take note of these words of mine.'

I.P. Chryssanthopoulos
Atlantis, New York, 5.1.1941

«ΕΙΜΕΘΑ ΟΥΔΕΤΕΡΟΙ!»

ἐφώναξε ἡ μικρὴ Ἑλλάδα στὸν φασιστικὸ γίγαντα. «Ἀλλ'
αὐτὰ ἦσαν ἑλληνικὰ (δηλ. ἀκατανόητα) γιὰ τὸν Ντοῦτσε», σχολίαζε ὁ Ἄγγλος γελοιογράφος· "Ἰλληνγκγοικαρθ.

'WE ARE NEUTRAL' cries small Greece to the fascist giant. But it was all Greek to the Duce,
comments the English cartoonist.
Eikones, 29.10.1965

24

INVITATION
MUSSOLINI: Get off from the plank of the British Guarantee and
come under my protection
Cartoon by Kem (Kemon Marengo), Great Britain and the East,
29.8.1940

Nevertheless, four months later:

"The purpose of the conference is to clarify the details of the offensive I have decided to take, along general lines, against Greece. This action in its first phase must include naval and ground objectives. Our ground objective is to capture not only all the islands in the Ionian Sea including the islands of Zante, Cephalonia and Corfu, but also Salonica. As soon as we have fulfilled these objectives, we will have improved our position against the English in the Mediterranean. The second phase, which will be executed either subsequently or simultaneously with the first phase, is the conquest of all Greece, so that it may be placed out of the field of battle and to ensure that it will definitely remain within our own political and economic spheres.

Since I have established the issue as such, I have also decided upon a date which, in my opinion, cannot be delayed for even an hour: the

25

26th of this present month. This operation has matured in my mind over the past few months, indeed even before our involvement in the war and even before the declaration of the war."

Statement made by Mussolini, President of the Council of War on 15th October 1940

It is announced from Berlin

With the title 'Anti European Decision' the newspaper Berliner Börsenzeitung writes among other things the following, regarding the Italian-Greek crisis:

"By rejecting Italy's demand to take over several bases, as a gesture of Greece's neutrality, and with the reassurances that Italy would withdraw, the Greek government has taken a decision which goes against its Italian neighbour, against the New European order and in favour of the enemy of this new order which is England. This decision, despite the historical events of the last 14 months, goes against the new European order and indicates that Greece has clearly submitted to the politics of England...

Greece had to ally herself either in favour or against the emancipation of Europe from England, in other words either in favour or against the European solidarity. The decision by its present government is to ally Greece against the New Europe.

Deutsches Volksblatt, Zagreb, Yugoslavia, 1.11.1940

Hitler to Mussolini

"In 1940 and in January of 1941, I decided to put a bolt on the western entrance to the Mediterranean. With this object in view I met with the President of the Spanish government. If there had been an agreement then, my great plan for the Mediterranean would have been realised. I was dumbfounded when I was suddenly informed that Italy was to declare war on Greece. This was the reason for my sudden trip to Florence on 28 October 1940. The unfortunate initial outcome of Greece's entrance into the war encouraged the English to attack Libya with success. And then for the first time, General Franco appeared hesitant. Since then, all our endeavours to persuade Spain to enter the war as our ally have been proven fruitless."

A letter from Hitler to Mussolini dated 27 December 1944 which was found among Duce's personal papers at the time of his execution.

Come and take them
A poster by Kostas Grammatopoulos

THE FEW AGAINST THE MANY

28th October 1940. The Greek dictator, General Ioannis Metaxas, was awakened at dawn by the Italian Ambassador Emanuele Grazzi who handed him an ultimatum: Benito Mussolini demanded the right to occupy the Greek territory.

Expressing the will of the entire nation Metaxas flatly rejected Mussolini's demands. That day marked the "OXI-Day" (No-Day) that is the refusal of Greece to yield to the powerful Fascist empire. A handful of Greeks dared to defy the mighty Axis. And yet that was one of the bleakest phases of World War II. Hitler had launched his Blitzkrieg and conquered in less than two months Norway, Denmark, Holland, Belgium, France. England found herself isolated facing the imminent invasion of the British Isles.

Against all odds Greece stood up to the challenge. Monday, 28th October 1940 aroused the enthusiastic decision of a people to live up to its centuries old tradition, its legendary passion for freedom. The war was on. The first Greek war communiqué of the General Staff announced that the Italian troops had invaded Greece and that the Greeks were "defending their fatherland".

The first Greek war communiqué

28th October 1940.
As from 5.30 am today, the Italian armed forces are attacking our troops protecting the Greek-Albanian border. Our forces are defending our native territory.

The first Italian communiqué

"At dawn on the 28th October our forces stationed in Albania crossed over the Greek border and gained entrance at several places. Our advance continues."

Today at 6 am war was declared between Greece and Italy.
The Greek armed forces are defending their territories.
From the collection of John and Nora Tsatsas

"My children, we are at war"

28th October 1940. At the end of the summer which we had spent in Kifissia with my father as we usually did, we - my husband and I - had taken up residence in Athens where we stayed during the winter. At exactly 03.30, it was still night, my father Ioannis Metaxas telephoned and woke us up. 'My children, he said, we are at war. Come to Kifissia.' When we arrived at 04.30 at our house in Kifissia we found only my mother. Ioannis Metaxas was at the Hotel Grande Bretagne in Athens - which was the headquarters of the General Staff, and he had summoned the entire Cabinet to an emergency meeting.

At 8:00 am the first bomb fell on Patras. Meantime, my mother had given us an account of what had happened since dawn. At 3 am Italian Ambassador Grazzi arrived at Kifissia and speaking French to the guard, entered the house through the back gate, the same entrance that Metaxas always used. The guard, not knowing what to do, announced that the French Ambassador had arrived. Metaxas sat in his usual couch with the Ambassador seated to his right. My father had had just enough time to put on a dressing gown. "I have brought you my government's ultimatum" said Grazzi to the Prime Minister. Metaxas took the telegram and read it. He had expected this of course but not at 3 o'clock in the morning. Grazzi continued in French: "You will allow us to cross through Greece!"

"No" replied Metaxas,"I will not allow your forces to cross through Greece."

"In that case, we are at war" said Grazzi.

Grazzi was upset and embarrassed because not only had he known Metaxas for some time but he had in the past repeatedly pledged friendship and promises of no intervention.

With the onset of the war and at my father's orders, our whole family took up residence at a hotel in Kastri since there was a possibility that Metaxas' residence might be a target of an air attack. We stayed in Kastri for a month. I was married to a surgeon, Professor E. Phokas and we had two children. I was recruited by the Red Cross as a first aid ambulance nurse who helped transport the wounded to hospitals. It was a difficult task because we had to drive at night without any lights.

My husband, being a Professor, became a chief surgeon.

Nana Phoca-Metaxa

The First War Aid

When Metaxas turned down the ultimatum of the Italians, he ordered the Ministry of Defence to mobilise the armed forces. At approximately 3.15 am on the 27/28th October, the moment we were all expecting, the order came. We started the mobilisation of the staff immediately. My assistants departed for Syntagma and Omonia where they requisitioned fifty taxi vehicles. They were used to transport the officers to and from Perama and Skaramanga. They travelled back and forth with such speed that it seemed as if wings had been attached to their wheels. At 6 a.m. we had finished transporting and stationing the officers at their posts. I had also sent out five hundred notices with only my signature. At about 6.30 a.m. I went down to the Ministry's main entrance and told the drivers they could leave and return at mid-day to collect their fares since there were no cashiers in the Ministry at that hour. The drivers set off cheering 'Long Live Greece!' At 12.00 no-one came to collect their fares. It was the first contribution to the Greek war effort made by the taxi drivers of Athens.

Nicholas Zorbas
Proodos, 5.11.1983

Reliving October 28th

Monday 28th October 1940 - Sirens were heard at dawn this morning. What was all this about? My mother came into my bedroom to tell me that our neighbour Madame Fifi, who had the habit of loudly announcing from her window all relevant and irrelevant news for the benefit of the neighbourhood, informed us that the Italians had declared war on us because Metaxas had not bowed to Italy's ultimatum and had said 'No'. I didn't believe a word of this. When, however, I telephoned a friend of mine to tell her that I would call on her, she asked me whether I was still sleeping or simply teasing her. "Havn't you heard the news!" she said with great emotion. "We are at war!" I didn't have time to reply. Far off cannon shots and the thunder of explosions confirmed the morning sirens and the tragic reality. War and slaughter had now begun for us. May God protect us.

I got dressed and set out for the centre of Athens. I was very impatient to live through this unknown adventure which was just beginning. On the trams and buses people were clinging from the doors and windows and many had climbed onto the roofs of the trams. Outside the army barracks in Kifissia Avenue the traffic became very heavy. The first air raid siren was heard at 10 in the morning. The streets were filled with people, who were undecided whether to go down the shelters or to take other cover. All were looking up at the sky hoping to see the enemy aircraft. Indifference and impudent valour. We were waiting for them to bomb us and we wanted to see them do it. I heard a little boy ask, "When we've defeated the Italians, what shall we do with Mussolini?"

From the diary of Maria Markoyianni

A lesson of unity

...The first great lesson taught on the anniversary of 1940 was the lesson of National Unity.

Within each society there are ideological, political, social and personal differences. But at a time when the nation is in danger, these differences, irrespective of their actual importance and significance, should not take precedence over the need to maintain the unity and freedom of the nation. At all times in the past, when the Greeks did not adhere to this principle, at all times when for personal or political interests and differences they did not comply with this commandment, they have paid a heavy price. The source of our triumph in the war of 1940 was our spiritual unity. ... It wasn't only a question of survival, but a question of honour to defend the mountains of Epirus. By their heroic resistance, the Greeks set an example. They offered invaluable

33

aid to the forces which fought for freedom and confirmed their great tradition, the tradition of the Greeks.

Vassilis Laourdas, Efthini, October 1973

Political Prisoners of the Greek-Italian War

Memorandum sent to I. Metaxas

...We the communists, putting aside the past, assume our positions in the front line under your command so that we may crush the Fascist advance and defend our country's integrity and independence. We are also prepared to confirm in person our position to you and ask you kindly to set a date so that we may meet for this purpose.

> Akronafplia 29 October 1940
> sent with our deepest respect
> and honour
> Ioannis Ioannidis
> Constantinos Theos

Antonis I. Flountzis
Arkronafplia and Akronafplians

A doctor's contribution

(Declaration)

"I belong to the non-conscripted age group of senior citizens and I desire with all my remaining strength to offer something for the cause of our country. I therefore offer my medical services free of charge at my clinic, or in their homes, to all impoverished families of all those who are serving their country and who reside in the entire area of Psychiko, i.e. the districts of Psychiko, of Euterpe and of Diavolorema and Ellinorosson.

Aimilios D. Kanoutas, Nea Ellas, 26.11.1940

The contribution of a pupil

The following letter was sent to the President of the Government: "This golden sovereign was placed as a gift in my crib when I was born and my father kept it safe so that he could give it to me when I grew up. But now that we are at war I send it to you so that you can make a bomb which will be dropped on Italy. I kiss your hand in reverence."

Mihalis D. Papayiannis, Primary School pupil, Form 3
Proïa, 9.11.1940

He offers his field

The following telegram was sent to the President of the Government:

"Not having any money to give to the war effort of our country, I give instead my field which is located at Variko, in the village of Liopessi Epirou and which is 5.5 acres. I humbly ask you to accept this, my only possible contribution.

Ahmet Tsapounis, Proïa, 10.11.1940

The women of Cyprus in the War

A main news article published in the 'Chronos' newspaper, Limassol, 14 November 1940

Gold is the only thing which will be able to maintain the stability of our currency until the end of the war. Women of Cyprus! Greece asks nothing of you. She asks only for the gold which you wear round your necks, on the fingers of your hands and on your heads as decorative objects and jewellery. Consecrate the sacred struggle of Greece for her honour by offering all the gold which you own and is a needless and useless decoration.

There were hundreds of such pleas from the Cypriot people. Patriotic words delivered from the pulpits of the churches. Meetings in the squares, stadiums, schools and cinema theatres.   Men, under age and of age, ready to go to Greece as volunteers.   But since the English did not allow voluntary enlistment to the Albanian front,   the newspaper continued its main articles directed to the women.   "Give that which you can give, since you   cannot give your husbands, your brothers, your children."   But the 'Chronos' was quickly disclaimed. With England's plea:

"Enlist at the Cypriot Regiment, fight for Greece!"   Cyprus gave not only money, gold, pledges and jewellery but also   husbands, brothers and children.   Even women! Without their jewellery!

In the first 7 weeks, 65,565 gold pounds and 14,112 gold pieces   were collected together with other valuables, despite the   economic plight of the people.   37,000 Cypriots put on the khaki uniform, of whom 6,000 served in Greece.

Kimon Haralambidis, Cyprus

The War of 1940 and Cyprus

During the first year of the war, in 1939, despite appeals by the British, very few Cypriots enlisted in the army and those that did was out of economic necessity.   Despite the lenient conditions, which had been put into effect to ease the complete standstill brought about by the war, the Cypriots did not believe in the declarations for freedom, since they themselves were not free.   Many supported Hitler because they believed that only a German victory could bring about the freedom of the island, as promised by German propaganda broadcast over the radio.   The prophet of Limassol, Karvounaris Mavroyangos, whose prophecy of a German victory in the First World War was never fulfilled, began preaching openly that his true prophecy was this war.   In the schools we were divided into different groups supporting different sides and we would argue heatedly in the yard during recess.   The school windows and the windows of all government buildings had been sealed with thousands of taped sheets to protect us from shattering glass in the event of a bombing.   There were blackouts at night in the city and in the houses which were accompanied by a mute impatience and anticipation of the unknown outcome of the war which was raging violently at the borders, at sea and in the sky.

As soon as Greece entered the war on the 28th October 1940, this dull indifference immediately disappeared. The walls which had divided us from the English crumbled. The desire for freedom became synonymous with the victory of the Allies. The supreme desire was for the defeat of the armies which had entered onto Greek soil and which would then be followed by 'the prize of victory' which was 'freedom' as proclaimed by Churchill. And then the mass of voluntary enlistments began. Collections were made in support of the Greek struggle. Thousands of volunteers. Everyone and everything in the struggle against Fascism, in the struggle for freedom and democracy as the Cypriots believed. And they gave everything, believing in those pronouncements which were never fulfilled for our small country.

Kimon Haralambidis
Embros, London, 31.10.1981

.

An unrestrained, irrational enthusiasm

We had not yet fully understood what an air raid meant. It took the bombing of Patras which resulted in fifty deaths and numerous injuries to make us understand that looking up into the sky to see the aircraft, even if they were those of the 'spaghetti eaters' was not a game nor a means of entertainment.

That morning at the school of Rythmics which belonged to Koula Pratsika, the girls met and sat together talking and trying to think of how they could help. Some of them had spent the previous night at a party. As a number of them had stayed up late, some of them had difficulty in waking up when the siren went off and frightened, they had run to the school. There, they all asked to be accepted as volunteer nurses for the Red Cross. They also organised several choir groups and then escorted the young recruits to the Larissa railway station. Later on this same group met the wounded soldiers who came from the front and went to the hospital to comfort and entertain them. From the very first day, students gathered at the Polytechnic and in the midst of their patriotic enthusiasm, those who had not already enlisted asked their

37

professors to allow them to volunteer. And with makeshift signs and banners which they had quickly put together, they started a procession down Panepistimiou Street. People gathered on street corners reading the general conscription notices which had been pasted on the walls. An unrestrained, irrational enthusiasm has taken hold of every man, woman and child. It's so contagious that even the serious minded and disciplined people are not immune. Some search for English flags, while others want to buy a picture of Churchill and the King. At regular intervals the streets are filled with the din of the regiments which march past, some wearing the khaki uniform while others still wear their civilian clothes. Their singing is met with applause from the people in the streets. Some of the male bystanders, in their enthusiasm, rush in and lift soldiers on to their shoulders shouting: "Death to the spaghetti eaters, who sank our ELLI!"

But if the streets were filled with overjoyed and enthusiastic people, behind some closed windows weeping mothers holding their children tightly in their arms, tried to remember the last minute advice of their departing husbands:

"Watch over the children, go to the shelters when the alert is sounded and if you don't hear from me, don't worry. I may be aboard a ship or I might be stationed in a village which is far from a post office."

At the railway stations there was indescribable confusion - wives, mothers, daughters, sisters, fiancées, all had come to see their men off. Eyes filled with tears, white handkerchiefs waving in the air and a thousand voices shouting all at once "Godspeed and Victorious!" The schools in Athens closed temporarily and the students, overjoyed that they would not have to attend lessons, pasted posters on walls. They helped their mothers during the blackouts. They taped the windows in the event of a bomb attack, with dark blue paper for the blackouts. Stationers did a roaring trade and there wasn't even one sheet of paper left in the shops, not even as a sample. Blankets, rugs, kilims and dark clothing, even these were recruited for the blackouts.

The china shops as well as the shops which sold kitchen items were

In the air-raid shelter 1940-1941
A sketch by Thalia Flora-Karavia

busy. Housewives bought any type of pitchers they could lay their hands on - glass, clay, ceramic, wooden - so that they could store water in the event of a breakdown of the water supplies through bombing.

The food shops could not serve the number of customers they had and they were always short of stock. Alas, the Greeks did not know of the hunger that awaited them and how insufficient was the food they were then buying! Electric torches also disappeared from the shops. No-one can possibly imagine what those first few nights of the war were like, when the darkness of war enveloped the city and made it vanish. The enormous squares of the houses became imperceptible shapes, the streets became long dark strips. People groped their way along the walls moving quietly and cautiously and they couldn't find the trolley or bus stop. They couldn't even find the door of their home. Hushed whispers trumpeted through the endless silence and a cough echoed across the vast void of the black night. The only bright points, and comfort and hope in the dark night which descended upon Greece, were the moon and the stars which could be seen on a clear night.

From the diary of Maria Markoyianni

Memories of a young boy

I was a young pupil then, but at an age when one remembers every-thing, I also shared in that joy, for it passed in my memories as a joy. Happiness, outpouring of emotions, a sense of enjoyment and humour without one bad moment. Joy when we heard the peeling of the church bells announcing yet another victory, an outburst of emotions when we raised our flags on the flag poles, and a sense of excitement when the sirens were heard and we ran to the shelters where we would talk with a whole group of unknown brothers - for we were all brothers and sisters then - conversations which were spattered with tasteful jokes about the Italians, who flew over our heads threatening us (ridiculous really) with bombs which we thought were certainly made out of tin cans. Games followed the all clear, screeched by the sirens.

The collection of bomb fragments which were scattered in the streets and in the fields were our pride and joy. And what a celebration we had if we came across the shattered remnants of an Italian airplane. Those were days that can never be matched again! And the news reports which we would listen to as we gathered around the radio with our heads bent, and those songs of Vembo and the speeches delivered by Metaxas urging us not to leave a single inch of land uncultivated, those speeches which had transformed us into farmers and our little gardens into tiny farmlands filled with spinach and aubergines and with chickens and rabbits.

What sunny days we had during that autumn in Thessaloniki! The women in the neighbourhood, seated on their front doorsteps or in their porches, knitting woollen garments for the army which shivered in the snows of Albania, talking quietly with one another, their former differences forgotten. And we the children and the old men - for the rest were at the front - would browse through the newspaper, reading

the main titles and laughing at the cartoons and throwing away those historical leaflets unaware of the greatness of the moments which they described.
Alexander Kalomiros

The Country's War Preparation

In October 1940, all Greeks - the King, the Cabinet, the army and the ordinary people came together without hesitation or differences, against Fascist Italy, determined to fight and to make whatever sacrifices were needed to maintain our freedom and above all our honour and dignity as a people, as a State and as a Nation.

... There were some who were reluctant and hesitant until the eve of the war. But how could there not be some reluctance and hesitation when all of Europe had either been conquered or had surrendered to Germany. France had been defeated, England was the only country in the battle and she could not help us. Hungary and Rumania had surrendered to the Germans, Turkey - despite the pressure of England -

"For the soldiers"
A poster by Vasso Katraki

41

would not promise anything to us, Yugoslavia withdrew (she deserted us, having received a promise that Thessaloniki would be her prize) and Bulgaria was preparing to attack at the same time as Italy would. In these circumstances were those who hesitated inexcusable, especially in view of the fact that Italy's military weakness had not yet been revealed? And were all those who were hesitant traitors and defeatists? Metaxas himself, unwavering in his decision, indicated in all his diary entries his anxiety and fears.

...But by August 1940 there was no reluctance and disagreement among the members of the Cabinet, as indicated by the phrase "Now everyone is with me" which was written by Metaxas himself in his diary entry dated 17th August 1940. From 1936 onwards the government had

'You who have remained behind, protect my family by buying the War Lottery'
A period poster designed by Pericles Byzantios
Contributed by Tassos Nollas

begun the military preparations of the country. The problems were great and the shortages immense and the necessary expenditures astronomical. Due to the problems which the European manufacturers faced in view of the impending outbreak of the Second World War, they could not satisfy our orders for anti-aircraft and anti-tank missiles, machine gun ammunition, tanks and above all aircraft. France and England put a hold on all Greek military orders. The army secured approximately 400,000 men fully supplied and equipped with what equipment was available at the time. An outstanding effort was also made in the area of military training, focusing on the training of both soldiers and officers. If our country's war preparations were inadequate, how was it that we were able to defeat the Italians?

General conscription and the establishment of the military was achieved in a matter of 16 days (28 October to 13 November 1940) despite air attacks carried out by the enemy. 309,000 men, 776 guns and 125,000 animals were mobilised. In addition, reinforcements, supplies, transport and hospital units, centres of departure, post office routes, heavy vehicle transport and maintenance of transport were also organised. During this same period the transport of food, ammunition, medical supplies and maintenance supplies were also organised. Efforts were also made to improve the roads according to the finances available at the time. It was during this five year period, from 1936 to 1940, that the road from Metsovo to Ioannina was constructed which connected Thessaly with Epirus. This road was used for the bulk of the military transport during the war and was later called "The road to Victory".

Athanasios Laspias, THE HISTORY OF THE GREEK NATION

Yiannis Papaioannou, one of the great bouzouki composers/players as a soldier, together with the musical instrument maker Joseph (left) 1940
Gennadius Library/the archives of Elias Petropoulos

"Conscription" Sketch by Spyros Vassiliou, Athens

We are impatient to reach the front

We are six children: George, Andreas, Yiannis, Manolis, Eugenios and Roxani. When war was declared we were the first four to be conscripted. According to the law, the first two brothers were relieved from serving at the front. We did not make use of this privilege. The first brother enlisted as a volunteer. He volunteered for the front line in Albania. The fourth brother was already doing his military service at the Bulgarian border and when war broke out all four of us were in the front line.

The fifth brother was under age. He was only 17 years old. On the 25th August I was called for further training. At the outbreak of the war, I was serving with the 44th Infantry Regiment at Rethimnon. Within a few days the regiment had left Souda in a convoy... We left Athens by train and disembarked at Amindaio. From there, in the midst of a terrible winter and difficult circumstances, we began the march to the front. We marched day and night with the exception of clear days when there was the danger of an air attack. We made several stops to rest and eat. The last stop on Greek soil was at Kolokinthou, after 31 hours of marching in terrible weather conditions. The roads were dirt tracks. In fact they were small lanes used by carts or simple footpaths which had been trodden by the horses. The surface was covered with snow and ice, and the soil had become muddy swamps. Everywhere you slipped. I remember we abandoned an exhausted horse which had sunk into the mud up to its belly and we could not get it out. The same happened to several soldiers, mostly mule drivers, but we could not abandon them.

Exhausted by the 31 hour forced marches in abominable weather and loaded down with heavy guns and ammunition, and with mules which carried weights beyond their natural limits, we eventually arrived at night in the first Albanian village of Kapetista or Kapetits. We entered the first house we came to, so that we could lay down our heavy burden and rest. We were completely overcome with exhaustion and hunger. The next day we sought out our units and regrouped. I will never forget the patriotic and enthusiastic speech delivered by Captain Halkiadakis to the troops. He said that it was the third time that he fought on these northern mountains and continued: "Men, we fought and won one of the most difficult battles which has ever been fought because our fight against nature was even greater than the battle against the enemy. I feel that with soldiers like you, we shall defeat any enemy."

We continued our march, with absolutely no means of transportation and communication and hampered by horrible weather conditions and with insufficient supplies. On many occasions we went hungry, but we were determined to reach the front. Unending marches and sleeplessness. I marched along holding the tail of a horse. I slept and dreamt. I woke up when I tripped or lost my footing and then once again I would fall asleep while stumbling along. My ears rang with the echoes of the Captain's speech about the battle against the elements and from this I drew strength and courage.

Andreas Z. Manouras

Evangelos Yiannaris. The first dead officer

30th October 1940. The dawn of the third day of war. The morning mist still hangs heavy. I can barely make out the silhouettes of the Hensel aircraft which belong to the 2nd Independent Flight. At the end of the auxiliary airport of "Lembet" which is situated above Salonica, I can just make out tents and the few wooden barracks which outline an enormous tableau with the village of Oraiokastro in the background.

...Pilot officer Yiannaris is notified that the Commanding Officer wants to see him. He and Warrant Officer Leonidas Tzantas appear together. The C.O. announces that their flight unit has been assigned a very interesting mission; to help the army unit of Western Macedonia. Three aircraft will take off with the purpose of identifying enemy units as far as the area of "Tren". The three aircraft which will carry out this mission will take part in bombing enemy targets in the area of Vourbiani, Pirsoyianni and Avgerinos. They will also support units of the 51st Regiment of Davakis which is stationed in the areas of Giftissa, Kato Arena and Tambouri.

...A little later our pilots board their aircraft and, together with their other colleagues, they take off for their targets. But everything around Pindos is covered in thick dark clouds. They fly through the clouds trying to find a way out, fighting against the elements of nature. Nothing frightens them. They must carry out their mission at all costs. At one moment, the crews of the aircraft lose all contact and break up their formation. Thus the Hensel 126 of Yiannaris and Tzantas is by itself. They have almost finished their mission. Engine trouble develops and ammunition is exhausted, so they set course for base.

Suddenly on the horizon, small dots appear. Five enemy Fiat 42 aircraft fly towards them. Tzantas begins to climb in order to avoid them. For the moment he has escaped. However, two of the five enemy aircraft pursue him. They are quicker, more manoeuvrable and better armed. They attack from the right. Then they are joined by three more which attack from the left. They machine gun incessantly, but the Greek aircraft manages to fly into the clouds where the enemy loses it.

The 24 year old Evangelos Yiannaris, however, has been killed by enemy bullets. He was the first Greek Officer to die in the great air battles of 1940.

Nikos Dendrinos

From an Athens Radio Documentary. Programme broadcast on 20.10.76

GREECE FIGHTS BACK

Despite the enormous superiority of the Italian armed forces the Greek army not only resisted the invaders fiercely but by a full-scale counter-attack on November 14th forced the Italians to a massive retreat into Albania. The redoubtable 3rd Alpine division, Mussolini's object of pride, fully equipped and skilled in mountain warfare, was compelled to retreat in panic to avoid being encircled. Some fell in the ravines, others were dispersed in the woods, others taken prisoner.

In the mountain of Pindos women of the neighbouring villages run to the assistance of the soldiers by transporting arms, food supplies and equipment on their backs. The fight is hard, yet the advance is vigorous. The Greek army, in a body, breaks the backbone of the entire Italian front and embarks on the road to victory. Their war cry is: AERA.

General Katsimitros writes

General Katsimitros writes
Eighth Division
The General   30th October 1940

My dear Eleni,

Do not worry, things are well. My plans are being put into effect as I had anticipated. Should you hear otherwise, do not take any notice since they will only be rumours. We are holding our position well and very soon we will deal with them appropriately. The performance of our artillery has been outstanding and numerous military vehicles have been destroyed and the greater part of the enemy's artillery power has been neutralised. I kiss you, Haralambos.

From a handwritten letter of General Haralambos Katsimitros sent to his wife
Epirotiki Eteria magazine, November 1981

The lance and the hand grenade only have the right of speech

On the second day of the counter attack (November 2), the commander of the unit, Colonel Davakis, preparing for an attack on the mountain of Tambouri, came under enemy fire on the mountain of the Prophet Ilias-Fourkas. He quickly climbed up to the summit so that he could identify the enemy unit. There he was wounded by a shot through the lungs fired by a trained marksman at a range of 500 meters and was taken to the summit's surgery.

Command was assumed immediately by the major in command of the army military league. Realising that the enemy was planning an attack with a force of about 2000 men in order to re-take the summit of the Prophet Ilias-Tambouri, I immediately decided to launch an attack along the same lines with a force of 600 men against the enemy's 2000. I withdrew to an altitude which was out of firing range, I spoke to the officers and men stressing the fact that should the enemy capture the hill then he would continue unhindered all the way to Metsovo. I allowed the advancing troops to reach an altitude of 200 metres, which was the safety zone, and then launched the counter attack. Our men began fighting body to body. Only the bayonettes and hand grenades had a say now and the fighting was vicious on the summit. Despite the overwhelming odds, the Alpinis began to retreat towards the valley of Sarantaporo and Albania. They abandoned many of their dead and wounded, together with large amounts of ammunition and 150 transport vehicles, on the field of battle.

On 3rd November, I again launched an attack with all my available forces on Tambouri which was captured and its defences were re-established. In this way, the communications of the enemy north of Smolika were cut, the rear and sides of the Julia division were threatened, and reinforcements from Albania were unable to reach the cut off Italian forces. The cleaning up of Pindos lasted approximately twelve days. It must be noted that in the battle of Pindos the finest Italian army units were defeated and our victory brought about a complete change of the Italian plans. It also secured the left flank of the Epirus Division and above all, it bought time for conscription and for strategic planners to meet and plan the strategy of the Greek Armed

Forces to realise further their already developed defensive strategy.

Ioannis Th. Karavias

From his speech delivered to the students of the Military Academy, 27.10.83

A letter to a warrior

Beloved,

... "T.T.41... somewhere on the peaks of Pindos...

Your rounded, well loved letters, are like lips that speak with tenderness ...

I am no longer a woman who waits, and trembles at the thought of reading in fine print among the triumphant 'communiqués' that for her the war and victory are over. With your courageous spirit you have stirred in me the Dorian blood of my ancient Cretan grandmother and the knitting needle has slipped from my fiery fingertips and I have felt the veil of the Sister of Mercy suffocate me....

Soldiers from the villages of the area Pogoniou
(county of Ioannina) near the border of Albania

This I write to you, my dearest.

Fight with two hearts for me without worry, because today I have enlisted with you and rush along with you in the paths of history.....

Sophia Mavroidi-Papadaki

ANTHOLOGY OF LITERARY EXTRACTS, 1940-1941

Private Ioannis Kavadas

The woman of Pindos

I will simply say that I saw her, when I found myself near her in one area of Pindos, at Zagori, where the initial battle and victory of Pindos took place from October 28th to November 10th. I will try to draw the woman of Pindos as my eyes saw her, as I came to know her with my own soul, so that I may give you a picture of what happened in the other areas of Pindos as well.

In November of 1940 I had to go to Zagori to see my parents. My mother was ill and I left my two children with a woman in Koritiani, at Katsanohoria. I began my journey by car as far as Dovra. There I learnt that all transport had been suspended. The Italians had arrived in Vrissohori and it would be dangerous for me to continue my journey nor were there any means of transport for me to continue. I saw that everyone was upset and in great confusion. But I could see no women.

"Where are the women?" I asked.

"The women", Warrant Officer Simetzis said, "are carrying the cannons and ammunition up to Grambala, while other women, on the other side, are carrying their loads up to Gamila."

"How is this possible?" I asked. I was amazed. "How can women carrying such loads possibly climb up those wild mountains? Only wild goats can climb up there! I've never heard of such a thing!"

"We tie thick ropes around their waists" said Simetzis, "and policemen standing on higher levels pull them up.... And these women, heavily loaded as they are, climb up like goats, now clinging to a rock, now grasping at stray roots, buckling under the weight of their load and always in danger of falling into the precipice which opens below them. They climb up and down continuously" he added, "and often throw rocks at the enemy below who have advanced as far as the huts of Tservatiotika....."

I listen to him with bated breath... My mind wanders in its attempt to conjure up this image! Perhaps I am dreaming, perhaps I didn't hear properly.....

In my mind I can hear a verse of a song:

> "Look at the Epirot women
> In the mountains of Pindos
> With stones and rocks they fight
> To keep their men and retain their freedom."

After a while I beg to be given an army horse and I set off. I enter Tsepelovo at night. Here too there is great confusion. Everyone carries a load in the middle of the night, ready to begin their route to the look-out posts. They see me and gather round. I ask them what is happening. They themselves are not too sure of what is happening either. Only that the Italians are very close and they are setting off in this direction so that they may break through the blockades and reach Zagori. They ask me questions anxiously and I tell them what I know. We go home... neighbours, friends and acquaintances... crying, as I cry and remember. I take off my wet clothes. They set the table. There is plenty of meat. They are slaughtering the animals (their only possessions) because they have nothing to feed them. All their annual yield of hay has been given to the army. I ask for a little bread. There isn't a crumb to be found... They collected all the bread and sent it with the women to the look-out posts.

Julia Zissi tells me that for days she and her daughters have not eaten so much as a crumb of bread, only hazel nuts, walnuts and potatoes... Nor will Julia ever eat bread again. Whatever flour she has left, she will bake into loaves and she and her daughters will carry the loaves up to Vrissohori......

Many of the villagers know that there are paths which are unprotected but dangerous. Many bridges are unfortified. Only yesterday Laiotis Bridge, which was a main avenue for the Italians, was finally burnt down. It was wet, drenched right through and would not burn... until a villager from Laiotis, the builder Charalambos Tsamis, took nine tins of petrol which had been smuggled by the women, and using their shirts as tinder, he burnt the bridge down one hour after midnight. And when, in the morning, the Italians arrived ready to cross over and saw the burnt bridge, they retreated in fear. Running to their commander they told him that the Greeks lie waiting in the forest and set fire to bridges and fields all around them....

Suddenly they hear the church bells peal. The doctor, the teacher, the priest and the officer explain to them that from a useless telephone - the other telephones had been taken - which had been assembled by the young telegraphist Giamalis (he was awarded a medal later) they had heard only moments ago the voice of the "giant" who was besieged at Vrissohori and who was desperately trying to get through to Yiannina shouting to Gigopoulos:

"For heaven's sake quickly send us food, clothing and ammunition!
The men are freezing, they are starving and they cannot hold out much longer!"

But Yiannina cannot hear because the lines have been cut... But even if they could hear, how could they reach them in time since the roads have been destroyed and cars can no longer travel on them. Let's therefore go as quickly as possible....

The village fills with smoke as if it had been set on fire. Ovens, fireplaces, stoves, small fires are all lit at once .... Even before the break of dawn women and young girls, boys, old men and women and their donkeys all carrying food, blankets, rugs and two shirts each, set off escorted by Captain Siaperas and his men. They pass Skamneli where they tell the villagers the news. They too rise up and ring the church bells in the same way. The women from here also gather together and with whatever food they can manage to collect they set off once more....

As they approach Vrissohori, they see more women from other villages working in great excitement. Some are cleaning the roads, shovelling the snow, carrying jugs of water, preparing supplies, boiling milk so that "the boys" may drink it hot, kneading bread and baking it, tending the wounded, washing and darning clothes and whatever other task needs to be done...! I watch all this, my eyes filled with tears. I make notes hanging on to every word they say. I want to stay longer but I have to leave in the morning.

I tend to my children and then return to Zagori. The roads have almost been opened by the women as far as Kapesovo, the end of the major road. Heavily burdened they reach the end of the road where they excitedly unload their supplies...! But from here, how will the accumulated supplies be taken? From where? From the footpath of Tsepelovo where mules slip and fall to their deaths?

Leaving, we cross through large pine and oak forests, an 8 to 9 hour march. There is mud everywhere and every now and then there is snow. We see groups of wounded soldiers dragging their feet through the mud, some heavily wounded tied onto the backs of mules which are being pulled by women or soldiers. There we hear about a woman from Western Zagori, the strongly built Garoufalia.

She saw a wounded man who was tied to the back of a mule but who was in such pain that he groaned as the animal was pulled along.

"Don't pull the animal like that, boys", she yelled out.

"The jolts of the animal only causes him more pain. Untie him and I will carry him myself. I too have a son at the front and I know what it means to be a mother...!"

And she takes off her heavy clothes, throws off her stockings and shoes and tenderly takes him onto her shoulders and carries him across the wide river... And other women carried many wounded soldiers as we later heard...!

What can one first remember? The incidents which record the heroism and patriotism of the people are legion .... I see again the old woman Argyri passing by, bent under the weight of her load, running to keep up with the others and her loaded donkey. For fifteen days she didn't stop to take a breath. "I go with ammunition and return with the wounded", she tells me. "I've not set foot in my house. I eat on the run whatever dry food I can lay my hands on and then I set off once again." "Rest a little!" I tell her. "Leave that heavy load and have a cup of coffee."

"You must be joking my young woman!" she tells me. "There is no time to rest. Tell me to run as long as I have any strength but don't tell me to put my load down and rest. I will continue to run and run until the evil which has besieged our country is gone and we have been liberated once and for all".....

Returning to Yiannina I showed my notes to the General Director who insisted on keeping them even though they were in rough drafts and disorganised. That same night he read them to the Prime Minister over the telephone who was left speechless. The next morning the Prime Minister read them to the heir of the throne and to Papagos whose eyes filled with tears. Two days later Pavlos Palaiologos, the columnist for the Eleftheron Vima, asked me for the official essays which were read by Papagos.

"Official essays..." I replied laughing, "they were only rough drafts which were written wherever I could put pen to paper."

"It doesn't matter," he said. And he reproduced the same small pieces of paper, printing them in the editorial column of 15th December 1940 and which, for the first time, informed the Greek people of the amazing events which were taking place in the mountains of Pindos.

From the notes of Frosso Ioannidou

Wood engraving by Tassos

Patriotic demonstrations by the Greek Jews

My beloved brother Benjamin,

I can imagine your surprised expression to see that I am writing to you from Lehonia. I arrived ten days ago as a refugee. We would not have left Volos despite the sirens and the bombings since our house had a shelter, but the Naval Committee wanted to use the house and they told us to hand it over to them by 5 p.m.

Wood engraving by Tassos

I was not upset by the request since I feel that at times like this we should all help the Government. We all set about collecting our personal belongings and I brought two boys from the factory to help us pack, a little chaotically, since some of our possessions were packed in trunks, some in wooden crates, while yet others were packed in suitcases. We handed the house over at 4 p.m. and we spent the night at a hotel and in the morning, as we were leaving, the air raid sirens went off and we stayed put. Fortunately, we were not bombed. Lehonia, Agria as well as Pilion are filled with people. In Volos those godless people dropped a large number of bombs on defenceless civilians...

Our young men fight valliantly and our beloved Greece, with the help of almighty God, will be victorious and the whole world will speak of our valour...

Our beloved Greece will never become enslaved because our brave youths fight with the cross over their hearts...
Your sister, Esther Z. Levi

Letter sent to her brother by a resident of the United States
Ethnikos Kirix, New York, 16.1.1941

Greek heroism and Fascist barbarity

By Cyrus L. Sulzberger, correspondent of the New York Times
IOANNINA - This war is above all a war of skirmishes, isolated battles, individual endeavours and anonymous tragedies which are hidden from the world behind the mountain range of Northern Epirus. Here are some incidents:

A Greek Officer narrated the first incident to the writer one afternoon when we sat close to the front and where we could hear the thunder of the 75 Greek artilleries and where we could see darkness spreading all around us. The last rays of the sun painted the snow covered mountain peaks blood red. The wind whistled through the forest and we drank cognac.

"....We set off", began the officer, "on a patrol with 54 men and we travelled far behind the Italian front line. The patrol was made up of hand picked men and able drivers. We travelled all night, sleeping in the forest and eating country bread with cheese and olives. We had with us hand grenades, guns, bayonets, ammunition and four men transported two machine guns. We had disguised ourselves as peasants and had smeared our faces with dark paint. We carried out surprise attacks, blowing up bridges, roads and we launched attacks on their petrol stations. We killed all enemies we encountered and those of us who did not make it back, never will. There were no wounded. Seventeen of our men were left behind."

To the readers, as to the writer, this may seem like propaganda which is why I requested that I be allowed to see these areas. Because it is not possible for anyone to believe that these people destroyed their own homes. I believe the officer's story to be true. The house of a doctor was utterly destroyed and only the outer walls survived. His medical books lay in torn heaps together with his surgical instruments and other household items which lay scattered about. The house of a merchant was filled with hay and spluttered with blood from slaughtered animals and there wasn't one piece of furniture which survived unscathed.

...If we eliminate - something which is almost impossible - the constant presence of aircraft and the occasional appearance of transport vehicles, I would have thought that this was the Balkan War of thirty years ago. The mules which carry the mountain ammunition, the soldiers who sit around the camp fires singing the songs of the encampment, the clatter of the horses and the presence of evzones with their traditional costumes and their shoes crowned with pompoms, all this seems incomprehensible in the age of machine powered catastrophes.

Sulzberger

Night movements at the front

The Battle of Morava

It was a dark moonless night. We walked along in the dark without being able to see a thing, including where we were walking. The only thing you could make out was the outline of the man who walked next to you and the whispers we exchanged trying not to make any noise which would alert the enemy. It had rained heavily earlier on and the earth had turned to mud. The different vehicles which had passed over the road ahead of us made walking difficult since with every step you took you found yourself in mud up to your knees and the only way you could take the next step was to pull your leg out with your own hands.

Sweat ran down our faces and our bodies gave off intense heat in our attempts to walk... The lice which covered our bodies would start to stir from the heat and suck our blood making us suffer even more. After untold hardships we arrived, without being seen, in front of the enemy and we waited to attack at daybreak.

As soon as the first rays of light appeared we heard the rat-tat-tat of machine guns which were firing at us. The machine guns were only about 100 metres away and they fired incessantly.

As soon as we realised what was happening, several of our men charged forward with their bayonets and within a few minutes the Italians, panic stricken, were forced to abandon their machine guns and to surrender to us with their hands held high over their heads. This was the Battle of Morava whose surrender allowed us to conquer Koritsa.

Stephanos I. Kasanovas

7th November 1940

"...In conclusion - even if an attempt is made to rectify the situation - our operation has resulted in complete failure (falimento completo)."

19th November 1940

"This morning, during the course of briefing, the Duce announced the Greek occupation of Erseka. Erseka is a vitally strategic location,

because it can cut off all communication and transportation and allows for a speedy and easy advance against Koritsa and which the Greeks are attempting to capture if they have not captured it already." Further developments have moved the Italians to a more critical position. Pricolo writes in his report dated 19/11 the following to Mussolini:
"The entire front is being pressured and is withdrawing from
Kalama up to Erseka and Koritsa..."

Extracts from the War Diary of Gen. Armellini, deputy Chief of the Italian General Staff

Article by G.H. Katsimitros in the magazine "History"

Italian postcard from 1940

THE FIRST ALLIED VICTORIES

The Greek offensive now becomes irresistible. One by one the Albanian towns fall into Greek hands. Predominantly Greek in population, large towns and villages, with thousand years of Hellenic culture and Greek Orthodox tradition, return to their motherland.

The conquest of Koritsa is acclaimed everywhere as a military triumph. A landmark; the first land victory of the Allies in the Second World War, victory of the free spirit over force. The occupation of Koritsa is followed by the capture of Moschopolis, Pogradec, Premeti, Ayioi Saranta, Argyrokastro, Chimarra. In the words of C.M. Woodhouse, "the Greeks won the first victories of the Allies anywhere on land, ahead of the British in North Africa".

A ray of hope gleams in the horizon now.

We will aid them in their struggle

History may have to record that the invasion of Greece was the beginning of the end of Mussolini's dominion. Certain it is that we have secured an ally of whom we may well be proud. "There is one small, heroic country," declared Mr. Winston Churchill in the peroration of his speech at the Lord Mayor's luncheon at the Mansion House on November 9, "to whom our thoughts today go out in new sympathy and admiration. To the valiant Greek people and their armies, now defending their native soil from the latest Italian outrage - to them we send from the heart of old London our faithful promise that amid all our burdens and anxieties we will do our best to aid them in their struggle, and that we will never cease to strike at the foul aggressor in ever-increasing strength from this time forth until the crimes and treacheries which hang around the neck of Mussolini and disgrace the Italian name have been brought to condign and exemplary justice."

The War Illustrated, London, 12.11.1940

The Greek Victories cause anxiety to the undefeated Hitler

Vienna, 20 November 1940
Duce,

... When I asked you to receive me in Florence, I set off with the hope that I could present my views on the commencement of your campaign against Greece, a campaign which was about to begin and of which I then had only sketchy details. I wanted above all to persuade you to postpone this operation for a later and more favourable date, or at least until after the American Presidential elections. I primarily wanted to emphasise to you the importance of putting off such an operation until you had quickly established the occupation of Crete. I desired to present you with my views regarding this operation, and to propose the use of one parachute division and one airborne division. As the situation has now developed today, its military and psychological consequences are of grave importance and it is imperative therefore that we must examine the resulting situation very thoroughly and objectively.....

The military consequences, Duce, are now extremely crucial. England will have under her control a number of air bases which will bring her closer to the oil wells of Ploesti and more directly to the whole of southern Italy and particularly to the harbours of Italy and Albania. I cannot even dare to think of the consequences of such a situation.

Extract from a secret correspondence written by Hitler and sent to Mussolini

LES LETTRES SECRÈTES ÉCHANGÉES PAR HITLER ET MUSSOLINI

Mussolini, humbly excuses himself

22 November 1940
Führer,

I am grieved that my letter of October 19th did not reach you in time

"Haunted"
Sketch by Low

so that you could have given me your opinion on the then planned campaign against Greece, an opinion which I would have respected and adhered to as I have done on previous occasions. The advance of the Italian army into Greece, which at the beginning was quick and whose results were reassuring, has now been checked and the Greek forces have succeeded in gaining the initiative. There are three major reasons for this:

1. Bad weather - heavy rain which has prevented the transport of artillery and ammunition. One armoured division was completely submerged in thick mud and made useless.

2. The attitude of Bulgarians, who allowed the Greeks to withdraw 8 divisions from Thrace in order to use them against us in Albania.

3. The complete non-cooperation of the Albanian troops, who mutinied against the Italian forces. In one particular case, we were obliged to disarm 8000 Albanian soldiers and sent them to the rear of the front.

All these events now belong to the past, and they should not cause us further worries, although of course I must admit that all these unforeseen events did have unfortunate consequences. However, now Italy is preparing 30 divisions, with which we shall utterly destroy Greece.

Extract from a secret letter sent by Mussolini to Hitler

LES LETTRES SECRÈTES ÉCHANGÉES PAR HITLER ET MUSSOLINI

A registered letter from Koritsa, with Greek stamps and seals, sent to D. Bezantakos in Athens, 19.12.1940

The New York Times

Reg. U. S. Pat. Off.
"All the News That's Fit to Print."
ADOLPH S. OCHS, Publisher 1896-1935.

SATURDAY, NOVEMBER 23, 1940.

KORITZA, AN OPPORTUNITY

Koritza, principal Italian base within Albanian territory for the invasion of Greece, has at last fallen. Rome admits that the town is in Greek hands. This is a suitable triumph for Greek arms. Argyrokastron, the second Italian base, a little more to the westward, is now under attack.

Roles have been reversed in the Pindus Mountains. It is the Italians, not the Greeks, who are on the defensive in this new stage of the conflict. Porto Edda is threatened, the advancing Greeks being only a scant thirty miles away. Valona is no longer safe. The sole port in Albania securely left to Italy is Durazzo, far to the north. British airplanes have already bombed Durazzo, but if the Italians are pushed back to the sea it may become their only outlet.

A good Italian-built road leads from Koritza to Durazzo, through Tirana, the capital. It is along this road that the Italians are retiring. But a good road for the Italians is also a good road for the advancing Greeks. With it in Greek hands, all the Italian forces in Albania could be outflanked, cut off among the mountains.

That is the present prospect indicated by Greek success—the Italians kept on the run, the Straits under British domination, and Yugoslavia nerved to resist German and Italian pressure. It probably needs only a comparatively small number of British divisions with accompanying artillery, tanks and airplanes to bring it to fulfillment. But where are the divisions and whence are they coming? Is British land armament and trained man power yet sufficient to spare enough for this providential chance? If the answer is affirmative, this may prove to be a turning point of the war.

We have liberated Koritsa

To: IX division 17.50 hours, The Infantry Office.
"I report that at 17.45 hours today the detachment under my command entered Koritsa and liberated it. Colonel Begetis."

The British Ambassador to Athens, Sir Michael Palairet, was one of the first to arrive and offer his congratulations to the Prime Minister. He notes in his letter:

Dear Mr. President and friend,

I cannot allow this happy day to go by without expressing to you my happiness and warmest congratulations on the occasion of the announcement of the capture of Koritsa, the first town to be held at the beginning of this war by the enemy. It is a triumph for which the Greek army should feel great pride. This heroic achievement, which the Greek armed forces have realised, has a vital and immediate impact on the world. I am pleased to have the privilege of representing, at a moment such as this, my country in Greece which moves forward at a quick pace carrying in her hand the flag of freedom..."

Kathimerini, 22.11.1985

The Greeks of Alexandria

The moment Mussolini attacked Greece, began the chain of events which are so important to us. In Egypt too, the entire Greek community gave its wholehearted support to the Greek effort. The same organisations which had been set up in Greece were also formed in Alexandria. The women joined the various organisations which knit sweaters and other clothing...

Our morale was very high. And when Koritsas, Pogradeç and Ayioi Saranta fell it was as if you were in Greece. You could not imagine the Greeks of Alexandria. 90,000 Greeks had taken up permanent residence there. We had our own schools, our own churches - we had a large church like the Metropolis of the Annunciation along with many other churches and of course the Patriarchate of Alexandria. The Greeks of Alexandria formed a closely knit society....

Greek flags were hoisted on flag poles, immediately after the Greek army's first victories! The whole of Alexandria was bedecked with Greek flags, something that had never happened before...

No, the Egyptians did not object for the simple reason that the Egyptians were on the side of the English.

Oral account of Leonidas Halkoussis

Bilhete Postale
"The March to Albania"
A cartoon published in
"The Daily Mail" and later
made into a postcard in
Portugal
From the collection of
John Tsatsas

Dimitris Papadimitriou. Leading grocer of Koritsa
Sketch by Patrick Leigh Fermor
From the collection of Natalia Mela
Contributed by Tassos Nollas

The first Albanian Meal ...

You cannot imagine the wealth which can be found in these times of shortages. Here life takes on another hue, accompanied by the rhythm of the cannon's noise which reaches into your inner soul and creates an acoustic perfection which is markedly different from the sounds of everyday life....

Yesterday evening I stayed in liberated Koritsa and my host for two or three hours was a simple but wise Greek. I tasted my first Albanian meal there which was an Albanian chicken pie. I found it remarkably tasty. But then again you cannot imagine how tasty the plain army bread can be at certain times....

From a letter written by Panagiotis Kanellopoulos to his wife on 7.12.1940
From the collection of Anastasios Kanellopoulos

The impressions of the English journalist Betty Wason

Athens, December 2

On the day that Koritsa fell the Greeks rejoiced as they had never done before. Everyone took part in the processions, waving Greek, English and American flags. The Greeks, as well as the Albanians of Koritsa, wildly cheered the Greek soldiers, especially the pilots and the Evzones. The songs of the celebration filled the air. In the hospitals the doctors are having difficulty trying to restrain the lightly wounded soldiers from leaving their beds. The sick and wounded are impatient to return to the front lines. I met a Greek pilot who was brought to hospital with two small head wounds. One night he got out of bed, changed and left the hospital unobserved. He made off in the direction of the nearest airstrip, boarded a plane which had been equipped with two bombs and took off towards the Albanian border. There he came across a convoy of Italian vehicles driving towards the front and he immediately dropped both the bombs on them, after which he flew to

Athens instead of the airstrip from where he had originally taken off. As soon as they saw him, they admitted him to hospital where he was impatient to recover fully so that he could continue his exploits.

Atlantis, New York, 5.12.1940

Mimis Traïforos remembers

The theatre Mondial, during those glorious and never to be seen again years, was not simply just a theatre. It was a national pulpit, a national arena. It was from the stage of the "Mondial" that I announced the surrender of Koritsa, Argyrokastro and Ayioi Saranta before an audience which jubilantly embraced and kissed each other while the orchestra of the immortal Souyioul and Thodoros Papadopoulos played our national anthem.

Unforgettable moments, hours and days. Those who lived through it and who have kept its memory alive are truly privileged. My ears still ring with the cheers of the audience after the announcement of military victory which was first made public at the theatre Mondial by that distinguished journalist Zerberas. I still see before me the scene at the Mondial overflowing with wildly excited people who kissed and embraced us all, all drunk with the wine of glory and victory.

The weekly magazine of the Rotary Club of Athens
Athens, 18/30.10.1984

In America it was an honour to say that you were Greek...

During the years of the Albanian war, it was an honour to say that you were Greek. I remember when the Americans would hear us speak they would ask us what our language was. Whenever we said it was Greek they would embrace us and kiss us... You cannot imagine the kind of things that happened. It was at that time that a spectacular show was organised and put on by the "Radio City" of N.Y. for the Greek War Relief. All the great stars from Hollywood took part in it. Some sang, some danced, all for the sake of Greece. "Radio City" accommodated an audience of 6,000 people and it was filled to capacity. There wasn't even any standing room available. All the Greek community attended. They had announced that they would establish a direct line with the Albanian front so that we could hear the actual fighting but in the end poor weather conditions and static broke down the radio link.

Oral account by Panos S. Fafalios

Ο ΕΛΛΗΝΟΙΤΑΛΙΚΟΣ ΠΟΛΕΜΟΣ
Η ΕΙΣΟΔΟΣ ΤΟΥ ΕΝΔΟΞΟΥ ΕΛΛΗΝΙΚΟΥ ΣΤΡΑΤΟΥ ΕΙΣ ΤΗΝ ΚΟΡΥΤΣΑΝ
ΠΑΡΑΣΚΕΥΗ 22 ΝΟΕΜΒΡΙΟΥ 1940

The Greek Italian War
The entry of the Greek Army into Koritsa
Friday November 22, 1940

Short Telegram

The Palestine Radio Station broadcast the following news item:
"The Greeks have captured 150 Italian soldiers and 300 mules.
The mules put up a great resistance!"

Eleftheron Vima, 22.11.1940

" 'A' as in Argyrokastron?"

"'A', as in Argyrokastron"
A cartoon by Alan Dunn 1940 (Copyright) 1968 The New Yorker Magazine Inc.

*A cartoon by
Nikos and Yiannis Lagakos
The Duce thought that he could
ride the Trojan Horse, but Hitler
sees another on his friend's back.
Look who is the donkey and
who is the rider now?*

ΣΚΙΤΣΟ ΤΩΝ ΝΙΚΟΥ ΚΑΙ ΓΙΑΝΝΗ ΛΑΓΑΚΟΥ.

Ὁ Ντοῦτσε ἐθαρροῦσε
ὅτι τὸ Δούρειο Ἵππο θὰ τὸν ἐκαθαλοῦσε.
Μὰ ἄλλον βλέπει ὁ Χίτλερ στοῦ φίλου του τὴν πλάτη,
καὶ ἄλλον βλέπει γάϊδαρο κι' ἄλλον γαϊδουρολάτη !

Young Greek American Children's Drawings Ethnikos Kirix, New York, 19.1.1941

*Sketch by G. Yialafos
He has stopped his boastfulness
and the Evzone gives him a good
lesson and poor Duce feels something
sharp a little below his
waist!*

ΣΚΙΤΣΟ ΤΟΥ Γ. ΓΙΑΛΑΦΟΥ.

Ἔπαψε νὰ καμαρώνῃ
κι' ὁ τσολιᾶς τὸν καμακώνει
καὶ ὁ Ντοῦτσε νοιώθει κάτι
παρακάτω ἀπὸ τὴν πλάτη..

Sunday Letters

The Young Greek Children

"Dear Teacher of Atlantis"

"We the Greek children who were born in the United States of Greek parents, and are brought up as Greek Orthodox Christians and taught Greek regularly, we were taught even in American schools about the glory of ancient Greece and how the Greeks were responsible for introducing the rest of the world to the culture of the mind, the arts, and the meaning of freedom and democracy.

But despite all these things, in the beginning we felt great shame when we were asked what our nationality was and often, with bent heads, we would say that we were not Greek!

All this occurred at a time when others, belonging to other races, considered it an honour to be called Philhellenes and gladly would become members of Ahepa and Gapa. But from October 28th and onwards, things changed completely. Mussolini had to move against Greece before the Greek blood which ran through our veins stirred and began to boil. It took approximately three months for our evzones and soldiers, our artillery, cavalry and pilots to beat the Italians into retreat and raise high once again our Greek glory....

And then another miracle happened. Here in the United States, no-one feels more proud than the young Greek generation. Each of us, without hesitation and with our heads held high, we proclaim "I am a Greek boy, I am a Greek girl". Everything we have read in the books about Greece and the Greeks is true. We see it with our own eyes. And we are very proud.

G.S. Papayiannis
Atlantis, New York, 9.2.1941

Children's Letters

... Me and my brother Constantine will give our savings to the Greek Red Cross. My mother tells us that the Greeks took from the enemy the village Droviani where she was born, which is in the countryside of Delvino and everyone in our house is happy.

I kiss your hand,
Eleni I. Koukouli
Haverhill, Mass.

Ethnikos Kirix, New York, 3.1.1941

"May you grow up to be as brave as your people in Greece are today"

Autograph of Eleanor Roosevelt to 6 year old Yiannis Stamou
Ethnikos Kirix, New York, 26.1.1941

American Article

"Either we act or we remain silent" ....

"Since we know the remarkable feats of the Greeks we should now take a look at our own deeds.

...Where is the aid which was promised by the United States to Greece? Not even one shipment of food or clothing has been sent by the U.S. despite the promise made last October. The time has come for us to make some decisions. Either we make promises to aid countries which fight for democracy and actually send the aid or else we must stop

Typical Advertisements from Greek newspapers published in the United States, translated on the following page.

78

making empty promises and leading countries into difficulties from which they cannot get out.

   The achievements of the Greeks prove false all the predictions made by our secret service agents. A small state surrounded by great and powerful enemies, whose sources of production are very small, has waged such a battle that they have earned the praise of all far more advanced countries. We, on the other hand, are a formidable power capable of defending itself against all countries and with countless sources of production, promise everything but offer nothing.
Either we act or we remain silent."

"BEACON", Wichita, Kansas
Ethnikos Kirix, New York, 12.5.1941

Now Playing - the finest Greek film with the lowest ticket!

By popular demand and for one last time
The Queen of the Greek Cinema
"The Little Refugee"
     starring Sophia Vembo

   A dramatic plot, with Greek songs that have the power to stir the heart and embue the great happiness, which is the Greek spirit. EXTRA War update on Greece. The Greek army's entrance into Koritsa. Spoils, as well as prisoners of war. Celebrations which were held in Athens will surely move you and much more.   As well, the defeat of the Italians in Libya.

Miami Theatre

47th Street and 6th Avenue, New York City
Continuous showings from 12 am to 12 pm
Tickets 40 cents, children 15 cents

A Great Dance held by the Cypriots for the needs of brave Cyprus

and for Greece, the mother country
Sunday night February 23 at Manhattan Center
311 West 34th Street New York City
A rich patriotic programme
Dancing until the small hours of the morning

The Greek Stage

A new production of the play entitled "The Heart of the Greek
Warrior"
Nikos Zapnoukagias
Sunday January 26th
8.45 sharp, at Palm Garden 308 West 52nd Street
Revue and dances
Tickets: Stalls $1.00

The Greeks of New York Celebrate

At the well-known Embassy News Reel Theatre
The first exciting film depicting the fall of Koritsa will be shown

Apollo Company Palm Garden

308 West 57th Street
Sunday, February 2
Lina Dorou and Nikos Patsis
In the patriotic and social drama
"THE SOLDIER'S MOTHER"
A play about the epic struggle of our country

The first good news

During 1940-1941 I was stationed in Northern Ireland. We were preparing to march south if the Germans landed there. Greece was a long way away. The news of the Greek victories in Albania was the first good news which we had since September 1939. We had, in fact, come to view our own retreats as "victories" and I believe that in a way they were! It was a period when the Greeks and the English stood up alone to face the Fascist tyranny at a time when others were either surrendering or negotiating with the enemy. This point should be noted by all people.

Walter Parkes, England

Daily Sketch, 30.1.1941

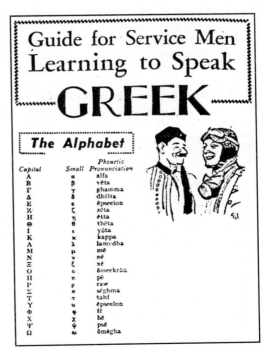

Guide for Service Men Learning to Speak GREEK

The Alphabet

Capital	Small	Phonetic Pronunciation
Α	α	alfa
Β	β	vèta
Γ	γ	ghainma
Δ	δ	dhèlta
Ε	ε	èpseelon
Ζ	ζ	zèta
Η	η	ètta
Θ	θ	thèta
Ι	ι	yòta
Κ	κ	kappa
Λ	λ	lamvdha
Μ	μ	mè
Ν	ν	nè
Ξ	ξ	xè
Ο	ο	òmeekròn
Π	π	pè
Ρ	ρ	raw
Σ	σ	sèghma
Τ	τ	tahf
Υ	υ	èpseelon
Φ	φ	fè
Χ	χ	bè
Ψ	ψ	psè
Ω	ω	òmègha

A Welsh Greek remembers

This event occurred during the war at the time when Greece was victorious against the Italians in Albania, at a time when all the other allied countries had either been defeated or had signed treaties with the Germans and which prompted Churchill to say:

"Our only ally in this war who stands by our side is glorious Greece."

The English had a very high regard for the Greeks. They would follow the activities of the Greek army and they even learnt the geography of the land.

One Sunday morning I was driving from Cardiff to Cheltenham to visit a friend. Passing through Newport - it was at dawn on Sunday morning - the town was quiet and sleepy. I must have been speeding because at one point a police car approached and signalled me to pull over. The typical questions then ensued: driver's license, where I lived, nationality etc. The police officer noted down everything. Quite suddenly, a second police officer got out of his patrol car and came over. He was a superior officer. He asked me my nationality once again. I replied that I was Greek. To my surprise, he then turned to the other officer and said: "Since he is a Greek, let him go on his way."

Oral Account by John S. Fafalios

In Sydney, Australia

Sydney Australia, 28 February.
(National Press Service. A special correspondent for the newspaper "Ethnikos Kirix") Sydney radio reported that a crowd of 18,000 people filled the streets of the city cheering the proud evzones and other Greek fighters. This parade gave the Australians the opportunity to express their admiration for the heroic people of Greece. Not since the outbreak of the war, continued the Sydney radio report, has anything made such an impression on the country as the heroic feats of the Greeks against the great armies of Mussolini.

Ethnikos Kirix, New York, 28.2.1941

And the Greeks of Africa

We, the undersigned, of Greek descent and residents of Dar-es-Salaam have gathered here today, the 8th December 1940, to determine a means of offering aid to the families of our country's enlisted children. We swear on our honour to contribute the herein stated amount as of this current month of December and for every month to follow and for six months after the cessation of the war as a means of aid and an example of the admiration for the victorious army of our nation and our sacred duty to our country.

Dar-es-Salaam, 8th December 1940

Atlantis, New York, 9.3.1941

Even as far as Honolulu, Hawaii

The local newspapers wrote lengthy articles on Greece and with large bold titles described the victories of our army. They spoke of the "eighth modern miracle". The radio stations and newspapers of Honolulu began to broadcast and report the first joyful news. They began, reluctantly at first, to talk about "resistance" but later to report about the victories of our army.

We started to rejoice on our country's victories and cheered together with our allies the Norwegians and later with the local inhabitants of Honolulu and indeed with all the world!

From dawn every day, dozens of vehicles full of curious people would arrive beside the dock where our ship was moored, who wanted to see what our flag and we Greeks looked like. They wanted to see what kind of people these Greeks were who, like in the past, fought against any enemy no matter how strong and mighty he might be.

One newspaper carried on the front page a colour photograph of the Greek flag which took up the entire page and in Greek letters the title: "LONG LIVE GREECE". The honour and joy which we felt and lived through during those days in Honolulu is probably a 'once in a lifetime' experience.

Michael Angelikoussis, Kardamyla, March 1986

Armies Cannot Slay The Spirit of Greece

THE ITALIAN ATTACK on Greece has aroused the old Greek spirit of national pride, freedom and personal courage. This spirit expressed itself in Greek philosophy, literature and arts that have been the basis of European culture. All European nations have gone to school to ancient Greek artists and philosophers. Roman art and Roman literature as well as philosophy started flourishing after the Roman armies had defeated the Greek Empire, rival of ancient Rome. Greek artists and poets were taken to Rome as teachers. Now, 2000 years late the Roman armies are on th march against Greek indepe dence. Modern Italy may defea the Greek army but the Gree spirit is deathless.

Greek Forces Take Chimara
Crush Italian Attempt to Halt Drive On Valona, Capture 800 Prisoners
ATHENS, Dec. 22

Greeks Triumph At Argirocastro
Occupy Third Albanian Base, Taking Over 1000 Prisoners
BITOLJ, Yugoslavia, Dec. 6

Porto Edda Is Captured
Italian Base Reported Fallen to Greek Armies
BELGRADE, Yugoslavia, Dec. 8

ITALIANS EVACUATE VALONA AS GREEKS PRESS FORWARD
ATHENS, Dec. 14

Greeks Battling in Sub-Zero Cold Force Enemy Retreat

Greeks' Skirted Evzones Best Duce's Bersaglieri
Battle Cry of Fierce Highlanders, 'Aera', Get Out, Rings Over Mountains
ATHENS, Nov. 14

Italians Take Heavy Losses as They Flee
ATHENS, Nov. 8

Naval Vessels Battle Off Corfu; Greek Army Captures 1200 Italians
ATHENS, Nov. 2

Koritza Falls To Greeks
New Base Threatened As Italians Flee in Haste
ATHENS, Nov. 22

Frank Daley, GREECE GALLANT GLORIOUS

A City in Mexico

The Greek Embassy is overrun every day, by school children requesting all sorts of information about modern Greece, a lesson which has been added to the curriculum of all secondary and post-secondary schools in Mexico. At a foreign embassy these words were heard from the mouth of the embassy's Councellor: "Ladies and Gentlemen, tonight's musical programme will commence with the playing of the national anthem of the world's most heroic country." And suddenly the enormous room was filled with the sweet notes of our national anthem.

Atlantis, New York, 10.5.1941

A letter from the Philippines

My dearest brother:

After a forty day journey we finally arrived in Manila. The first thing that made an impression on me, as soon as I had disembarked, was the fact that all the newspaper vendors on the streets were loudly announcing the contents of their newspapers.

There were large bold headlines on the front pages. My curiosity was so great that I asked one of the vendors in English what was happening and why he was yelling out the headlines. Slightly annoyed, he replied: "Where do you live! Haven't you heard that little Greece is defeating the Italian Empire?"

I asked him if he could read out all the titles to me. "Little Greece is defeating Great Italy" ... "The feats of the ancient Greeks pale before the feats of the modern demi-gods" ... "The Greek Navy and the Greek submarines attack and sink Italian transport ships full of Italian soldiers"... "The Italian army is retreating in disorder."

My dearest brother, you cannot imagine what I felt when I heard the newspaper vendor's reply. Tears filled my eyes.

Letter from a Wireless Operator of the Merchant Navy

Naftiki Ellas, November 1945

*Argyrokastro 1941. Five journalists who were sent to the front
to cover the war as correspondents. From the right: Kostas
Triandafillidis (Asyrmatos), Thomas Malavetas (Ethnos), Pavlos
Palaiologos (Eleftheron Vima), Sotiris Matantos (Typos),
Theodoros Doganis (Vradini).
From the collection of Vassos Tsimbidaros*

Postcard sent from Argyrokastro by nurse Athena Messolora to her family in Athens
From the collection of Alexandros L. Zaoussis, Athens

Rome, April 1930. Edda Mussolini waves to the crowd of wellwishers as she leaves for the
church where she will marry Galeazzo Ciano. Benito Mussolini, the bride's father, can be seen on
the left. In honour of his daughter, Mussolini renamed the harbour of Ayioi Saranda 'Edda'.
The Greek army seized the harbour on 6th December 1940.
Archivio Rizzoli Editore, Milano

The "Albanian" General to the Great Spagettini

Tirana	Koritsa
Durazzo	Moshopolis
Valona	Pogradec
Elbasan	Erseka
Berat	Konispolis
Tepeleni	Ayioi Saranda
Argyrokastro	

– Why don't you just tick off the entire list and be done with it?
  Cartoon by S.K. Bezos, Proia, Athens

An example of bravery

Greece has set an example of bravery for all the world.

Bahit, Turkey

Alexander Papagos

The Italian general, Gariboldi, told me that Italy's attack on Greece was a crime and a grave political miscalculation. He blamed Count Ciano for the attack since it was he who urged that the plan be put into effect as quickly as possible and boastfully called the war against Greece "my war". So certain was Ciano of victory that he had chartered a special ship and had sent out invitations to his closest friends that they may accompany him on his triumphant entry into Athens.

Alexander Papagos, TWO YEARS IN HITLER'S ARMY CAMPS

General Cavallero zum italienischen Generalstabschef ernannt

Marschall Badoglio auf eigenes Ansuchen enthoben

General Caballero has been appointed General-in-Command of the Italian general staff. General Badoglio asked to resign.
Deutsches Volksblatt, Zagreb Yugoslavia, 7.12.1940
Cartoon by S. Polenakis

The Two Fools

Italy's supreme war council convenes
Cartoon by S. Polenakis

Goebbels makes a note

Wednesday 4th December 1940
The Italians are pushed back by the Greeks; one defeat after another.
The entire Italian plan is rotten right through.
Wednesday 11th December 1940
I am discussing the Greek campaign with Jodl. His views on the
military situation are not hopeful. Rome has truly slowed down our
plans.

From the diary of Joseph Goebbels

Greece will always have a special significance for my countrymen

I am not thinking solely of recent history, although my generation has
good cause to remember Greek valour in our common struggle against
the Fascist dictators forty-five years ago. How could we forget our
shared experience when, after the fall of France but before the United
States entered the war, our two peoples stood alone in Europe against a
monstrous tyranny? I still recall the excitement on hearing that the
Greek army had thrown back the invaders from Albania. No wonder
that Churchill said of the Greeks at that time - this was "their finest
hour".

Nor have I forgotten how the combined heroism of Greeks, Britons
and men from the Commonwealth delayed Hitler's attack on Russia
and altered the course of the struggle.

Sir Bernard Braine, MP, Leader of the British Parliamentary
Delegation speaking in Athens in November 1982

The worth of a few

Valorous Greek people! Can you understand what meaning you hold
for us today? For these past few horrible months we have known many
failures and disappointments, the shattering of the values of which we

had once been proud, and our hopes... and suddenly, as if from the depths of a beloved past, your voice as dearest as no other, is heard to rise and rest upon the thunderous noise of hell. What joy, what feelings of rapture sweep over us as we listen to the voice of Greece. For us, you represent the triumph of the virtuous generation, of true worthiness, the worth of only a few. And what gratitude we feel for you, you who gave back to all of humanity, the strength of faith in man, of admiration, of love and of hope.

André Gide, France (from a letter sent to K. Th. Dimaras from Cabris, 31.12.1940

Basel, 2nd February 1941
Dear Katie,
I thank you warmly for your good wishes. The letter took a long time to reach me. If it had arrived sooner, I would have written to you earlier. I am following the struggle of the brave Greeks with admiration and sympathy.
I honour every country which fights for its freedom. God will bless this struggle for it is sacred.
I sign off with my best wishes to you, your dear family and your country.
A letter written by a Swiss, Ella Frei
From the collection of Katie Lentakis

92

A Small Nation

Greece, our ally, is a small nation but one whose bravery changed the course of the war.

Ernest Bevin, British Minister of Labour
From his speech given at a press conference on 20.12.1940
Le Messager d'Athènes, Athens, 22.12.1940

From a 1940's deck of cards

A turning point in history

Greece's 'NO' which indicated the Greek people's challenge of the Axis powers was not a simple war: It was a turning point in mankind's history for freedom in our century.

Oral account of Lord Jellicoe
Anglo-Hellenic League, London, 3.3.1981

Great admiration

Churchill had great admiration for the way the Greeks fought in Albania. I would speak with him about the expeditions and he would listen with great interest as I narrated to him the details of the battle. I think that until then he had no idea how desperately hard was the battle on the Albanian mountains.

From a letter to the authors by Sir David Hunt, Private Secretary to Churchill in 1950

The Glory of Greece

The Greeks inflicted the first defeat of the Fascist axis. Even if Greece were crushed tomorrow, her military contribution would not loose its stature. It will be to the glory of later Greece that she vanquished the myth of the invincible Fascist axis and gave to all free men confirmation of the value of democracy.

New York Times, 28.11.1940

A few moments of fun for the Greek soldiers on the front line
Alexander Papagos,
THE WAR OF GREECE
1940-41

THE WAR ILLUSTRATED

3d Weekly

Edited by
SIR JOHN HAMMERTON
Editor of THE WAR ILLUSTRATED (1914-1920)
Writer of the famous War Film FORGOTTEN MEN

One of the Kilted Greeks Who Beat the Italians

AT THE PEAK OF GLORY

Christmas 1940. New Year 1941. So different from the previous years. The unsung heroes of the front have no other companions than the solitude, the suffering, the anxiety for their beloved ones. "Peace on earth"!

The capture of Klissoura on the 10th of January 1941 has been regarded as a feat. In his congratulatory message to the Commander-in-Chief Marshal Alexander Papagos, General Wavell stated: "The Greek army occupied Klissoura which was universally considered as impregnable".

Twenty days after the occupation of Klissoura Metaxas suddenly dies. The unexpected news when Greece was at the peak of her glory spread consternation and insecurity at home and abroad. A turning point in the Greeks' bitter fight for freedom.

A well with good drinking water

From the day we occupied Pogradec and all through Christmas and the New Year the Italians did not bother us and we did not bother them. On good days they could see us and we could see them. The Italians must have been 1,000 metres away from our camp. There was a small village in no-man's land which consisted of about 20 houses. To the left of the village, as seen from our perspective, there was a well with good drinking water. The few inhabitants of this village - we and the Italians - drew our water from the well. We were the last to know about this well having seen people coming from it through our binoculars. We nevertheless approached the well cautiously in case our soldiers met theirs. This silence, which was an unsigned ceasefire, lasted until the last ten days of January. Then one day the Italian artillery started to fire with more precision at our camp. Four died and ten were wounded. The wounded were sent to the hospital of Pogradec and the four dead were buried in the area between our camp and the well.

Oral account by Dimitris Syllas
Contributed by Tony Hatzigeorgiou

December 24, 1940

I cannot sleep. My mind wanders to my beloved country, to my mother and father, my sister and my beloved fiancée. In past years we were happy sitting around the festive dinner table, listening to music and playing tombola. Life smiled upon us and everything was beautiful, the complete opposite of what it is today!

From the diary of an Italian prisoner of war
Atlantis, New York, 18.5.1941

Christmas 1940 in Albania

Christmas Eve 1940. My unit was stationed in a small village near the harbour of Ohrida, the northern most point of the front, close to the Serbian monastery of St. Naoum. The weather was wet and cloudy, the sun shining through for only a few minutes before disappearing behind the clouds again. At least the cutting wind, which took your breath away, was not blowing. It was a very good day, one of the few that we had spent in this barren and inhospitable land. A group of soldiers passed our tent. One was a professional dancer but an example of composure and understanding, the other two were singers in Athenian choirs.

They had earlier visited our captain and had sung Christmas carols, and they were on their way to sing more carols to the colonel of the 22nd Regiment of Mytilini who was quite near us. They persuaded us to join them and we all went along to see the colonel. When the colonel heard what we wanted to do, he was deeply moved and opening his army trunk took out a picture of his wife and daughter together with an icon and we all started singing carols, using spoons and forks as "triangles". He offered us cognac and whatever sweets he had, and wished us a "good victory and may the following year find us home".

We then set off to visit Father Dedes of the 22nd Regiment, a true clergyman who had just returned from Pogradec after performing the last rites on the dying and who was soaked through to the bone from the rain and snow. He received us with much kindness and asking to be excused went to change his clothes. We lit a small fire so that we could keep warm and dry. We sang our carols which were then followed by the traditional offerings of drink, sweets and good wishes. Night mass followed which was performed by this saintly man and in which the choir participated as well. After mass, Father Dedes heard confessions since he had earlier announced that mass would be held the following day in a field and anyone who wanted to take Holy Communion could. And indeed Christmas mass and Holy Communion were held the following day but under terrible weather conditions. It snowed and the wind blew violently. As soon as mass was over we learnt that a delivery of army bread had arrived and that we had been given half a loaf each. This made us all happy since the bad weather had cut off all communications and transportation behind the front line.

Pericles Z. Kitrilakis

Buon Natale

The chivalry of the Greek warriors. A gift to the Italian soldiers.

The famous radio commentator Gabriel Heatter, speaking on Christmas Eve from the radio station WOR said the following with great enthusiasm:

'Among the many dark news reports which come in to us from the tempestuous world, we received a bright message from the Albanian front which verifies to the despairing world that the ancient customs of chivalry which we read about in books have not died but live in the lion hearts of the children of Greece. Fifty taxi drivers of Thessaloniki volunteered to transport to the Greek fighters on the Albanian front hundreds of crates of brandy and other festive gifts for the Christmas celebrations. All the taxis arrived safely at their destination and the precious gifts were distributed to the Greek soldiers who fight so courageously for the freedom of their country in the snow and ice of the hostile Albanian mountain ranges.

When the Greek soldiers had drunk the brandy and had warmed

themselves, they exchanged wishes of a speedy and final victory. One of the Greek officers suddenly thought of the Italian soldiers who were on the other side, holding their guns in their frozen hands, and perhaps with hungry stomachs. Like a true knight and a Christian, he decided to send some of their gifts to the enemy. Today Christ was born, he who brought love to all men, thought this kindly Greek officer. As this thought ran through the gallant officer's mind, the hate of war left his soul.

One of the taxi drivers, who spoke Italian, quickly offered to carry out this dangerous mission which the charitable Greek officer had ordered. Within minutes the taxi driver had attached a large white handkerchief onto his car and fearlessly drove towards the Italian lines where the soldiers of Benito Mussolini were sitting shivering with fear and hunger. They froze even more when they saw the vehicle with a white handkerchief stop a few metres away from their positions and the driver jump out and salute them while he shouted 'Buon Natale, soldati Italiani - Merry Christmas soldiers of Italy'.

The Greek taxi driver then unloaded several bottles of brandy from his car which were more than enough to warm the fifty Italian soldiers who were posted there. He once again saluted them and once again shouted 'Buono Capo D'Anno, soldati Italiani -Happy New Year Soldiers of Italy' before getting into his taxi and driving off. In the meantime both the Greeks and the Italians who had followed this emotional scene from a distance uttered a sigh of relief and expressed their pleasure by applauding. This moving scene has not ended nor will it be forgotten. When one day this war is over, those of the fifty soldiers who have survived and were stationed at this part of the Albanian front will remember the Greek gesture for the rest of their lives. And when the passion of war dies out, they will sit around their fireplaces and tell this story to their children and their grandchildren. A story which will sound like a fairy tale and which will speak of the chivalrous gesture made by their enemy, the soldiers of Greece, on the day of Christmas 1940.

Ethnikos Kirix, New York, 3.1.1941

An Italian card which was given to us at the front so that we could write to our families
K. Maris

Twelve men and one loaf of army bread

We were never short of ammunition but food provisions sometimes could not reach us because there was a shortage of mules. Often these animals would die in the snow on their return journey from the front. I remember on Christmas day, twelve men shared a loaf of army bread (2 kilos of brown bread) and three herrings, and nothing on the next day.

They say that the Italians did not fight in Albania. This is not true since at the battle of Koritsa, before we seized one of the heights we were driven back twice. The same happened at the battle of Kleissoura, where the fighting was fierce and lasted for ten days.

Philip Messinezis

Italian bombing of Corfu on Christmas Day 1940

On 24 December 1940 at midnight, we thought that we would have at least twenty four hours of peace. Not only for us, who had been bombed incessantly by the Italians but also for all people who were elsewhere. A beautiful day dawned. In the morning, R.A.F. aeroplanes flew over Corfu town dropping packages of gifts to its wretched inhabitants. Leather coats, boots and food parcels. This was made known to all the island.

At Stavros, where we then lived, we felt great joy. It was a gesture which made us happy. In the afternoon it was quiet and since there was no fear of an attack, a young group of friends met at the National Bank's shelter and held a dance. Perhaps it was the music that prevented them from hearing the sirens, or if they did hear them they may have thought it was not serious. Others went out into the streets, thinking that the approaching planes were English and carrying more gifts. One of the bombs (at the time they called it an airtorpedo) fell on the roof of the National Bank, passed through the upper rooms penetrating the floor before exploding among the dancers. No-one survived. Their remains were taken to the First National Cemetery where they were buried in a mass grave. Only the body of one man, whose family was able to identify him was buried in a separate grave.

The tombstone of the mass grave bears the names and ages of eighteen victims. All, with the exception of two, were under the age of 40. Among them were eight young people between the ages of 13 - 19, two children aged 4 and 8 and a mother with her two daughters aged 17 and 13.

Very early the next morning I heard the news on the BBC. Its first report was of the Christmas Day bombing of Corfu by the Italians. The news report began with the following words:

"What may be termed the Christmas massacre, took place in Corfu yesterday afternoon when Italian bombers...."

Oral account of an anonymous Corfiot

My very dear Daddy:

This year Santa Claus will only come to you in order to warm you up and sweeten your life. Mother and I are sending you a little crucifix so that it may take care of you and bring you home to us soon.
Kisses from your Paki

Letter to Evangelos Nomikos by his daughter
Contributed by Paki Spinelli

From the diary of a Sergeant

I am sending you extracts from the diary of Sergeant Diamantis K. Stafilakas from Inousses, Chios. I was deeply moved at that time (1940-1941) when I read the diary surrounded by my Swiss luxury and realised what the Albanian expedition was actually like. I was deeply proud of Greece and of the human emotions which welled up from these few pages.

From a letter of the Hellenist Samuel Baud Bovy to the authors, Geneva 29.7.1986

3.1.41

The time is 9 p.m. and I am assigned to command. All night I remain

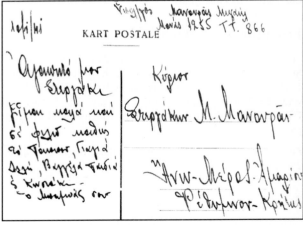

awake changing the guards every two hours. The cold is bitter. We shiver like leaves. Our altitude is 1553 metres. We step into the snow and sink into it up to our knees. At the end, in the morning I drop into my bed and fall asleep for a while. On top of all the hardships we have to endure, we also have the lice. Finally, I leave to take a bath, wash my hair and I return frozen!

Wednesday 8.1.41

Today I got up again at around 9. I eat and set out for my duties. On my way there I meet a friend who had a nervous break-down. He lost his voice and his hearing because of fear... When we get up we see the bodies of many Italians lying all over the place, some sitting, some on their backs and others flat on their faces. It breaks my heart.

Wednesday 15.1.41

I leave to take off my boots and notice that my feet are frost-bitten. You can't imagine the pain I feel. The weather is the same. We've not eaten anything today.

Saturday 18.1.41

It has finally dawned thank God. The door of our shelter will not open because of the snow. The strong wind sweeps the snow up against it. It is raining again today. We are drenched through. It's pouring outside again. In the end there is no possibility of a fire since the smoke blinds us. During the nights my pain is excruciating. In the end I go outside and I walk about the place. I try to make another shelter, I managed to dig it down to about 20 cms before the snow began again. I give up and leave. I go and ask to be put up somewhere else. They take me in and at last the dawn breaks and finds me sitting. Earlier we had chanted hymns for a while and then went to sleep.

Sunday 26.1.41

The day is cloudy today. It is raining. The snow has melted and one can see the bodies of our men and those of the Italians scattered around our shelters.

From the war diary of Sergeant Diamantis K. Stafilakas
Contributed by Samuel Baud Bovy, Switzerland

The old veterans

The Committee of the Union of Old Veterans of Macedonia visited the 3rd Army Corps and appeared before the Army Corps Commander asking that the old veterans of 1912-1922 be taken on as volunteers for the duration of this sacred struggle.

Atlantis, New York, 15.1.41

Our Greece may be poor, but it has the soul of the Greeks

From Pandalogia, this very Greek town of Northern Epirus, my daily missions began, either alone or with others near the line of fire. I will never forget the first mission which we carried out on Thursday, 9th January 1941. I went out with Second Lieutenant Michalopoulos, a civil engineer who, like me, had studied in Paris. Our objective was to scout around and establish whether the retreating enemy army had mined the bridge they were abandoning.

We set out at dawn under a barage of unending canon fire. Our motorcycle took us as far as the narrow road of Kleissoura which was still enemy occupied. We left very quickly since the road was constantly under fire. We started to climb up the right hill, but with great difficulty because we were covered in mud and every time we heard a shell explode near us we fell on our faces. It was raining and fortunately aeroplanes did not appear overhead. The ambulance showed us the least attacked pathway so that we could reach the commander of our unit which was in the process of an attack. The Captain, scantily protected, was in a state of excitement since he was preparing to launch an attack at that particular moment.

"You've arrived early" he told us, "Look at this", and he gave us his binoculars through which we saw the enemy tanks moving about unhindered.

"How will you attack the tanks when you've no anti tank missiles?" I asked uneasily.

"Listen carefully Lieutenant" replied the platoon officer who stood next to me and who was preparing for the attack.

"Our country is poor and does not have the appropriate ammunition, but it has the soul of the Greeks. We will attack them with that."

This was the brave young man's reply. He was a teacher in civilian life. He did not survive that day.

Solon P. Kydoniatis

At the hospital of Kleissoura

The place was filled with beds full of pain. Under the grey army blankets were legs that would never walk again, and hands which would never be able to touch again other hands with tenderness and love. On white pillows among bandages and groans there were always two eyes which shone with the light of God......

As soon as the order was given for the assault on Trebesina, the whole hospital was in an uproar. The wounded who had taken part in the first battle to win the mountain, some on their deathbeds and whispering the last few words to Death, tried to throw off their blankets and get up, to grab their weapons and to run and climb up the mountain. Many bandages were in danger of coming off and a little further away several plaster casts cracked so that the arms and legs could be freed from their restricted confines. And a lieutenant who had just come out of surgery and was recovering took hold of the metal bars of his bed and threw himself half a metre high in mid air, like a Greek flag unfurling before the battle.....

"We want to go as well!

We want to go to Trebesina!

All of us, so that we recapture our mountain......"

Takis Doxas, ANTHOLOGY OF LITERARY TEXTS FROM THE YEAR 1940-1941

From a Greek Soldier's War Diary

On the 17th January we left for Kleissoura. We only travelled during the night because of the enemy war planes. Rain and snow. We marched for three nights until we reached Erseka where we stayed for two nights. We broke into a warehouse and took some beer bottles, a cask of wine and some other things. We then left and began setting up camps and we established 12 of them. Then we captured Leskoviki and several other villages in Albania.

We reached Kleissoura on the 28th January and set up camp. We pitched our camp on a hill. Snow! We had set up our tent over a trench which had been lined with rocks. We were exhausted. During the night, the snow fell heavily on our tent and collapsed on us. If we hadn't woken up we would have all died. We then dug the snow out and went under the tent. We had no water, so we tried to drink the snow but the more we drank the thirstier we became.... We lit fires because we were drenched right through and the enemy scouts spotted us and first thing in the morning we saw hoards of planes which started to bomb us. We lay on our faces all day. They killed quite a few men, but not from our unit. At night we left and went to another ravine....

On the day of the Trion Ierarhon, this day will remain in my memory for ever - dawn broke and what do you think we saw? Italian aeroplanes which were dropping three bombs on our unit which killed fifteen men and wounded another twenty, not counting the men in the other units. I was in a tent with two other men, Diakakis and Mousadakis, and Diakakis was wounded. The explosion sent a shell hurling which took off his hand. They began to run up along the ascent. I stayed where I was, but above my greatcoat I don't know how many shells there were. When night fell we took the wounded to the road so that the vehicles could take them and we buried our dead and left for Trebesina. Nothing but cold and snow as we marched along. They had given us one glove for the hand which held our rifle while the other hand was kept in our pocket. It was so cold that if someone cut our cheeks with a knife we wouldn't have felt a thing. We travelled by night because we were afraid of the Italian planes.

Eventually we reached a place where we could set up our camp. It was all thick mud. We cut branches from the trees to lay on the mud, so that we could sleep relatively dry. But it wasn't dry, just mud.... I was in Trebesina in the snow for ten days. On February 13th at dawn we launched our first attack and seized Boundanori. I can't tell you what really happened, except that the Italians took the mountain from us three times and three times we took it back before finally taking it for good.

From the war diary and an oral account of Pantelis Markoyiannakis

Sketch by Yiannis Moralis

He didn't know how to hate the enemies of our country

The worst memory I have was of a 50 kilogram bomb which fell on the house opposite ours and which killed 17 members of a family. Only one member survived and that was because he was not in the house at the time. Our dowry, the dowry of all young brides, had become rags which were hung up in a tree full of holes. I remember the glow of the fire, the noise and the dust which followed the explosion and the fear because I was very young and I had never seen a bomb explode.

The fierce battles for Kleissoura took my closest childhood friend. He died after they amputated his legs three times because he had contracted gangrene. I shall never forget the pain he felt. The irony of fate was the fact that he had studied in an Italian school and of course could not bring himself to hate these enemies of our country.

M. Aslanoglou, Australia

We Surrender

Kleissoura, 23rd December. Woken at 7.30 by heavy thundering of enemy machine guns. Suddenly a soldier comes running in and asks for the doctor. I run too. A lance corporal, whose eyeballs have come out of their sockets, has lost his senses.

... He is mad!

9th January. A day of hell for our Regiment. From dawn till dusk, non-stop firing from enemy artillery, deafening...

At 19.00 hours I am summoned to the battalion command. The major informs me immediately, that we must retreat in silence, in complete order and with as much equipment as possible. I call my colleague Del Anna and order him to announce this to the troops. I didn't have the courage. We begin marching.

The march continued into the next day and the officer goes on: Shortly the enemy artillery concentrated its fire on our section. What a massacre! What a sight, seeing frightfully dismembered people and dead whose features are unrecognizable because they were hit by gunfire. I had to see them all because I had to gather the names of the dead and wounded. What a catastrophe! I remained silent and sad. Around midnight, a messenger arrives from the Division. Once more our battalion will abandon its positions.

15th January. Our positions at altitude 807 are now established. An enemy attack occurs in the afternoon... Ordered to march to the front line, nobody moves. Then I was obliged to push the sections forward with my gun in my hand. The major and I managed in the end to push them forward. I have not eaten for two days.

16th January. Around dawn, a hell of a firing against the Alpini and the Tuscan Wolves. These forces held out till the 12th but eventually all the sections ran off leaving our left flank exposed. However, the order from the regimental commander is that we must die in situ and not retreat. A second line is being formed and the third battalion still holds out. The Regimental command has already left. We are still in our places. What a sorry sight it is to be present at a disorganised retreat.

23rd January. The 9th and 12th companies have surrendered, being completely surrounded. I send a man to see what has happened, but as soon as he stuck his head out he saw Greeks very close to the command. I try somehow to organise a resistance but there are so few of us! The major, myself and some men from the command. I address the major: "Major, all is lost! Give the word and we are ready!" The major says tearfully: "Put down your arms! The sacrifice is pointless! We surrender!" We ascend to the watershed and I see that all the prisoners are already gathered in one place. But out of a force of four hundred and sixty men which the battalion had the day before, only ninety are present. The rest are either dead or wounded. We are surrounded and with the officers at the head, are lead to their command.
The Greek officers behaved very politely to us officers.

From the war diary of a captured Italian officer
Atlantis, New York 18.5.1941

The Duce speaks, the first military operations in Epirus

Comrades,

Today is a very important and unforgettable day. It brings to an end
one year since we went to war. One year full of vital events, and
amazing historical developments.

The march on the peaks of Pindos of the 'Julia' Division was very
difficult. The middle motorised unit had broken down completely
because of the rain and mud and could not take part in the defence of
Kalpaki. The flood of Kalamas River halted the Siena Division for five
days. On November 6th the High Command ordered the 'Julia' to
withdraw from Konitsa. The 'Julia', which was one stop from Metsovo,
withdrew and several times was forced to open the road ahead, with
bloody clashes. With the withdrawal of the 'Julia' began the Greek
counter-attacks. By mid November they had reached Koritsa and
Argyrokastro by December. One can consider that the period of Greek
initiative ends with the conquest of Kleissoura and the so called 'Line of
Mali' which stretched from Kiarista to Spandarit. From that moment
on every Greek attempt to reach the critical military objectives of
Elbassan, Berat, Valona - especially Valona as the English desired - was

112

repelled by the steady resistance of our forces (Joyful applause).

From a speech delivered by Mussolini and reported by the newspaper L'Avvenire d'Italia, 11.6.1941

From the American War Correspondent Leland Stowe

Interview with Metaxas

A little before my departure from Greece I had an interview which lasted a half hour with Prime Minister Metaxas. I am, I believe, the first foreign correspondent whom he has received since the outbreak of the war. It was New Year's Eve and two comments that he made during the course of our conversation left a deep impression on me.

"No, the honour of Greece's decision to resist is not mine" said Metaxas. "I know that any Greek from whichever part of my country and from whichever social class, who found himself in my position at that time, would have taken the same decision. I know that no Greek would surrender the freedom of his country without fighting to guard it. For these reasons the decision to resist was not a difficult one to take. There was no other way for the people of Greece."

Prime Minister Metaxas spoke very slowly and later added this:

"Above all for us the Greek Orthodox, death is just an episode." From that moment onwards his words have always remained in my thoughts. In all sections of the Albanian front, and also behind the front lines, from Salonica to Thebes, Athens to Patras, I met only one kind of Greek - men, women, even children, for whom freedom is the very breath of life, and death just an episode.

Ethnikos Kirix, New York, 24.2.1941

An Englishman in Chania

I found myself in the Section sent to Crete at the end of December 1940.

My first impressions were unfavourable. We were under canvas in an olive grove beside the main Chania-Suda road, and it rained incessantly; our encampment became a morass, and we were wet and miserable.

The sudden death of the Prime Minister, General Metaxas, whose heroic rejection of the Italian ultimatum on 28th October 1940 brought Greece into the Second World War as Britain's only ally at that time, caused consternation in Chania. I have never, before or since that date, seen people crying openly in the streets, and this was the more remarkable in, of all places, Chania, the birthplace of Venizelos, whose followers professed then, as their successors still do, hatred for the right wing in general and dictators in particular.

Ralph Stockbridge, England

The death of Metaxas

When we received the news that Metaxas had died, we all broke down. We were completely paralysed. Yes, we Cretans, were always against Metaxas! Everyone, all of us! But it didn't matter. Then we were all one body. The army stood as one. We didn't have political parties nor pro-Metaxas groups because here we were faced with an external danger. And I tell you this, our leader has died at the most crucial moment. Now what shall be done?

Oral account of Pantelis Markoyiannakis

The New York Times consider the death of Metaxas a loss of worldwide significance

The loss of such a leader at this moment, writes the New York Times, is a great loss for his compatriots, his allies and for all those who fight the war against the Nazi domination. The most surprising fact about Metaxas was that he received his military education and training in

INSIDE INFORMATION

● Death of Dictator Metaxas will make no difference to Greece's war effort, nor will it cause any internal dissensions.

*   *   *

● King George of Greece, we learn, is unofficially to take the place of the Dictator until the newly - a p p o i n t e d leader, Korizis, the banker, gets into his stride.

*   *   *

● It may take Korizis some time to impress himself on the Greek public, to whom he is so far comparatively unknown as a personality.

*   *   *

● The King supports him, so do the Army, all political parties, and the financial interests in the country.

*   *   *

● British and American financial circles are also on his side. All these facts are of prime importance in the Greek war. They mean that the new Premier has all outside support as well as all home support.

*   *   *

● Moreover, Greek war momentum and enthusiasm are now so strong that what would have been a disaster at the beginning of the Albanian war will now have no effect.

*   *   *

Daily Sketch, London, 30.1.1941

Germany according to traditional practice and he ruled the country for the last five years as a dictator and hardly loved by the fanatically democratic people, yet he died as a national hero, with all the people and all the political parties at his side.

When Greece was attacked, it was not the Prime Minister who dissolved Parliament to rule the country militarily, nor was it the General who planned the defence and reinforced discipline over the chaotic political situation which ruled, but rather the Greek spirit enshrined in the will of the people to live as a free nation.

... As the leader of a small and militarily ill-equipped country, he repelled the powerful invader beyond the Greek borders, destroyed the myth of the invincibility of the Fascist Axis and opened the way for the triumphant English assault in the Mediterranean. No-one will ever forget that Metaxas was the victor of the first military victory against the Axis.

Atlantis, New York, 30.1.1941

The Greek Miracle gave new faith to the world

London, 30 January. The article published in today's "Times" is significant not only from the point of view of the late Prime Minister but from the point of view of the triumphant Greeks. The writer notes that the Greek miracle gave new faith to the world, wisdom to the free and temporarily enslaved nations and encouraged the Allied armies in Egypt to defeat the Italians in Libya. The writer notes the British aid which has been given to Greece but at the same time clearly states that the first triumphant victory of Pindos is due entirely to the Greeks who hardly received any English aid at the time. The French, with renewed faith, set up a gigantic sign across the frontier of the Italian occupied Menton, which said

"Greeks, here begins the French border". Other British papers also comment in a similar vein.

KESSARIS, correspondent of Ethnikos Kirix in London

Sketch by Alexandros D. Alexandrakis, THUS WE FOUGHT 1940-41

THE PRICE OF FREEDOM

For the Greek soldier the winter of 1940/41 was the harshest enemy, more implacable and cruel than the enemy himself. For fifty years Albania had not experienced such a cold, merciless winter. The temperature dropped to 15 degrees below zero. The snow reached three metres in height. Some soldiers were buried alive under its white shroud. Frost-bite proved more deadly than the enemy opponents' bullets and mortar bombs. Amputations were often imperative.

And yet the Greeks fought on. "As a war correspondent", wrote Leland Stow, "I had the great privilege to work and live next to the Greek soldiers, and even sometimes to share their dangers; to live with a people for whom freedom is the very breath of life, and death just an episode."

An unpaid debt

As machine-gun corporal at the Albanian front, I tried to retain any stirring daily impressions in the form of sketches. Some of those sketches were made under relatively calm conditions, in tolerable quarters with materials that I had taken with me. Others however were done hurriedly, on whatever piece of paper I had in front of me and in terribly difficult circumstances.

Many things have concerned me in my art. But the pictures of the front and of our superhuman effort in that overwhelmingly one-sided struggle, keep coming back to my paintings again and again, like an unpaid debt.

Manuscript of Alexandros D. Alexandrakis

THUS WE FOUGHT 1940-41

Despite the terrible exhaustion

At dawn on the 12th February, our Regiment with its second battalion, took part in the first battle of the front, on the adjacent snow-capped peak of Trembesina. We broke through the enemy front with a vicious attack and began the pursuit.

However, a terrible snow-storm broke out, rendering the pursuit impossible, due also to the steep anticlines. Thus the battalion was obliged to halt and to withdraw somewhat in order to reorganise itself. One of the companies of the first battalion, together with the first machine-gun unit which I belonged to, went to hold the summit. The snowstorm was so fierce that we were obliged to dig a trench in the snow for our protection. At dawn the next day the entire Regiment continued with the attack.

The battle lasted all day, overthrowing one Italian resistance after another and pursuing them to the gully where the village Artza de Sobra was, behind the village of Psari; there then began the hardest part of the operation. This was because the Italians occupied advantageous positions on the very uneven and inaccessible mountain sides towards the ridge which overlooks Tepeleni, where the legendary Boudanor with its great losses is also found. The enemy machine-gun and mortar activity was continuous, but our attacks were also continuous and persistent.

With the war-cry AERA AERA (Forward Forward) we had occupied all the peaks before nightfall. At the last leap of Boudanor, the supplier of my unit's first machine gun, Ioannis Terzidakis, lowered the tripod from his shoulder and told me: Sergeant, I can't go on... I can't bear it any more... It was a crucial moment, make-or-break. I immediately grabbed the tripod and ran forward with excess energy. But I didn't last long either. Exhausted, I put down the tripod and the filler, who had been following me on foot, took it immediately, and we continued the attack.

Despite the terrible exhaustion, the ferocious weather and the nightlong torrential rain, we immediately began organising ourselves and consolidating our positions in order to repulse the expected enemy attacks which did indeed ensue. As we shifted the machine-gun during the night, to a supposedly better position, we hit on something soft. It was Italian corpses. Until daybreak, when we were able to see the formation of the terrain in front of us, the mountains and gullies echoed AERA AERA, with machine gun-fire and Italian hand-grenades which we had seized in quite large quantities. And all that was into the unknown as we had no idea what was in front of us or where the enemy was. Simply to break their morale and raise ours. When day came we buried the two Italians in the snow. We cried over our own dead... We felt sorry for the two Italians as well, victims of people with paranoias and foolish ambitions. They too had mothers waiting for them...

I was so exhausted that I was overcome by a sort of rheumatism and I requested my new captain to give me some leave so that I could go to the doctor, because I could not sleep. As soon as I felt slightly hot, the pains were unbearable, and he said to me:
"Since you cannot sleep I feel happier about our safety" (I was in charge of the machine-guns on the heights). "Anyhow, the rules do not cover your case. Only open wounds and frost-bite."

Andreas Z. Manouras

Χειρόγραφο τοῦ Ἀλέξανδρου Ἀλεξανδράκη
ΕΤΣΙ ΠΟΛΕΜΟΥΣΑΜΕ 1940-41

Letter to our family
Alexandros D. Alexandrakis, THUS WE FOUGHT 1940-41

My horse's eyes

"What, dear colleague, is the one thing you will never forget from that war?"

My colleague had been in the cavalry.

He looked at me, took the tongs and gave a gentle poke to the fire which blazed in front of us and replied:

"My horse's eyes"

Then he continued.

"We had been chasing the Italians for days. We had got them off our territory, which they had entered and were following them on foot in that hell-hole, Albania. Our horses, weakened by exhaustion were now finding the snow and the precipices difficult. I saw many fall, the men stroking them a little and leaving them where they had fallen to continue chasing the Italians on foot. Then came the turn of my horse. My grey got stuck in a ditch, covered with so much snow that it was invisible. I jumped off the saddle. The horse tried to get up, couldn't and fell down further. Starving, drenched to its bones, tortured by the endless running on the rocky ground, it was doomed to stay there. I picked up the things I had in my saddle to follow the others on foot. I stroked the back of its neck a little and kissed it. Then I set off. After a few paces, I turned to look at it one last time. It might have been an animal, but it had been my companion in war. We had faced death so many times together, had lived such days and nights together as can never be forgotten. And I saw it looking at me as I left.

What a look that was, my friends. It revealed so much complaint, so much sadness. I wanted to cry, but the tears did not come to my eyes. War doesn't leave time for such things. For a moment I thought of killing it. But I couldn't bear to do it. I left it there. And it stared at me until I disappeared behind the rock.

Spyros Triantafillos, Acropolis 1941

From the Front

"Vraka"

What I am sure you don't know is that the soldiers at the front bring out a newspaper. I saw it circulating in the wild, in the line of fire, and being read to the accompaniment of enemy guns. It is written in ink, printed by duplicator, has its article, chronicle, verses, sketches and cartoons. Despite all the marching, the fatigue, the snow and the battles, our soldiers are still good-humoured enough to write and issue this paper which has the colourful title "Vraka" (Cretan trousers) - it is issued by the young men of that heroic Great Isle - and with the following charming statement: "Newspaper of... such-and-such Regiment, published in an undefined place whenever operations allow and Mussolini's donkeys aren't braying. Director, the Cretan wit; owner, the entire Regiment." They serve it to me at the top of a tall wooded hill where we are camouflaged, among the dense and large wild arbute trees. A healthy northerly breeze, descending from the snow covered mountains strokes our faces - strong like those words which we read in the main article, written by our very own fighters. Who better than they to give us the true spirit of the struggle?

Spyros Melas

Archive of Anastasios Kanellopoulos

An eventful burial of the dead

I was one of the 18 men entrusted by our Battalion Commander to bury the dead. Eight of us carried the four dead on stretchers. Three had the tools for burial, I held everyone else's weapons and the Battalion Priest held the Gospel. We chose a spot and dug four holes as quickly as possible. Then the priest started to read and to chant. I told him: Father, be quick, the Italians are right in front of us. When he had finished his chanting and his readings, the priest took some papers out of his pocket and started reading a speech to the brave soldiers who had fallen in battle.

Again I said to him: Father, be quick. He interrupted the speech and said to me: Corporal, I will report you. Just as he finished the sentence, a mortar exploded 20 metres away. The priest folded his papers and we all ran for it. Fortunately we had had the time to cover our dead. When we had got quite far away, another 5-6 mortars fell on the burial spot. Thus I was not reported because the priest confessed that I had been correct.

Oral account of Dimitris Hadjigeorgiou
Contributed by Tony Hadjigeorgiou

"Don't cry, Stathi..."

At around ten this morning, they opened some barbed-wire and let out a company of Italian soldiers. They were told to march in line till they arrived at the free villages where they were to demand asylum from the inhabitants. But they had not gone very far when they were pelted with mortars and guns.

Many remained on the road. A bloody horde arrived at our village, with rags and small boxes made of planks on their feet for shoes, and eyes half-closed from hunger. The village women poured out into the streets to help them. Aunt Yiangaina, who had lost her eldest son, Stathi, at the Albanian front, came out too. She was crying and her aged face wrinkled even more.

"Stop the sobbing, they were the ones who killed your son" Lucas, the idiot café owner confronted her.

But she neither replied nor looked at him. She bent over an Italian who was leaning against the café wall and who cried, "Bread, mother" as he stared at her. A piece of shrapnel had eaten away his clothes and the skin on his back and he was battling with death, but he kept on asking for bread.The old woman cleaned his bleeding wound with a white cloth dipped in raki, while crying and talking to him: "Don't cry, Stathi. Yes, I am your mother. Don't cry. I've got both bread and milk."

Kimon Farantakis: SCATTERED DIARY OF A YOUTH AT KISSAMOS

Greek nurses at the front

ATHENS - 1st January - (PM) by Betty Wason - While Greek soldiers
throw themselves into battle with their arms and bayonets in order to
keep Greece free of invasion, the nurses carry out a task which is equal
in bravery and self-denial to that of the army. Undaunted by the
adverse weather conditions they continue the task of providing every
possible treatment to the injured and the sick. The hospitals consist of
tents in the snow, usually within earshot of the gunfire. These
makeshift hospitals follow the army everywhere. The tents are folded
and transported by lorry, many of them even by mule while the army is
on the move. Whenever a move is necessary, the operating instruments,
the storage heating, the mobile stoves, the folding beds, chairs and
tables are loaded instantly. The nurses then take their own belongings.
Normally, whenever they have to cross rivers whose bridges have been
destroyed, the hospital articles are transported to the opposite shore by
ropes and wheels, while the doctors and nurses cross the river on
horseback or on foot.

Atlantis, New York 4.1.1941

*1941. Marika Kotopouli in the salon at Tatoi, for the disabled
and all the troops.
Photograph from the Museum and Centre for the Study of Greek Theatre, Athens*

The sound of wooden stumps on the concrete floor

Every Sunday we used to go to the hospitals for the wounded of
Albania, together with fellow actors, singers and dancers, in order to
entertain them. The point of the entertainment was to give a little joy
to those limbless (and abandoned) bodies and to make them continue
to feel that their contribution had been both great and justified. Our
programme had a patriotic content, with folk dances and both folk and
klephtic poems and songs.

I remember one of our visits in a ward with some Cretans with amputated legs. The National Theatre dancer, Eleni Papayiannopoulou,
was with us, together with her dancing troupe. At one point, when they
started dancing the Cretan dance, the disabled Cretans lifted their
bodies in delight, grabbed their "wooden stumps"*, put them on and
were swept into the dance. The tragic sound of the wooden legs on the

concrete floor still lingers in my ears and it will never die away.

*These wooden legs did not have a foot. They ended in a piece of wood like a walking stick. This episode happened during the Occupation.

Olympia Papadouka

How I decided to establish a blood donor's clinic

When the wounded started to arrive in great numbers from the front and especially when frostbite, our second enemy - often accompanied with gangrene - we suffered a great loss of life because of the shortage of blood in the hospitals, P.N. of Pireaus and in the Tzaneion Hospital. I was the head of the laboratories of the two hospitals. We had so much work, both the staff and I, that we would often stay up all night to finish the day's work.

And that is why I decided to establish a blood bank clinic, which after all was only a drop in the ocean. One afternoon I was going round a ward which was full of wounded soldiers just brought in from the front.

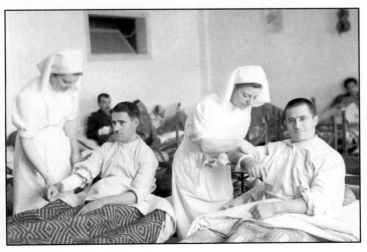

From the collection of Amalia Pitt

An Evzone speaking with a wounded soldier from the Albanian War.
Keystone Press Agency, London

They were to be operated on the next day and I had to determine which patients needed urgent tests before surgery. I stopped at the bed of a wounded evzone who had developed gangrene in one leg as a result of frostbite. His condition was serious and he was scheduled to have his leg amputated the following morning. He was a handsome young man. Despite his condition and his fever he said to me:

"Doctor, whatever happens to me I shall return up there. I still have a couple of things I'd like to tell those spaghetti eaters."

He continued "Please come a little closer. I have something I'd like to ask you." Then he said, "I know that they are going to cut my leg off. I'm engaged to Maria... A lovely girl, full of virtue. We've been in love ever since we were children. Doctor, do you think she'll still want me after they've cut my leg off?"

"You are being very silly" I replied. "Don't you know that they now make artificial limbs which differ very little from the limbs that God gave us. I promise you that you won't even realise the leg is artificial. And you won't have a limp, I give you my word about that"

The operation took place the next morning. Unfortunately he needed blood. Without blood his life was in danger. When I was informed, I jumped into my jeep and drove as quickly as I could to the National Blood Bank of Athens. I made a tremendous fuss but blood could not be found. They asked me to wait and they would see what they could do as quickly as possible. Unfortunately they were not quick enough and the young man died.

That night, I remember, I didn't sleep at all. It was then that I decided to do what was at the time thought to be the impossible. To establish a blood donor's centre. Even though my schedule was a heavy one and I lacked the appropriate facilities and staff, the Blood Donor's Centre was a great success. It made up for the shortage of blood which we had, and its popularity spread to the civilians. The number of daily blood transfusions were almost the same as those at the National Blood Bank of Athens. (The National Blood Bank of Athens gave 10-15 more blood transfusions a day). The staff of both hospitals received the establishment of the Blood Donor's Centre enthusiastically. And as for the donors, they all came with great enthusiasm and they were not only the staff of the hospital (sailors, officers and privates) but also the staff of the Tzaneion Hospital. One nurse who worked at the Tzaneion Hospital was rejected as a blood donor. When she was told this she burst into tears and pleaded with me not to deny her the honour of giving blood. I took a little blood and told her that I would use the plasma which was equally as important as the blood itself. The general public received the Blood Donor's Centre with enthusiasm. People came happily to donate their blood and we became very popular.

George Pangalos

"UNITED WE FIGHT"

When we talk about the Greek victories of 1940 we do not only talk about the army. Its triumphs had not overshadowed the equally worthy achievements of the Navy, the Merchant Marine and passenger ships as well as those of the small but valiant Airforce. "The Greek miracle" was a triptych: the soldier, the sailor and the airman. Together they won the right to be free and the world's praise.

But even after the collapse of the front and the occupation by the German invader, the Greek flag was not taken down. It continued to wave on the masts of warships, thus symbolising the uninterrupted fight on the sea front which never surrendered to the crushing might of the enemy.

On the 23rd of April 1941 when the activity of the Greek fleet virtually started in the Middle East, 16 warships manned by 210 officers, 440 non-commissioned officers and 3000 seamen left the mainland to continue the Battle of Greece from Egypt, the Middle East and Malta.

Once more in the annals of Greece freedom survived, mainly thanks to her Navy and Merchant Marine, these "wooden walls" as described by Themistocles, which have always been indissolubly bound to her fight for independence.

The Airplanes of 1919

The war of 1940 found me at the airbase of Larissa. As soon as war was declared we immediately began our preparations and proceeded to the airbase at Kozani. Our aeroplanes were the "Bréguet" scouting planes which were lightly armed. They were old French planes which had been manufactured between 1919 and 1920. They could be equipped with four bombs along the wings and a machine gun was attached to the tail which seated one gunner.

We left Larissa and went to Kozani. At Kozani there was an airfield which did not have a runway, in fact it didn't have anything. It was made up of a field which had been temporarily cleared so that the planes could land and take off from there.

Our commander was Elias Koutsoukos, a very good and brave officer. Although our aircraft were old, our pilots were brave and they did their job well. During one flight the commander left us and went on a scouting mission by himself. He wanted to take some photographs of the Italian encampment so that the bombers could then fly out and bomb them. But he was unfortunately detected and pursued by Italian fighter planes. They shot his plane literally to pieces and he was obliged to make a forced landing in the fields. He was unhurt but his plane was littered with holes. Despite this he managed to land it somehow in the fields. He walked back to base and we then went out to retrieve his plane. As soon as we saw the holes in it we all wondered how it hadn't exploded. We returned to our base....

I don't quite remember exactly if we had 8 or 9 aircraft but this one of course could not fly in the state it was in and so we took it to Athens. We were then left with 8 planes and as I said earlier, they were all old French planes which had no ignitions. To get them started you had to use a wrench and turn the propeller several times to get a start. We needed about one hour to start an engine. Around the end of November, enemy aircraft, which I think were flown by German pilots, flew over our airbase. They blew the place up. They hit and burnt all the planes except one. It was the oldest and it had the name "Ellas" written on its side. They had shot so many holes through it, through the wings and tail, through all of it, but it didn't catch fire. The rest were completely burnt out. In March or April the English arrived. An entire troop of English arrived there. They set up their camp a little further away from the airbase. We would go there often. Most of them were Cypriots who were very keen to fight, but they didn't get a chance, because the German forces came and they were forced to retreat. We kept our position until the Germans came within 500 metres. We then set fire to our barrels of gasoline - there were about sixty barrels in all - and we then retreated on foot into Yugoslavia.

Oral account of Heracles Doliotis

Hydroplanes engage in single combat

On the following day after our arrival at Paloukia of Salamis, I was on my way to the base. Suddenly I felt a slap on my back and turning

A morning scene at an airbase in Greece.
Pilots prepare for their daily flight. Official photograph of the R.A.F.
From the collection of Lambros Koromilas

around I saw that it was my commander, Ioannis Arabatzis, now a Group Captain of the Greek Airforce. He took me into his office and pointedly said to me: "As you know, the situation is critical and I need your co-operation. We must carry out more missions each day but unfortunately we do not have enough navigator gunners. So I'm asking you to carry out two missions a day whenever necessary. One in the morning and another in the afternoon." I raised no objections and told him that I would gladly offer my services whenever my country had need of them. Pleased, he slapped me on the back once more and I left.

From the following day I went out on two scouting missions each day, one in the morning and one in the afternoon. At noon we were at the base, eating quickly and then leaving again. During one mission in late November 1940 we were on our way to reconnoitre the area of the Icarian Sea, from Samos to Kos. The weather was clear and we could see what was happening on the northern Dodecanese which were then occupied by the Italians. When we finished our reconnaissance we set course for our base. As I sat in the gunner's seat with the machine gun in my arms and looking out towards the tail of the hydroplane, I saw an Italian Catalina bomber hydroplane which was heavily armed approaching us.

This type of plane was equipped with twenty five automatic machine guns. Its speed was twice our own and it was so powerful that to engage it directly was futile. I told the pilot that an enemy "fly" was on our tail. As soon as he saw it he said: "You call that a fly. That's the devil himself. So we've got to be heads or tails." "The Catalina", he added, "is too heavy and can't climb fast. So we'll go above it. If we don't succeed then we are going to do a suicide dive on the Catalina, while we scramble out with our parachutes." So we climbed higher, while the Catalina tried to follow us, but unsuccessfully and passed underneath us. I continued firing at it. Then my pilot prepared our plane for the suicide attack. We turned and dived at the Catalina. But the moment the Italian pilot guessed our intention, he made a quick about turn and a few seconds later we saw the Catalina making for the Dodecanese. As soon as the Italian plane had distanced itself my pilot told me that the Italian High Command had issued orders to all pilots to avoid all Greek planes which attempted a suicide attack. This had happened with many of our pilots in Albania. We then assumed a lower altitude and flying across the Cyclades we set course for our base at Salamis.

Two days later ships carrying soldiers were scheduled to depart from Samos for Alexandroupolis. Our mission was to reconnoitre the Icarian Sea once again. We signalled that the sea from Samos as far as Chios was free of enemy dangers. As soon as the ships had departed for the straits of Chios, we received new orders to patrol south of the islands of Fournoi.

In the afternoon we were patrolling to the south, in the area south of Icaria, estimating that our ships were at that time entering the straits of Chios. Suddenly the same Catalina hydroplane appeared once again. We identified it by its markings and no doubt the Italians identified us from ours. Before it approached us we increased our altitude and carried out a series of attacks until nightfall, when we received orders to return to our base. There we learnt that our ships had passed Chios and reached their destination without the Italians attacking them on their way.

This was my last mission in the eastern Aegean area of Chios-Samos-Dodecanese. All the men of my unit went for three days without a mission, something which made us anxious. When our commander was informed of our anxiety, he called us together and said:

"Up to now we've carried out our missions successfully and without any losses. All the army units which were stationed on the islands have been moved to Northern Greece and are even now preparing to fight in Albania. Therefore we now have no further missions to carry out here. Soon we will be engaged in new and better missions at the front, in order to pursue the enemy who is retreating. Thank you gentlemen."

Oral account of Ioannis E. Spinos
Contributed by Tony Hadjigeorgiou

The Funeral of the First British Soldier

In the streets of Athens I followed the funeral of the first British soldier who had fallen in battle during the Greek-Italian war. The dead man was a British Airforce pilot. As soon as the funeral procession approached, the Greek people showed their true feelings and continued to express their grief even after the body had been laid to rest in the shadow of the Acropolis.

The Greeks are very curious of the British and very friendly towards them, securing the best houses for their use. At the British Army Headquarters, from where all the machinery of war is set in motion, I am informed that even the British commanding officers did not expect such a spontaneous reaction from the people. In the streets one can see young people aged 15 to 20 wearing the blue uniform of the anti-aircraft unit. Whenever soldiers arrived the Greeks approached the English with joy greeting them with a friendly 'Hello', 'Are you alright?' 'Is there anything you'd like?'

The windows of the houses and buildings in Athens are criss-crossed with pieces of paper just like the houses and buildings in London. Anti-aircraft guards constantly patrol the streets. Soldiers in automobiles or on bicycles go from place to place and graphic Evzones who wear the traditional Greek tunics walk along the streets from time to time.

Report from Athens by James Alderidge
Atlantis, New York, 12.11.1940

Greek soldiers surround the grave of one of the first two British pilots who fell in battle at the beginning of the Greek-Italian War
Hellas, London, 12.5.1944

The Funeral procession of the first British pilot who was killed in action
Keystone Press Agency, London

The British Pilots

With the British Airforce somewhere in Greece (A special assignment of the Eleftheron Vima).

We had a 90 mph wind against us the entire journey. We increased our altitude so we could get out of the clouds. It was the worst weather we have encountered to date up in those mountains. In the end we were forced to turn back. An abrupt change of weather after such a lovely morning. Perhaps some of the others managed to get there. I don't know.... The cheerful face of the Squadron Leader had left a great impression on me when I had first met him. Now he no longer wore the same expression. One could see the fatigue of the flight drawn on his face as he entered the mess and collapsed into a chair....

In the club lounge the conversation is as calm as that which prevailed in the clubs of pre-war London. The crews of the bombers come in in groups of twos and threes and sit down to take a cup of tea......

Each day the British Air Force sends out bombers or fighter aircraft over the Albanian mountains under the worst conditions which at times are more dangerous than the air warfare which occurs in Europe or Northern Africa....

One can be certain that there are few air crews from the European War theatre who can be compared to the men of the British Airforce who fight over Albania today - and of course none who are better than they.

Leland Stowe
Eleftheron Vima, 15.12.1940

Greek sailors at the altar of their country

Even though Greek sailors did not fight in the Albanian mountains as our soldiers did, they continued their battles at sea, even after the German occupation of our country. In any case, the first shot in 1940 was not fired in Epirus, but was the cowardly launching of a torpedo by the Italian submarine which sank the ELLI on August 15th in Tinos where it was anchored in honour of the Main Feast of Christianity.

137

The hundreds of victims deserve recognition and remembrance. Didn't our merchant fleet also fight and produce victims with the torpedoing of our ships? It is, of course, not possible to mention everyone by name who gave their life in the struggle, but we should remember them.

Manuel E. Kulukundis

The destroyer PSARA

We took part in night bombardments of various targets on the Albanian border and a little more to the north always with two other destroyers. It was quite unforgettable. Our enthusiasm was boundless, once we knew that the shells which we gently caressed as we loaded them into the guns, were destined to cause death and destruction to the devious invader.

We often took part in many convoys which guarded the transports full of soldiers from the large islands of Crete, Lesbos, Chios etc. to Northern Greece. During one of these convoys to Chios we arrived at night and stayed outside the harbour patrolling the waters until the transport ship was ready to depart. I tried to be included in the crew of the motor boat which would take the captain to shore where he would receive further orders, so that I might be able to see my family, but I was not included. When my father (God rest his soul) heard that the destroyer was the PSARA, he brought large quantities of Chiot sweets and distributed them among the crew of the motor boat.. He also gave them some sweets for me with his blessing and asking me to share them with my colleagues on the destroyer. He was very proud that his son was fighting for the freedom of Greece.

Nikos G. Pittas

"The Silent Service"

The Activities of the Greek Submarines

Many people have christened the submarines, the "Silent Service".

138

The adoption of this name is characteristic of the reticence and the modesty of submarine crews, and which contributes little to their reputation. It is also indicative of the vast silence which prevails around them as their ships move invisibly and silently in the depths of the sea. But above all perhaps, the term is indicative of the silence within the vessel itself when it moves in to attack. Nothing stormy like the soldier's cry "Up and at them". Nothing as magnificent as the brightness, the smoke and the explosions of mortar shells, with wounded lying on the ground and the drunken exhilaration of the forceful advance of the Infantry, the armoured unit or of the pilot.

... These gifts of patience, of the cold calculation of the danger in an atmosphere which does not offer incentives of advance and enthusiasm, but mandatory patience and an absolute discipline to the rules of group effort and altruism. For here, in the silent service, there are not famous heroes, only a handful of famous names: PAPANIKOLIS, KATSONIS, PROTEUS, NIREUS, TRITON, GLAUKOS, MATROZOS and PIPINOS.

These were the names of the eight Greek submarines which took part in the Second World War for five consecutive years and where our Navy showed her presence next to the other democratic nations which fought against the dictatorships of the Axis for the preservation of freedom and human values.

In this way, the names of our heroic submarines became legendary; names such as the PAPANIKOLIS which was the first to return crowned with laurels after its successful activity in the Adriatic. It was successful, after an intensive patrol, and it took advantage of the information obtained from a small enemy boat it had sunk. It then positioned itself in a suitable location and waited for the arrival of the fully loaded Italian convoy. It fired its torpedoes and sank the transport ship FIRENZE. After that, each successful sinking of an enemy ship was attributed by the people to PAPANIKOLIS throughout the entire war.

Christos Soliotis

Naftiki Ellas, November 1984

PAPANIKOLIS

*The submarines PAPANIKOLIS, PROTEUS and KATSONIS in the dockyard at Salamina
from where they would depart during the years 1940-1941 to guard the shores and to obstruct
enemy sea transports sailing towards the Albanian front.*

Contributed by Dimitris Papageorgas

The Greek newspaper ELLINIKON MELLON

*"The submarine PAPANIKOLIS sank three large enemy ships which were in a convoy carrying
troops and supplies from Brindisi to Valona in the Adriatic.
The total displacement of the sunken vessels was 25-30,000 tons.*

140

They unanimously reached a decision

The detailed broadcast of Captain Iatridis' heroic action links his name with the epic deeds of Dimitrios Papanikolis, naval hero of the 1821 revolution against the Turks - and is typical of the courage and faith of today's Greek fighters. Before the submarine PAPANIKOLIS departed from its base, the Captain called together the thirty eight men of his crew and told them that their mission was highly dangerous. He further declared that if there were any who were reluctant to risk death, they were free to leave. But no-one asked to be excused. They unanimously decided to risk death. Before they departed the telegram notes that "We have received the Holy Sacrament and we have called upon the aid of The Blessed Virgin and of Saint Nicholas, the patron of all seamen."

Ethnikos Kirix, New York, 3.1.1941

PROTEUS

The submarine PROTEUS (Y3), under the command of Lieutenant Commander Michael Hadjiconstandis (Gold Medal of Bravery) on the afternoon of 26 December 1940, departed from the navy yard of Salamina to execute an offensive patrol in the area of the Adriatic with the objective aim of destroying enemy transports and to prevent reinforcements and provisions reaching the Italian army in Albania.

How Greek Submarine Sank Italian Tanker

(Press Association War Special)
ATHENS, Monday.
A GRAPHIC account of how his submarine sank an Italian tanker of 5,000 tons by gunfire in the Adriatic has been given to the newspaper "Kathimerini" by the vessel's commander, Captain Spanidis.

ἐφ. South Wales Echo and Express, 6.1.1941

Suddenly, at 10.00 on December 29, the Greek transport ship IONIA which belonged to "Elmes" transmitted an SOS signal to the Naval High Command which was followed by a signal indicating that it was under attack by an enemy submarine. Its signal indicated that it was located in the Bay of Valona, in the exact area where the PROTEUS was patrolling.

Furthermore, from an announcement which was broadcast over the radio station of Rome and from the information obtained from officers who were taken prisoner at the Albanian front, it became known that the PROTEUS, on the morning of 29 December 1940, attacked an Italian convoy just off the coast of Valona which included the transport ships of SARDEGNA - ITALIA - PIEMONTE and which were heavily guarded by an escort of Italian warships.

Also made known was the fact that the PROTEUS fired a series of torpedoes at the convoy, which struck and sank the largest transport ship, the SARDEGNA, an 11,452 ton ship carrying troops and supplies. Following the successful torpedoing of the Italian transport, the PROTEUS itself was sunk with all hands on board after it was rammed and struck by depth charges fired by the Italian torpedo boats which escorted the convoy and counter attacked immediately.

Dimitris Papageorgas
Naftiki Ellas, December 1985

— Ή Ἀδριατική εἶναι δική μας. Γεμάτη ἰταλικά πλοῖα, γεμάτη ἰταλικό στρατό !...

Invincible operations - The Adriatic is ours, full of Italian ships and Italian soldiers

The people shower congratulations upon the Greek Navy

New celebrations in Athens on 7 March 1941 after the submarine NIREUS, commanded by Lieutenant Commander Vrassidas Rotas, attacked and sank an Italian transport in the Adriatic during the night of the 23rd to the 24th February. The Greek Naval successes these last few months have been many and the Athenians, whenever they happen to see a sailor in the streets, lift him onto their shoulders and carry him along in triumph. They also organise small celebrations. These displays are becoming more frequent, especially now that soldiers of the British Expeditionary Force can be seen in the streets of Athens. In Piraeus there are almost daily arrivals of reinforcement units from the British Navy. The convoys begin their journey from the harbours of Africa and are guarded by large British cruisers. The Greek ships of "The Mediterranean Lines", the IONIA, the CORINTHIA and the ELLAS also joined the convoys which transported the British troops.

Yiannis Kairofilas, ATHENS OF 1940 AND THE OCCUPATION

The "invisible" ones

To the sad list of losses of our merchant shipping throughout the duration of the war, one will meet a group of unusual ships which have been lost and which are characterised as the "invisible ones". These are the cargo ships which were lost in the depths of the ocean while transporting precious supplies for the provisions of the people and the struggle of the allies, without leaving a trace behind of the tragic end they met, almost as if the sea opened up and swallowed them. These "invisible ships" which were lost without trace amount to twenty.

Naftiki Ellas, November 1945

TETI NOMIKOU

Even though the role of the Greek Merchant Marine in the war is not sufficiently mentioned, it is nonetheless a crucial and significant one, indeed the Merchant Marine has been called the "Fourth Weapon".

Allow me also to mention its significance in the following narrative from my personal diary.

On 26 January 1941 the Ministry of the Merchant Marine appointed me as second mate aboard the merchant ship TETI NOMIKOU. On February 3rd we received orders to set sail with a convoy towards an unknown - for us at least - destination. We received directions as to the changes in the course of the convoy from the leader of the convoy. On February 4th we passed Crete along its western shore and on February 7th we arrived at Port Said where we weighed anchor and awaited further instructions. On the next day we were given orders to proceed to Famagusta in Cyprus without an escort. It was a particularly dangerous journey since we were travelling without an escort and we could become an easy target for the enemy. God, however, was on our side and we got to Famagusta safely on the 10th of February. There we learnt that we were to receive a shipment of mules for the Greek army.

We were the first Greek ship to visit Cyprus after the war had begun. You can't imagine what this meant for our fellow countrymen of Famagusta. The reception they gave us was truly moving. They did everything they could to entertain us and many would invite us to dine with them at their homes in the evening.

On the 15th of February the loading was completed and we prepared for our departure. We had with us many young Cypriots who wanted to enlist as Greek citizens in the Greek army despite the fact that they were exempt from military service. It is not an exaggeration to say that literally all of Famagusta came to the harbour to see us off. The next day we set sail for Port Said again unescorted, arriving there two days later. We moored and waited for the formation of the convoy which would depart for Piraeus. On February 26th we sailed with the convoy, but this time escorted by three British destroyers and on the second day when we reached open waters we saw a powerful naval squadron which belonged to the British navy approaching from the west. As we learnt later the squadron was assigned to prevent the exodus of the Italian naval units which a few days later were forced to about turn after the Italian naval forces were utterly defeated at the Battle of Matapan by Admiral Cunningham. On this occasion our journey was highly adventurous. A sudden rise of bad weather, similar to that described in

From the collection of
Christos Soliotis, Athens

the Acts of the Apostles during St. Peter's journey to Rome (Acts Ch.13, 14), broke out and the convoy was scattered. Our ship was very light, the only weight we carried was the mules. The wheel was turned completely to the left but it could not keep its prow up. We were knocked about violently. Many of the mules in the hold became untied and were cruelly killed as they hit themselves against the stands and the walls of the hold.

A British destroyer came up alongside of us and asked us what was happening. When we explained they instructed us to continue towards the lee of Crete and from there to continue as best we could (Do your best when under the lee of Crete!) Thankfully night fell and in the morning we found ourselves three miles off the coast of Crete. We stopped there, opened the hold and threw the dead animals into the sea. We then continued along the coast until we reached Palaiohora on the south western shore of Crete.

We weighed anchor there and waited for daybreak. In the morning we raised our flag and immediately a motor boat approached us and we asked them to send a telegram to the Admiralty (the use of the radio was forbidden) for further orders. Thus we received the order to depart for Suda Bay where a Greek destroyer would meet us and escort us to Piraeus. But our adventures were not over.

When we reached Suda and prepared to weigh anchor, at the last moment the Lieutenant Commander changed his mind as to the location of where the ship should cast its anchor and we continued another 500 metres towards the coast and dropped anchor there. No more than 10 minutes later we heard the roar of guns from the neighbouring mountains which was the signal of an air attack. Almost immediately a squadron of Italian aircraft appeared and flying low dropped their bombs at random over Suda Bay. One of these bombs fell exactly on the spot where we would have initially dropped anchor. If we had remained there we would have been hit. Sceptics may say that it is coincidental. I believed it truly was a miracle that we survived. Finally, the next day, March 4th, the destroyer LEON arrived and after taking in coal we departed for Piraeus under escort, arriving safely on Friday 7th March.

Georgios A. Perris

5.4.41
Sketch by A.N. Loizos

146

MUSSOLINI'S
SPRING OFFENSIVE

9 March 1941. The Duce launched his Spring Offensive, the famous "Primavera". Present himself in the Albanian mountains. The Greeks defend themselves to the last man. On March 14th, General Caballero decides that the Italian forces are not able to break through the Greek lines. He advises Mussolini "to stop the offensive until a better season".

"The great Spring Offensive" says Angelos Terzakis, "ended in complete and utter defeat for the Italians, before the very eyes of the Duce. Twelve Italian divisions, with powerful air backing and abundant supplies, threw themselves into battle against the six Greek divisions which had no airplanes, no food and were exhausted. Yet the Italians made no gains. This phenomenon transgresses the limits of logic and enters into the realm of miracles."

A Six hour truce

When the battle started on the 3rd of March we did not budge from the left of Pogradec. Where I was, the slope was covered in snow and as the Italians fell dead, they remained there. One day an Italian priest who held the rank of a Major arrived and requested a ceasefire so that they could bury the dead. His translator was a young Italian, aged 18 - 20, from Rhodes who spoke Greek fluently. Rhodes was under Italian occupation at that time. They asked for a six day truce. They blindfolded the officers. The young Rhodian remained. They spoke to the headquarters. They said six hours, and not six days.

The Italians started to bury their dead. Six hours had scarcely passed when we opened fire again. Then the Italian boy from Rhodes said: "We are men of God as you are. A mother gave birth to you as a mother gave birth to me. And now I will cross over to the other side so we can continue to kill each other."
I shall never forget his words.

Oral account of Gerasimos Lendarakis

The earthquakes at Larissa

I belonged to the automobile squadron. To begin with I slept in a tent in the snow outside Larissa for a month without taking off my clothes, not even my shoes. Then Harilaos Roufos, a doctor, arranged for me to go to this small room in air-defence and we lived there together. Until the earthquakes hit Larissa. Many houses fell then. Ours, the air defence had turned into a building site. That evening we all met in the restaurant and said: "Did your house fall down? Mine too." It's comforting to know you're not the only one. With the earthquake, the wall fell on Harilaos' bed but thank goodness he was at the hospital, otherwise he would have been crushed. I had frozen. Stones fell on my bedding. I remember how later we pulled the dead out from under the stones. During the entire time, Larissa was being bombed continually. People wanted to get to the shelters but they were afraid of the earthquakes. There was someone in air-defence. One day the look-out informed him that four planes were approaching. He said "they're ours" because they were expecting some of ours and they thought they were Greek. Only they were Italian. They skimmed over the square, killing some coachmen and horses who had gathered there with their carriages.

Oral account of Private Themos D.

"Now you are the head of the family"

One day, during that unforgettable March of 1941, my mother, my young sister and I boarded the same train as my father and the whole Regiment, which was retreating from the border region of the river Evros in order to be deployed in central Macedonia. They had to hold out along the Axios Valley, from which the German attack was expected.

My father kept us at the seat of the Regiment, whose Commander he was until the eve of the German invasion and we were obliged to travel by military train so as not to create panic amongst the local population.

Since my father was visibly moved and my mother, with her arms around my three year old sister, was shut away in her indescribable misery, my father's groom was my only companion on that endless train, which carried a whole Regiment, its arms and supplies in its pile of carriages, towards what they all expected to be a hopeless struggle for the nation's honour.

I still see before me that railway with the innumerable carriages, loaded with soldiers who sang marches with enthusiasm and who would get out at the stations en route to stretch their legs from the long journey. At the junction of Plati, after Salonika, we parted from my father, descended from the military train and waited for another one at midnight to take us to Athens. My father and his Regiment would press on from there to their battle positions. I remember my mother, thrust in his arms, with my sister wedged between them crying. His words still echo in my ears: "Everything will pass and hopefully we will meet again. Look after the children. Careful, Athens is full of traps. Costas (my father's younger brother) will be waiting for you at Larissa station". Then my father lifted us up in his arms, first my sister, then me, hugged us tightly and kissed us.

It was the first time I saw tears in my father's eyes, who till then I had known to be strict and rigid. "Now you are the head of the family" he said to me, and I shut his command deep in my soul.

This picture of my father, with his campaign uniform, brought to a close my memories of the 1940-41 war.

George I. Christoyiannis

Extracts from the Italian Archives

The observation post where Mussolini arrived was filled with generals who hoped that the day would bring their first victory in a war which had until then been nothing more than a series of defeats. Geloso, and Ranza, the Chief of the Air Force, were there as was General Gabara who wore a most strange short coat which was not part of his proper uniform but which he wore because he said it had brought him luck in

Mussolini and General Ugo Caballero together with other officers inspect the Italian Greek Front
Publifoto Notizie, Milano

other battles.

Visibility was excellent. Cavallero gave Mussolini several explanations, showing him the snow and cloud capped peaks of Trebesina
and Sindeli where so much Italian blood had continued to be shed. The
artillery barrage had already begun and was spreading along the entire
front. Orders had been given that every gun was to open fire, even
towards areas which had not been planned for the attack. This was
done so that the Greeks would not know where the advance would
begin. However General Papagos knew, because one of our officers
who had been taken prisoner had in his possession written directions
which revealed the locations along the front from which we would
launch our attack. The bayonet and the hand grenade, the weapons of
the final stages of an assault, were the real protagonists of those bloody
battles...

Mussolini, however, realised quite early that the situation was getting
worse, despite the optimism of those who surrounded him. He said as
much to General Pricolo: "If an attack is not successful in the first two
or three hours, then it never will be!"

To Vima, Athens, 28.10.1965

150

The decisive wound was dealt to the Greek Army from March 9th to 14th

(This is the Italian version)
Letter of the Commander of the Armed Forces in Albania, to Mussolini.

"Duce, in this theatre of war where scenes of fierce fighting have been played out for six whole months, there is a small area which is deeply scarred by the fierce struggle which has taken place there and where the efforts and the courage of the Italians were joined together dynamically. This area includes the height 731 and the hill of Monastir. Yes, Duce, you know these areas, you were a witness to the heroic sacrifices of our armed forces who fought there last March. That narrow mountain path which extends for several kilometres as far as the plain of Desnitsa is the place where a fierce battle was fought and which proved to be decisive. Every grain of soil bears the scars of grenades and mortar shells, both our own and those of our enemy, as well as broken and abandoned weapons, rifles cut in half, the enemy's light artillery guns destroyed by our own fire. Hand grenades and rounds of unexploded ammunition are scattered all around.

The enemy trenches which were taken and retaken obstructed the enemy's forward advance against us and were found filled with bodies. No other place could offer a stronger token of the patience with which the victorious attack of our armed forces was conducted in March. This attack, which was directed and supported by you dealt a fatal blow to the main body of the Greek army and sapped its vigour and rendered it unable to launch a counter-attack."

HILL 731. Symbol of Greek Resistance

Like ghosts, blackened by fire and bleeding from superficial wounds, they clambered up the hill for the second time, holding their submachines which spat out hot lead into the trees that hid retreating Italian soldiers. Masses of dead flesh covered the slopes of 717 and 731, and after each failed attack, the Italian artillery would start up again

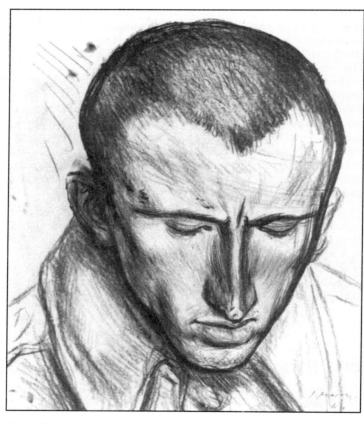

Greek Soldier
Sketch by Yiannis Moralis

with greater frenzy. No one could possibly believe that men could stay alive on hill 731. Yet they lived and waited for a respite, and then they would start again their own killings. Losses in dead and wounded were tremendous and one or two men went mad, not because of fear, but because of disgust at seeing flesh being torn to pieces and limbs being thrown all around them. Something inside them cracked, revolted at the carnage.... and sanity was only restored when the enemy guns started up again. But now the Italians got their range all wrong, and were killing only Italian soldiers at the bottom of the hill....

Achilleas Tagaris, MARS NARRATING

Mussolini speaks to the Italian Parliament
(His speech was broadcast by Rome Radio)

When I went to Albania at the beginning of March, I felt the prelude of victory in the atmosphere. Due to the tireless efforts of General

The Italians try to retake Hill 731
Soldiers of the 31st Regiment on their way to replace their exhausted comrades who impatiently await their arrival
Publifoto Notizie, Milano

The scene of horror on Hill 731 where many Italian soldiers met their death. The ground is littered with dead bodies and weapons, which one group of soldiers (visible in the background) are trying to collect.
Publifoto Notizie, Milano

Mussolini documenta
i vittoriosi sviluppi della guerra

all'epilogo della campagna di Grecia alla nuova sistemazione terri-riale balcanica

Mussolini shows documentation of the victorious developments of the war.
From the epilogue of the Greek campaign to the new
Balkan territorial systematization
L'Avvenire d'Italia, 11.6.1941

Caballero, who had assumed command of the armed forces on December 30, the army in Albania was organised, fortified and prepared for the attack (loud and persistent applause from the audience). The soldiers' morale was high. The lines of communication were in perfect order. A force of power which was truly impressive. If my visit was the army's reward, then they earned it completely. My meetings with the soldiers allowed them to show their complete trust in me, something I shall never forget. The same may be said of the thirty thousand workers who work along the roads, often under enemy attack. The last Greek desperate effort to attack took place at Voiousa and was crushed the moment it began by the regiment "Julia". During the week of March 9 to 16, which saw the undertaking of the Italian initiative, the Greek army ceased to exist as a force capable of fighting. This was also acknowledged by the Greek government itself....

It must be noted that many Greek detachments fought bravely. We are not fully aware of the exact Greek losses, but the indications are that their losses were far greater than our own. While the Italian army was preparing to finish off the Greek army, Yugoslavia indicated by her betrayal what her real feelings were. The Axis war against Yugoslavia thus became inevitable. The armed forces of the Axis acted in perfect synchronisation and with lightning speed. While the 2nd army of the Alpinists came down along the length of the Dalmatian coast in rapid marches which tried the endurance of their soldiers, the Greeks retreated with their rear guards engaged in battles and in the end tried to stop us at the border of Albania with the cunning of Odysseus himself. They offered a truce to the Germans and not to us. We brought them round to reason and they finally surrendered without terms.

(Parliament is on its feet shouting Duce, Duce)

Greece, an Italian vital space

Countries whose population includes several multilingual elements live a difficult life. At times this may be unavoidable due to military security reasons. But special treatment must be given to these countries provided of course the loyalty of its citizens is guaranteed. Of course, when nationality does not agree with the geography, it is the nationality which must depart. The exchange of populations and the emigration of part of the population is dictated by divine providence because it causes the political borders to coincide with the racial borders.

The Refugee. "You disobeyed our orders. We told you to leave Europe once and for all!"
Punch, London, 2.4.1941

According to the agreement made with the German administration, all of Greece, which includes the city of Athens, will fall under the occupation of the Italian armed forces. This brings about many problems, more notably the problem of provisions. However, we will face these problems and we will try to relieve as much as possible the wretchedness of the Greek people brought about by a government which is now a prisoner in London, considering that Greece is now part of the Mediterranean territories which belong to Italy.

(Parliament jumps to its feet - long ecstatic applause).
L'Avvenire d'Italia, 11.6.1941

Honour to the Greek name

All the free countries owe a great deal to modern Greece. Up until now, Greece was considered a small country in terms of wealth and population. Today, thanks to her bravery and virtue, she deserves to be recognised as a great power....

No other page in Greece's glorious history honours the Greek name more.

Daily Telegraph, London, 25.3.1941

The Greek people fight for their freedom

In the name of the gagged but living French people, the free French send their greetings to the Greek people who are fighting for freedom. 25th March 1941 finds Greece at the height of her heroic endeavours and at the summit of her glory. Not since the battle at Salamis has Greece achieved such greatness and glory as she has today.

General Charles de Gaulle, France

Cinderella, you keep your eye on the pot....!
Cartoon by Kem (Kemon Marengo), England

Η ανέλπιστος σωτηρία.....

The Times, London, 3.3.1941

The unexpected Rescue....
Cartoon by Stamatis Polenakis, Athens

"OPERATION MARITA" -
THE GERMAN INVASION

The "lamentable mistake", as Hitler called the Italian invasion of Greece, forced him to order the Wehrmacht to make preparations for the only battle he wanted at all costs to avoid: the Battle for Greece. Not only out of admiration for the classical Greek spirit and for the Greek soldier, but also for strategic reasons because his armies for months were making preparations to invade Russia as early as spring 1941. In his mind, it was inconceivable to launch his "Operation Barbarossa", the invasion of Russia, so long as his south flank, the Balkans, remained vulnerable.

The continuous defeats of Mussolini's armies by the Greeks had the inevitable effect. On April 6th 1941 Hitler's mighty forces invaded Greece without warning. For the Greeks the hour of the second OXI (refusal to yield) had struck. The first impact was the "Metaxas line", which was the fortification all along the North frontier. Twenty-one strongholds resisted with valour the formidable mechanised German forces.

"After a ferocious resistance", remembers General Zacharakis, "we were compelled to raise the white flag of surrender. At the exit of the stronghold we were taken by surprise: A German detachment was lined up presenting arms in honour of the Greek defenders. The Commander of the German Regiment congratulated us for the stronghold's defence".

Greece was now fighting on two fronts. The beginning of the end.

Memorandum No. 143, 9.3.1941

With the entry of the German forces into Bulgaria, Greek public opinion now feels threatened directly by Germany. Resistance is pointless, but for reasons of national honour it is deemed inevitable. It

159

is, however, in keeping with the Greek mentality in that it does not want to avoid the pressure nor break the forces of the resistance now that the German army is approaching.

Despite the unpopularity of the English, which of course is not reflected in the press, the Greek people believe that they will not allow the German forces - even if it is only to disperse the English - to enter the country without a battle. For this would have broken the Albanian front and the so called sacred war which up until now has been waged successfully against the hated Italians, and which would have been lost. It is true that the trust in the Führer and the role of the German nation in a new Europe, with the national honour of Greece secured, has been shaken in many circles. However, it is still so strong that sincere guarantees against the Italians could influence public opinion.

Ehrbach (German ambassador to Greece). From the official documents of the Ministry of External Affairs of Germany

The Great Pretence

Telegram from the Minister of External Affairs of the Reich to
the German Embassy in Athens
Berlin 5 April 1941 Time 21.05
Coded message for the secret affairs of the Reich

Personal - To the Ambassador

On Sunday April 6th, at 5.20 German day light saving time, please notify the Minister of External Affairs there that you have an urgent announcement to make and therefore request to see him immediately. As soon as this has been done, please make the following declaration.

"In Berlin at this time, the Greek Ambassador to Berlin was delivered a note on behalf of the Minister of External Affairs of the Reich and in which a memorandum was enclosed.

These documents mention that the Greek government's non-neutral position from the onset of the war and the presence of strong British forces in the country, has brought about the present situation which

leaves Germany no other choice but to act. The Government of the Reich consequently has given orders to its army to expel the British armed forces from the soil of Greece. All resistance to the German army will be ruthlessly crushed. In the note, it is emphasised that the German Army does not come as an enemy of the Greek people and it is not the desire of the German people to fight the Greek people as a nation and to annihilate it. The blow which Germany is forced to strike on Greek territories is against England."
Ribbentrop

From the formal Archives of the German Ministry of External Affairs-Volume V

February-June 1941

The Greek Dance of Death
To what good is ancient disguise
No one is saved by ancient glory
Before the destruction of today.
To dance with death means - to die
Der Stürmer, Nuremberg, 21.11.1940

Typical young Nazis, now prisoners of war, as they go through
London to prisoner of war camps.
Daily Telegraph and Daily News, Sydney, Australia, 23.5.1941

A speech by Goebbels

Hitler's proclamation to the German Army announcing that Germany was at war with Greece and Yugoslavia was read by Dr. Goebbels over the Berlin radio at 6 am today in the presence of journalists, who were summoned specially to the Foreign Office to hear it.

Dr. Goebbels said: "In the name of the Führer I am reading the following Order of the Day to the German Army in the east:

162

Soldiers, of the south-east, you now take the interests of the Reich under your protection. You will do just as well in the south-east as your comrades did in Norway and on the western front. You will be no less courageous than the German divisions which in 1915, on the same Balkan soil, fought so victoriously.

You will be humane only where the enemy is humane to you, and where he confronts you with brutality you will beat him back with the same weapon. The fight on Greek soil is not against the Greek people, but against the arch enemy, England.

The prayers, thoughts and very life of the Germans are again in the heart of every German soldier."
Signed Adolf Hitler, Commander-in-Chief.

The Colonist, Queensland, Australia, 12.4.1941

The lost speech of George Seferis (later a Nobel Prize winner) delivered to foreign correspondents one hour after the invasion of the Germans, 6.4.1941

Today at 5.30 the armies of the "Great Reich" attacked Greece, small Greece, a small country which for months now has fought victoriously against the treacherous invasion of the Italians. On October 28th Greece decided either to live freely or to die. This decision was never questioned, not even during the first months of this war. It still remains firm today when this second crisis appeared a few days ago. And today we are still determined to live freely or to die.

Kathimerini, 26.10.1984

Thoughts...

To this day David, after thousands of years, is the only one who has defeated Goliath. And for a thousand years perhaps Greece will be the only country which has stood firm in the face of two Goliaths who have attacked her. And when all else has been forgotten, this shall remain.

Eleni Vlachou, Kathimerini, 28.10.1965

The First Greek to Meet the Germans

From ALEXANDER CLIFFORD, Daily Mail Correspondent

ATHENS, Monday.

IN a sunny, cheerful hospital ward to-day I found the first man who saw the Germans attack Greece.

He lay with his head swathed in bandages, a slim, dark peasant from Macedonia called Gregoris.

From his little iron bed he told me his story—a story which must have been repeated a hundred times along the frontier.

At 4 a.m. on April 6 Gregoris was standing sentinel on a spur of the Belashitsa mountains. The night was cold and wet and dark, and he strained his eyes northwards towards the Bulgarian frontier.

German troops were only 300 yards away. For days he had heard them trying to make themselves understood by Bulgarian soldiers, seen them cooking and cleaning equipment.

The previous day a German plane flew over taking photographs. Something was going to happen.

Without warning the night became filled with dazzling white flashes and detonations. Hand grenades fell all round him. The Germans had attacked.

*The Daily Mail,
London, 15. 4. 1941*

GREECE "INDIFFERENT TO THREATS"

POPULAR ANGER OVER BULGARIA

FROM OUR BALKANS CORRESPONDENT

ATHENS, MARCH 2

The news of Bulgaria's adhesion to the Axis as well as the official entry of the German troops have caused little surprise in Greece, if only because the public had been plainly forewarned by Mr. Churchill's latest broadcast speech. Nevertheless the public is deeply impressed if not indeed positively angered by the news.

I was on board a Greek hospital ship when the B.B.C. announcement was heard by the wounded. All, however severe their wounds, were unanimous that if Greece were faced by a new threat they were ready. One legless man, asked how he felt, replied that he had no regrets for his wounds, except that they prevented him from going back to fight for his freedom. Another badly wounded, but not maimed, swore that he longed for the day when he could return to the front to meet whatever new aggression might threaten Greece.

That attitude is typical of the vital spirit of resurgent Hellas.

*The Times,
London, 3. 3. 1941*

Greece
The mythical deeds of the ancient Greeks live once again, those
deeds which revealed the heroes' daring. The German army's
heroic advances today casts a shadow over all that once used to
dazzle the world.
Der Stürmer, Nuremberg, 22.5.1941

The Olive Branch from Mount Olympus
Hitler's new Balkan adventure gives satirical point to this
memory of the Olympic Games in Berlin barely five years ago, when
he received an Olympic olive branch from a Greek, a winner of the
famous Marathon race.
Daily Sketch, London, 7.4.1941
The Photo Source/Fox Photos

An open letter to Adolf Hitler

...We cannot believe that a mighty nation of eighty-five million people will make a flanking attack on a small nation struggling for its freedom and already fighting against an empire of forty-five million.

What would your army do, Mr. Chancellor, if, instead of infantry, artillery and divisions, Greece sends as sentries to her frontiers 20,000 invalids, with no legs, with no arms, with blood and bandages to confront it? Would there be an army to attack such soldiers? But no, that cannot be. The many or few Greek soldiers who can be sent there will stand in Thrace as they stood in Epirus. There, too, they will fight. There, too, they will die. And they will await from Berlin the runner who came five years ago to receive the light from Olympia, now, with the same torch, to set on fire this small in size yet great country, which once taught mankind how to live and now will teach it how to die.

George Vlachos, Kathimerini, 8-3-1941

'Our weapons - on Olympian ground'
A picture taken by the German Reich war correspondent, Roth,
which was issued as postcards by the German Government
From the collection of John Tsatsas

The hour of history

...This unanimity with which ten million Greeks faced the terrible fact of war is, I think, the most significant phenomenon in the entire history of our nation. Greece united in body and soul, stood before the open book of fate and dictated this new chapter in her history.

This did not come about by force or threats. Ten million Greeks offered their bruised egos, their wounded pride, their political ambitions, their hates and their passions, their personal envies and vanities, their differences and their conceit together with their ideologies and their theories of neopolitics, they have offered all these on the altar of Greece like the young couples who gave their gold wedding rings, like the poor servants who offered their savings. In this way the five hundred thousand young men of the army offered their youth and their lives with complete free will and with all their hearts.

From the other side of our border, a people of 45 million strong strikes at us. We are defeating them because we are a strong and free people and they are a people of 45 million slaves. This is an unequal struggle and the nations of the world, be they friend, foe or indifferent, follow it with astonishment. What will its outcome be?

This outcome hardly matters. Our total vindication was realised at the beginning. How we all fought this war, this is the victory of our people....
Stratis Myrivilis

ANTHOLOGY OF LITERARY TEXTS FROM THE YEARS 1940-1941

No-one is discontented

N.C.O. Dimitris Mavromatis writing to his brother, Private Mavromatis M.:

"We have received the postcard which you sent as a soldier. The joy and pride we felt cannot be described. Now all three brothers are eagerly doing their duty to our country. I am happy that the lot has fallen to all of us at the same time. So no-one will be discontented, nor

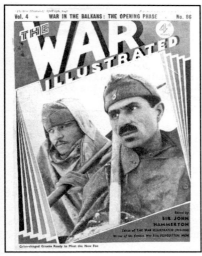

will one feel envy for the others. Let us all three shout out together: 'Long live Greece! Long live the Greek Army!' We affectionately send our love. Your brothers Evangelos and Mitsos."

Proia, 5.4.1941

How the Greeks reacted to the Invasion of the Nazis

"We do not fear the hordes nor death. I assure you quite sincerely that I would prefer to die now while offering my life on the altar of my country, rather than later, when death will come naturally...

With these thoughts and this decision that I have made, I send you my last will and testament which I have drawn up myself and which has the same validity as one which has been drawn up by a lawyer."

A letter by Private A. Economakos to his brother who was a resident of the United States. The sender had enclosed in the letter his last will and testament, in which he divided all his possessions among his brothers, determined to sacrifice himself on the altar of his country.

Ethnikos Kirix, New York, 8.7.1941

HITLER STRIKES

...

He will get a warm reception, warmer than he antici-
pates judging from his braggadocio. We have every confidence in the courage and military skill of the Yugoslavs.
The Greeks have already established theirs.

Daily Sketch, London, 7.4.1941

Operation "Lustre" - the British mission to Greece

There are those who maintain that Lustre should never have been
mounted and that Greece, in effect, should have been left to her fate.
At moments even Churchill, as he anxiously revolved the pros and cons,
drifted in that direction. One must have a point of view, so it must be
stated unequivocally that both honour and expediency summoned
Britain to Greece in 1941. The appeal of honour was felt by all those
responsibly concerned with decision. From the point of view of
expediency, it must simply be asserted that Britain's status in the Middle
East, already so vulnerable, could hardly have been preserved if the
Germans had been allowed to sweep down to the Parthenon and the
Peloponnese unopposed....

Wavell was right when saying to Liddell Hart that "from the political
and psychological point of view Operation 'Lustre' was justified."

Ronald Lewin, THE CHIEF

It was our duty to intervene

There was no doubt that our Greek campaign would end in disaster.
Long before any formal announcement had been made, it was a well
known fact that we had armed forces stationed in Greece, but I could
not find even one person who believed that the campaign would be
crowned with success. On the other hand, everyone felt that it was our
duty to intervene. It is a well established fact that we cannot fight the

170

Germans in Europe but at the same time we could not abandon the Greeks to their fate.

George Orwell
Partisan Review, July 1941

War is an option of difficulties

On 13th January, General Wavell, the British Commander in Chief in the Middle East, came to Athens secretly to see the King of Greece,General Metaxas and General Papagos. Wavell then put forward proposals for British support for Greece based on what might be made available from his forces in the Middle East.

General Metaxas, while appreciative of this British approach, concluded that the forces available would be inadequate for halting a German attack and that it would subject Greece and Britain to losses out of proportion to any gain. On 29th January General Metaxas died. On 22nd February, Wavell came for a second secret meeting at Tatoi. Now for my second and very marginal comment. Before that meeting, Wavell lunched at the Legation, only Sir Michael Palairet, the Military Attaché, Colonel Blunt and myself being present. In talking to Wavell of the forthcoming meeting, we emphasised two points. First, the final decision would lie with the King. But secondly, that decision would depend on whether His Majesty and his service advisors considered that the degree of British assistance available would give a reasonable chance of holding the German threat. Wavell, for a proverbally silent man, became eloquent. He said that the question was not how many divisions the enemy might be able to count on. The question, on the contrary, was how many could be deployed and brought to bear. In North Africa this had been amply shown. The Qatara depression left only a narrow passage between it and the sea. This meant that in the forward area the number of divisions which could be immediately engaged was severely limited. In the case of Greece, an enemy attacker from the North would be limited in much the same way, geographically that is, by the number of routes which mechanised columns could follow through the mountains.

—by Illingworth.

The interest of this is to confirm what was not at first believed, namely that General Wavell, unlike Marshall Badoglio, was himself not pushed by Churchill into a campaign for political reasons which on military grounds he would not have risked. This has recently been brought out notably by Ronald Lewin in his book about Wavell entitled THE CHIEF.

For a variety of reasons, the plan then evolved in February for the defence of the so-called Olympus-Aliakmon line was never fully carried out. In fact, it could not be since, amongst other things, on our side through our being unable in the event to provide the support, in particular air and logistic support, which had been intended. On the

172

Greek side, there was the misunderstanding over the withdrawal of Greek troops from the Albanian front and Macedonia which had been envisaged so as to be able to build up a consolidated and continuous front.

I say misunderstandings, for there is no doubt on our side that we thought that Papagos had agreed to such withdrawals. Equally there is no doubt, to my mind, that in the circumstances of March and April 1941, it was a manoeuvre unrealistic for Papagos or any other military commander to have attempted, complicated as it was, first by the uncertainties over Yugoslavia and then by the collapse of Yugoslav resistance. General Wavell may well have recalled one of his own favourite quotations from General Sir John Wolfe: "War is an option of difficulties."

Going over these times as I may in my mind's eye, I always return to what Winston Churchill said in the House of Commons a week after the evacuation of Greece:

"Looking back over the sad course of events, I can only feel that if we had again to tread the stony path, even with the knowledge that we possess today, I for one would do the same thing again and this is the view of all my colleagues in the War Cabinet and the Defence Committee."

Harold Caccia, England

From a speech delivered at the Royal Overseas League, London, on the 13th May 1982, for the Anglo-Hellenic League

A special order sent by General Bernard Freyberg to the New Zealand Second Division

In the desert, Helwan army camp
March 1, 1941
Special order on his departure for Greece

Before leaving Egypt for the front, I had planned to say a few words.* But events have overtaken me and I was not able to do so. For this reason I send you this note enclosed within a sealed envelope, to be opened on the ship after the voyage has got under way. Within a few days you may find yourselves fighting to defend Greece, the cradle of civilisation and learning. We shall meet our real enemy, the Germans, who have proclaimed that their objective aim is to destroy the British Empire. It is then obvious that wherever we may fight them, we fight not only for the defence of Greece but for the defence of our own homes."

*General Freyberg and the New Zealand division left Alexandria on board the HMS YORK on March 6, arriving in Athens the following day.

From the official history of New Zealand during the Second World War. DOCUMENTS, Volume 1 (War History Department,Wellington, 1949)

April 6th Sunday

A beautiful day, glorious and warm. Glad to be alive. Germany has declared war today I believe. A few air raid warnings have boomed out from Athens, and we have gone on washing our clothes as usual! We all got ready last night for anything that might come our way.

A glorious sunset is now making a beautiful scene more beautiful. A rippling sea close to us, dotted with islands. Fast bombers are going out. I wonder where or for what they go south and come back cheerfully, or so they appear.

The quiet dark-skinned people of this great jewel of a country go about quietly, wounded men never seeming to worry anyone, never an angry word anywhere.

Yes, a lot of brave fellows come and go. Fathers, many of them - one shot through his left arm, on his vaccination spot, then into the ribs and out at the right kidney. He is cheerful, and only stiff in the arm. His kiddies are glad to have him home, also the mother who is proud to show the bullet holes in the coat etc. From where I'm sitting I can see a great flock of pigeons roosting on a shed roof. Dear things. Must go off now and buy some good eats!

April 7th Monday

Awake all night. Athens bombed. Rotten. Have had to take down tents at midnight ready to move. Now on machine gun post with mates. Expecting German planes at any moment, and effects thereof! Glad to have a go at them.

From the War Diary of Harold Loftus, New Zealand
Contributed by Alan Loftus, New Zealand

'Aussies' hail the Greeks

Order of the Day issued by Lt. Gen. Sir Thomas Blamey to the Australian Forces in Greece.

Just twenty-six years ago the Australian Army carried out the first operation on northern Mediterranean shores, when our kinsmen landed at Gallipoli.

We have now landed again in these regions, to fight at the side of the Greeks, and to overthrow once more the German effort to enslave the world.

The Greek nation - the smallest and the poorest of all the nations that the Axis sought to bully into submission - alone refused to submit. Their efforts, along with our own, have already destroyed one of the Axis partners as a Power and forced the Germans to take control of Italy's destiny.

There can be no doubt also that their valiant and successful struggle had a great effect in determining Yugoslavia, after she had yielded to German bullying, to arise and defy the Axis powers.

In Australia we know little of this valiant nation. I am sure that as you get to know the Greeks the magnificent courage of their resistance will impress you more and more. It is not unlikely that the action of this small and noble nation may prove in the end to be the beginning of the final downfall of Nazi tyranny.

Before you have been long in Greece you will realise that every Greek man and woman, every pound of Greek money, is being put into the war effort. They are undergoing great privations and willingly making great sacrifices. We come as comrades-in-arms, and they welcome us as such. Athens, April 14 1941

The War Illustrated, London, 2.5.1941

The First Australian unit on Greek soil

We finally embarked at Piraeus, the Athens' port. We were the first Australian Unit to set foot on Grecian soil in this campaign, and we gave ourselves airs accordingly. Coming off the boat we were accorded due recognition for the history we were making by the Official War Photographer.

A K.L.M. bus took us through Athens on a ten mile journey to the Athenian health resort, Kaffisia (sic), where we were to spend the next eight days. We naturally expected to go under canvas and were pleasantly surprised when we were taken by an English liaison officer to an ornate mansion with all modern conveniences, complete with marble staircase, central heating and sunroof. From this house, three days earlier, was evicted none other than the brother of Hitler's erstwhile chief lieutenant, Herr Rudolph Hess. He had been ordered by his irrate landlord to make certain repairs. He replied that "a German takes orders from no-one". But the landlord had the last word even though he was Rudolph's brother.

The Greeks' welcome could only be described as tumultuous. During this week in Athens we were hailed and handclapped wherever we went and the Greeks' friendship was with us to the end, despite the fact that we had more evidence of fifth column activities than anything else as they tried to upset our getaway. Sometimes the warmth of the Greeks could be very embarrassing. Entering Zonar's, one of Athens' leading cafés, to meet one of my brother officers, I was very disconcerted to receive a handclap from roughly a hundred people assembled. I did not know whether to imitate royalty as they move through a concourse of cheering people, so with an air of "I'm blowed if I know who your're clapping", I reached my friend, who was laughing at my discomfiture.

J. Baskin, Australia
The Greek Gazette, London, November 1982

A sailor's story on board HMS PERTH

Monday 7th April 1941

01.00 - Arrived Piraeus Station and found everything in confusion large fires everywhere and the waterfront ablaze and surrounding shops and houses wrecked. Explosions were taking place all around in the harbour and numerous ships were on fire. We hurried around to No. 5 freezone the jetty where we had to pick up our pinnace back aboard. On the way there we had to push through mobs of fleeing inhabitants of the town who were pushing barrows full of household property and large bundles of gear tied in blankets on their shoulders. On arrival at the jetty gates we were met by officers who told us to get the hell out of the vicinity as quick as we could as the ship alongside which was burning furiously was full of ammunition T.N.T. explosives and liable to go up at any moment. We were to report back to HMS CALCUTTA which was alongside on the other side of the harbour.

We got there without mishap and reported on board. We were told that the PERTH had shifted well outside into the outer harbour and that we would spend the night on board.

Monday 7th (cont.)

We were asleep for a while and it must have been about 02.30 or maybe later when a tremendous explosion rocked the harbour and town for miles around. The CALCUTTA was lifted bodily out of the water and thrown back in again. Everyone standing was blasted to the deck. We made our way on deck to see what had happened although it was not hard to guess that the ammunition ship, a "Clan" Line boat, had blown up. The sight was terrible. Nearly every ship in the harbour was alight and sinking. Two hundred yards away from us was a large Greek ship loaded with oil blazing furiously and every few minutes oil drums would explode in her. The water was one mass of flame where burning oil had spread over the surface and upon this were all sorts of small fishing boats, wrecks and debris on fire and drifting about starting more fires. I could count at least fourteen capital ships afire. Beside us were two Greek hospital ships on fire one sinking by the stern. Helpless men were seen trapped and their cries for help going unheeded for nothing could be done for them.

By this time we had all broken up into five parties for we were surrounded by fire also. All the jetty we were on was burning and burning materials were dropping out of the sky from the big explosion. Large pieces of steel and twisted girders, parts of ship were dropping all around us as we worked. Some of these pieces must have weighed many tons. One piece that landed about 20 yards from where I was working was about 15 ft long, 5 ft wide and twisted like a corkscrew. The fire had spread to the roof of the building we were working on and four of us with an officer were sent on top to see what we could do. There was a Breda machine gun nest on top and we had to cover the ammunition up. The crew had been wiped out earlier in the night and the "Ammo" was laying around loose. The gun had half a tray loaded as it was left. We were stamping the fire out and shovelling sand about when one of the boys picked up a burning glove which he couldn't stamp out but he soon dropped it for it had a hand in it. The affair was very amusing at the moment though tragic.

We got the fire under control and broke the sand bags around the nest and toppled them over the "Ammo" on the deck. We found a little white puppy there which we rescued and took below with us. Just as we got below another terrific explosion sent us scurrying into holes and what didn't go to earth got blasted there. Some ship had exploded just along from us and some more steel came whistling down around us. We had all the fires in our sector well under control and the AJAX was fighting her way out of the harbour. She was alongside the ship full of oil and had to get out of it. It was good work on the part of the skipper in manoeuvring out through that blazing wreckage, oil and mines that had been dropped in the harbour. The CALCUTTA slipped them and all miscellaneous things were mustered ashore.

We then marched through the wrecked streets until we were a safe distance away from the waterfront. People were starting to put in an appearance now to watch the fires. Fire engines and army trucks were still screeching through the streets onto the scene. We halted in front of a beer garden sort of place where we were fell out and told to settle down. I started looking for "Darky", Jack and Vic. I found Jack and Vic and we were worried over "Darky" for we couldn't find him. Outside of this place where we were there were a few tables and chairs on which the boys were settling down. We broke down the doors and went inside. Then after a while when everyone had made makeshift beds out of chairs and tables I managed to find a large overcoat behind the counter also a cushion on the chair. For these I was thankful for it was very cold. All windows were blown in and the floors were littered with broken glass but I crawled under the tables and went to sleep.

We were all awakened about 06.00 by an ammunition dump exploding around in freezone area. It shook everything for miles around and left flame and debris in the air for nearly 15 minutes or more. Large columns of thick black smoke darkened the city for the rest of the day. Pieces of brick, timber and other debris were showered down on us standing nearly a mile away from the area. Lt. Palairat who had mustered and taken command of us found a phone in the shop and rang up the Naval Attaché for information and orders. We were ordered to march out of the town to Salimus (Salamis) Bay where PERTH was lying.

The night explosion at Piraeus and its aftermath. The ship CLAN FRASER which caught fire was loaded with explosives. The explosion a few hours later caused widespread damage as can be seen from the photograph above. ACTIVE SERVICE - WITH AUSTRALIA IN THE MIDDLE EAST

The march is one I will never forget. The town was still blazing and wreckage all along the waterfront. Truck loads of A.I.F. "Tommies" were rushing to the scene and refugees were streaming out of the town. It was a pitiful sight to see young and old alike trudging along with despair written all over their faces. Some were injured but they still carried on. As we marched through we were cheered and clapped by everyone. "God save the King" and patriotic verses were shouted from all round. The effect it had on the people to see British sailors marching through the streets was amazing. They have highest regard for the British and Australian forces. We marched on over the hills and down into the bay. (07.30) There were two big shell craters near the oil tanks but they had been very badly aimed and were well short. Our pinnace picked us up and took us aboard.

Monday 7th April (cont.)

09.00 - Arrived on board and had breakfast.

17.00 - In company with AJAX and CALCUTTA we left Salimus Bay and headed for Suda Bay, Crete.

From the war diary of J.K.E. Nelson, Australia

I was ordered to collect some British diplomats

At dawn on April 9th Yanni, my Greek driver, and I, a Captain in the Intelligence Corps, left Amyntaion in our lorry. My orders were to collect a party of British diplomats who, in flight from the German offensive in Yugoslavia, were expected to reach Florina. We drove through the British front line at Klidhi in the Kirli Derven pass. The road - the only one to the frontier - was a mass of potholes, and it was further encumbered by dumps of stones, intended for repair work. Yanni zigzagged slowly northwards to Kaliniki crossroads, where we were told that German motorised troops were on the way to the Monastir Gap. Little time was left. Yanni drove fast down the side road to Florina. There all was chaos. The Headquarters of the Greek Division was being abandoned and the Staff papers were being burnt in the street. Civilians with their valuables were leaving for the hills. The Colonel in command of the Headquarters was just about to leave - he led me to suppose towards the gap west of the British line at Kirli Derven, but in fact he and most of his men went westwards towards Koritsa in Albania. He had heard nothing of any British diplomats. At midday I decided that we could not wait any longer. We took on board two Yugoslav Air Force officers and some wounded Greek soldiers, for whom no provision had been made. Yanni drove like the wind to Kaliniki crossroads. No Germans were in sight. So we turned south ahead of them.

The road was congested. Some Greek troops were travelling in battered buses, and others were driving the ox-carts and mule-carts which were carrying their stores and ammunition. As we passed slowly through the Kirli Derven pass, the British troops were preparing for action. At Amyntaion, in rain and sleet, there were Greek and Yugoslav troops apparently in some confusion, and I could not find any officers of the unit to which the wounded soldiers belonged. So we went on together through the night into Thessaly, where the asphodels on the hillsides were astonishingly beautiful in the bright moonlight. We rested by day and drove by night in order to escape the worst congestion and later to avoid the strafing by German aircraft on that one main road. At Athens I reported to British Intelligence, and I expressed my opinion that the Germans would exploit the gap west of the British line and that an armoured column could pass via Grevena into northwest Thessaly and proceed from there to Ioannina in Epirus. The Intelligence Staff thought otherwise.

My personal knowledge of the terrain was discounted, and I was told that the route via Grevena was impracticable for armoured vehicles. I only wish it had been so. A fortnight later I was sent to destroy the cotton stocks at Haliartos during the last night of the British withdrawal. Our time on the Greek mainland was running out.

Nicholas Hammond, England

Die Deutschen Truppen 120 km vor Saloniki
Am Montagabend wurde die griechische Grenze erreicht - Die bulgarische Bevölkerung begrüßte die Deutsche Wehrmacht in freudiger Erregung

The German forces 120 klms from Thessaloniki
On Monday night they arrived at the Bulgarian/Greek border The people of Bulgaria greeted the German army with delight Deutsches Volksblatt, Zagreb, Yugoslavia, 1941

On the frontier

... The long-anticipated German attack materialised in April. The Wehrmacht cut through the gorges of the Rhodope Mountains and swept across the Pelargonian plain. Among the first of the endless stream of wounded trundled down to Athens in a blacked-out train were two enormous Cretan youngsters from the olive-growing district of Rethymno whose division, held in reserve after its initial mobilization, had gone on hunger strike until it was sent to the Albanian front and was later transferred eastward to meet the impending German onrush.

Lying side by side in a hospital ward, they said: "We were up on the Bulgarian frontier when they started their advance and their infantry came forward in a psychological attack, standing up straight while we lay behind rocks. Christo said to me: 'These cannot be men or they wouldn't stand up that way. It isn't right. Do you think that our bullets won't hurt them?' So I said: 'I don't know. We must try.' And we shot and two of them went down. Then another two. But there were so many of them"...

C.L. Sulzberger "The Glory that IS Greece"
LEST WE FORGET - THAT NOBLE AND IMMORTAL NATION . . . GREECE

The progress of the German Army
VON SERBIEN BIS KRETA

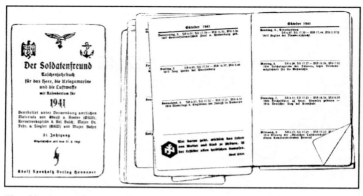

The soldiers' companion
1941 pocket diary for the use of the German armed forces
From the collection of Ray Sandover

The ambulance trains

A nurse's mission is clearly a woman's mission because it needs a great reservoir of love and, above all, a strong faith and self sacrifice. Hand in hand with the women behind the front, they give courage to our suffering brothers. One of the many responsibilities that the nurses undertook with great courage was the Ambulance Train. I lived within one of these trains for the entire war of 1940-41. What were these trains? An ambulance train consisted of 20 coaches which could accommodate 190 wounded. These coaches didn't have windows, were without any conveniences, only one door and although the door was the only means of ventilation, it had to be kept shut at all times, not only because of the cold but also because of the black-outs. The trains only travelled at night. As one can very well imagine, the atmosphere with the wounded - and some wounds had become gangrenous - was very suffocating. The coaches did not have connecting doors and each time something serious occurred to a wounded patient, say in coach number 20, the nurse had to stop the train, get off and run, in the snow or heavy

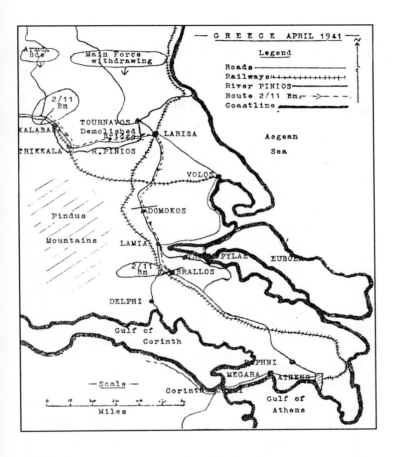

— G R E E C E   APRIL 1941 —

Legend

Roads
Railways
River PINIOS
Route 2/11 Bn
Coastline

rain, to coach number 1 where the doctor happened to be. To these trains our wounded would arrive after the hardships they had already endured and where they would begin to feel the first rays of happiness in the midst of this suffocating atmosphere.

I make a particular note of the 7th medical train. This was named

"Glorious" because throughout the war it transported 7000 wounded men without losing one of them during transportation.Its last and historic journey was on 8 April 1941. The train on that day carried 431 soldiers rather than 190, all of whom were seriously wounded. The train left Florina for Athens, but a short distance from Veria at Skidra the train encountered a blockade because the Serb front had collapsed, followed by all the subsequent events which led to our enslavement. The amazing courage of the nurses once again saved the day. Even though the head nurse knew that on the afternoon of their departure, exactly two hours after they had left Florina, all the bridges that they had to cross would be blown up and that the entire city of Florina would be evacuated, she kept calm and was able to give encouragement to the other nurses so that they could carry out their duties calmly and with determination.

While the bridges were being blown up, the 7th medical train, by some miracle, reached Skidra. No-one, with the exception of the nurses, knew that the Serb front had broken. The arrival, however, of the medical train coincided with the arrival of a Serb train. Fleeing the wrath of the invaders, it had managed to depart for Monastir carrying with it Serb officials and their Patriarch. The tragic truth was made known. The wounded could not believe what they heard. The collapse of the front broke their wings and for a moment panic reigned supreme. The tightly packed train began to empty. All those able to walk or limp or even drag themselves left the train so that they could save themselves from captivity. At this most critical moment the German Stukas flew over Skidra and began bombing and straffing.

The driver abandoned the train. The wounded fled as fast as they could, those who were handicapped called out for help and in the midst of this hell, a place to stay had to be found - a temporary hospital had to be established. This hospital was organised and equipped with supplies, thanks not only to the four nurses but also to the residents of Skidra. Throughout the events of these few days, when the wounded soldiers of the 7th medical train were at Skidra, many anonymous patriots showed their courage and patriotism by risking their own lives in order to save the lives of the wounded soldiers. All the population of Skidra and its surrounding countryside - which consisted largely of Greeks from Pontos (on the Black Sea) - offered invaluable aid in helping and saving the lives of the handicapped.

"Ολαι αἱ εἰδήσεις τῆς νυκτός
Ἐσωτερικοῦ καὶ Ἐξωτερικοῦ

ΕΛΛΗΝΙΚΟΝ ΜΕΛΛΟΝ

Τὸ πρωϊνὸ τηλεγραφ...
Ἀσύρματος καὶ Ραδιό...

Η ΧΘΕΣΙΝΗ ΓΙΓΑΝΤΟΜΑΧΙΑ ΠΡΟ ΤΩΝ ΟΧΥΡΩΝ ΜΑΣ

Συνεκρατήθησαν καὶ πάλιν οἱ μηχανοκίνητοι ἐπιδρομεῖς

ΑΡΜΑΤΑ ΜΑΧΗΣ ΣΥΝΕΤΡΙΒΗΣΑΝ.- ΑΙ ΥΠΟΓΕΙΟΙ ΣΤΟΑΙ ΤΑΦΟΙ ΤΩΝ ΓΕΡΜΑΝΩΝ

Τρίτη 8 Ἀπριλίου 1941

ELLINIKON MELLON (THE GREEK FUTURE)
Yesterday's gigantic battle in front of our strongholds
Motorised units were again held off
Army tanks crushed. The underground passages become graves for the Germans.
Tuesday 8 April 1941

The conquest of territory, a trench along the Metaxas line
VON SERBIEN BIS KRETA

Especially moving was the case of a Pontian doctor, father of four children, who had left Veria which was still unoccupied by the Germans to come to Skidra when the Germans had already occupied the town, bringing with him precious medical supplies, when we had none, and had resorted to washing patients suffering from gangrene with salt water. The 93 wounded aboard the 7th medical train remained in Skidra and after 12 days were transported to Thessaloniki, together with seven more wounded soldiers, 6 Italians and one German. They all arrived on Easter Sunday. The symbolic day of the Resurrection was celebrated in a brotherly way, because human pain knows no barriers between the victors and the vanquished.

Sophie Meria

Anti-tank obstacles

German war report on the battle for the Greek forts on the METAXAS LINE
6.4.1941

.... Two 7.5 cm guns of the 2nd Battalion/95 SOP, (Lieutenant Colonel von Kaufmann), were also used, which immediately fired on the Greek artillery positions. The most significant problems, the transport of the heavy guns, were overcome by the tremendous efforts of the sections involved, efforts which surpassed the bounds of human endurance. By continuous work both by day and night, temporary artillery positions were established.

Our attack commenced at 05.20 on 6 April 1941. However, within the plan of our attack, the improvement of our positions was not achieved. The only thing that was accomplished was the capture of Hill 1389 by the Second Battalion/85 SOK, which was then used as the regiment's look-out post. At the same time, the Greeks had reinforced their look-out post, KONGUR (1951) without us realising it, and the first attack by the 1st group of commandos (85 SOK) ended without its seizure. The battle for Kongur was fierce and caused the first casualties of the regiment.

At 05.40 the preparations for the artillery attack began with a round of trial shots. The 3rd battalion/85th SOK had, after a 30 minute daring attack, taken the fort Istimbay and by neutralising the fortified Greek artillery positions along its western slope. The 3rd battalion's immobilization of Istimbay was achieved immediately by the Greeks. Having realised the strategic importance of Istimbay's position within her lines of defence, the Greeks succeeded in neutralising the 3rd battalion by directing intensive artillery fire on the fort.

The 1st battalion/85th SOK's attack on Popotlivitsa was not able to neutralise the forces on the height of Soultanitsa. The Greek artillery was set up on the southwestern slope of this height. The 3rd battalion's position on Istimbay worsened hour by hour because of the constant pounding of the Greek guns. The Greek artillery units managed to free several besieged artillery positions and they launched a strong defensive attack with automatic weapons and hand grenades. We suffered heavy casualties, especially among the officers (3 dead, 4 wounded).

Curt, grim and with a mute arrogance

.... They sent me to the army hospital in Athens. I was suffering from temporary blindness brought about by the snow and the ghastly conditions. I remember that I lived through the terrible explosion of April 1941 in the harbour of Piraeus while I was in the 'Mistriotis' ward. This explosion occurred when German Stuka bombs blew up a ship filled with ammunition.

When I was discharged from hospital with my eyesight restored, I was sent to Thessaloniki because I could speak German and I was to accompany the first German prisoners who were taken along the Metaxas line to Rupel under heavy guard.

There were 42 men and three pilots all curt and grim, their mute arrogance was reflected on their faces. We brought them to Athens. A few days later the grim, dark and endless night descended upon Greece. However, we carried the sun within us.

P.K. Enepekidis

Memories from the War Period 1940-1941

According to the strategic plan, upon the declaration of war, I had to appear before my unit which was the 26th Army Regiment of the city of Drama. It was difficult to travel and I arrived three days late. When I arrived at the Regiment's headquarters, my commanding officer, Lieutenant-Colonel Adam Adamopoulos, reprimanded me curtly... 'Father, you should have been one of the first to arrive and not one of the last....' and with a small but kindly smile he continued 'You ought to be court martialled! But there is no time for that right now, go to the supplies officer so that he can issue you your clothes, take off that priestly cassock and put on the khaki uniform.'

... Our regiment manned the forts of the Falakro sector of the 7th division. At Volakas, Lysse, A3, Granitis, Vrondou and at the plateau of Nevrokopi we spent an entire hard winter from the 2nd November 1940 to the 6th April 1941 when the Germans then declared their own war upon us. Our defence held for four days. It was a body to body war which gained the admiration of a high ranking German officer.

Metropolitan of France Meletios

The stronghold of Rupel

The General Staff chose ten officers from the Corps of Engineers, put them through a one year academic course taught by the professors of the Polytechnic and other specialists on fortifications etc. and then sent them to build the Metaxas line based on the plans which they had drawn up earlier.

To Second Lieutenant Engineer A. Sougaridis was assigned the task of building the fortifications of Rupel. The workers came from distant locations with their eyes blindfolded or within an enclosed vehicle and they were not allowed to communicate with the outside world. They were not to know where they were working so that there would be no possibility of information leaking out. When the fortifications were well under way, General Metaxas with his ministers and Chiefs of the General Staff of the Army, Navy and Airforce came for an inspection.

When they reached a certain area, Sougaridis said to Metaxas: "Mr. President, I have orders not to allow entry to anyone except yourself, the Minister and the Chief of the General Staff of the Army, Mr... and Mr..." "Of course" Metaxas replied, and only 4 or 5 people continued the inspection. The rest, Ministers, Chiefs of Staff etc. remained behind.

During the summer of 1938 I was the First Mate aboard a submarine which had travelled with the fleet to Thessaloniki. I had no hope of seeing my friend because he rarely left the fortifications to come to Thessaloniki. He would come down for only two or three days every three months. By chance, however, we did meet. "How is the building progressing Thanasaki?"

"What can I say, Alexander. We have finished about two thirds of the entire construction." And he added, emphasising each word, "At this moment I can hold off an entire army corps"....Tears came into my eyes.

The Germans who had easily broken through the Maginot line and countless other lines in other areas of Europe, could not break through the Metaxas line. They entered Greek territory through Yugoslavia. The Greek army, fighting against two dictators, that of Italy in Albania and Germany here was finally exhausted and surrendered. The Germans surrounded the Rupel fort but even then they could not take it. Finally, the end came. When the defenders of the fort were ordered to surrender, they - covered in soot and gunpowder - came out with their heads held high. The Germans, who wanted to honour them, stood at attention and presented arms!

Lieutenant General Athanasios Sougaridis, Honorary General Inspector of the Army, is no longer among us. As soon as he had finished the construction of the fortifications he was transferred to another unit. In this way he did not have the good fortune to actually see what he had so long believed in and to enjoy the fruits of his labour.

Alexandros D. Rallis

I forbid the press to defame the Greeks

9th April 1941: The Greeks are fighting very bravely. I forbid the Press to underrate, to defame them. The Führer admires the valour of the Greeks. He was sorry he had to fight against them.

From the War Diary of Joseph Goebbels

Bravery and Heroism

We had heard from many people about the bravery and heroism of the Greek army. But we could never have imagined the bravery and heroism which you soldiers have shown.

General Böhm, Germany

They were true men

Here I must cut short my speech and pay tribute to the outstanding gallantry of those Greeks who defended the forts of Macedonia and Thrace. They were completely isolated yet they continued to fight until the very end knowing that all hope had been lost. These were true men, and we know that their deeds live and will continue to live as long as there are free people who live and breathe.

Lord Alexander, England

THE NEW THERMOPYLAE

The battle of the Metaxas forts was followed by the last battle, the struggle for the "body" of Greece as it has been called. The Germans, having broken through the line situated between the rivers Strimon and Nestos, now march south. Conditions on the Northern Epirus front are desperate. Despite the fighting which continues, the front is collapsing. The General Staff however refuses to surrender. The Greeks and the British Expeditionary Corps link their forces and create a new front along the Aliakmon River.

Thermopylae is the last attempt to establish a new front. The Greeks and the British together manage to hold the legendary area for three days. On the 16th of April, orders for the retreat of the Allied forces from Thermopylae are given. The Allied forces then begin night retreats while continuing to fight strongly.

Evacuations of various harbours are also beginning, all of which are located in mainland Greece but primarily in the Peloponnese. The destination of the troops is Egypt and Crete where, together with the Greeks who have managed to flee, they will continue the struggle for freedom. In Athens, on the 18th of April, the Prime Minister, Alexander Korizis, commits suicide. On the 19th of April, it is decided that the Greek government be transferred to Crete. On the 20th, General Tsolakoglou arbitrarily signs the terms of surrender at the front.

The last war communiqué, on the 23rd of April, is like the mourn-ful tolling of a bell, announcing the general pull out of all the Greek armed forces whose unequal struggle, ended with "our surrender to the German forces on the evening of April 20th".

The communiqué concludes with the reassurance that at the moment of surrender to the Germans "the Italian forces were held in check by our forces in Albania, who did not allow the Italians to step back on Greek territory". According to the statement made by Churchill: "The Greek military honour remains unblemished."And then begins the unending retreat. The gloriously defeated return to their 'homelands'. The front of victory in Albania and Epirus subsides and changes appearance. Weapons and firearms are destroyed. Dreams and hopes are shattered. On April 25th and 26th, for the first time in war history, German parachutists land at Corinth. At the same time, German mechanised units arrive just outside Thebes. From there the road to Athens is open. It is the road to sorrow, to misfortune and despair.

General Sigmund List's armoured convoys are located close to the gates of the capital. At 9.00 in the morning of April 27th, the first German armoured column appears, the first motorcyclists of the armoured division. Along their way they find all the window shutters tightly closed. The people of Athens refuse to receive them. The surrender of the city then follows. And the convoy continues for its destination - the Acropolis. On the 10th of May, the swastika is raised in the air with the blue Greek sky in the background. At exactly 10 a.m., the same moment as the swastika is raised, the well known author, Penelope Delta, drinks poison, no longer able to bear the insult. She is the first to die in the Greek resistance foreshadowing the revolt of the Greek spirit against the conqueror.

Ambulance Train No. 1

April 11, 1941. I am aboard the Ambulance Train No. 1 at the small station of Palaiofarssalo, in Thessaly. The commander is Lieutenant Doctor L.S. Morton, R.A.M.C. and I was his interpreter. When the war with Italy broke out and we pushed the Italians into Albania - it is a vicious lie that the Albanians resisted the Italians; far from it, they helped the Italians as much as they could, because they hated the Greeks as they still do - the Greek Medical Corps decided to establish Medical Trains. The Greek Medical Corps must have been stupid since they chose to use refrigerator carriages to carry the wounded. When they had set up the stretchers and added a small radiator, they then realised they had a problem on their hands.

The carriages had no doors at each end and so communication was only possible when the train stopped. Therefore they needed 31 nurses for the 31 carriages! Furthermore, if the need arose, which it often did, for the doctor to be present in a particular carriage, they had to stop the

196

train in the dark with rain and snow falling and the doctor had to search for the required carriage tripping over stones and bushes. The call for the doctor was made via an internal telephone which resembled a child's toy. Often, by the time the doctor arrived, the wounded soldier had died! When the British Expeditionary Corps decided to establish two Medical Trains, it first sent two English officers of the Corps to St. Ioannis Rendis who found carriages which had access to one another. They converted the carriages into what looked like the interior of a hospital and instead of 31 nurses and an assisting staff, the English did the same job with a staff of 9 in total!

Aboard the Ambulance Train No. 1 at Palaiofarsalo, we would await the arrival of the English wounded so that we could then transport them to Piraeus and to hospital ships there. The scene we saw was Dantean. Greek soldiers in groups would descend from the nearby hills, some armed, some not. Those who carried arms threw their guns, their cartridge belts and their helmets to the ground in disgust, where they formed a small shapeless mound. They all wanted a means of transportation so that they could go further south. But the only means of transport was our train and that was without a steam engine. The only existing steam engine was taken by some railway men who had departed leaving behind a man named Akritas - I can't remember his first name - whom they had sent to the village to get food and whom they had abandoned.

At one time I saw a Greek Captain go up to a small hill and thousands of soldiers gathered around him. The captain shouted in a loud voice, "Men, unfortunately our country has lost the war!" And then an eerie nightmarish outcry of "ZETO" was heard which froze my blood. And yet the panic stricken soldiers who fled before Hitler's deadly war machine broke out with this "ZETO" ('hurrah') which their panic stricken souls felt. "ZETO" meant we are alive and that we continue to live!

Dusk was starting to fall. The mob, for it was truly a mob, sought any means of transportation. But there were no other means of transportation but our train, without an engine, waiting to receive the wounded English. The exhausted Greek soldiers entered the medical carriages and lay down on the stretchers to sleep. In vain did we plead with them to leave, because the stretchers were reserved for the wounded. They drove us away with the most awful insults. Then the first ambulance arrived and it did not know where to leave the wounded. I can still hear the groans of the boys from Albion who had come to defend our country. And then the commander, Lieutenant Morton, frightened, made the most insane decision. He called me to his office and gave me his greatcoat with its two central stars on the shoulder straps, his helmet, his revolver with its thick khaki strap, a large electric torch and a letter written on a piece of blue paper which bore the letterhead, signature and stamp of the Ambulance Train No. 1 and ordered me to remove all the intruders who were on the train and to load the wounded and to depart for Pireaus.

The evacuation was easily accomplished. I took six Greeks who were assistants on the train - I still remember their names - and collected all the rifles and helmets and emptied the carriages one by one. This time the insults came from us and the intruders retreated like wet cats. The stretchers filled with the English wounded. The only thing which remained was the steam engine. Akritas helped me. We tried to contact Shimatari using the toy telephone. A woman's voice replied which sounded like a grammophone recording: "This is Larissa, the Germans have entered the city, please hang up." This was repeated several times monotonously. If the Germans had entered Larissa, then it would not be long before they reached Palaiofarsalo. I became very alarmed. The message later proved to be the work of the surprisingly active 5th Column. In the meantime, a steam engine had arrived from Shimatari with two - hear ye, hear ye - Australian engine drivers! We set off. At each bridge Akritas and the Australians would get off and search it in case it was wired with explosives. We reached Domokos. It was almost dawn.

The Australians told me that the steam engine had no more water. They walked towards a cistern. Like a lizard one of the Australians climbed up and shoved the canvas pipe into the engine's opening. As soon as it was filled with water we prepared to resume our seats. In the dim light of the lanterns a Greek Second Lieutenant stopped me roughly, these were tense moments: "Listen to me. You are going to take me along with my group to Athens."

"It's not allowed" I replied, "this is an English Medical Train", and I made to move off.

He took hold of my sleeve and said: "Come here you .... I'll .... whatever you hold sacred!"

I am not a violent person, quite the opposite, by nature I'm quite mild tempered, but the tension, the exhaustion, the fear and above all the extreme sense of responsibility I felt looming over my head, made me lose my temper. I pulled out my gun, put it against his stomach and shouted: "Who do you think you're talking to like that?" There was a long cold pause, and then I heard a most polite voice: "Mr. Murat, are you an officer of the English army? I'm sorry. My name is Klavdianos, civil engineer! "I also apologised and we became friends and overlooking the regulation, I managed to take him and his group on board the train.

The following afternoon we arrived at Shimatari. The small station had been bombed earlier by German planes and it had sustained many casualties. Lieutenant Morton woke up and cleanly shaven, received all the items he had given me and we set off for our final stop and our bitter farewell.

Last year the British Embassy in Athens telephoned and informed me that Dr. L.S. Morton would be visiting Greece during the summer and that he would like to see me at that time. I expressed my pleasure at seeing a friend from those difficult and very tense days. But he did not come to Greece. I don't know why. Perhaps he was taken ill or worse. I never found out. Perhaps we shall meet in the next life where we will exchange our memories of that difficult, frightening, but above all, young period of our lives.

Dimitris Murat

Greek campaign

I will try and write down a few of the things that happened, as this is the first time I have had a table to write on, and I am afraid the other scrappy letters I got away were destroyed.

I will start at the beginning. We had one wild night in Alexandria after

199

being pulled out of Libya and I was woken up and told to report to a ship at 8 o'clock. We all knew we were going to Greece though it was all "very secret". To my delight I found I was to be M.O. to a ship and she was not leaving for two days, so I had two days more or less in Alexandria and bought you a handbag etc. and went to the pictures.

When we arrived at Athens we found the rest of the unit had not come yet so Bill Gunther, Ian Roberts and I had several days and a car. The Acropolis is one of the few things that comes up to anticipation value, and we went up and saw the sunset from the Parthenon. There was still a bit of snow on the mountains and the skies were blue and the sight of green fields and olive groves was much better than Pot. Brom. for the nerves after four months in the desert. The people behaved just as the newspapers said, threw flowers at us and smiled, and were generally charming. The high percentage of incidence of fairies and the scenery made me think of those charming people Woodhouses. The old Prof. knew a thing or two!

After a week we moved north and all through the villages the people gave us drinks of wine. One of Greece's main troubles appears to be that it has too much scenery and too much weather. I can honestly say that I have never seen such glorious scenery as we saw from the convoy up.

I had a seat in a car most of the way, and we stopped for lunch overlooking Mt Parnassus one day and Olympus another. I knew I would know all about it some day as I bought a book costing 56/-. Then an interesting thing happened. We were told one morning from a "secret but authoritative" source that hostilities with Germany would commence at 5 a.m. This was at 2 a.m. and we had to be packed and ready to move by 5. I had had three days in bed with flu, and felt pretty weak, but we got it done and remained at one hour's notice to move for a day. We moved up into position and I had the extreme pleasure of eating Caviar (yours) and biscuits and tea from my thermos in the snow.

Everything was very lovely but owing to Fifth Columnists I think, rumours of all kinds were rife. Finally I was chosen to march with a section of a brigade which did not have an M.O. I was not feeling too strong but was glad I got the job as it was part of the old Battalion, and the boys said they were pleased to see me.

200

One very regimental sergeant said, "My word, it is good to have you with us, Sir, we all have more confidence when you are with us", which repaid me for many things. We set out at 11 p.m. with certain field ambulance personnel and ten donkeys laden with medical stores. The position was that transport had to be withdrawn quickly, and the men were to march cross country to trick the Jerries who were in danger of breaking through on the left flank and cutting us off. We marched all night in a light snow storm mostly uphill, and the donkeys fell over and had to be unloaded, lifted and loaded.

Suddenly we looked down three thousand feet and across to Olympus at about 1 a.m. with a ghostly moonlight seeping through the snow clouds. One of the most unlikely dropscenes I have ever seen. We came down to river level and on the way, as we had had donkey trouble, Major Hooper came back to see if I was alright as I was about half a mile behind the others. The Engineers gave us hot tea and we crossed on a punt pulled by the "ginger beers" who would not let anyone help them, saying "You've done your job, this is ours." The boys were still singing though it was now 4 a.m. On the other side of the river was Bill Gunther and a truck for my sick or wounded, and a bottle of whiskey!! There were very few sick and none dropped out as they had been warned that they would have to be left in the snow.

From a letter by Tom Selby, Australia, 4.5.1941

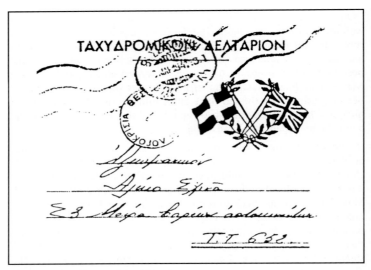

From the collection of W. Moseley, England

Sketch by Bailey

They would see the smoke and open fire

I had an exciting adventure when we had assumed a position of rearguard in Greece, at a place which was called Kokinoplo where we marched during the night somewhere in the area of Mount Olympus. There was a lot of mist and fog and we sat around talking. We were sitting in half opened trenches, which were not very deep, and the Huns opened fire. We didn't know what was going on. It was a strange feeling. We took refuge into our small holes. The Germans seemed to be aiming at my trench, and I couldn't quite understand why. Later on I realised that as I was smoking my pipe - something which I've done all my life - they could see the smoke and they opened fire. As soon as they approached, we suddenly realised that they were very close and then we opened fire on them as well.

Ray Minson, New Zealand
Transcripts of interviews made for the documentary film, "Touch and Go - the Battle of Crete, May 1941", written and directed by Tom Steel and produced by Jeremy Isaacs Productions for the New Zealand Broadcasting Corporation

An Australian war diary

10th April

The vessel which was to carry us to Athens was the SS PENNLAND, a large Dutch passenger ship fitted out as a transport, and fairly comfortable though very crowded.

In the late afternoon we moved from the wharf to an anchorage in the outer harbour. As we passed close to a British cruiser one of the sailors called out, "You'll be alright. We'll come up next week and bring you back." Ominous words. We sailed at 2200 hours in company with SS CAMERONIA being duly escorted by HMS COVENTRY and three destroyers. We were the last convoy to leave for Greece. The voyage was uneventful, the food good, the weather pleasant. The trip took forty hours, and we were not attacked.
12th April

An ammunition ship in Piraeus harbour had been bombed and exploded a couple of days before, devastating the whole harbour. So we could not berth there, and it was decided to land the troops at Phaleron Bay, disembarking them in the local fishing vessels known as 'caiques'. But the tide was out when we got there, and the caiques could not get alongside the jetty. So the last few yards had to be done by dinghy.

The troops who had landed were taken in trucks to Daphni where they spent the night in tents under the pine trees. I was tired and the scent of the pine needles induced a deep slumber.

13th April

Trucks called for us in the afternoon and took us to the railway station where we entrained. I had been warned that there was much traffic on the road and it might take 24 hours to get to Larissa. Our train left in the late afternoon on a journey that should have taken about fourteen hours. Athenian residents lined the railway track and cheered as we went along. This was much appreciated by the troops. We made slow progress during the night.

14th April

Dawn found us at Brallos, about half way to Larissa. We were on the foothills of Mount Parnassus and the scenery was magnificent. Thereafter halts were frequent and long. We eventually crawled into Larissa in the late afternoon. A sizeable town rebuilt after a recent earthquake.

We were told that the main force was withdrawing through Larissa, and our job was to take up a position on the road west of Kalabaka to cover the withdrawal of the British Armoured Division from the Aliakmon line, and block the road against any advance by the enemy on Larissa from the west. The trucks would take us to Kalabaka, and we would move on tomorrow by foot to a selected position.

15th April

We moved on through Kalabaka marvelling as we went at the Meteora - the rock pinnacles with monasteries at the top.

The original plan was that we should take up a position on the Aliakmon road, but when I looked at it with Brigadier Savage we found it quite unsuitable. It was thickly timbered with plane trees with no field of fire, and the Germans if stopped could just walk round the flanks. So we went back and selected a much better position three miles west of Kalabaka in a defile athwart the road and the railway, and with our left on the Pinios river, an impassable tank obstacle. We saw Greek women repairing the road down which refugees were streaming.

It was an uneventful day.

16th April

Some B Echelon vehicles from the Armoured Brigade came through and I tried to get some reliable news from their front. They still seemed to be on the Aliakmon line, and had had no contact with the German army. But they had been bombed from the air. We discussed plans for a withdrawal the following night.

The road was completely blocked by refugees and soldiers who were so tired that they did not care if they were run over or not. Here and there engineers were preparing demolitions. It was an anxious time, and I did not sleep well.

19th April

We set off promptly at 0300 hours and had a clear run over the eight miles into Larissa. The town had been heavily bombed, and was deserted by the inhabitants. The only living person that we saw was an MP who directed us through the town and on to the main South road.

We had no sooner started than planes came over in relays bombing vehicles on the road, and machine gunning the sides of the road where any troops had taken cover. This lasted some hours, and we made slow progress to Lamia. From that town on to the foot of the Brallos pass there is a long straight stretch of road on a causeway. I was dreading this, but fortunately by the time we got there the Germans had used up all their bombs for the day, and we had an uninterrupted run across the causeway, and from there on to Brallos where we found the men and vehicles of the Battalion assembled.

The bivouac area at Brallos was just a place for the night. It was congested and on swampy ground. But the cooks were able to prepare an evening meal. I had a conference of company commanders and ordered that at first light the vehicles were to be dispersed. I also warned them - as I had been told by the Divisional commander - that next day the Battalion would have to take its place in the Thermopylae line, with New Zealanders on the right down by the sea. Having done this the strain of the last few days, plus the shock of being shot up took their toll, and I cracked up. My left arm was numb and temporarily useless, and the RMO insisted that I must go to hospital next day. So in the morning I departed after handing over the command of the Battalion to Major Sandover.

T.S. Louch, Australia
The 2/11th (City of Perth) Australian Infantry Battalion
Edited by Bill Brown

Guns in the mountains

Finally, south from Kozani, the Germans were blocked again when Australian sappers blew up a bridge over the Aliakmon river. The approach to the bridge was flat, and again the Germans came over in masses. "I would not have believed it," a young Australian machine-gunner said to me. "They came up the side of the road like flies, shouting something. We were giving it them from all sides and they went down like you see in the movies. It was just like a movie". Every time the Germans tried to repair the bridge they got smashed about more from the big gun sitting up on the mountains. The Germans sent up infantry to get the guns but they were beaten back every time. Finally, the big 105's came up, but the British guns had already done their job and withdrawn.

"I have spoken to men coming back, and they have all got individual stories that are unbelievable unless you are here with that artillery going off before you, the rain sizzling down, the cold and the wet, the rumbling and the silence making the background of battle. The whine of the transport up in the hills. The deep dark valleys showing the flash of the battle below. The shells bursting in a red flash. And you tense and waiting for the sound to reach you seconds later but never hearing it because the deep mocking laugh of the explosions is continuous.

THE CAMPAIGN IN GREECE AND CRETE issued by the Ministry of Information

The Germans at the harbour of Kavala
Keystone Press Agency, London

Contributed by Jean-Louis Roba, Belgium

The first refugees
The Greek Gazette, London, October 1983

A hectic experience

The forces to which I was attached came under 'Jerry's' tender attentions at a place called Ellisona or Ellison, in the Mount Olympus area, about April 14, when we had several air raids. These continued for two days, one being of a particularly spectacular nature, when at 7 pm, just at sunset, 35 German heavy bombers, flying low and almost wing-tip to wing-tip, were good enough to visit us. Fortunately the damage was slight in comparison to the weight used, but the raid followed within an hour of the issue of orders for us to come back to a place called Levadia, about 150 miles south.

That trip was a hectic experience. The road is very narrow, and goes through two main passes, one north of Lamia and the main Thermopylae Pass. These were very steep, winding roads, and were crowded with military transports and Greek refugees, on foot and in cars and carts, intermixed with cattle and sheep and household goods of all descriptions - the latter a very pathetic sight that one will never forget.

From a letter by Crofton Stephens
The Mercury, Adelaide, Australia, 2.6.1941

Thermopylae, 30.4.1941
Contributed by Herman-Otto Greiner, Germany

Night at Thermopylae

Stars in their thousandfold splendour
And Earth exuding breath of spring,
Pines, cypresses and agaves pointing skyward
In all their glory.
But, lo! This idyll of flowering nature
Is shattered now by dazzling lightning,
For only a brief moment, but then -
Guns roar - their echo climbing mountains
Is held awhile, withdrawn - then flees
As if escaping from itself and runs
along the hills.
Soon fades the rumbling but is followed
By crashing, evil spraying steel and stones, and meteoric
charges hiss and glow and die.
Silence returns and faith and thoughts borne by the stars
And fairy night awakes and nightingales rejoice in song.

Hans Ulrich Plath, Germany
VON SERBIEN BIS KRETA

VON SERBIEN BIS KRETA

210

Helmeted German motorcyclists advance through the Pass of Thermopylae on April 25th
(Radio picture received in New York from Berlin)
Keystone Press Agency, London

Retreat from Thermopylae

The soldiers were still working on the job when they were attacked from both sides by parachutists and there was air bombing and machine guns. Both a vital road and the bridge were attacked.

...Suddenly there was a terrific explosion and the bridge disappeared. As far as can be ascertained from the scanty evidence, a New Zealander, finding that the electric wiring had been cut, strolled down the road under heavy tommy gun fire, lit the fuse and went down with the Bridge. He died upholding the standards of individual sacrifice.

BBC Archives, Imperial War Museum, London

A good deal more experience

19th May 1941

Dear Dick,

Thought it about time you heard from me again. Since writing last time we have had a good deal more experience than that gained in the first gentle campaign in Libya Italiana.

We boarded the train for Northern Thessaly. The train was somewhat overcrowded and I found myself with three other Australians, four Greek soldiers, mules and horses. The mules under the care of the Greeks were bound for Albania, the truck being roped off into three sections with the mules occupying positions 1 and 3 with the eight men in the middle. Olives, barley bread, Greek cheese, wine and koniak formed our diet.

Hour after hour we wound through the mountains with their deep gorges and snow-capped peaks until we arrived at Larissa, the rail junction for Albania, Thrace and Yugoslavia.

Retreat...

The straight road to Larissa was dive-bombed and machine-gunned every hour of the day but travelling at night was safe as the planes would not venture among the mountains. But from the crack of dawn until 20.15 hours, life was hell.

The great passes through Larissa to Lamia and the pass of Thermopylae were narrow, the road churned into thick gluey mud and embellished on both sides with burning and tipped-over transport artillery put out of action, dead horses, mules, sheep and cows. Greeks walking and riding in wagons drawn by all types of motor and animal power.

We passed through Thebes, once the capital of Boetia, which had been badly hit. Larissa was a pancake and Lamia a shambles. The whole while our chaps and the New Zealanders fought a rear-guard action dynamiting the bridges over the gorges and blasting away at the German tanks. It was rendered all the more difficult by dive-bombing and machine-gunning aircraft. We had no sleep for days and I marvel now how we managed to keep going day after day with practically no food or sleep. We never changed our clothes or had our boots off for a fortnight.

From a letter by R.C. Robertson, Australia
The Greek Gazette, London, May 1983

Capture

18 April

On 18 April 1941 I took a detail of 20 vehicles to evacuate the 21 New Zealand Battalion which was fighting a rearguard action at Anglimos(?), East of Larissa, Greece. When I got there I had to wait till the troops were collected. In the late afternoon the Germans landed parachute troops in Larissa and cut off our retreat to Volos, in the Gulf of Pagasetikos. We were ordered to leave the vehicles and make our way on foot to Volos, the road being jammed full of vehicles as a result of a German road block.

I eventually ordered my men to disperse, but shortly afterwards the traffic began to move again. I had remained beside the vehicles with my driver and a few more other ranks, and we now tried to get across country through marshes in some of the vehicles. After driving all night we got stuck in the marshes. I had then got with only two vehicles to a blind road, and found that there were Germans on either side of us.

20 April

I destroyed the vehicles and we then walked across the mountains to Volos which we reached about 20 April.

21 April

Volos was by then deserted, but we managed to get an old Greek cart, two mules, and a horse and made our way towards Lamia (21 April). Here we found a battle raging in the Lamia Pass, and we could not get through. With the help of Greeks, however, we got a Greek schooner on which we made our way to the island of Evoia, landing on the north west point. By this time we were a party of about 200, all of whom had crossed from Lamia in the schooner, most of us being New Zealanders and Australians with a few British troops.

From the north western point of the island about 40 of us went to Edipsos, across the bay, in a motor boat. The Greek officer who took charge of the party insisted on the Greek crew taking us under threat of shooting. During the crossing there were German stukas flying around us almost continuously.

22 April

From Edipsos Greeks arranged for 400 or 500 of us being taken by light schooner by night to Khalkis, which we reached on 22 April. Khalkis is connected with the mainland by a bridge which we crossed by vehicle, under instructions to proceed to a dispersal area. After several hours here, we were sent to an entraining point from which we were eventually taken by train to Argos (arrived 23 or 24 April).

23/24 April

Here we were put in the sea evacuation area, whence we were sent to Tolo Beach. At Argos I was placed under the command of a Lt. Smith, 21 New Zealand Battalion, having joined up with the remnants of that battalion and various waifs and strays. I still had 16 or 17 of my own men with me.

On the first evening at Tolo we formed up on the beach, where there was a naval officer and several British officers of high rank. They were in touch with the Royal Navy by radio. We waited two or three hours on the beach till a destroyer sent in a landing craft. We formed up into groups of six and the landing craft was filled. I was among those left behind. We were ordered back to our dispersal area just off the beach to await the next boat.

We spent the next day in the dispersal area under cover. At night we formed up again on the beach, but no ships came in. Next day at 07.00 or 08.00 hours, we were told that the Germans were advancing on us and we had orders to prepare to defend ourselves. The radio set was destroyed, all communications with the Navy being thus cut off. We organised ourselves into first and second lines with a few Bren and Lewis guns and rifles we had. My men and I were ordered to the first line of defence on a ridge. In the morning the Germans (parachute troops), came down. We kept them off most of the day, and several of my men were killed and wounded. About 15.00 hours there was a lull in the fighting, and a man bearing a white flag approached. One of our sergeants went to meet him. He turned out to be one of our own men captured at Argos. He had a message from a German officer ordering us to capitulate by 19.00 hours, otherwise we would be bombed.

28 April

We were then ordered by the senior British officer (possibly a brigadier) to capitulate. There were then 500 or 600 of us in the area.

After the wounded and officers had been removed in captured British trucks, the rest of us were marched to Nafplion, where we were put into an improvised camp in the playground of a school.

We were here for two or three days, and were then removed to a camp in Corinth, where I remained till 7 June.

From the war diary of Bruce Joshua Crawley, New Zealand
Contributed by Jean-Louis Roba, Belgium

I walked 160 miles

I have got permission from our "Skipper" to mention our escape from the Huns. The first escape was not so bad, we only had to walk about 15 miles before the transport picked us up. We were also under shell fire all the way along the railway track. This was on 15th April. It is now 29th April and we're still running away! The second escape was a bit worse. For six days and nights we walked from village to village, buying Greek cheese, goats milk and Greek bread which is hard and dry. I walked about 160 miles.

From a letter by Ken Little to his family, New Zealand

We're prepared to stand

Without striking a note of mock heroics, it can truthfully be said that we would all have preferred to stay there to the end rather than shamefacedly continue our withdrawal. Air Force or no Air Force we were prepared to stand.

Testimony of an Australian Officer
The Advertiser, Adelaide, Australia, 27.5.1941

The Secretary of State for Dominion Affairs to the Prime Minister of New Zealand

20 April 1941

Both the Greeks and the Imperial forces have fought magnificently and from all accounts have maintained their positions well and have inflicted heavy casualties both in men and material on the enemy.

OFFICIAL HISTORY OF NEW ZEALAND IN WORLD WAR 2. DOCUMENTS, Volume 1

Hitler 'throws everything' into Battle of Olympus
MOUNTAIN GUN-TANK DUELS
April 18. *Laron Special Correspondent*
ATHENS. Thursday.

From a period newspaper
Frank Daley, GREECE GALLANT GLORIOUS

Adolf Hitler at the Macedonian front

London, 20 — According to German radio stations, Hitler today celebrated his 52nd birthday at the Macedonian front among his Chiefs of Staff. Thus at the Macedonian front, Hitler saw his columns fighting against the heroic offsprings of small Greece who defend their territories in such a way as to provoke the admiration of the Germans themselves.

From a newspaper of the period
Demosthenes Koukounas, THE GERMANS IN GREECE

Our poor flag!

The Germans were approaching from all sides. That is why all civil servants were ordered to evacuate Koritsa. The departure was a sudden decision. I started to run, together with Second Lieutenant D. Karras, to the garrison's headquarters to catch up with them. As we ran, the trumpet announced the lowering of the flag at the town hall. As always, we stood to attention. The scene was truly moving. Behind us stood quite a few soldiers and one of them was heard to say with a sigh: 'Our poor flag....!'

From the war diary of Panayiotis Kanellopoulos
THE YEARS OF THE GREAT WAR 1939-1944

We burnt the flag of our regiment

With the entry of the Germans from Doirani into Thessaloniki, we found ourselves cut off and forced to surrender our weapons. We all shed tears as we burnt the flag of our regiment and vowed to continue our struggle silently and to raise once again our flag over free Greek soil when the blessed moment of final victory came.

The Metropolitan Meletios of France serving with the Greek forces in the forts of Macedonia

Order

2nd Army Division
General's Office
Number A.P. 45

Officers and soldiers,

The General German Army has given to us, the Division commanders, the decision of the Führer to accept our petition to treat us generously. No-one will be considered a prisoner of war and there will shortly follow a general demobilization.

Enemy actions have ceased.

Tomorrow a German Division, which will be led under the direction of our officers, will be stationed here between the Greek and Italian Armies.

We are given the right to withdraw within the next 10 days to our borders which we shall maintain.

I wish to emphasise to everyone that we must present an image of pride and bravery as befits those who carried out their duties towards their country. It is imperative that we give the impression of a well organised and disciplined army.

Easter 1941, Georgios Bakos, Major General

Ioannis A. Vernardos, TREBESINA

Incredible

The Germans had issued an order: "To disarm the entire army. The officers only to be allowed to keep their revolvers". They issued an order that we were to throw our rifles into a heap. But I broke mine, why should I surrender it?

Incidentally, the only division of the Greek armed forces which was not disarmed was the Cretan Division. Anyway, after a few days of marching we arrived in Psathopyrgos near Patras. We were all exhausted, hungry, wretched and full of lice. But we went in columns.

The Italians followed in 50 to 100 trucks. The Italians had broken into a cigarette factory in Aminteo and had taken thousands of packs. As they passed us, they threw packs of cigarettes at us, but we let them drop on the ground and refused to pick them up. This made the Italians mad. So they threw more and more at us and we continued to ignore them, which incensed them more. Even as prisoners, we still made them feel inferior.

Anyway, we marched on. Now we were passing Preveza, Arta, going towards Messolonghi. This took place in May 1941. Just as we approached Messolonghi, we saw a parked limousine as if waiting for us. An Italian colonel came out. He looked spick and span, with shining boots. He asked who our commander was. Ours was Papanicolaou. He was on a mule, with a long wretched beard, dirty clothes and full of lice. Papanicolaou got off his mule, when he was told that the Italian colonel was in charge of the Italian troops who some days ago had fought against us for about a week. The two men met and greeted each other. The Italian asked, "Which was your sector?" and the other replied "Across from Kleisoura." They found that they had fought each other and they began to talk about their past lives. Now everything had finished, no matter what happened. "I want to meet your gunners, because I admire them", said the Italian Colonel. "Their shots would come directly into our boilers. It was incredible!...

Fine gunners, I want to congratulate them!"

Oral account of Pandelis Markoyiannakis

To Arms

Friday morning 18.4.41

Today is the 8th day of our retreat. I am so tired, I cannot begin to describe the sufferings of this march, nor of the horror which no-one knows how long it will last. We march day and night continuously; we cover the retreating forces of the sector and we are on duty continuously. The Italians have almost caught up with us. I write this in haste, as there will be a battle.

I continue: The Italians have come very close, we climbed up onto a hill and engaged in a skirmish, we will fight, that is certain. We covered the retreat of the army and now we are the last, a handful of men without any firearms and food to defend ourselves.

I fear that we may be taken prisoners.

Saturday morning 19.4.41

... The battle has begun. They are trying to surround us from the sides.

After a few hours: we are fighting, we are fighting and the mortar shells are exploding very close to us. My ammunition is almost finished, most of the men have left and only a handful have remained.

Saturday noon: The battle continues.

They're coming, they're coming, our machine gun has jammed. What will happen now? Reinforcements must come; there are too many of them. The small hill which lies across from us has been taken. Now they attack us from both sides. My thoughts are with my mother, my father and all my loved ones. To my right from the top of a hill, some machine gun has me targeted. It keeps shooting at me, sometimes individual shots, sometimes whole rounds. It won't allow me to look up even for a moment, but I'll get a chance to see where he is and then we shall see. My gun isn't working, I can't load it. I try to fix it. Damn, I can't.

We've just received the order to hold out for another three hours at whatever cost. It is now 5 p.m., we will ... hold out but what about ammunition? The thunder of battle is incredible; machine guns, bombs, both artillery and aircraft, a hell of fire and steel. I gave my sub machine gun to a companion who is beside me to see if he can fix it. He's an old and experienced fighter. Still nothing, it is horrid to be at war without any arms. He shouts that my gun is now ready. I get up and crawl out of my trench immediately. They shoot at me. I interrupt. I keep loading, loading continuously. My weapon has jammed again. I clean it as best I can. The Italians have been reinforced with one more gun.

Dusk: Everything is the same.

After an hour: The bullets fly around me, really close and large bombers fly overhead. German probably. They dive bomb us.It is close to 8.00: We will be retreating soon. They continue to fire at us but we don't fire back; only once in a while because we don't have that much ammunition left.

From the war diary of volunteer soldier, George P. Bisbas

2002, Advanced Air Force

April came but we still hadn't received any orders to attack. 20 more British fighters with their crews have arrived increasing the total number of the airforce in Yianina to 32. We are given the name "2002 Air Force of the Albanian front".

At dawn on April 6th we were informed of the German attack on Greece. In the afternoon of the same day 60 German heavy bombers appeared escorted by 30 fighter planes. We did not engage them because it was not possible to do battle with the 12 modified airplanes we had. The English planes took off and I saw the most horrific scene of the war. I was on a small hill near one anti- aircraft gun defending the airport. The air battle was vicious. The noise of diving aircraft, the rattle of machine guns, the noise of anti-aircraft guns, bomb explosions and fire everywhere. A perfect hell. I saw 15 - 16 German planes and 7 - 8 English planes, all wrapped in flames and smoke crashing to the ground and taking to their death all their crews. I didn't see even one parachute open. This went on for two hours. The airport was literally dug up by the bombs of the 60 German bombers. Of the modified hydroplanes ten, together with mine, were destroyed. Only two survived intact and able to fly. When the air attack was over, I saw the two planes take off from the bombed runway and head south.

Unfortunately, the German attack called off all the pre-arranged plane reinforcements to the front for the commencement of the Spring Offensive. In two days, 8 April 1941, we prepared to move behind the lines. In fact the retreat along the Albanian front had already begun. We got into a car and were transported to the airfield at Agrinion where I saw the two surviving aircraft of our unit. If I remember correctly, it was Good Friday, perhaps May 1st, when they told me to take two airmen with me and to go to the city so that we could shop for Easter.

221

We filled two army sacks with food and set out from the town in the direction of the airbase, as the locals called it. As soon as we reached the clearing of the airfield and were approximately 800 metres from the other end where our unit was, we saw a German fighter bomber flying low and approaching the area where our planes and unit were hidden. We threw down our sacks and fell into a trench which was horizontal to the course of the plane. It opened fire a short distance before reaching us. As soon as it had passed overhead, I looked up and saw that it had turned and changed its course so that the shots could hit us along the trench. I told the boys to follow close behind me and taking cover behind the trees in the wood just as the plane came towards us. Its second attack allowed for a better firing line and the bullets ripped through the trench we had lain in during its first attack. As soon as it passed over I yelled out "Boys, follow close behind and distance yourself from me as it will return." The woods were muddy because of heavy rain and as a result we were unable to cover the distance which was required. For its third attack the German fighter bomber dropped bombs close to where we were. Mud splashed into the air by the explosion and we were covered from head to foot. On its fourth and fifth attacks, it dropped bombs along a wide area, as if it knew that at the end of the runway we had hidden our two airplanes and the entire unit. Luckily, our appearance indicated that the unit was on the other side of our base, otherwise the unit would have sustained heavy casualties. After its final attack, seven in all, our food provisions lay scattered on the ground.

After the attack, even though we were covered in mud, we returned to Agrinion to buy more food. When we returned to the base, our commander told us that we three had saved the entire unit. They had followed the attack and it seemed that the pilot thought that this was the location of our unit, at the end of the runway, since that entire area had been thoroughly ploughed up with bombs and artillery fire.

Night had not yet fallen when we received a new order to move to the airbase at Elliniko (Athens). We reached Elliniko on the same night via Eleusis, the Sacred Way, the Acropolis, Syngrou Avenue and the coastal road of Faliron. There the procedure to surrender our arms began. The German would place each rifle on a step and with his foot break it in half. It was our misfortune that one of the last fifteen men got angry with the deliberate destruction of the arms and was ready to kill the German officer.

I seized him quickly and turned his weapon away, while at the same time the translator, with great courage, took hold of the German's hand which was moving towards his revolver. He explained to him that the man was a little insane and he knew this from earlier incidents. Of course it was a lie. In reality the young man was a brave fellow. The German immediately withdrew smiling and when our man was left disarmed, he gave him a friendly slap on the back. Then he told us, through a translator, to go to the base's headquarters. As we were approaching the headquarters, we saw a large column of German tanks and vehicles coming towards the airbase. It came from the coastal road. When the column came to a halt outside the headquarters, the German commander got out of an armoured tank and with his escort climbed up the stairs. I did not see the meeting with our own commander. He was squadron leader Yiannaris. The German commander asked Yiannaris to order us to clean up the runway which we had destroyed the day before, with the promise that they would take us in German cars to Omonia Square, from where we could then catch a local bus to return to our homes. We refused the offer and chose to go on foot. After a short while we dispersed and began to walk, taking the coastal road of Old Faliron, towards Athens. After 20 minutes German motor cars caught up with us and using a loud speaker, and in Greek, they invited us to get on, so that they could take us to Omonia. We did not believe a thing they said, thinking that they would return us to the airbase to repair the runway we had damaged the previous day. The translators persisted, insisting that the Germans were polite and kept their promises. A few started to get into the automobiles and in the end we all accepted the ride.

Since I was more suspicious, I was one of the last to get on. In fact they did take us to Omonia and told us: "For you the war is over. Go to your homes and your family. No-one is stopping you."

Oral account of Ioannis Spinos
Contributed by Tony Hadjigeorgiou

223

Retreat from Pogradec, Albania

At 10 pm on April 10th a friend, whose name was Klimis, and I decided to leave for the rear lines. It was 10.15 pm when we agreed to abandon everything taking with us only a blanket, a sack filled with some food, our guns and four hand grenades. We set out at night in the same direction that the Regiment had taken. All night we walked towards the rear lines often confusing the footpaths and getting lost. At dawn we heard the thunder of the Italian attack from behind. We must have been close to where we had started and we had not travelled as far as we should have done during the night. In the light of day we were able to orientate ourselves and began to either run or walk briskly. We had grown quite hot and sweaty from running. In the afternoon we saw the dust that was raised by the Regiment as it marched along 5-6 kilometres in front of us. When night fell we could not hear the artillery of the battle. Klimis and I agreed to rest a while. I don't know how long I slept, but my anxiety and nightmares woke me up before the dawn of April 12th. The night before I had laid out a mark and before daybreak Klimis and I continued along the same route. My companion started to slow down because his feet had swollen badly from frostbite. The Regiment was steadily leaving us behind. I wonder what happened to the 63 men who had been left behind at the front. I never found out, because I never saw them again.

On April 14th we entered Greece, following the Chios Regiment, exhausted from the slow progress of Klimis. Even though that night the Regiment continued south, for Klimis' sake I was forced to stay at a village called Ieropigi where we were given hospitality by the village priest. He cooked us soup and rice and gave us wonderful bread. We washed, changed our underclothes and slept on some soft bedding.

The following day, April 15th, we headed south having lost touch with the Regiment. That night we slept in a hayloft. The following day, April 16th, we continued our march. After mid-day we saw, on the slope of a mountain, another small village.

Klimis, his eyes filled with tears, said: "Jimmy, I cannot walk any longer. Leave me before you are taken prisoner. I shall walk slowly along on my own and reach that village. Some good Christian will help me."

It was then that I threw off the blankets, sacks and weapons. I took Klimis on my shoulder and two hours later we arrived at the village. It was Aghia Kyriaki. They put us up at the community's office and gave us stewed potatoes, bread and a place to sleep. Very early the next morning I woke Klimis up so that we could leave. He told me that he would stay in the village and he gave me a letter, a photograph of himself and the address of his mother so that I could visit her at Kokkinia of Piraeus. They showed me a central road which led to Kastoria. I said goodbye to my friend, thanked the good villagers and departed on my own.

I ran through a plain which had few trees for approximately four hours and then came across a small village. A man asked me where I was going and I told him the whole story. Our native villages in Asia Minor were next to each other and he offered me wonderful hospitality. Food, sleep, a bath, civilian clothing. I gave him all my army clothes which he wanted. And so, in civilian clothing now and free of lice, I set out along the central road for Athens. I met many Germans along the way whom I greeted without raising the least suspicion that I was an officer of the Greek army. It took me several days to reach Larissa and Lamia, always with short stops along the way, but not with as good hospitality as before. At Lamia I bought cigarettes and a little food, cheese and bread. I still had quite a bit of money on me because my brother had given me some before we separated at Hotsika.

As I was resting on the side of a small bridge, I saw a small convoy of German cars coming from Lamia towards Athens. The convoy came to a halt near me. I started calmly to walk towards them and the Germans got out of their cars for a rest. Their Officer asked me something but I couldn't understand. I realised he was Austrian and that he needed a guide who would take him to Athens. I undertook to show him the way and offered him a Greek cigarette. I was very lucky because the Austrian took me as far as Thebes. I understood that he could not take me as far as Athens. I remember I spent Easter at Thebes.

There I learnt that the Germans had already reached Athens before me. I did not know what had happened to my Regiment. Nor did I dare tell anyone that I had come from Albania. I stayed in Thebes for 4-5 days and gave my good clothes, which the man from Asia Minor had given me, to a machine shop and bought second hand clothes so that I would not arouse suspicion. The man at the machine shop gave me plenty of food and a train ticket for Athens.

By the time I reached Athens I realised I was full of lice once again. From Athens I went to Kokkinia and gave Klimis' mother the things he had entrusted me with. Then I went to Piraeus hoping to find some means of transportation to Chios, my island. Close to the old clock at Piraeus I entered a barber's shop to have my head shaved. The razor dripped with blood from the lice which were caught in its blade. Before I had finished, an old friend of mine, Likoudis, came into the shop and after I told him all the hardships I had gone through, he took me to his home. We bought ointment and powder for the lice, he set up a huge pot of water to boil and a bath tub and gave me new clothes. This time I finally got rid of the lice once and for all.

Oral account of Dimitris Hadjigeorgiou
Contributed by Tony Hadjigeorgiou

Despite the orders issued, some officers surrendered to the Germans

.... At Ioannina on the night of the 16th April I first met General Pitsikas. He kept me with him.

On the 18th April - Good Friday - he asked me to attend a meeting of his staff as a political adviser. There was silence all over Athens.

In the evening of the same day we received the news of Prime Minister Korizis' suicide. The meeting took place in the after-noon. Pitsikas and his staff - among whom were Major General Platis, the then Colonel Grigoropoulos and the then Lieutenant Colonel Balodemos - stood firm by their decision to continue the war until Athens ordered the contrary. After the meeting - which took place while the German planes were bombing Ioannina - General Pitsikas and I remained alone together. I told him that he should go down to the bomb shelter. He refused. I shall never forget the tranquility of his expression. He said: "I realise that to continue the struggle is in vain. But I will continue the fight until

I receive an order stating otherwise. The honour of the, until yesterday, victorious Greek Army and the solidarity towards our allies, the British, compels me to take this decision."

On Saturday of Holy Week, Ioannis Pitsikas issued his final order to all the units. He demanded that the struggle continue. But on the afternoon of Easter Sunday, April 20th - a memorable day which was not lit up by the candles of the Resurrection but by the flames of deadly airbombs - the officers under the command of General Pitsikas surrendered to the Germans without his knowledge and contrary to his order. At 4 am, the morning of April 21st, General Pitsikas asked me to accompany him to Athens. We sailed through the Corinthian Gulf in a ship, from Naupaktos to Psathopyrgos. I still have as a sacred heirloom a photograph. At that moment the Germans were bombing the harbour of Patras, my birthplace. Before we arrived at the Isthmus of Corinth, General Pitsikas fell ill. It was impossible to continue. He told me to go on to Athens and to report to the King - we did not know if a new Prime Minister had been sworn in - all that had happened.

This I did at midnight on the 21st to the 22nd April. The King was pleased to hear that General Pitsikas remained firm and did not surrender to the Germans. The King had not been informed yet of what had happened. The information which came down from the front was unclear and contradictory...

Panagiotis Kanellopoulos
Kathimerini, 8 .6.1975

Chaos reigned supreme

It was Holy Week of 1941. In Athens chaos reigned supreme. No-one knew if there was a military front or not and if there was, where it was located. It was Thursday if my memory serves me right. I went to call on some of my friends who were serving in the G.H.Q.(It was then in the Grande Bretagne Hotel). I found all the officers not in their offices, but standing in the corridors smoking, drinking coffee and talking, some nervously and some with a sickly indifference. I found my friends. No-one knew if there was still a front and where it could possibly be.

Telegrams which had been sent by the G.H.Q. to the front, remained

April 21, Lieutenant General I.Pitsikas seated. Standing from left to right are: P. Kanellopoulos, Lieutenant (lawyer) Leonidas Pitsikas and the then Captain Elias Papagiannopoulos Panagiotis Kanellopoulos, THE YEARS OF THE GREAT WAR 1939-1944

unanswered. The situation was desperate. I left there and went to the English G.H.Q. It was located at the Marasleion School. I had an old friend and school mate from the Academy there - the then Wing Commander George Tzannetakis. He was the Greek liaison officer in the English G.H.Q. where he also had his office. I found him in his office and we talked. He asked me if he could repeat what I had told him to a friend of his, a Lieutenant Colonel whom he had met while he was in England on a Greek government scholarship to study internal fuel combustion engines for aircraft and fuels. This Englishman was serving at G.H.Q. in Athens. I told him that he could tell him my account. The next day I would pass by the School of Marasleion to find out his answer.

I went the next day and Tzannetakis told me: I informed the Englishman who told me that yesterday evening there would be a general meeting of the staff in the presence of the English Ambassador, Palairet. He asked me if he could bring the issue before the council.

I told him that he could and Tzannetakis continued: Today the Englishman came and saw me. He told me - as a reply - this and that. And he then added: Unfortunately George, nothing can be done. Yesterday (17.4.41) we went to Skala Oropou and brought back King George who had left Athens and had boarded a yacht which belonged to Bodosakis and whose captain was Admiral Voulgaris.

Themis Moschatos

A stark black night descends upon our country

I was serving at the Ministry for Air when on the second day after the declaration of war, I was notified to present myself at General Headquarters. I found myself before a company of our 'high ranking officers', headed by the King, and learnt that I was to be the interpreter for an English RAF Officer who had just arrived for his first meeting to discuss what aid could be givenby G.H.Q. Middle East to embattled Greece. We quickly realised, both he and I, that we had been old school mates in 1931-1932.

I include this detail because Williams, that was his name, requested that I be appointed Liaison Officer with the Greek authorities. After a while Prince Peter, a remarkable man whom I would say was burdened by the royal blue blood which coursed through his veins, assumed the duties of Chief Liaison Officer with the English military mission as it came to be called. I remained liaison officer only with the R.A.F. It was from this position that I learnt, perhaps from Prince Peter, or probably from some English officer who had told me that "We exerted great pressure on your King, so as not to leave from Oropos at the crucial moment." My information comes from a second source and so I cannot give you any more information.

For myself, I went from airbase to airbase, from one Greek airforce unit to another, trying to subdue the panic which arose from conflicting and pointless orders. To burn our fuels, to destroy the airbases and so forth. One would have thought that these orders were coming from the Germans and their friends and not from the Greeks! I went to the Ministry for Air in the hope of tracking down the source of these peculiar orders which hindered the departure of the Greek and English units from the front. I could find out nothing. It was then that I asked myself if I should throw off my uniform and follow the fate of all the Greeks or whether I should go back to my position with the others and become a paid clerk. It was at this crucial moment that I met Moschatos. He said to me: "George, a black night descends on our country. If you feel you are like a small candle, a small oil lamp, then you must give your light, however small it may seem, for the use of the Greek people. If, on the other hand, you feel it is your duty not to abandon your position with the English forces, then take them as far as their embarkation point, if it is their fate to abandon Greece and to create a new Dunkirk."

The RAF Headquarters was leaving Athens for Nauplion. They waited for me until the last moment. There it was decided that the non-fighting personnel were to be divided into two groups. One group, led by an English high ranking officer, would leave for Crete or Egypt from Kalamata. The other, much smaller and led by myself, would try to find whatever local transport was available, even small caiques, and try to reach Crete from Githeion. The mission they had assigned me was carried out successfully and with no losses. As a matter of fact, my group increased by four young Greek airforce officers.

Oral account of George Tzannetakis

Alexandros Korizis

Alexandros Korizis was the first Prime Minister, during those crucial hours, who presented before the British the issue of Cyprus. Korizis, fully aware of the oncoming tempest, talking to the British Foreign Minister Anthony Eden on March 2nd whilst the latter was visiting Greece, pointed out the need for the transfer of the Greek government and King from Athens in the event of a German invasion. He noted that Crete was not the ideal location for the Greek state leaders and added that the issue could easily be resolved if Great Britain would generously offer Cyprus to Greece, given the fact that only on Greek soil could the King exercise his royal perogatives.

Korizis reminded the Greek Ambassador to London of this conversation and added that Eden had given this reply: "Your request will be examined more closely and upon my return to London I shall present it before the Prime Minister." Korizis had asked that the issue be brought before Winston Churchill himself. Several days passed, most likely there were British cabinet meetings, and even though the Germans continued to march on Greek territory, Korizis received his answer from London that "The position of the Greek government would be, in this case, the same as that of all the allied governments temporarily based in England and that the British Government will not hand over the island which it governs." This occurred on April 13th, while the Germans were advancing south. It was the first refusal which Korizis naturally did not accept. He modified his original request, as it was later made known, asking for a small part of Cyprus to be added, a request which Ambassador Palairet promised to pass on to London immediately.

On the following day, April 14th, Eden - speaking to the Greek Ambassador in London - replied that he was grieved to announce that he could not fulfil the Greek request. H. Simopoulos had been instructed by Korizis to insist on the issue because it came at a crucial period. To this insistance, the British Minister promised that he would once again discuss the matter in the cabinet, but hastened to add that the Greek Ambassador "should not raise his hopes high because the issue was complicated and delicate."

The issue did not go any further because the Nazi military machine had occupied the Greek capital and the King and the government of Tsouderos had already departed for Crete which later proved highly secure and was one of the last Greek outposts to be occupied by the Germans. It is to the honour and credit of Alexandros Korizis that he tried desperately to sway Britain's attitude towards Cyprus at a time when Greece was sacrificing everything she had for the sake of the common good.

Dimitris Chronopoulos, GREEK TEMPEST

The Death of Korizis

On Good Friday, 18th April at 2 p.m., I received a telephone call from "Evangelismos Hospital" to go immediately to the residence of Korizis. He had shot himself with a revolver through the heart. He was the second victim after Metaxas. I did not know the reasons for his self sacrifice, but knew well his sensitive nature. I was certain that his collapse was associated with his position as Prime Minister as well as the unfortunate position Greece had been placed in after the decision of the Government and the King to leave Greece. The death of my dear friend Korizis, with whom I had close emotional ties, brought me great grief.

Marinos Yeroulanos, MEMORIES 1867-1957

The Government in Crete

The inaugural speech of the new President of the Government: To the Greek People: At this difficult and very crucial moment, during which I depart with the heroic King of our country who is a worthy symbol of this great struggle, a struggle which the nation continues, I feel that it is my duty to say that I am truly proud of this political action, which symbolises fully the uncompromising Greek spirit and loudly proclaims the firm will of all of us not to submit to the invaders.

Greeks, we are fighting against an unjust and unprovoked attack which was launched on our rear by a most powerful enemy in order to salvage from utter defeat their cowardly associate Mussolini.The unauthorised signing of surrender in Epirus to the German army was a hurried gesture of exhaustion, excused only by the unequal but nonetheless victorious struggle which lasted for six whole months. The struggle is full of material damage and of cowardly wounds inflicted on the unarmed population.

Persevere with fortitude. Only in this way can we strengthen the morale of our country, for which soon a new and greater future will be created. Nations which maintain their honour and respect their obligations towards their friends gain in prestige and stature - a stature we acquired in blood and superhuman efforts. We have a responsibility to respect and guard our honourable name and prestige. Rest assured that soon the day of our nation will dawn. It will be the greatest day of Hellenism.

E.I. Tsouderos, President of the Government
Athens, 23 April 1941

Under Tsouderos regime

Lieutenant General Alexandros Papagos has submitted his resignation to the Greek government which is located in Crete and which was accepted by Royal Decree and published in Athens on 23rd April 1941.

....His self imposed retirement is accepted with regret. For the many years of service given by Lieutenant General Papagos, the King expresses his deepest gratitude since he was the Commander-in-Chief in charge of the Greek army during that most brilliant and glorious epic.

Alexandros Papagos, TWO YEARS IN HITLER'S ARMY CAMPS

Lieutenant Generals Pitsikas, Bakopoulos, Kosmas and in the middle Papagos outside Dachau concentration camp where they were held for several months

233

Don't worry about us - you have to save yourselves

On April 25th we were informed by General Heywood that the last moment had arrived and that our point of departure would be the church at Daphni at 15.30... At 15.30 we met at the famous Monastery of Daphni, along the Sacred Way - General Heywood, Admiral Turl, Mr. Maniadakis and myself...

We stopped at Kineta. German planes patrolled the road which was littered with the remains of the last bombing. Many of our party descended and took cover as soon as they found more appropriate shelter. I looked around completely lost in my thoughts.

General Heywood pulled me along asking me not to draw the enemy pilot's attention with my naval uniform. We went to Corinth. I watched as the city and railway station were bombed. There was no resistance either on land or in the air. I can still hear the shrieks of women and children who had boarded the train to leave Corinth as it was shattered by a bomb which fell on the station. The road from Corinth to Argos was constantly being bombed.

...Nightfall found us at Miloi, on the road from Argos to Tripoli beside the shore and opposite Nauplion. One villager, one of the many good men who are found on Greek soil, approached me. He was returning from the neighbouring mountain, along with his other fellow villagers, where they had taken shelter under the trees during the day because they feared the bombings. He thought I was English and with hand gestures asked me where I would spend the night. I explained who I was and told him that I was with other English officers. He pleaded with me to use his home to rest for the night. He prepared a dinner with the best that was available and he and his wife served us themselves. He filled his glass with wine and drank to our health saying: "Don't worry about us - you have to save yourselves. Don't be afraid of anything, we will crush them." General Heywood was deeply moved by this sincere declaration of the villager. As for myself, I sat and thought that this was the way the Greek people spoke, thought and expressed their feelings during that black period when they were faced with the spectre of slavery.

At dawn on Saturday 26th April, we said goodbye to this hospitable house and its owners and we went back to the large olive grove where the headquarters of General Wilson had temporarily taken refuge. We waited there the whole day while German fighter pilots flew over the area looking for targets. At about 11 pm, a Sunderland flying boat which would later take us to Suda Bay landed near the seashore. A couple of hours later, General Wilson, his staff and the rest of us boarded the Sunderland. At about 2 am on Sunday 27th April, the flying boat top heavy with 62 men and their luggage on board managed to take off for Crete...

Admiral Alexandros Sakellariou, GREECE'S POSITION IN THE SECOND WORLD WAR

Memories of a German War Correspondent
With the paratroopers in Corinth

We set out with the German advance army along the road from Thebes to Athens. We stop at one of the many bomb craters which the British had created on the road so as to slow our progress. They were being filled in by the soldiers and we waited patiently for them to finish the job. Fifty soldiers worked at each crater. They started to work at midnight and it was now 7 a.m. After watching them for a few moments I told my photographer and driver that I would continue on foot. If we were separated, then we would meet to celebrate at the German School of Archeology in Athens where I had spent a blissful ten days as a student seven years earlier. Only 100 kilometres remained before we reached Athens.

At the next crater, which had a width of 30 metres and a depth of 5 metres, two soldiers and an officer from the Engineer Corps were trying to work out how they could overcome this obstacle as quickly as possible. From what they said, I understood that the paratroopers had already arrived in Corinth and I had to meet them there without any delay. A few minutes later, I came across an abandoned English motorcycle and I set out along the pass towards the sea. The dangerous points along the road had been marked out with white letters on a black background by the British. The bomb craters did not prove an obstacle for my motorcycle. The few residents I saw in the villages I passed through were waving a piece of white cloth tied to a stick over their heads.

I could now see the deep blue sea in the distance, at first like a long narrow ribbon among the grey mountains and the island of Salamis. There is a crossroad at Mandra. The road ahead leads to Eleusis and Athens and the road to the right leads to Corinth. I passed by dead mules whose blood had thickened and turned black as it had drained from their bodies. They were still saddled. Abandoned British lorries. Many of them were in the ditch between the road and the sea, overturned with their wheels facing upwards to the sky. I continued between the olive groves along the side of the road to a flat green plain filled with trees and green fields in which were hidden the remains of lorries which had been abandoned by the British army. Their windscreens were shattered, their petrol tanks torn; they were the remains of the "victorious retreat". After about 100 kilometres the Isthmus of Corinth lay before me. The time was 11.15 am exactly. Crossing through two craters and the railway lines which ran along their sides, I descended to the beach and climbing another 50 metres had almost finished my job. But I didn't trust the Tommys. It could have been one of their old tricks; to let the enemy cross over unhindered and then to attack those who followed. We would see soon enough. The wide ribbon of the Isthmus whose length was many kilometres, was in front of me. It is a plain which stretches out like waves between the mountains with an elevation of several hundred metres and which protects it like a solid wall.

The Isthmus of Corinth resembles a bridge between the mainland and the Peloponnese and from 1893 it was divided by a canal which allowed the passage of ships. I asked myself if we had taken the bridge over the canal. It was over this bridge that the railway lines and the road travelled and linked Northern and Southern Greece.

Suddenly I saw paratroopers coming out of their shelter. "Look" one of them said, "the first German soldiers." I was immediately surrounded by a sea of smiling faces. Each one gripped my hand tightly. Cameras turned on me and I was asked to strike a pose. Their eyes shone with great happiness because our meeting proved that the road between Corinth and Athens was free of the enemy. In the meantime, the photographers from the weekly newspapers took pictures from the bridge.

Further down I meet some English war prisoners. "You've lost the

Derwegne Fallschirmjäger

1. Der - weg - ne Fall - schirm - jä - ger, ent -
schloß-ne Waf-fen - trä - ger, be - gei - stert, rasch und
jung, mit don-nern-den Mo - to - ren em -
por, ge-fahr-et ko - ren, be - reit zum küh-nen Sprung.

2. Der Flug der Luftsoldaten, hebt, Sonnenkameraden, früh an vor
Tag und Tau. Wann sich die Schirme spannen, beginnt der Sieg,
wir bannen den Feind wie Wetterschlag.

3. Der Flug erklimmt die Höhen, die Länder, Ströme, Seen durch-
braust ein Lied von Erz. Wir bahnen Kampfentbrannten, den grau-
en Unbekannten, den Weg ins Feindesherz.

Worte: Sibelius. Weise: Hans Baumann. Eigentum des Ludwig Doggenreiter Verlages
Potsdam. Aus „Kameraden, laßt uns singen" (Neue Soldatenlieder)

The paratroopers song
'Morgen marchieren wir' - Liederbuch Der Deutchen Soldaten
Potsdam 1939
From the collection of Michael Xilas, Athens

game" I say to them. "No, sir" they reply with disdain, "we've still got Winston Churchill".

I leave them and carry on towards the bridge. I meet many more paratroopers, and their commanding officer. They fought very bravely to capture the bridge and suffered great losses. They were still digging two more graves. We had no flowers to put on the graves as the ground is very dry. But our love will follow them and our gratitude to all those dead boys will never wither.

I now stand on the northern end of the bridge and look at the other end. There is nothing in between them, except brown green feathered

Hauptmann Piehl,
GANZE MÄNNER

birds that fly hither and thither. Parts of the wrecked bridge lie in the gap of the canal, other parts submerged in the blue sea waters. In between the wreckage of the bridge there are bodies of German engineers who had gone to get rid of the explosives laid by the English and had died in the effort.

Suddenly a flare rose high into the sky. There was a huge explosion and the remnants of the bridge sank further into the depths of the Isthmus. A few hours later the Isthmus of Corinth was in the hands of the Germans.

Kurt Pauli, VON SERBIEN BIS KRETA

At the Isthmus of Corinth. At the last moment...

The complete success which we were expecting to achieve at the most crucial moment of the parachute operation against the Balkan campaign was lost in a most dramatic way. The bridge over the Isthmus of Corinth, which we had just captured, blew up.

Helmut Treffner, Germany

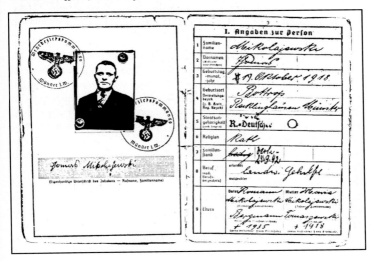

Military identification card of the German parachutist Thomas Mikolajewski or Mikfeld, who fell in Greece during the spring of 1941

Corinth: Tactically a success, strategically an error

The airport at Larissa in Northern Greece was small and crowded with units of the German Air Force. Among other aircraft there, arrived a large cargo plane JU 270 with its large gliders and carrying the 2nd Engineer paratroopers under the command of Colonel Sturm. The paratroopers' assignment was to capture the bridge over the Corinth Canal with a quick attack so that they could cut off the roads which led

239

to the harbours in the Peloponnese from the British Expeditionary Force.

At 5 am sharp on 26th April 1941 the first JU 52 began cautiously to tighten the rope which connected it with the attack glider DFS230. The glider moved forwards. Then the three engines of the JU revved up to full power and the propeller scattered dust and sand up into the morning sky. The two aircraft picked up speed. The glider was the first to take off even though the cabin struck the runway several times before it actually lifted. Then the pilot gently pushed the lever forwards to help the JU to take off.

Finally they were both airborne and after circling several times he increased their altitude. Each glider carried nine seated paratroopers. No-one was wearing their parachutes because there was no room for them. Only the pilots' seats had a small space which accommodated a parachute even though the pilots, out of respect for their comrades, never used them. One unit of the 6th Company, under the command of Lieutenant Norbert Haeffner, whose plane had in tow a glider, was heading in the direction of the Corinth Canal. As soon as they reached the point which had been agreed, the gliders were unlinked and they glided towards their targets. They saw a huge column of English and Greek soldiers travelling from the bridge towards the harbours and from there to Crete. The wheels of the gliders hit the ground hard as they landed and came to a stop on either side of the Canal. One glider crashed into a pier along the bridge, wounding all the crew aboard. The paratroopers quickly over-powered the guards at the bridge and then began to cut the wires which were attached to the charges which had been placed on the bridge. Two British anti-aircraft guns to the south of the bridge opened fire on to the paratroopers who had landed on the northern side. Lieutenant Tensen and his unit attacked the guns and successfully neutralised them.

In the meantime paratroopers climbed down the bridge and disconnected the explosive devices, putting them in a heap in the middle of the road. At the same time Tensen and his men marched to the southern end of the bridge where another gun, a Bofors 40 cm, opened fire. The paratroopers took cover behind a cliff.

It was then that the British realised that there were only a handful of

Germans. They brought up more ammunition and tried to retake the bridge. Tensen quickly wrote a note to his commander. Just as he was tearing the page from his notebook he looked up to see the bridge which at that moment, according to the orders of Lieutenant Haeffner, they had started to take away the explosive devices. Tensen saw the war correspondent, von der Heydten, take a picture from the bridge while the British were shelling it. Suddenly a big explosion was heard which was followed by pro-longed thunder. There was a flash of lightning and thick smoke billowed up from both sides of the bridge. The bridge broke in half and tumbled into the depths taking with it all the soldiers who were on it.

Later on, the war correspondent's camera was found on the edge of the Canal. The last negative showed the bridge as it was exploding.

There are various accounts as to how and why this happened. The opinion of the Germans was that the British anti-aircraft fire struck the explosive devices on the bridge while the official British report states that two New Zealand soldiers had slipped towards the bridge and set off an explosive device which had been overlooked by the Germans, thus sacrificing their own lives.

According to the report of a British war prisoner, two British officers, Tyson and Phillips, apparently slipped along the bridge and set the charges off. For this gallant action, they were awarded the Victoria Cross.

The German accounts are fewer because most of the men from the Engineer Paratroop Unit, including Lieutenant Haeffner, were killed in battle a few days later in Crete. A few German soldiers claimed that they had seen a British officer running towards the bridge but it was difficult to shoot at him because the British had sent up a smoke screen.

The ruined bridge of course prevented the passage of ships and as a result the airbases for the invasion of Crete could not be refueled as quickly as was necessary. But above all, it was soon obvious that Operation Corinth had been delayed by two days. A large body of the British Expeditionary Corps had already passed over the bridge of Corinth. 42,000 British soldiers had left Greece and many of them reinforced the defenders on Crete. Corinth tactically was a success, strategically an error which General S. would have of course avoided - if he had been informed about Operation Corinth.

From the German series: THE WEAPONS OF THE SECOND WORLD WAR
Special edition: The Third Reich - Crete

The Demolition of the Corinth Canal Bridge

26 April 1941. From what I can remember the chain of events occurred as follows. Wilson shot at all the Germans he saw trying to approach the bridge. It seems that one of them managed to slip by him and get under the bridge and he later reappeared holding a long shaped object in his arms. As soon as the German was hit, the object he was

The Demolition of the Corinth Canal Bridge

carrying exploded and then the bridge blew up. Wilson didn't know if the explosion was caused by the German soldier or if it was the work of a New Zealand sergeant and another man, who broke through the line of fire to set off the dynamite. The sergeant was hit and killed and so was the other man with him, whose identity is not known. Kensal, however, believes that the destruction of the bridge was their accomplishment. No-one else has told me of any other person who could have set off the dynamite.

Edward Lillingston, Prisoner of War
Oflag IX, 16.2.1944
Imperial War Museum, London

Flight over the Isthmus

I was with 4 Company, 1 Battalion, 2 Parachute Troops Regiment. Our C.O. was Captain Morawetz. 1 Battalion was located near the village of Male-Konare. Our tents were put together from pieces of tent cloth which every soldier carries in his pack. There were 18 of us to a tent, hence conditions were very cramped, and there was still snow on the ground. There was a shortage of straw. We had spent Christmas Day still in barracks, No 2 AA barracks, Berlin-Doeberitz, near the Olympic Village. Shortly after New Year's Day we boarded a train for Baden near Vienna.

From there, we were moved in a goods train through Hungary and Romania to Bulgaria where we arrived four weeks before Easter 1941. Roman Catholic Easter and Orthodox Easter a week later was spent by us in Male-Konare. I don't know when the Defence Forces High Command became aware that there were no British in Lemnos (nothing was said about this), nor did we know why we were where we were.

We were kept constantly in battle training and had no spare time for going out. There were a lot of rumours about places where we were supposed to go into action etc. About two days before being committed to action, chaplains of both denominations visited us. Whoever wished to attend a service and take communion could do so. After this, and this was customary with us, we had to write our wills. After Larissa had fallen we were issued with parachutes. In the evening we moved to

Plovdiv airfield and flew to Larissa where we slept under the aircraft. Reveille was at 0300 hours. Hot tea was handed out. We buckled on our parachutes and enplaned. Orders had been issued before this.

Our battle tasks and air photo pictures of our operational sector had been passed to us by platoons. We were flown from the direction of Patras to our jump-off area, a cornfield at the eastern exit of the Corinth Canal between the railway line Athens-Corinth and the Athens-Corinth road. We jumped between 0500 and 0530 hours. While flying over the Canal we almost skimmed the water.

A slight interlude: Our 3 Platoon Commander, 4 Company, 1 Battalion, 1 Parachute Troops Regiment was Lt. Huetter, a Tyrolean and a great guy. This was his first experience of going into action. He was 21 years old, had a placid character and a strong sense of duty but not overmuch dash. I had been detailed for liaison duties and if need arose as Commander of the Company HQ troops. He was the first to jump with me as No 2 after him.

When we had been airborne for some time we had some AA fire coming at us. The pusher-off gave the order: "Hook in chutes!", and when our Lieutenant stepped to the door he got pale in the face and cold around the feet and I saw that he had difficulty with his nerves. I tapped him on the shoulder, unhooked his ripcord, pushed my carbine hook to the No 1 position and his to my No 2 one. He thanked me with a nod and stepped behind me.

After 10 minutes he recovered his composure and returned to No 1 position for jumping. When we came over the Canal he got busy and began pushing out my foldable bicycle packed in a container which was to be thrown out before we jumped. However, I was not happy about losing my mount and pulled it back. Some seconds passed which seemed an eternity, then the airstream seized the container with my bike in it. I never saw it again.

The aircraft pulled up to the altitude at which we had to jump, i.e. 100 metres. The signal to jump came at once and all went off without a hitch and according to plan. As I was the fellow who had to pass on orders for the C.O. I jumped with the field telephone(?) and had to float along the railway embankment. Here I saw a camping tent 10 metres away. Two men and two women were sleeping there quite unaware that we had arrived. They were our first prisoners. My platoon accomplished its combat task within an hour. After this we were kept for a special task assignment.

After some time we were ordered to reconnoitre the country in the direction of Athens. There was fierce fighting raging along the Corinth Canal up to 10.00 hours. Steps were taken at once for a makeshift crossing over the Canal to replace the bridge which had been blown up. We continued taking prisoners. There was a very long queue of civilians, soldiers and refugees coming from the direction of Athens.

Towards evening Captain Kroh, the CO of the battalion called a sergeant and twelve men to the Battalion Command Post and announced that Corinth had capitulated and that they were to support the Greek police unofficially but with full authority until the official arrival of German troops.

We were taken in a lorry to Corinth at about 21.00 hours and took up our quarters in the town hall. Teams consisting of one German paratroop soldier and two Greek policemen went on patrol in the town. The Greeks carried no weapons. German units had already passed through Corinth before the arrival of the Army SS, and until these arrived the town Mayor ordered us to look after law and order as there was no military police presence yet. We were to stop commandeering and illegal activities regardless of the rank and status of persons concerned and if need be with the use of arms.

After four days my company was moved to Loutraki on the bay opposite Corinth, and billeted in hotels where bed bugs made sleeping impossible and caused us much pain.

We were moved to tents in an olive grove near a primitive military airfield in Megara, where we were only a few hundred metres from the sea. From here the company was taken on a visit to Athens, but apart from this we were out of touch with the population. Every time we wanted to go out we had to get the CO's permission.

Our day: Reveille 0700; breakfast; internal economy, light battle training etc.

Heinrich Sturm, Germany
Contributed by Jean-Louis Roba, Belgium

The Victorious and the Defeated

This photograph was taken at the beginning of May at the harbour of Nauplion in the Peloponnese a little after my parachute drop in the area of the Corinth Canal on 26 April 1941. The photograph shows English and German soldiers after the battle.

The picture is of great interest because it does not distinguish who are the victors and who are the vanquished. A blow up of the picture reveals that one of the English soldiers is reading a German newspaper. In the group one can also see me - I am the one wearing the helmet.

Adolf Strauch, Germany

24th April 1941

It seems that this time it is the end of our prisoner-of-war camp. The entry of the German army into the capital - unfortunately - is imminent. But let me not go on... Many emotions fill my soul. Emotions of joy and elation for the imminent realisation of the most significant possession: FREEDOM....

I think of the trials of the Greek people. I completely sympathise with the Greeks when I - God what irony - on the other hand will enjoy 'our' much longed freedom.

Mario Cantoni, WITHIN THE BARBED WIRES

At the hospital with the wounded

I served at the hospital of Loutraki from 20 November 1940 to April 1941 when the Germans invaded. Most of the wounded pleaded with the doctors to shorten their treatment so that they could return to the front. They asked us not to record a high temperature on their charts so as to mislead the doctors!

The attitude of the wounded towards our English allies was equally moving as was their attitude towards the young German paratroopers (800 boys between the ages of 17 - 19) who had been brought to the Pallas hospital, all sustaining wounds after the battle at the Corinth

From the collection of Fani Mavroudi-Theodoropoulou

Canal. They treated the young Germans with kindness and compassion and to the English, they tried at all times and in all ways to express their gratitude. There were many examples of chivalry and hospitality. I remember a second lieutenant who had lost both his legs (below the knees) and who dragged himself - they had not yet given him wooden legs - to the wards of the English to offer them cigarettes, candies and to tell us, the nurses, "Take care of them. Reduce our mess and give it to them because they are used to butter and marmalade, while we are used to sparse meals."

Today this second lieutenant, with the wooden legs, walks and proudly leads the procession at every military parade.

Fani Mavroudi-Theodoropoulou

"THE FEW AGAINST THE MANY"

An announcement which was issued by the British Headquarters for the Middle East stated: "Despite the heavy enemy attacks, our fronts in Greece have not been broken through anywhere. The heroic Greek army which fights at our side has a major role."

The Colonist, Queensland, Australia, 26.4.1941

You are listening to the voice of Greece

"...The Athens wireless was still on the air on Saturday night but, contrary to the usual practice, the Greek National Anthem was not played and there was no music to herald the news bulletin. This was read by the announcer in a quiet, dignified voice. He began by saying, "You are listening to the voice of Greece". The following appeal to the nation was also broadcast from Athens during Saturday night: "Greeks, stand firm, proud and dignified. You must prove yourselves worthy of your history.

The valour and victory of our Army has already been recognised. The righteousness of our cause will also be recognised. We did our duty honestly.

Friends! Have Greece in your hearts, live inspired with the fire of her latest triumph and the glory of our Army. Greece will live again and will be great, because she fought honestly for a just cause and for freedom.

Brothers! Have courage and patience. Be stouthearted. We will overcome these hardships. Greeks! With Greece in your minds you must be proud and dignified. We have been an honest nation and brave soldiers."

The Times, London, 28.4.1941

Special report on Mount Olympus
Das Reich, Berlin, 27.4.1941

A Dead City

For days Athens could hear a fierce march approaching its gates. It had stopped for a short while in Northern Greece; there it could not pass unhindered; dipped in blood, it lost a little of its strength. Then it continued more easily; it passed through large and small cities, it descended and descended and everyone heard and counted the heavy steps which continued to grow in strength, and everyone estimated the distance.

- They are in Livadia!

- Rubbish, Livadia! Can't you hear them? They have already passed through Thebes.

South Wales Echo and Evening Express, 26.4.1941

Norddeutsche Ausgabe

VÖLKISCHER BEOBACHTER

Kampfblatt der nationalsozialistischen Bewegung
Großdeutschlands

Athen in deutscher Hand

Fallschirmtruppen besetzten Korinth – Leibstandarte „Adolf Hitler" nahm Patras

Athens in the hands of the Germans. Parachute troops have captured Corinth.
The Army Corps of 'Adolf Hitler' has seized Patras.
Völkischer Beobachter, Berlin, 28.4.1941

GERMANS OCCUPY ATHENS

SWASTIKA HOISTED ON THE ACROPOLIS

APRIL 27.

ADVANCE INTO PELOPONNESUS.

LAST HOURS IN ATHENS

A SILENT CITY

The Times, London, 2.5.1941

German army vehicles in Syntagma Square

They were the foreign soldiers, made of steel, who did not know resistance and who made the earth tremble with each step they took.

...Who could get any sleep? And who allowed sleep to embrace him? These fierce steps had become a heartbeat which would not slow down. Everyone heard them, each time closer and closer, and their breath had the rhythm of a step which is fast and threatening.

...When daybreak came the steps could not be heard. The foreign soldiers had arrived outside the gates of Athens.

...The time passed, as did the soldiers along the main streets of Athens, riding on their vehicles; but the German soldiers couldn't see any people or hear the faintest whisper. The Germans lifted their eyes to the windows, to the balconies. Everything was shut, everything was empty, as if the city had not awoken yet.

...And the windows always remained shut. They hid the hate of the people but they also demonstrated the city's deep mourning. It was an old Greek custom. A house which mourned never opened its windows. And that day every house in Athens had a death, the same death.

...The hours went by, dusk came and then night came. But night did not resemble the normal night. It was the beginning of a different kind of night, one which no-one knew how long it would last, how many misfortunes it would conceal, how many tears and laments it would hear and what kind of a dawn it would eventually bring forth.

Petros Haris, THE LONG NIGHT

Athens surrenders...

Von Stumme at the Archdiocese

After the departure of the King and the Government from Athens on April 25th, the Greek authorities which remained in the capital, the military commander and the Mayor of Attikobeotia and the Mayors of Athens and Piraeus began to think of the best way to hand over the city to the Germans, who were now approaching the city after the surrender of the army of Epirus by General Tsolakoglou.

They then asked Archbishop Chryssanthos to be part of the committee which would receive the Germans and which would hand over the city.

The Archbishop, without one moment's hesitation, said that "Greek priests never hand over a Greek city to foreigners." Furthermore, several lightheaded compatriots who groomed themselves to take part in the first "occupied Greek" government had asked the Archbishop to conduct a thanksgiving service at the Metropolis to mark the end of the war with the Germans. In a fury the Archbishop dismissed this idea too. But because he feared that some stupid cleric might be persuaded to allow the service to take place - without his authority of course - he ordered the Dean of the Metropolis to lock up all doors and to hand the keys to him in person. Indeed, as soon as he got the keys, he decided - for obvious reasons - not to keep the keys himself or hand them to one of his bishops, but gave them to me who, as Secretary of the Synod, was of no great importance. He gave me strict orders not to hand the keys to anyone without his express permission. These are the events which occurred before the arrival of the German, General von Stumme, at the Archdiocese.

On April 27th, the morning when the Germans entered Athens (it was St Thomas' Sunday), I had just returned to my home, after celebrating Mass. Then I listened to that last and most tragic programme which was broadcast by Athens Radio, and heard the highly esteemed voice of the announcer say: "Brothers, hold your heads up high. Greeks place Greece above all else! We will continue the war. After this, do not listen to this radio station; it will no longer be Greek. Long live the army. Long live freedom", and with our national anthem the radio programme ended. This was the end of Radio Athens - as we knew it - from 27.4.1941 until 12.10.1944...

I had not yet recovered when the telephone rang. It was the secretary of the Archbishop who told me to come to the Archdiocese immediately as the Commander of the German forces, General von Stumme, was on his way there. I set out at once and without any difficulty arrived at the Archdiocese. Just as I was about to cross over Panepistimiou Street, where the National Library is, I saw the first column of German tanks which was heading towards Omonia Square. There were a few pedestrians walking along the pavements but none of them turned to look at the conquerors. They ignored them. This was the Athenian reception of the occupation army as they saw them a little after the occupation of the capital of their country. I confirmed this with great emotion and a justified national pride. It was the first gesture of our national resistance to the then powerful conquerors.

As soon as I arrived at the Archdiocese and presented myself to His Emminence, he asked me if the keys of the Metropolitan church were still in my possession. I reassured him that the keys were in my hands. Then, because I was the only one there who knew any German, he gave me instructions as to how to receive the General; "with dignity, he said, but also with great pride and aloofness."

It was around midday when the General arrived. I ushered him into the reception room on the upper floor where His Emminence was waiting for him together with the assistant of the Archdiocese, Bishop

Talantios, the later Metropolitan of Thessaloniki Panteleimon, his canon Gervasios Paraskevopoulos and his personal secretary, Constantine Papazonis. The Archbishop rose as soon as the General entered but did not leave his place.

After the courteous gestures of greeting were exchanged, the Archbishop, without showing any particular signs of courtesy, sat down in his chair and indicated to the General the chair to his left and which was the seat of the Bishop's assistant or the canon of the Archdiocese. The General who had come in with a certain air of superiority continued to maintain it after he had sat down. He began by saying how much he had always wanted to visit Athens, of which he had learnt so much at school and Military Academy, and where he had so many friends. At this point the Archbishop interrupted him and said: "Indeed, before the war Germany had many friends in Greece, among whom I was one". The General froze as soon as he heard this and he suddenly lost his air of superiority. He stayed a few minutes longer, then got up, saluted the Archbishop and looking very shaken he left. He was leaving behind him the first formal manifestation of our national resistance. Von Stumme also learnt that in Greece he might meet a few Quislings, but he would not find any friends!

Former Archbishop of Athens Ieronymos

Sull'Acropoli sventola la bandiera d'Italia

Dopo una marziale sfilata il gen. Schoerner trasmette al gen. Berardi il comando di Atene

The Italian flag waves in the breeze above the Acropolis. After the procession of the army, General Schoerner hands over the command of Athens to General Berardi.
L'Avvenire d'Italia, 26.6.1941

German soldiers at the Parthenon

Formal announcement from Australia

(Cable of the International News Service)
Melbourne, Australia, May 2
It is noted that during the time when the German army was raising the swastika over the Acropolis in Athens, the Greek army was fighting fiercely to cover the retreating British, since the retreating forces were making their way through mainland Greece and the Peloponnese so that they could board transports and depart.

Atlantis, New York, 2.5.1941

And the last hope was lost

Whoever has seen the Greeks fight can only admire them and feel compassion at their moment of anxiety. Their small built and slender soldiers are so brave and disciplined. Their women and children accept the hardships which the war has imposed on them with a brave heart. The Athenians themselves react more like children. I spent days in Athens when no-one smiled, neither men nor women, because the news from the front was depressing. And I saw joyful celebrations break out only because they had received a report that afternoon announcing some victory. Now their last hope is lost. The decision to withdraw the Imperial Army from Greece had been made that same day, and even though the Athenians had not been informed at that time, they must have felt that defeat was in the air.

The Times, London, 2.5.1941

At the Oracle of Delphi
It is all your fault! You were the one who had prophesised that the foreigners who would come to this country would be defeated and driven out.
Yes - and ??
Das Reich, Berlin, May 1941

257

The Gazette

Montreal, Canada

Modern Spartans

··· If this gallant force is to be over-whelmed, which Heaven forbid. it will leave to the British Empire and to the world as proud a message as did the Spartans of old. who died obedient to the trust reposed in them.

*The Gazette,
Montreal, Canada
Frank Daley, GREECE
GALLANT GLORIOUS*

The evacuation

I was told I was to go to Greece. Evacuation had already been decided on. I was to be Jumbo Wilson's "GSO 1 for Evacuation". I knew him well from Staff College days and also his B.G.S., Brigadier Sandy Galloway (Cameronians).

At Athens we went straight to General Wilson's headquarters at the Grande Bretagne Hotel. Here I found Sandy Galloway. He was at his best, large, cheerful and unruffled. He greeted me with a broad grin; it was the first time we had met since he was a GSO 3 and I was intelligence officer.

We began by having reconnaissances carried out of the embarkation beaches, their approaches and assembly points for the troops; and we allotted two selected officers to each. It may here be mentioned that Jumbo, when appointed to this rather dicey command, asked first for maps of the Peloponnese, as he was sure that an evacuation was inevitable. He told me this himself with his gargantuan chuckle, long afterwards.

Sandy and I went together to visit the rearguards. Jumbo spent most of the time in Athens, so as to be in touch with the Greek government

258

and high command. The Greek army, which had more than held its own against the Italians, was crumbling under the pressure of the Germans. But fortunately, as we withdrew, the frontage in Boeotia got narrower and the danger of having our left flank turned receded.

We went first to the rear-guard on the Australian front, which was commanded by a British gunner brigadier, Dee. He was full of confidence; I was sorry to hear, a couple of years later, that he had died soon afterwards. The Bralos Pass, north of Lamia, was a formidable position and could have been held indefinitely, given reasonable air support. From there we went to the New Zealand front on the right, where Hargest's brigade was holding the pass of Thermopylae. This too was a strong position and could have been held, and Hargest too was full of confidence. In fact German pressure on land was never of great consequence. It was their absolute control of the air that caused the trouble and they exploited it to the full.

The R.A.F. in Cairo, when the enterprise was being planned, had undertaken to provide seventeen fighter squadrons. In the event, they sent only six. As the serviceability of these ran down, it was decided to keep the last dozen aircraft in hand, to cover the evacuation in the few hours after dawn when ships would be easy targets for air attack. Unfortunately, instead of being well spread out on their landing ground, they were parked in a huddle and destroyed in a single bombing attack.

One of the first jobs I had to do was to pick the meeting place for a conference at which Wavell was to tell Blamey (Commander of the ANZAC Corps) and Freyberg of the New Zealand Division that the force was to be evacuated. Jumbo of course already knew, but Commonwealth politics made it desirable that the Australians and New Zealanders should be told by the Commander-in-Chief himself.

The selection had to be from the map, which was not very good, and it had to be within easy reach of Blamey (near Thevae), not too far from Athens (Jumbo) and somewhere easy to find in the dark and near enough to Athens to allow Wavell, who was due in the Piraeus by flying boat in the evening, to get back to the Piraeus so as to be in the air by dawn. It was also preferable not to have the conference on a main road because of the noise of passing traffic, usually heavy at night. So I chose the bridge over a small river at the northern edge of Erythrae village and there the conference was held at midnight.

After the midnight conference Sandy and I went back to the Grande Bretagne to write the operation order confirming the conference decisions. I did the writing while Sandy kept pinching me to keep me awake. We were due to leave at 0800 hours for the advanced HQ at Thevae, where we were to take on the direct control of the two divisions and the 1st Armoured Brigade. The manuscript was in the hands of the typists bit by bit, and my part was finished by 0600 hours. It seemed pointless to sleep then, so I took a car up to the Parthenon to see the sunrise. It was exhilarating and I shall never regret it.

On the evening fixed for the large scale evacuation from Kalamata, there were 10,000 men there, including 6,000 unarmed Yugoslavs who had found their way south and a number of 4th Hussars without their tanks. Eleven destroyers came in soon after dark and gunfire was heard in the distance to the north. The Germans, having parachuted the Corinth bridge, had sent one gun and a small covering party through Tripolis and down the Kalamata road. The gun opened fire and some R.A.S.C. drivers held it up with rifle fire. When the naval lieutenant arrived on the harbour and found the brigadier, he was told that the enemy were just coming in, that evacuation was impossible, that he had given the order to surrender and the destroyers would not be needed. They went away. The final disgrace was that officers were ordered to stay with their men so that the handover to the Germans should be orderly. There were many individual escapes to Crete.

I only learned the details of this story some time afterwards. I am glad I have forgotten the name of the brigadier. Chronologically I am adrift, because this calamity had not taken place when we closed down the headquarters in Athens and transferred to Miloi in the Peloponnese, some twenty miles from Navplion. All movements of troops towards their embarkation points in Attica were well on the way and finally Sandy and I left the Grande Bretagne for the last time and for some reason I have forgotten, in a car provided by Prince Peter, with his own driver.

We had hardly started when we realised that we had no food with us. As we were just passing a confectionery I stopped the car and went into it. In two visits to Athens since then, I have tried to find it and failed. I asked for a couple of slabs of chocolate. The pretty girl thrust a whole box of slabs at me. The manageress came to the counter and added a huge box with a blue satin ribbon suitable for a prospective mother-in-law. They refused to take anything and said they were grateful to us for coming, and the Germans would take it from them anyhow (I remembered the little suburban grocer in Belgium who had said the same about my bread and cheese). So, overloaded with chocolates, I returned to the car, round which a crowd had gathered, in an emotional state which included smiles and tears. One stem of sweet pea, with three rather tattered washy pink blooms, was thrown through the car window; it meant more than any of the sweet peas I have since seen at the Chelsea Flower Show.

The New Zealanders too, on their way to the beaches, had flowers thrown to them. This must have been one of the only occasions when an unsuccessful army, in its retreat, has been given a triumphal exit; for that is what it was. Little did I think, then, that I should be in command of the first British troops to come back to Greece and that I should be the first to fulfil the promise that I made to the janitor of the Parthenon and to the chocolate shop, "We shall come back."

Freyberg had now arrived at Miloi and was to command the final evacuation from the Peloponnese and Sandy was to stay with him.
Jumbo was to go off the same evening to Crete in a flying boat. The HQ staff and clerks were to go off in the convoy from Navplion. Either I or David Belchem was to take them and the war diary by sea; the other of us was to stay with Sandy, and Sandy made us toss up for it. I went by sea from Navplion.

I had already been along to Navplion that morning, just to see the arrangements for the assembly and embarkation were alright. I spoke to some Australians, who were taking cover in the scrubby hills, which reminded me of Anzac. A few of the older soldiers had been there and agreed with me. The harbour had been empty except for the burning hulk of the bombed freighter, ULSTER PRINCE. When we got there at night she was still burning and the hull was glowing, red-hot.

George Davy, Scotland

Lieutenant Colonel George Davy during the evacuation of the British forces on board HMS HOTSPUR

Brigadier Leonard Parrington was taken prisoner by the Germans during the retreat of the British army on the 29.4.41 at Kalamata From the collection of the Imperial War Museum, London

Imperial War Museum, London
The catastrophe at Kalamata
Berliner Illustrierte Zeitung, 26.6.1941
From the archives of E.L.I.A., Athens

Short notice to move off

The force stayed at Levadia until April 22, when we got short notice to move off in an hour and to take only arms, ammunition, rations, and such things as towel, soap, socks and other articles which could be carried on ones back in a haversack.

So off we set in motor transport with practically just what we stood up in.

The point for halting was near a beach chosen by the Navy and Army for an embarkation.

The order was given for Corps Headquarters to embark. We went into the water up to our armpits. Many were knocked down by the surf but were helped up by their comrades. Ultimately, the craft got away, the men packed on it like sardines, moving out in the darkness. We could see by our watches that it was then 4 am and we knew the transport would be gone. The Naval Officer in charge of the craft then summoned all the officers, and told them that we would have to be put back ashore, as a transport would not be waiting for us.

The craft was then run to Didymoi beach - "a lovely spot" - where we were disembarked, and took cover with the utmost speed, as daylight was near, and we knew that the German bombers would soon be at hand.

The following evening when at last the sunset and twilight started to deepen, we moved down the valley through the scrub to the assembly points on the side of the road. There was a cold wind blowing and the sea looked grey and misty with no sign of ships.

Suddenly, far out at sea, a lamp flashed as a destroyer signalled to the Navy men on shore and soon after one could distinguish grey shapes of destroyers creeping in shore out of the sea mists.

I admire the Greek people as a whole, and feel sad for the bulk of them, who are not pro Germans.

The Fifth Column element is strong, active and efficient, particularly in cities and large towns, especially at rail and road junctions and key points; but the kindness of the country folk on our later day travels - the gifts of bread, eggs and water when they knew that in a day or two they might be starving -those things we will never forget.

From the letters of Crofton Stephens
The Mercury, Adelaide, Australia, 2-5.6.1941

3 May 1941 - A ship transporting British soldiers during the evacuation from Greece
Imperial War Museum, London

Thessaloniki on fire - exodus by caiques

... Caiques, as the Greeks call their small fishing boats, were the principal conveyances from the burning Salonika waterfront, which we reached by taxi at the moment when the fiercest night raid by the Germans was directed against the port.

The first left Salonika Bay three hours before the Germans arrived, with firing already audible in the suburbs, and with an unearthly glare from the oil tanks fired by the British demolition experts reddening the sea. Two large buildings topping the peninsular cliff were walls of flame.

...The sea retreat was organised upon the waves. Majors and colonels upon poops of dozens of craft, most of them less than 40 feet long, talked over the situation with old island salts. Meals consisting of soft black bread and oranges, with hard tack as dessert, were served by passengers tossing food from hand to hand.

On the second night the sea grew rough, and the cold was too great for sleep upon the rainswept crowded decks. Before dawn came the craft had picked her way into the harbour of a land-locked island far to the south.

The harbour was crowded by dozens of caiques, and a worried portmaster was pacing the stony quay endeavouring to persuade the skippers to leave promptly so as to eliminate the danger of air raids.

...In the starlit morning we set out in a tiny motor boat for a small bay on the island of Euboea, which we reached about noon, and after a two mile hike to the nearest village a motor car was procured which brought the entire company to one of the principal towns in central Greece. After the mayor himself had turned out the constabulary to find a taxi, I set forth on the long drive to Athens.

The War Illustrated, London, 2.5.1941

Bundesarchiv-Militärarchiv, Freiburg, Germany

Bundesarchiv-Militärachiv, Freiburg, Germany

The ships will come tonight

Monday, 28th April

Left benzine guard station in trucks for a port 130 miles north west of Athens. Place was bombed, also boats, so set out for this place. Further north about 130 miles over a great pass or really over about 5 passes.

Are being bombed and machine gunned heavily all day. Not one of our planes has come to help us. About a thousand boys got aboard Sunday night. We came down to embark but ships have not come so here we are going through the same dose.

It is Monday, 28th April I suppose. I understand the ships will come tonight. We are in a great orange grove. Wrong place really as it is a great target for the cursed Huns that speed past and bomb all the time.

My pulse is still normal I hope! even if I do dig my nails into the earth when a bomb is coming down with its nice whistle! What a great pity to have death sailing round in such a beautiful country. This curse surely can't go on. I hear the Hun plane coming again so must get down flat.

Monday night

Our men were signalling to ships to come in, but our signaller had been taken prisoner and so our men had not the code. So the navy were not taking chances. Besides, the Germans sent out two shells, out to sea at the navy.

At last at 3.30 all hope of getting the ships in seemed hopeless. About 4 or 5 boats set out and myself and 6 men got a big heavy water-logged boat, found some lumps of timber for oars, and set out to get the navy to come in, but when about 2 miles away we heard what I believe were the ships going away, as it was morning.

We then decided to make for a headland, and get away best way possible, but the tide sent us right across to the other coast, about 20 miles off, where people were good, and found us food. Made a couple of oars, rough but good. We pushed off towards Crete and today are in a cove in a lovely little harbour, and are resting. We have our rifles and gear yet.

Last night we heard ships passing far out, probably coming to rescue

My dear sister Elli,
May we meet in moments of freedom. The password is "Long live Greek freedom".
Affectionately, Manolis 28.11.1941.

Postcard of the period
From the collection of Fani Mavroudi-Theodoropoulou

our men. About 6000. They would be without food for two days. We all were foodless, only having a tin of beef and emergency rations in a small tin. Our bread truck had broken down the first day. The mistake was that all bread was on the one truck, so we have had no bread for at least nine days.

Bombed and machine gunned every day while in the olive groves waiting to be taken off. One cannot be blamed for getting off in boats if they can, though we are suffering badly now as our boat is too ungainly to work without a sail. We have had bread given to us twice now but can't buy anything as we don't see any shops.

This evening we head out for some islands towards Crete, our only hope to get back to our boys.

From the war diary of Harold Loftus, New Zealand

The journey is over. Soldiers are transported to Alexandria,
30 April 1941
THE MEDITERRANEAN FLEET - GREECE TO TRIPOLI

So ended the Greek campaign

For two days we worked at our R.A.F., and provision was made for us to get away on the last official night of evacuation, providing we could take our wounded with us. This we did, and at about 2 am we boarded a cruiser, the ...., notable anti-aircraft ship of the British Navy. You cannot imagine the relief we felt that we were actually aboard a ship. We were given a marvellous reception by the sailors, who gave us refreshments, gave up their bunks and did everything possible to make us comfortable.

In three hours during our journey from Greece to Crete our ship threw up over a thousand shells at Dive-Bombers. I was oblivious to it all. Off the hard ground for the first time in weeks I slept from 3 am to 11 am.

... So ended the Greek campaign. Men who were in the evacuation of Norway and Dunkirk with us in Greece said that the Greek show was the roughest of them all, but I don't think any of us would have missed it for the world.

J. Baskin, Australia
The Greek Gazette, London, November 1982

A Greek remembers with eyes filled with tears of rage

The 28th April found me in Preveza. The war on Greek Epirus had just finished. The territory of Northern Epirus had been gained by our army through a series of hard but victorious battles against the Italians, but we were obliged to vacate it again with a tactical withdrawal, under the threat and pressure of the German troops who, during those days, had already pushed their feelers out towards our rear.

Well, that morning, I had to run over to the Headquarters of the 3rd Division, to the ancient Nikopolis, 6 kilometres north of Preveza. By the time I returned, our Unit had dissolved. During the morning, a rumour from the "Arvila (Boot) Agency" spread, saying that the Germans had gone back on their word and were now going to let the Italians occupy Greek Epirus, including Preveza.

That rumour swept everything clean away. How? Why? Don't ask me. I cannot offer an explanation. But when I got back to Preveza near lunchtime, our quarters were empty. I could find no officers or cavalrymen from our Unit. Nor could I find my horse, my groom or my campaign kit. The IY Reconnoitering Team, the last organised section which existed in the region of Preveza, had ceased to exist. It melted like wax, and became one with the human torrent which flowed disorderly towards the south.

Well, I was walking alone on the main road returning to Preveza from Nikopolis at ten in the morning. I wore my folder with its maps and my binoculars over my coat, while on the inside, in my trouser back pocket was my pistol. As I walked along, I would come across small German patrols of three men every 50-100 metres who had obviously come to supervise the evacuation of the road.

I had almost reached Preveza, when the final patrol, which I had passed without incident a short while before, shouted wildly at me to stop and, brandishing their arms, took my map folder, my binoculars and my pistol and then made signs to force me quickly off the road. I ran up a small slope covered with vineyards to the left of the road; when I reached the top I didn't dare move so as to see what was happening because, meanwhile, the sound of car engines descending on Preveza was reaching my ears. And what did I see? Three German cars in front, then a small Italian phalanx, with beards, plumes and a triumphant air, then two more German cars in the middle, the rest of the Italian formation and finally a German rearguard. Then I remembered bitterly the Arvila Agency, how sad yet how right they had been, as well as the order we had received from the Division on the 22nd April as we were holding the last line of retardation north of Konispoli, which said, amongst others:

"I am letting you know that a truce has been signed between Greece and Germany and that the Germans will intervene between the Italian and Greek armies". At the same time, the Divisional Chief of Staff informed us verbally that "The truce has been signed between the Commander-in-Chief of the German forces in Greece and the Commander of the Greek Forces in Epirus and the Army Corps Commanders under them, with the following conditions:

1. Guarantee of the integrity of Greece's borders.
2. Immediate demobilization of the country.
3. Surrendering of arms and all matter of army materials into Greek stores.
4. A request, in the form of the fourth condition, is issued by the German Military Command to the brave Greek army to allow the passage of a German Regiment "which can intervene between the Greek and Italian forces to avoid any incidents".

With eyes filled with tears of rage, I got up from my hiding place on the top of the slope with the vineyards and descended towards Preveza through fields and footpaths.

Andreas Hoerschelman

'Η έπιστροφή τῶν ἡρώων. (Σχεδίασμα τοῦ κ. Π. Βυζαντίου)

The return of the heroes
Sketch by P. Byzantios

I feel as if I'm living in a dream

Tuesday night 29.4.41. The Germans treat us like prisoners of war even though they reassure us that we are not. This morning Telemachos and I were discussing our departure with several others when suddenly, a loud voiced German lieutenant appears and gathers us together for fatigue duty....

Sunday 18.5.41. I have been in Athens since last Thursday, for the last eleven days I have been living near my parents, eating as much as I want at a table with cutlery, sleeping on my soft bed and going out every afternoon with my Elli. We go to the cinema or for endless walks in Kifissia or Halandri. I feel as if I'm living in a dream, that I'll wake up at any moment and find myself back in Albania, in my tent at the outpost.

Wednesday dusk 21.5.41. I feel constantly tired, my kidneys hurt a bit, I don't feel like doing anything and I keep feeling this need to cry. I am bored, bored to death, perhaps it is my nerves... At night I have nightmares, many times I wake up frightened in my sleep.

From the war diary of volunteer soldier George P. Bisbas

Rest. Sketch by Yiannis Moralis

The Greeks were not at fault for anything

April 30, 1941: With the Führer. Discussions about the situation. The Führer feels saddened by the fact that he was forced to attack Greece. The Greeks were not at fault to deserve such punishment. He intends to treat them as humanly as possible.

From the diary of Joseph Goebbels

From Adolf Hitler's speech to the Reichstag 4.5.1941

Greece, who needed this guarantee less than anyone, was also prepared to obey the tempting English invitation and link its fortune with that of the sponsor and commander of her royal Master. Because even today - I feel I ought to say this for the sake of historical truth - I am obliged to make a distinction between the Greek people and that corrupt aged ruling class which, inspired by a King subordinate to England, is less concerned with real duties and with ruling the Nation, and more with appropriating the aims of British war policy.

This fact has genuinely saddened me. For me, a German who, due to the manner of my education when young and to my profession later, harboured a deep respect for the civilization and arts of a people, from whom in the past the first light of human beauty and dignity originated, it was difficult and bitter to follow the development without being able to do anything about it at all.

...We perceive and are well aware that a large percentage of those successes belongs to our allies. Italy's struggle against Greece, which lasted six months and was waged under the most arduous conditions and cost the greatest sacrifices, did not only immobilize the main mass of the Greek army, but exhausted it so much that its collapse was rendered inevitable.

...For the sake of historical justice, however, I am obliged to confirm that of all the enemies who have faced us, it was the Greek troops who similarly fought with intrepid bravery and the highest contempt for death. And they then surrendered only when further resistance proved impossible and therefore pointless.

We feel genuine sadness for the defeated and wretched Greek people. They are the victims of the King and of a small blinded class of rulers. They fought so bravely, however, that it is impossible even for their enemies not to grant them respect.

...The number of Greek prisoners, amounting to approximately 8,000 officers and 210,000 men must not be compared to the number of Serbian prisoners, because as far as the Greek forces of Macedonia and Epirus are concerned, it has to be said that they were forced to surrender only because of the joint German-Italian operations by which they were totally surrounded. The Greek prisoners have been, or will be freed further, due to the general brave stand of their soldiers.

Hitler's speech delivered at the Reichstag on 4th May 1941:
"The year 1941 will remain a milestone in the history of the Nazis."

BEYOND DEFEAT

The battle is over. Another battle now begins. The battle for survival within the adverse circumstances of the four year occupation. A battle against starvation, imprisonment, enslavement. In the darkness of the occupation the soul awakens, waits, hopes, loyal in the belief of a final victory, it brings together the many-coloured mosaic of the resistance. Every Greek, each with his own 'weapon', adds another stone to the temple of freedom.

HITLER: "So, YOU SEE — YOU'VE LOST EVERYTHING."
GREECE: "NOT MY SOUL."

AFTER THE FAMOUS
'PUNCH' CARTOON BY SIR
BERNARD PARTRIDGE, OCT 21ST 1914

To save the Greek flag

Cairo, Sunday

Costa Kukidis, a Greek soldier, was guarding Greece's blue and white flag on the Acropolis, in Athens, when a squad of uniformed Nazis marched up to him. "Haul that down", they said, "and run up this Swastika banner". Costa slowly hauled down his country's colours. He paused a moment, with eyes fixed on the German officer. Then he wrapped the flag round his body and hurled himself over the 200 ft high battlements. That story has just reached me through Greek channels.

Daily Mail, London, 9.6.1941

The awakening of the soul

The composer George Kazasoglou fought in Albania... "Four preludes of the return from the front" is the title of his creation - his own return of course... And as he later wrote:

"Gloomy, emotionally inaccessible, full of thorns, of protests, dejections and of intolerable grief is the road back, for the heroes and the victors, from the Albanian front of the war..... Is it fate or the designs of evil people, which chose to seal our glories and our superb victories in this dismal way. This is the emotional tone of my work."

"Four preludes of the return from the front" which were written in 1941, and performed for the very first time during the period of the occupation..."

The Germans, however, did not allow the performance - at the 'Pallas' on Sunday 5 March 1944 to be performed by the National Orchestra - of the fourth part. Because in this part it is clearly implied that the time of our liberation was imminent! The moving introduction of the National Anthem in the fourth prelude was an excuse for the Germans to forbid its performance.

Athena Spanoudi. From the programme 'Musical themes' which was recorded on 17.10.1983.

Atene — Il Comando delle truppe italiane rende omaggio alla Tomba del Milite Ignoto

The monument of the unknown soldier in Athens
L'Avvenire d'Italia, 29.6.1941

GREEKS FLOUT THE INVADERS

GERMAN FLAG TORN UP
FROM OUR CORRESPONDENT
ISTANBUL, JUNE 2

DEATH PENALTY

Anti-German Activity In Greece

CAIRO, Tuesday.—The German commander in Greece has proclaimed the death penalty for numerous offences in Greece such as the removal or destruction of German flags, the hiding of food, sales of food to the Germans at twice the usual prices, talk against Germany, and assistance to British prisoners by supplying them with food.

A German flag recently was removed from the Acropolis. The Germans declare that the Greek authorities are doing nothing to prevent such incidents.

The Mercury, Hobart, Australia, 4.6.1941

The heroic lowering of the Nazi flag from the Acropolis
by Manolis Glezos and Lakis Santas

After we cut off a piece of the Gothic cross with our penknives - one piece for each of us, because the rest of the flag was so big, we hid it in the cave of Agravlos. So that they would not arrest anyone else, we left our fingerprints on the crossbar and departed. The Germans threatened the commanders of both police stations which were located in the Acropolis area as well as the policemen stationed as guards that night on the Acropolis. All of them. And of course they also issued the announcement in which they condemned us to death. This was our first death sentence!

"We condemn them to death in abstensia."

As for us, we heard our death sentence pronounced over the radio.

Oral account of Manolis Glezos

The first resistance

I don't believe that my companion, Lakis Santas, and I were the first. Perhaps what we did, the fact that we took down the German flag from the Acropolis, was somewhat impressive but it was not a first. I have

Anniversary of the 25th March
Wood engraving by Vasso Katraki

280

certain information that at whichever part of the country the occupiers entered and the nation collapsed, the Greek population would instantly start up acts of resistance made up of a variety of people, evidence that the population wanted to resist the conquerors... In my mind, one episode is significant. The closing of shutters as the Nazis entered Athens was for me the first act of resistance. Now, the fact that some Nazis appeared at the start of the Holy Way, because I was in the area, and a very small number of people, probably no more than a handful, welcomed and applauded them, that does not deny the existence of a national resistance, on the contrary it confirms it. As far as I am concerned, it is a first broad resistance by the Athenian population, directly after the collapse of the official Greek state by the Athenians... I still remember a policeman from Samothrace standing on the beach, holding the Greek flag, and when the German occupiers appeared there in a landing party, he fired at them with flag in hand and they killed him. That is an act of resistance. And I believe that there are other similar acts which stand as evidence to that broad spirit of resistance which, in my mind, existed from the first day of the occupation throughout the country, not just in Athens.

Oral account of Manolis Glezos

A wood engraving by Spyros Vassiliou for the work entitled
"Inside the walls" by Sotiris Skipis, which was secretly circulated in Athens in 1943

Tomb of the Unknown Soldier
On the anniversary of Greek Independence, March 25, 1942, the humble people of Athens, their spirit undefeated, laid flowers on the Tomb of the Unknown Soldier (The Evzone guards at the Tomb were the only Greek soldiers permitted by the enemy to bear arms)
Phokion Demetriades, SHADOW OVER ATHENS

The high significance of the Battle of Greece

...It is generally accepted that the Battle of Greece, on the one hand saved England's military position in the Middle East and on the other delayed for two months the German invasion of Russia. This last claim was officially announced by Mr. Eden before the British Parliament. It aroused great emotion and was applauded by all. At a lecture which was given in London and which was published under the title "The Greeks change the course of the war", Mr. Raymond Offroy, former Consul of France in Thessaloniki, confirmed that with the steadfastness and courage which was shown by the Government, the army and the people of Greece, Greece changed the German time schedule and frustrated Hitler's Mediterranean plans.

Costas N. Hadjipateras, HEROISMES ET DROITS DE LA GRECE

With the passing of years, men have forgotten Greece's contribution to the last war. But history does not forget. The words of great and lesser men of the period about the exploits of the Greek Armed Forces and the Greek nation are recorded in the historical and political archives of many countries. Here are some quitations.

Unarmed against armed

You fought unarmed against those who were strongly armed and you were victorious. You fought, the small against the great, and you were successful. It could not be otherwise, because you are Greeks. We Russians won time to defend ourselves - thanks to your sacrifices. We are grateful to you.

Radio Station Moscow, 27.4.1942

A first class fighter

The Greek is a very good soldier and a first class fighter especially when he believes in the struggle for which he is fighting. The Greek has once again today confirmed these virtues and has defeated the Italians with his spirit and his bravery. And he continues to defeat them.

Lloyd George speaking in the House of Commons, 21st December 1940

Prototype of history

Heroic and chivalrous Greece, by her struggle and the example set by her people, serves as a prototype in the history of nations throughout the centuries.

... Let Greece rest assured, she will receive all that she deserves and she will live proudly and heroically among the victors.

Winston Churchill, February 1943

Before winter had caught up with him

The Greeks have done their duty. Only now does the free world

Greece's claims will be discussed
(Promissory note. The victory of Albania to the credit of Greece)
- But I'm Greece, I thought you'd recognise me ...
- No ma'am. Bring your identity card and two witnesses
Sketch by Spyros Polenakis
Laoutzikos, 20.9.1945

realise what this small and honoured country has offered it. If Greece had succumbed to the Italian demands, perhaps today we would all be living in a different world. The Eastern Mediterranean would have become a lake for the Fascist Axis. The borders of England in Asia would have disappeared and Hitler, without the open wound of the Greek Italian war, would have been in Moscow before winter had caught up with him.

Cedric Foster, Radio Station commentator USA, 28.10.1945

With Honour

You were not defeated but rather succumbed after a struggle, which covered you with honour.

Anthony Eden, 10.5.1941

In letters of gold

A small country has once again written history in letters of gold for all the world to read.

Viscount Halifax, British Ambassador to the United States of America
Excerpt from address, January 1941

Our only fighting ally

I would like to stress the fact that, without excepting either the Soviet Union or Great Britain or the United States, no country fought in World War II with greater bravery than Greece. We want to remind the world that from 1940 to 1941, with the exception of the British Empire, Greece was our only fighting ally who opposed the enemy and defeated him.

At a time when everything and all hope seemed lost, Greece made available not only her territory but also her arms and military effort at the disposal of the Allied struggle. We must not allow ourselves to forget it today.

Ernest Bevin, Foreign Secretary, speaking to the Security Council of the U.N. in 1946

Confounding the prophesies of disaster

In the Balkans for six months the Greeks more than resisted the weight of the Italian attack. Although, according to ordinary mathematical and military calculation, the overwhelming comparative strength of the Italian empire made almost inevitable the early defeat of Greece. But the Greek army, by heroic achievement and magnificent strategy, confounded the prophecies of disaster. Greece, with a spirit of independence, fighting alone on land, for six months resisted and repulsed the vaunted might of Italy. The plain fact is that the heroic Greeks, as long as Italy was the only nation in arms against them, magnificently succeeded in fighting their own battles.

Prime Minister of Canada, W.L. Mackenzie King
Excerpt from address to the Canadian House of Commons, 28.4.1941

When the time comes

Greece has saved Moscow and Caucasus. When the time comes any ingratitude towards the Greek people will amount to betrayal of all Europe.

Pierre Bourdin, BBC French Service, 30.5.1942

Faith in the victory of our struggle

We owe much to Greece, to the military and naval aid which she offered us. We owe her far more than that, however, because in a dark hour she proclaimed to the world her faith in the victory of our struggle. That was a spiritual advantage which no man among us should ever allow himself to forget.

Harold Nicholson, The Spectator, 9.1.1942

Like Greeks

We are used to saying: "Greeks fight like heroes." In the future we shall say: "Heroes fight like Greeks".

Manchester Guardian, 19.4.1941

Postscript

As a sort of postscript, I should like to add a further eye-witness account of the battles for freedom of the Greek nation, this time as seen from an entirely different angle - from LONDON.

We of the Greek Section of the BBC in Bush House - 12 Greeks, 9 young men and 3 young girls - followed every moment of this titanic struggle. We were witnesses and at the same time reporters of the events and their consequences. We shared the fears, frustrations and the joys of 1940-41 (all of us had families in Greece and some of us had relatives in the Greek Armed Forces). At first we were nervous and apprehensive, then gradually, as the Greek army pushed back the Italians into Albania, our fears and anxieties were transformed into joyful announcements and eventually into delirious tributes. KORITSA, POGRADEC, AYIOI SARANDA, ARGYROKASTRO, KLEISSOURA. What fantastic news, what joyful commentaries to broadcast each day in our six daily transmissions. This was the first Allied victory in Europe. No-one expected it, no-one could quite comprehend it. We felt proud to be Greeks and proud to be addressing those gallant Greek soldiers who were then deep into the wintry Albanian territory. And each Sunday we would give vent to our feelings of pride and joy with emotive tributes which were always followed by the Greek National Anthem. Many of us had tears in our eyes.

One recalls many moving events, but I always remember with particular delight two special occasions.

The first was my chance encounter in Bush House with General Charles de Gaulle. One evening I was in a great hurry to get to our studio for our evening transmission, when accidentally I opened the door of another studio. There in front of me stood that tall monolithic figure of de Gaulle in the sparse Free French uniform adorned only with the Cross of Lorraine. He was waiting for the Czechoslovak Ambassador who was also late. De Gaulle was sombre and not agreeably surprised that I had barged into his studio. Then, when I explained who I was, his face lit up and he proceeded to shake my hand vigorously. "Tell the Greeks" he said emphatically, "that they are fine, brave soldiers. The whole world admires them. We wish that they would throw Mussolini's army into the sea." I left the wrong studio feeling as tall as de Gaulle!

The second unforgettable occasion was even more euphoric. On the 11th January 1941, the Greek War Relief Fund and the Greek Red Cross held a Midnight Matinee at the London Palladium. It was a theatrical and musical extravaganza and many well known actors, singers and musicians took part. The theatre was packed to the ceiling. Royalty - Princess Marina was among the distinguished royal guests - politicians, diplomats, representatives of the Allied armed services, the press, the BBC, the London Greek Community, in fact everyone that mattered was there. The atmosphere was one of elation and high spirits and all the famous participants were cheered to the echo. This was indeed a celebration of Greece and its gallant fighters, with the spoken word, song and music.

The highlight, however, of the show was the star singer, Florence Desmond, who sang "WHAT A SURPRISE FOR THE DUCE, HE CAN'T PUT IT OVER THE GREEKS". This was a satirical ditty which made a laughing stock of Mussolini and his pompous prattle that he would conquer Greece in one week and enter Athens on a white charger.

The audience absolutely loved it and after the first encore everyone joined in the singing. At the end of each refrain there was a delirious ovation, with people standing, applauding, throwing flowers on the stage, and shouting "More, more, Flo more". After the fifth or sixth encore, I can't remember which, an emotionally drained but radiant Florence came to the edge of the flower strewn stage and spoke to the audience. "Thank you, thank you very much", she said, "You are all having a wonderful time; but I am gradually losing my voice! I think that after this, I should really fly to Athens and sing this song to those brave Greek boys at the front. They deserve your applause; not me!"

And to prevent any further encores, the whole theatre orchestra rose to its feet and struck up the National Anthem of Greece followed by the British one! As evidence, I still have the lacquer disc which the BBC recorded during that unforgettable night in 1940.

George Angeloglou, then Head of the Greek Section BBC

288

BIBLIOGRAPHY

Αλεξανδράκης, Αλέξανδρος Δ. Έτσι πολεμούσαμε. 1940 - 1941. Αθήνα, 1968.

Βερνάρδος, Ιωάννης Α. Τρεμπεσίνα. Αθήνα, Αλικιώτης, 1955.

Γερουλάνος, Μαρίνος. Αναμνήσεις 1867 - 1957. Επιμ. Μαρία Μ. Καΐρη, Κυρ. Ντελόπουλος. Αθήνα, Ελληνικό Λογοτεχνικό και Ιστορικό Αρχείο, 1981.

Δόξας, Τάκης. "Τρόπαιο στην Τρεμπεσίνα." (Ανθολογία λογοτεχνικών κειμένων Έπους 1940 - 1941. Επιμ. Πάνος Ν. Παναγιωτούνης, Παύλος Π. Ναθαναήλ. Αθήνα, Ώρα, 1954).

Δημητριάδης, Φωκίων. Σκιά πάνω απ' την Αθήνα. Μαρής, 1970.

Καιροφύλας, Γιάννης. Η Αθήνα του '40 και της Κατοχής. Αθήνα, Φιλιππότης, 1985.

Κανελλόπουλος, Παναγιώτης. Τα χρόνια του Μεγάλου Πολέμου. 1939 - 1944. Ιστορική αναδρομή και κείμενα. Αθήναι, 1964.

Κούκουνας, Δημοσθένης. Οι Γερμανοί στην Ελλάδα. Η γερμανική εισβολή και η συνθηκολόγηση. Απρίλιος 1941. Αθήνα, Μέτρον, 1983.

Μαυροειδή - Παπαδάκη, Σοφία. "Γράμμα σε πολεμιστή." (Ανθολογία λογοτεχνικών κειμένων Έπους 1940 - 1941. Επιμ. Πάνος Ν. Παναγιωτούνης, Παύλος Π. Ναθαναήλ. Αθήνα, Ώρα, 1954.

Παπάγος, Αλέξανδρος. Δύο χρόνια στα χιτλερικά στρατόπεδα συγκεντρώσεως. Αθήνα, Ο Κηφισός, 1984.

Σακελλαρίου, Αλέξανδρος Ε. Η θέσις της Ελλάδος εις τον Β' Παγκόσμιον Πόλεμον. Νέα Υόρκη, 1944.

Σκίπης, Σωτήρης. Μεσ' από τα τείχη. 2η έκδ. Αθήνα, 1945.

Τάγαρης, Αχιλλεύς. Ο Άρης διηγείται... Αθήνα, 1945.

Φαραντάκης, Κίμων. "Σκόρπιο ημερολόγιο ενός παιδιού". (Άνθρωποι και ίσκιοι. Αθήνα, 1975).

Φλούντζης, Αντώνης Ι. Ακροναυπλία και Ακροναυπλιώτες. Αθήνα, Θεμέλιο, 1977.

Χάρης, Πέτρος. Η μεγάλη νύχτα. Αθήνα, Βιβλιοπωλείον της "Εστίας", 1969.

Χρονόπουλος, Δημήτρης. Ελληνικές θύελλες. Αθήνα, 1972.

Casson, Stanley. Greece against the Axis. London, 1942.

Hadjipateras, Costas N. Héroismes et droits de la Grèce. Paris, Librairie Générale de Droit et de Jurisprudence, 1946.

Hauptman Piehl. Ganze Männer; vom Leben und Erleben der deutschen Fallschirmjäger. Leipzig, Verlaghaus Bong & Co., 1944.

Sulzberger, Cyrus L. "The Glory that is Greece."

Documents related to New Zealand's participation in the Second World War 1939 - 1945. Wellington, War History Branch, Department of International Affairs, 1949.

Les lettres échangées par Hitler et Mussolini. Introduction par André François Poncet. Paris, Éditions du Pavois, sd.

The Goebbels diaries 1939 - 1941. Translated and edited by Fred Taylor. London, Hamish Hamilton, 1982.

The Mediterranean Fleet. Greece to Tripoli. London, His Majesty's Stationery Office, 1944.

Von Serbien bis Kreta. Graz, Steirische Verlagsanstatt, 1942.

Also many unpublished personal war diaries.

INDEX

C000220787

Bologna &
Emilia-Romagna

Shona Main & Nick Bruno

Credits

Footprint credits
Editor: Jo Williams
Production and layout: Emma Bryers
Maps: Kevin Feeney
Cover: Pepi Bluck

Publisher: Patrick Dawson
Managing Editor: Felicity Laughton
Advertising: Elizabeth Taylor
Sales and marketing: Kirsty Holmes

Photography credits
Front cover: claudio zaccherini/
Shutterstock.com
Back cover: claudio zaccherini/
Shutterstock.com

Printed in Great Britain by 4edge Limited,
Hockley, Essex

Every effort has been made to ensure that
the facts in this guidebook are accurate.
However, travellers should still obtain advice
from consulates, airlines, etc, about travel
and visa requirements before travelling.
The authors and publishers cannot accept
responsibility for any loss, injury or
inconvenience however caused.

Publishing information
Footprint *Focus Bologna & Emilia-Romagna*
1st edition
© Footprint Handbooks Ltd
April 2013

ISBN: 978 1 909268 09 8
CIP DATA: A catalogue record for this book
is available from the British Library

® Footprint Handbooks and the Footprint
mark are a registered trademark of
Footprint Handbooks Ltd

Published by Footprint
6 Riverside Court
Lower Bristol Road
Bath BA2 3DZ, UK
T +44 (0)1225 469141
F +44 (0)1225 469461
footprinttravelguides.com

Distributed in the USA by Globe Pequot
Press, Guilford, Connecticut

All rights reserved. No part of this
publication may be reproduced, stored
in a retrieval system, or transmitted, in
any form or by any means, electronic,
mechanical, photocopying, recording,
or otherwise without the prior permission
of Footprint Handbooks Ltd.

The content of Footprint *Focus Bologna &
Emilia-Romagna* has been taken directly
from Footprint's *Bologna* guide, which was
researched and written by Ben Donald.

Acknowledgements
Thanks to Ben Donald for his excellent text. Thank you also to Elena Dall'Argine for all her he
in the updating of this book and for being the best ambassador for Emilia-Romagna there
Also to Giorgia Zabbini of Comune di Bologna; Zio 'Cinque Pance' Giovanni for his advice o
where and what to eat and drink; Pepe the bus driver for his history lessons; and Dave Petri
as always, for assisting us in all aspects of our research.

Contents

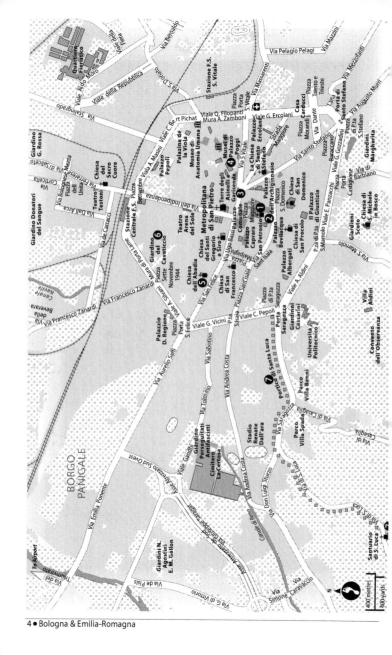

With streets like embroidered cloth, threaded with the arches of continuous colonnades, the heart of Bologna is a giant cloister. Under processions of classical columns and in the shadows cast between the half-moons of its winding alleys, the city inspires a furtive combination of intimacy and wandering, revealing her secrets to the unhurried visitor prepared to be led astray. Above and behind its chiaroscuro porticoes, Bologna is a rose-red city of bombastic churches and vainglorious palaces, lasting testaments to the architectural flattery bestowed by the papal and civic forces that vied for control of the city. Striving for immortality, these patriarchs commissioned lavish chapels, frescoes and tombs, creating in the process one of the most influential schools of Italian art and bequeathing to the city a litter of monuments and masterpieces. These remain in good condition and accessible, not ominously *sotto restauro*, as elsewhere in Italy.

Beyond Bologna, to the south and west lie the hills and mountains of the Apennines, rich with Etruscan history, fortifications and breathtaking vistas. Along the flat old Roman road of via Emilia, the historic towns of Parma, Reggio Emilia and Modena are handsome and affluent, famous for their huge hanging hams, wheels of cheese and sweet fragrant vinegar. Moving westwards along the might River Po is Ferrara, once the stronghold of the Este family. On the lower lip of the sultry Po Delta is Byzantine Ravenna whilst 30 miles but another world away is Rimini, one of Italy's most famous beach resorts.

This guide is intended for those who want to see, eat and feel Bologna but who may like to learn a little more about the relatively understated but strikingly diverse region of Emilia-Romagna.

Planning your trip

Best time to visit Bologna and Emilia-Romagna

Italy's climate makes it an attractive holiday or short-break proposition virtually all year round. However, Bologna can get extremely hot between May and September and there can also be regular and spectacular downpours of rain, especially in spring and autumn. In both cases the city's arcades really come into their own for shelter and shade. If there is a bad time to visit, it is August when many of the city's museums, buildings and – worse still – restaurants close, sometimes for the whole month, sometimes just for the middle two weeks. All year round, visitors staying for a long weekend are advised to make the most of the weekend days as many sights, shops and restaurants close on a Monday. Many shops also close on Thursday afternoons.

What to see in Bologna and Emilia-Romagna

A weekend
Most of Bologna's main attractions are within a short walk of each other. However, there might be a temptation to cram in too many sights. Time is equally enjoyably spent simply strolling around the arcaded streets. That said, a weekend visit will comfortably allow for a snapshot of the principal sights in the heart of Bologna's old centre, while still allowing time for shopping and lounging in cafés. Starting in piazza Maggiore, look inside the Basilica di San Petronio and climb up the Torre Asinelli before wandering around the streets of the university quarter. Head down via Zamboni and into the beautiful church and oratory of San Giacomo Maggiore before ending up in the Pinacoteca gallery, the best introduction to the Bolognese school of art. If it is Friday or Saturday, the market on piazza VIII Agosto will make a lively antidote to the painting. You should also make time to look around the serene cloisters of the Santo Stefano church complex. Finally, you'll probably want to walk off all the mortadella by taking a Sunday stroll up the colonnade to the shrine of San Luca, where you can enjoy panoramic views over the city and lower Apennines.

One week or more
A week will give you time to enjoy the essential sights at a more leisurely pace and to linger in some of the city's interesting districts such as the Mirasoli at the end of via Castiglione, the via del Pratello and the canal area around via delle Moline. If you are particularly interested in Bologna's watery and underground past, you could visit the fascinating canals that go right under the city. You might also want to inspect the treasures of the Chiesa di San Domenico and the magical hidden Chiesa della Madonna del Colombano in via Parigi. The Jewish ghetto and the Museo della Musica are also interesting historical diversions that will lay open the city. If you go up to the shrine at San Luca, the surrounding hills offer many lovely parks, monasteries and villas, such as Parco di Villa Ghigi and San Michele in Bosco. Bologna is also an excellent springboard for day trips or even one-night stopovers to Italian cities such as Modena and Ferrara. Parma, with its world-famous cheese and ham, is less than an hour away, as is the coastal resort of Rimini. Ferraris are made just up the road at Maranello and raced on the Grand Prix circuit at Imola just south of Bologna, while the hills southwest of Bologna offer spa towns, trekking and winter skiing, all within

Don't miss...

1 **Basilica di San Petronio**, a hulk of a church with an amazing astronomical clock, page 18.
2 **Palazzo dell'Archiginnasio**, the old university building with an anatomical theatre, old library and walkways encrusted with the heraldic shields of former alumni, page 23.
3 **La Torre degli Asinelli**, one of the two towers; the climb to the top is worth the effort for its superb views, page 26.
4 **Palazzo Poggi**, university museum with the Specola dell'Osservatorio Astronomico and Museo di Astronomia, full of instruments from the early days of star gazing, and the Museo di Anatomia Umana, full of very moving and very gruseome wax models, page 28.
5 **Cineteca di Bologna**, a former tobacco factory, now the nerve centre of this city of film, page 36.
6 **MAMbo**, a former bakery, kitted out in marble and wood showing stunning contemporary art exhibitions, page 37.
7 **Portico di San Luca and Santuario della Madonna di San Luca**, for a memorable walk up this porticoed road to the much-loved church, page 39.

Numbers relate to the map on page 4.

easy reach by both public and private transport. Such is the embarrassment of choice in the city that you may wish to organize your visit into themes, such as art, food, technology or simply shopping.

Churches, art and architecture
Be daunted by the basilica of San Petronio (page 18), awestruck by the delicate interwoven churches of Santo Stefano (page 31). See the abundance of sculptures and frescoes by Bolognese and Renaissance masters in San Domenico (page 31) and San Giacomo Maggiore (page 27). Discover the exquisite secrets upstairs in the Chiesa della Madonna del Colombano (page 36). Get an overload of Bolognese masters at the city art gallery, La Pinacoteca (page 29) and the Collezioni Comunali d'Arte in the Palazzo Comunale (page 19). For a trip into modernity, visit the MAMbo, Bologna's answer to Tate Modern (page 38), and the Museo Morandi (page 37), dedicated to Bologna's answer to Cezanne. For more of the modern, check out the Manifattura delle Arti cultural centre (page 37) in the former industrial sector, home of the Cineteca and Lumière cinemas.

Food
Take a culinary tour of the city's delicatessens and restaurants; see fresh pasta being made; see the food markets of the Quadrilatero, especially Tamburini (page 54); and visit the cheese makers of Parma (page 63).

Technology
Visit the Ducati museum (page 38), the Ferrari museum at Maranello (page 67) and the Formula One circuit at Imola (page 70). Go to the university museums and relive

the pioneering of Marconi and Galvani (page 26). Visit the Exhibition Centre in the Fiera district to attend one of the city's many important trade fairs, especially the Motor Show (page 52).

Shopping
Shop and window-shop for Italian fashion in an array of classy, chic and costly designer boutiques around town (page 52). Seek out some more experimental and hip stores offering innovative Italian takes on fashion trends. You can also browse for books (page 53) or buy up delicious ingredients at the city's well-stocked delicatessens (page 54).

Getting to Bologna and Emilia-Romagna

Air
From the UK You can fly from Edinburgh (**Ryanair**), London Heathrow (**British Airways**), London Gatwick (**easyJet**) and London Stansted (**Ryanair**). Return fares with the budget airlines can be as low as £60 as long as you only take hand baggage. If booked ahead, British Airways might only cost a fraction more and includes generous cabin and hold baggage (24 kg) in the price, not to mention a free glass of wine (or hot drink) and nibbles as you admire the Alps from 25,000 ft.

From the rest of Europe Bologna is well connected to the major cities of Europe, with budget lines such as **easyJet**, **Ryanair** and **Transavia** or scheduled airlines such as **KLM** and **Iberia**.
   You can fly into Bologna from any of the major Italian cities south of Rome (Naples, Bari, Palermo and Cagliari, plus others) with **Alitalia**, **easyJet** or **Ryanair**. Connections to cities north of Bologna are by train only.

From North America, Australia and New Zealand There are no direct flights from North American airports. However, you can take a connecting flight to Bologna from the main intercontinental hubs of Paris, Frankfurt, Zurich or Rome. If you fly into another Italian city there are quick and inexpensive connections by rail (for example, Rome three hours, Milan two hours, Florence one hour and Naples four hours).

Alitalia www.alitalia.com
British Airways www.britishairways.com
easyJet www.easyjet.com
Iberia www.iberia.com
KLM www.klm.com
Lastminute www.lastminute.com

Ryanair www.ryanair.com
Skycanner www.skyscanner.net
Transavia www.transavia.com
Travelsupermarket
www.travelsupermarket.com

Bologna Airport Named after their favourite son, Bologna's **Aeroporto G Marconi di Bologna** ① *via del Triumvirato 84, T051-647 9615, www.bologna-airport.it*, is well connected to Italian and European airports and even better connected to Bologna; it's only 6 km away from the city centre. (Gone are the days when the budget airlines flew to Bologna-Forlì, an hour or so away by train.)
   At the airport there's a tourist information desk, car hire desks, cash machines, a newsagent (*edicola*) and eateries. There are also some souvenir shops but if, on the way back, you are thinking of taking wine, spirits or cheese home with you, it would be much cheaper buying it in a supermarket or cheese shop and packing it (very) well in

Bologna Centrale

Bologna Centrale train station is sadly only too well known as the scene of the worst bombing in Italian post-war history. On 2 August 1980 a bomb, thought to be carried in a suitcase, went off in the main concourse, killing 85 and injuring 200. The Brigate Rosse (the Italian left-wing militant group) were blamed for it but it's now believed it was carried out by a small neo-fascist group. A huge crack in the marble pavement just outside the main entrance has been left as a reminder of the city's loss.

your hold baggage. Remember, restrictions on liquid make taking liquids home in your hand luggage impossible. Even if you buy it after security, you cannot take it onto any connecting flight – it will need to go into your hold luggage (unmanageable if your luggage is set to automatically transfer).

If you have a disability before flying to or from Bologna you'll need to notify your airline of the kind of assistance you require. For the best level of service do this 48 hours before the departure of your flight. When you arrive at the airport let them know of your arrival by using one of the help phones at the entrances of both terminals. You can also request help at the information desk on the first floor, at check in or on Level 2 of the car park.

There are 10 car hire companies at the airport including: **Avis** ① *T199-100133, www.avis. com*; **Europcar** ① *T051-6472111, www.europcar.com*; **Hertz** ① *T051-6472015, www.hertz.com*.

All arrivals come into Terminal B. The **Bologna Aerobus-BLQ** ① *www.atc.bo.it/orari/ aerobus*, can be found outside the arrivals door for the 25-minute trip to the train station. It leaves every 12 minutes after 0700 (before which it runs every 30 minutes) until 2000, when it runs every 15-30 minutes. It costs €6 each way and tickets can be bought on board. If you want to get a taxi, the taxi rank is near the door. Expect to pay around €14 to the Centro Storico. If you want to book a taxi you can call **COTABO** ① *T051-372727, www. cotabo.it*, or **CAT** ① *T051-4590, www.taxibologna.it*. There's a €1 supplement for a booking plus a further €0.50 for each piece of luggage.

Rail

Located on piazza Medaglie d'Oro on the north edge of the city walls, **Bologna Centrale station** ① *T892021, www.trenitalia.com*, is a major hub in Italy's train network. At the time of writing is was undergoing refurbishment to accommodate its ever-swelling passenger numbers. With high-speed links to Naples, Rome, Milan, Florence, Turin, Venice and Verona you are never more than a three-hour train journey from Italy's main cities and European destinations (such as Paris and Brussels via the TGV, Eurocity or Euronight). The **Frecciarossa**, **Frecciargento** and **Frecciabianca** lines all pass through Bologna as well as the old **Regionale** trundlers, which offer the cheapest if slowest way to travel to outlying towns. There can be long queues to buy a ticket but you can avoid them by using the easy-to-negotiate ticket machines or buying online and picking them up at the machine.

Road

Whilst their drivers have a – sometimes unfairly – bad reputation, Italy has excellent roads so expect fun fun fun on the *autostrade*. Bologna is linked to Milan (two hours), Florence (one hour) and Rome (three hours) by the A1. The A13 will take you to Venice and Padua or, if you want to head down the south coast, the A14 links Bologna to Rimini, Ravenna and Ancona. The tolls on these roads can be quite steep so if you want to save money get a

Traffic control system

Popular with visitors but not so popular with the locals is the Limited Traffic Zone (ZTL), a large area located within the historical centre of Bologna where cars, taxis and delivery vans are restricted daily from 0700 to 2000 except on Saturday. The entrances to the ZTL area are monitored by Sirio, the so-called electronic traffic warden. There is, however, special access to hotels, B&Bs and public garages.

map and use the *strade statali*, or dual carriageways. For information about driving in Italy the **Autostrade per Italia** (www.autostrade.it/en) have a good online guide in English.

Transport in Bologna and Emilia-Romagna

Most of what you want to see will be inside Bologna's city walls. Add this to the fact that it is a flat city and you will find that it is compact enough to get around by foot. For example, to walk from the train station to Piazza Maggiore will take 20 minutes while strolling leisurely from one side of the city's walls to the other it can take about an hour. Furthermore, street upon street of porticoes means that you can wander around protected from wet weather or the hot midday sun.

Bicycle

You'll soon notice that bikes are everywhere. If you want to hire a bike, go to **Astronolo** ① *via O Regnoli 2, T051-308828, www.astronolo.net*. A bike for 24 hours will cost €15 (city bike), €24 (mountain bike) or €18 (electric bike). Weekends cost €25, €45 and €30, respectively. The Comune di Bologna (the municipal council) have an excellent leaflet *Tutta mia la città* which, although in Italian, has some maps of bike paths and interesting little cycle routes around the city. You can download it from their website, www.comune. bologna.it, or pick it up from the tourist information office in piazza Maggiore.

Bus

It is fun and cheap to take the bus – and two can travel on one ticket. All tickets must be validated on board by stamping with the yellow machine (if there are two of you stamp your ticket twice). You can buy tickets from a *tabacchi* or *caffè* before boarding the bus at a reduced cost of €1.20. If the bus you are getting on has a green plate at the entrance it means you can buy a ticket on board for €1.50. If there's a red plate, you can't.

These tickets are valid for 60 minutes or 70 minutes between 2030 and 0630 or 90 minutes during the two-week holiday in August.

A day ticket costs €4 and after validating can be used as much as you like until 2400. A city pass costs €11 and allows you 10 trips. For information and maps of the bus routes see www.tper.it (Trasporto Passeggeri Emilia-Romagna) or pick up a map from the main tourist information office. Many of the maps given out by hotels and B&Bs have details of bus routes on them.

Car

The ZTL (see box, above) make this a bad idea and would also deny you the opportunity to experience the beauty of Bologna's porticoes. If you have a hire car, you can park it in one of the numerous car parks which are outside the zone. There is a list of these in the Tourist

Price codes

Where to stay

€€€€ over €300	€€€ €200-300
€€ €100-200	€ under €100

Prices refer to the cost of two people sharing a double room in the high season.

Restaurants

€€€ over €30	€€ €20-30	€ under €20

Prices refer to the average cost of a two-course meal for one person, including drinks and service charge.

Guide section at www.bolognawelcome.com; be prepared to pay around €20 a day for covered parking. Alternatively, your hotel or B&B may be able to advise and they might even offer free parking.

Taxi

A taxi from the station to a hotel in the Centro Storico will cost around €7. Due to the traffic control system it may not be able to drop you off or pick you up from right outside your hotel. If you want to book a taxi you can call **OTABO** ① *T051-372727* or **CAT** ① *T051-4590*. Fares for a hailed cab start at €3 (or €4.60 between 1800-2200 and €5.60 between 2200-0600). There's a €1 supplement for a phone booking plus a further €0.50 for each piece of luggage.

Where to stay in Bologna and Emilia-Romagna

Being a centre for business, tourism and academia, Bologna is well stocked with hotels. During trade fairs, capacity is quickly exhausted, so book well in advance. Every effort should be made to stay in the old centre, since this area is the focus for both sights and atmosphere. If you are looking for a view, ask for a room high up to allow for the porticoes and narrow streets. For insulation from mopeds, forgo the view for a room over a courtyard. Most rooms have en suite bathrooms although dimensions often dictate that they will have a shower rather than a bath. Breakfast is usually included in the tariff. For a more authentically Italian experience start the day with a coffee and pastry at one of the city's many bars.

From 2012 Bologna introduced the hotel tax (*imposta di soggiorno*), so adding €1-4 per night depending on the room tariff. Children under 14 are not included in this tax.

On paper, Italy has a star classification system akin to other European countries, but the reality on the ground doesn't quite reflect the ratings. Amenities that have been listed often don't exist or don't work and sometimes you'll find staff more interested in looking good than looking after their guests. The hotels are graded from one- to five-star deluxe, but a well-run, well-positioned three-star can often offer a better experience than a five-star filled with self-absorbed staff or a position on the outskirts of the town centre. In one- and two-star hotels (sometimes called *pensioni*) you often have to share bathrooms, but some of these properties can be full of atmosphere, with genial hosts. The three-star options almost always have an en suite bathroom and air conditioning – strongly recommended for the sticky summers. If a place is described as a *locanda*, which

Regional specialities

Broadly speaking the region's cuisine can be divided in two: Emilia, the western part is known for its cured meats and cheeses, while Romagna in the east has a variety of elaborate fish dishes. By way of an antipasto (starter) there are almost as many kinds of salami and prosciutto as there are towns. The world-famous prosciutto of Parma should not obscure other variants on the cold meat theme such as *culatello*, also from Parma, mortadella from Bologna, *zampone* (stuffed pig's trotter) from Modena and pancetta and *coppa* (both types of ham) from Piacenza. On the side, to help you assuage your hunger before the main dishes arrive, you will probably be offered *cresentine*, delicious, poppadum-like discs, usually topped with mozzarella and mortadella.

For the *primo piatto*, Bologna is the home of stuffed pastas, such as tortellini, *cappellacci*, *andanolini*, as well as the old favourite, lasagne. The famous cheese of Parma, *parmigiano*, is an essential ingredient, not only to sprinkle on top of your pasta but also, when added to milk, to make the many sauces and baked pasta dishes *alla parmigiana*, which define the region's cooking.

Parmesan is not the region's only cheese, however, and visitors should try the equally pungent *grana padano* and also the beautifully soft cow's milk *squacquerone*. On your side salad, drizzle a little *aceto balsamico* (balsamic vinegar) from Modena, and wash it all down with a glass of Lambrusco, Albana or Sangiovese. Hearty eaters might be tempted to find room for a delectable dessert, from the almondy and crunchy *torta sbrisolona*, or spiced *spongata* (sponge cake) to the *torta di riso* (rice cake), or the perversely named *zuppa inglese* (English soup), which we simply call trifle.

---

traditionally referred to an inn or a restaurant with rooms, these days it simply means a hotel and it can have any star rating. A bed and breakfast can be no more than a room in someone's residence (for better or worse).

If you are intending to spend more than a week in one place and you're not planning on bugging the concierge every 15 minutes for directions or restaurant bookings, seriously consider renting an apartment for your stay. Not only will you save money if you're looking at anything from mid-range or above, but shopping for groceries at the local markets and living like a local in a city that you want to get to know better can be just as enjoyable and rewarding as seeing a major attraction you've always dreamt of visiting.

Food and drink in Bologna and Emilia-Romagna

Bologna's third nickname, *la grassa*, the fat, does not refer to the gait of its populace (who are, largely, lean and groomed). It refers to the surfeit of produce and of dishes that the Bolognesi cook up. Whilst all Italians love their food, *la cucina Bolognese* is *molto particolare*. There is meat, and lots of it. Vegetarians may find Bologna a bit of a challenge.

When you're eating out, names like *ristorante*, *trattoria* and *osteria* are interchangeable; it's really the reputation for food and the prices that matter. Nevertheless, the old values of home-made and handmade dishes, prepared with fresh, local and seasonal produce, according to recipes handed down over generations, is what makes Bolognese cuisine.

Despite the abundance of restaurants, it is advisable to book ahead. Watch out for days when restaurants are closed and, if visiting in August, be prepared for many restaurants to

Bolognese ragù

The Bologna Delegation of the Accademia Italiana della Cucina have a solemnly declared recipe for *ragù* which was deposited to the Chamber of Commerce Bologna, Palazzo della Mercanzia, by notorial deed on 17 October 1982. They take the matter very seriously but so they should, as to those of us not lucky enough to be born of a home-cooking Italian mamma, it's a revelation.

Ingredients
300 g beef skirt minced
150 g pancetta or bacon cubed
50 g carrot finely diced
50 g celery finely diced
50 g onion finely diced
5 spoons tomato sauce or
20 g tomato purée
½ glass white or red wine
1 glass whole milk
salt and pepper

Method
• Fry up the pancetta or bacon in a frying pan.
• When it starts to colour add the onion, celery and carrot to the bacon fat. Once they are soft and fragrant, add the minced meat and brown.
• When the meat is brown, add the wine and tomato sauce/purée, mix well then bring to a simmer.
• Leave it simmering for two hours. Add a little milk every so often and check the seasoning.
• This sauce goes best with a pasta that will hold it, such as tagliatelle. Serve with a light dusting of Parmigiano Reggiano cheese.

be closed for holidays. Lunch is usually served between 1200 and 1500 and most places will not open in the evening before 2000, with their kitchens closing at around 2300.

Festivals in Bologna and Emilia-Romagna

Celebrating has always been important for the Bolognese, as befits a people who regard every meal as a feast. In the past, the city was never shy about celebrating its independent spirit at each overthrow of a pope, tyrannical lord or invader. Any victory and its anniversary was a licence to throw a party. In medieval times, the streets would fill with jesters and revellers and jousts would take place. Bologna even had its own *palio*, a horse race around the piazza Maggiore, similar to that which still runs in Siena. Another famous festival was *la festa della porchetta*, held on the same day, at which a suckling pig was thrown down to the masses from the window of the Palazzo Comunale as a gift from the nobility. Napoleon failed to see the funny side of either festival and banned them both during his occupation of Bologna.

These days, whilst the old traditions of a Catholic and university town continue, it's the whole spectrum of the arts – with the increasing presence and popularity of film festivals – that shape the cultural year.

Essentials A-Z

Customs and immigration
UK and EU citizens do not need a visa
but will need a valid passport to enter
Italy. A standard tourist visa for those
outside the EU is valid for up to 90 days.

Disabled travellers
Italy is adapting to the needs of disabled
travellers but access can still be very
difficult due to the age of many historic
buildings or the lack of careful planning.
For more details and advice, contact a
specialist agency before departure, such
as **Accessible Italy** (www.accessibleitaly.
com) or **Society for Accessible Travel
and Hospitality** (www.sath.org).

Electricity
Italy functions on a 220V mains supply.
The plugs are the standard European
2-pin variety.

Emergencies
Ambulance: T118; **Fire service**: T115;
Police: T112 (with English-speaking
operators), T113 (*carabinieri*);
Roadside assistance: T116.

Etiquette
Bella figura – projecting a good image –
is important to Italians. Take note of public
notices about conduct: sitting on steps
or eating and drinking in certain historic
areas is not allowed. Covering arms and
legs is necessary for admission into some
churches – in rare cases even shorts are
not permitted. The Bolognesi are decidedly
punctual and the queue is largely observed.

Families
The family is highly regarded in Italy
and children are well treated (not to
say indulged), particularly in restaurants
(although more expensive restaurants
may not admit children). Note that
lone parents or adults accompanying
children of a different surname may
sometimes need proof of guardianship
before taking children in and out of Italy;
contact your Italian embassy for the
current details on this (Italian embassy
in London, T020-7312 2200).

Health
Comprehensive medical insurance is
strongly recommended for all travellers
to Italy. EU citizens should also apply
for a free **European Health Insurance
Card** (www.ehic.org.uk), which replaced
the E111 and offers reduced-cost medical
treatment. Late-night pharmacies are
identified by a large green cross outside.
To obtain the details of the 3 nearest
open pharmacies dial T1100; out-of-
hours pharmacies are listed in most
local newspapers. The accident
and emergency department of a
hospital is the *pronto soccorso*.

Insurance
Comprehensive travel (and medical)
insurance is strongly recommended for
all travellers to Italy. You should check
any exclusions, the excess and ensure that
your policy covers you for all the activities
you want to undertake. Keep details of your
insurance documents separate. Scanning
them, then emailing yourself a copy is a
good way to keep the information safe
and accessible. Make sure you are fully
insured if hiring a car, or, if you're taking
your own vehicle, contact your current
insurer to check whether you require
an international insurance certificate.

Internet

Be very careful to avoid roaming charges when in Italy as these can be extortionate. The good news is that many hotels, restaurants and *caffès* offer free Wi-Fi. Just remember these are not secure connections so it is not advisable to use them for online banking or other financial transactions.

Money

The Italian currency is the euro (€). To change cash or traveller's cheques, look for a *cambio* (exchange office); these tend to give better rates than banks. Banks are open Mon-Fri 0830-1300 with some opening again 1500-1600. ATMs that accept major credit and debit cards can be found in every city and town (look around the main piazzas). Many restaurants, shops, museums and art galleries will take major credit cards but paying directly with debit cards is less common than in the UK, so having a ready supply of cash may be the most convenient option. You should also keep some change handy for toll roads if you're driving.

Be sure to check ATMs for scanning devices and always cover your hand when entering your pin. If you are paying in a shop or bar do not let your card out of your sight.

Opening hours and holidays

Shops, churches and many sights close for a long lunch at around 1230 and may not open again until 1600. Many places (particularly clothes shops) are closed on Sun and/or Mon. Family-run restaurants or bars may also shut for a day during the week. Eateries will often stop serving after lunch (around 1400 or 1500) and sometimes as early as 2100 in the evenings; don't expect to be able to order meals at any hour. Aug is the Italian holiday month when shops, bars, restaurants and even some sights can be closed for a fortnight or longer. They'll also close for Christmas, New Year and some of Jan. See Money, above, for details of bank opening hours.

Police

There are 5 different police forces in Italy. The *carabinieri* are a branch of the army and wear military-style uniforms with red stripes on their trousers and white sashes. They handle general crime, drug-related crime and public order offences. The *polizia statale* is the national police force, dressed in blue with a thin purple stripe on their trousers. They are responsible for security on the railways and at airports. The *polizia stradale* handles crime and traffic offences on the motorways and drives blue cars with a white stripe. The *vigili urbani* are local police who wear dark blue (in summer) or black (in winter) uniforms with white hats and direct traffic and issue parking fines in the cities. The *guardia di finanza* wear grey uniforms with grey flat hats or green berets (depending on rank). They are charged with combating counterfeiting, tax evasion and fraud.

In the case of an emergency requiring police attention, dial 113 or approach any member of the police or visit a police station. If it's a non-emergency, dial 112 for assistance. See also Emergencies, page 14.

Post

The Italian post service (www.poste.it) has a not entirely undeserved reputation for unreliablility, particularly when it comes to handling postcards. You can buy *francobolli* (stamps) at post offices and *tabacchi* (look for T signs). A stamp for a postcard (up to 20 g) costs from €0.70 for both EU and transatlantic destinations. For letters over 20 g and parcels, there is a maze of prices and options.

Safety

Statistically, the crime rate in Bologna is lower than in Italy as a whole. However, it is always advisable to take general care at night or when travelling, especially around train stations: don't flaunt your valuables; take only the money you need and don't carry it all in one wallet or pocket.

Pickpockets and bag-cutters operate on public transport, so try not to make it obvious which stop you're getting off at, as it gives potential thieves a timeframe in which to work. Car break-ins are common, so always remove valuables and secure other luggage in the boot. Beware of scams, con artists and sellers of fake goods; you can be fined a considerable amount of money for buying fake designer goods. In general, don't take risks you wouldn't take at home.

Telephone
The dialling code for Bologna is 051. The prefix for Italy is +39. You no longer need to drop the initial '0' from the area codes when calling from abroad. For directory enquiries call T12.

Time difference
Italy uses Central European Time, GMT+1.

Tipping
It is increasingly common for service to be included in your bill on top of the cover charge. Where this isn't the case (and, sometimes, even when service is included in the bill), tipping is expected but don't tip unless you are genuinely happy with the service: you do your fellow travellers a disservice if you do. There is no need to tip when buying coffees or drinks but a token of appreciation for good, smiling, grudge-free service, is always appreciated.

Tourist information
Bologna Welcome Tourist Offices, Piazza Maggiore, T051-239660, www.bologna welcome.com, Mon-Sat 0900-1900, Sun and public holidays 1000-1700, and the airport, via Triumvirato 84, T051-647 2113, www. bolognawelcome.com, Mon-Sat 0900-1900, Sun and public holidays 1000-1600, have piles of leaflets and maps and information about the city, including walking tours, wine tastings, cycling maps and public transport. You can also purchase the Bologna Welcome Card (see box, page 19).

Emilia-Romagna
Emilia-Romagna Turismo, www.emiliaromagnaturismo.com.
Ferrara, Castello Estense, T0532-2020 9370, www.ferrarinfo.com. Mon-Sat 0900-1300 and 1400-1800.
Modena, via Scudari 8, T059-203 2660, www.turismo.comune.modena.it. Mon 1500-1800, Tue-Sat 0930-1230 and 1500-1800, Sun 0930-1230.
Parma, piazza Garibaldi, T0521-218889, www.turismo.comune.parma.it. Mon 1300-1900, Tue-Sat 0900-1900, Sun 0900-1300 and 1400-1800.
Ravenna, via Salara 8, T0544-35755, www.turismo.ra.it. Mon-Sat 0830-1300 and 1430-1800, Sun 0900-1200.
Reggio Emilia, via Farini 1a, T0522-451152, www.municipio.re.it. Mon-Sat 0830-1300 and 1430-1800, Sun 0900-1200.
Rimini, piazzale Fellini 3, T0541-704587, www.riminiturismo.it. Mon-Sat 0900-1300 and 1400-1800 Sun 0900-1200.

Contents

Places in Bologna

The heart of Bologna is still its Roman core, piazza Maggiore, at the confluence of the city's two main roads: via Ugo Bassi and via Rizzoli. These two roads are the contemporary face of the old Roman road, via Emilia, which once traversed the whole of the region. The area now referred to as the Centro Storico or old centre is defined by the *circonvallazione*: the busy main perimeter road which follows the line of the city's old extremity walls, joining up the 12 city gates.

The Centro Storico: piazza Maggiore and around → *For listings, see pages 41-57.*

The two adjoining piazze Maggiore and Nettuno are the social hub of the city. Piazza Maggiore is where you will inevitably start or end up. Standing in this piazza you can feel the power and prestige Bologna once had. The tall, thick and crenellated masses of the Palazzo Comunale and Palazzo Podesta and the forbidding weight of the Basilica di San Petronio, whose faceless façade makes it more like a fortification than a place of worship, all reveal Bologna's former might. These buildings stand upon the ruins of the Roman forum when it was known as Bononia. But whilst the executions and Papal parades are no more, it remains a place where the Bolognesi meet, drink, protest, celebrate and entertain themselves.

The perimeter of piazza Maggiore and the area beyond its eastern flanks called the Quadrilatero once constituted the entire extent of the original Roman settlement. The Quadrilatero is now a grid of teeming market streets full of colours, smells and bustle by day, and lively chic bars by night.

Fontana del Nettuno

Bologna's bronze statue of the Roman God of the Sea has become a symbol of the city and a favourite backdrop for posing visitors who appreciate his chunky buttocks and the mermaids at his feet. Completed between 1563 and 1566 and known affectionately as *il Gigante* due to its size, the statue is the work of the Flemish sculptor Jean de Boulogne (known in Italian as Giambologna). Legend has it that prior to commencing work on the design of the Fontana, and preoccupied with the ample nudity of the pagan God, Giambologna sought an approval from the pope. "For Bologna it's OK" came the answer, an early confirmation of the city's fame in Italy as a centre for more liberal attitudes and emancipated thinking.

Basilica di San Petronio

① *piazza Maggiore, T051-231415, www.basilicadisanpetronio.it. Open 0800-1230, 1500-1800. Free.*
The building of San Petronio cost huge amounts of money and numerous lives, and required the demolition of many churches and houses – yet its ambition was never fully realized. Funded by public money, the basilica, which is a civic temple not a cathedral, was conceived by the elected city council as a monument of opposition to the Papacy and was

Museum passes

The **Bologna Welcome Card** is available from the tourist offices at piazza Maggiore and the airport. It costs £20 and lasts for 48 hours. It grants you admission to all the Genus Bononiae historical buildings (San Giorgio in Poggiale, San Colombano, Chiesa di Santa Cristina, Santa Maria della Vita, Palazzo Pepoli, Palazzo Fava, Casa Saraceni, San Michele in Bosco) and the following museums: MAMbo, Museo Morandi, Museo Archeologico, Museo Medievale, Collezioni Comunali d'Arte, Museo della Musica, Museo del Risorgimento e Museo del Patrimonio Industriale. With it comes a pass for 24 hours' worth of travel on public transport or a return ticket for the BLQ shuttle bus to/from Guglielmo Marconi airport in Bologna (so it's only any use if you buy the Bologna Welcome Card at the airport just as you arrive).

It also allows you offers and discounts at the main tourist services and at over 200 nightclubs, shops, restaurants, spas and leisure facilities.

originally intended to be larger than St Peter's. The Papacy grew fearful of this ambition and diverted money and land to the construction of the Archiginnasio and founding of the university. At 132 m in length, it is still one of the largest churches in Christendom. Designed in a late Gothic style by the architect Antonio di Vicenzo, the first stone was laid in 1390 and the current state reached only after several centuries of labour.

Inside it is vast. And bare. That said, God is in the details and, on closer inspection, the basilica does have many redeeming features. The first of these are the unfinished figures in the half-moon above the central portal. Begun in 1425 by the Renaissance master Jacopo della Quercia, they depict the Madonna and Child, St Petronius and St Ambrosius and, either side of the door, stories from the Old Testament.

It's in one of the 22 side chapels that the intact skull of St Petronius has been preserved: in the second left-hand chapel, where there are also frescoes depicting the saint's life. The astronomical clock created in 1655 by Gian Domenico Cassini and Domenico Guglielmi illustrates the links between the basilica and the city as a centre of exploration and discovery. As a direct result of their studies of Galileo's theories at the city's university, the two men conceived of this outsize sundial, whose length, precisely 67.72 m, equals 1/600,000th of the earth's circumference. At noon the sunlight entering by means of a hole in the ceiling hits this line and throughout the year travels from one end to the other, enabling measurement of the exact date of the summer and winter solstices. The marble slabs along the line indicate the days and months and also the signs of the zodiac. It was this line which led to the discovery of the anomalies in the Julian calendar (in 1532 the spring equinox arrived too early) and ultimately to the invention of leap years and the reform of the calendar by Pope Gregory XII, after whom the modern Gregorian calendar is named.

Palazzo Comunale

① *piazza Maggiore 6, T051-219 3998 www.comune.bologna.it. Tue-Fri 0900-1830, Sat and Sun 1000-1730. Galleries €5; over 65s €3; under-18s free.*
Built in 1287, this grandiose garrison shows just how prepared for attack town halls needed to be in medieval times. Commissioned by Cardinal Anglic de Grimoard in 1336, the considerable defences were conceived as a show of strength by the Papacy and to defend it from warring Ghibellines.

1 Central Bologna

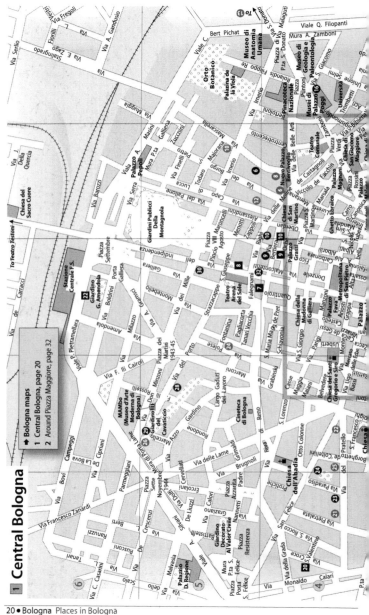

Bologna maps
1 Central Bologna, page 20
2 Around Piazza Maggiore, page 32

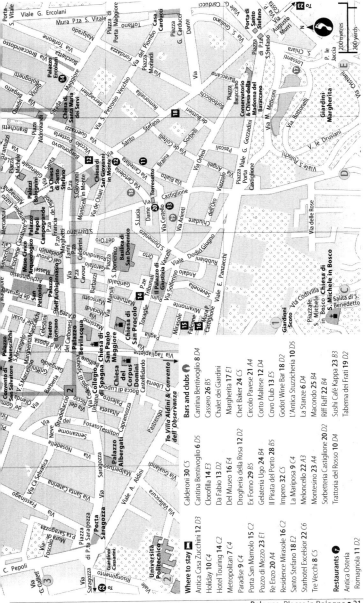

Where to stay

Antica Casa Zucchini 12 *D3*
Holiday 10 *C4*
Hotel Touring 14 *C2*
Metropolitan 7 *C4*
Paradise 9 *C4*
Porta San Mamolo 15 *C2*
Pozzo di Mezzo 23 *E1*
Re Enzo 20 *A4*
Residence Mirasole 16 *C2*
Santo Stefano 18 *E2*
Starhotel Excelsior 22 *C6*
Tre Vecchi 8 *C5*

Restaurants

Antica Osteria
Romagnola 11 *D2*
Calderoni 30 *C5*
Cantina Bentivoglio 6 *D5*
Clorofilla 14 *E3*
Da Fabio 13 *D2*
Del Museo 16 *E4*
Drogheria della Rosa 12 *D2*
Ex Forno 29 *B5*
Gelateria Ugo 24 *B4*
Il Pirata del Porto 28 *B5*
Impero 32 *C5*
La Mariposa 9 *C4*
Meloncello 22 *A3*
Montesino 23 *A4*
Sorbetteria Castiglione 20 *D2*
Trattoria del Rosso 10 *D4*

Bars and clubs

Cantina Bentivoglio 8 *D4*
Cassero 26 *B5*
Chalet dei Giardini
Margherita 17 *E1*
Chet Baker 24 *C5*
Circolo Pavese 21 *A4*
Corto Maltese 12 *D4*
Covo Club 13 *E5*
Godot Wine Bar 18 *D2*
L'Antica Stuzzicheria 10 *D5*
La Stanze 6 *D4*
Macondo 25 *B4*
Riff Raff 22 *B4*
Sushi Café Kappa 23 *B3*
Taberna del Frati 19 *D2*

Of Guelphs and Ghibellines

The conflict between the Guelphs and the Ghibellines was a major feature of 13th-century Italy. Guelphs were followers of the pope, while Ghibellines supported the emperor, Frederick the Great. Alliances for each side divided the country's many controlling family dynasties. In Bologna the two families to whom the conflicting factions allied themselves were, on one side, the Geremei, who were Guelphs, and, on the other, the Lambertazzi family, who were Ghibellines.

Following their victory at the battle of Fossalta in 1249, the Guelphs took control of the city and submitted it to the control of Pope Nicholas III, who from 1278 ruled the city by proxy from Rome. However, despite this yoke, Bologna was always allowed to enjoy relative autonomy for fear of further insurrection.

Bologna's buildings tell of a history of oscillation between papal and imperial forces. They were usually conceived as statements of the pre-eminence of one power over the other and were often altered by a new incumbent in deliberate architectural snubs.

Perhaps the most famous example of the Guelph-Ghibelline conflict, however, lies further north in Verona, where, at the same time as the battle of Fossalta, two young lovers were trying to transcend their families' different allegiances. Their names, of course, were Romeo and Juliet.

The clocktower was built in 1773 by Rinaldo Gandolfi whilst the large classical ground-floor window is the design of Galeazzo Alessi below which are two marble eagles, the left of which is attributed to Michelangelo. Rather amusing is the huge finger-wagging statue of Bologna-born Pope Gregory XIII (he of the calendar) produced by Menganti between 1576 and 1580. Bologna spent centuries in defiance of papal control but this statue, commissioned at a time when Bologna was controlled from Rome, was designed to leave the citizens in no doubt as to who was boss. The ground floor of the palazzo was once used as a market and warehouse for grain. Look for the plaque, which sets out the decreed standards of measurement in medieval times (the foot, the double arm and the perch) to avoid cheating and arguments between traders. The magnificent first-floor hall is reached via the sloping wooden causeway, so designed by Bramante for easy access by noblemen on horseback or in sedan chairs. At the top of these stairs is the Sala di Ercole ('Hercules' room', after the terracotta statue of the hero there by Lombardi) with beautiful frescoes, among which Ludovico Carracci's *Phaeton's Fall* and the *Madonna and the Earthquake* by Francesco Francia. The inside courtyard contains interesting rooms, many of which are open to visitors. The most important of these rooms, the Sala Farnese, is home to the Collezioni Comunali d'Arte, the city public art collection, which includes paintings and frescoes by many masters of the Bolognese school such as Signorelli, the Caracci brothers and Jacopo di Paolo, and works by Tintoretto.

Palazzo Podesta and Palazzo Re Enzo

① *piazza Maggiore. Closed to public except during exhibitions.*

Before becoming the governor's residence, the Palazzo Podesta was originally designed in the early 13th century to house the city's law court. The belfry with its *campanazzo* (literally 'bloody great bell' – it weighs 4700 kg) was added in 1453.

Built in 1244, Palazzo Re Enzo takes its name from the man who was its prisoner for 22 years. Enzo, the blonde young king of Sardinia, was the illegitimate son of Frederick the Great, ruler of the occupying imperial army. In 1249 the papal Guelph forces (see box, page 22) won a historic victory over Frederick at the battle of nearby Fossalta and took his son prisoner. He was detained in this building until his death in 1271. The building became known as Enzo's *dorata prigione* (golden prison) on account of the luxury in which he was kept, complete with cooks, maids and lady visitors to keep him entertained.

Palazzo dei Banchi

ⓘ *piazza Maggiore. Closed to the public.*

Completing the enclosure of the square on its eastern side, the Bankers' House (1412) is so named after the bankers and money lenders who used to have *banchi* (benches or stalls) under its arcades. Originally a row of jumbled buildings, they were brought together in the 16th century by the architect Vignola to create the present harmonious façade. Underneath the façade is known as il Pavaglione. In the days when the piazza was used as a weekly market, this area was where the cocoons of the *pava* (silkworm) were sold under a large protective marquee or pavilion.

Il Quadrilatero and il Mercato di Mezzo

Il Quadrilatero is the name given to the grid of narrow streets that were home to the small businessmen of medieval Bologna and each street still bears the name of the powerful associations of artisans and merchants it was known for: *orefici* (jewellers), *clavature* (locksmiths), *pescherie* (fishmongers), *drapperie* (textile merchants). Today these are still among Bologna's liveliest market streets with the food-lovers' **Mercato di Mezzo** ⓘ *Mon-Sat 0700-1300 and 1630-1930 (closed Thu afternoon).*

Santuario di Santa Maria della Vita

ⓘ *via Clavature 10, T051-236245. Tue-Sun 1000-1900.*

Originally built in the late 14th century to house the ill and impoverished folk of the quarter, this tiny church became home to one of the unrivalled works of beauty in Bologna's treasure chest of fine art: the dramatic *Three Marys Lament over the Dead Christ*, by the sculptor Niccolo dell'Arca. Mary's desperation was once described by the poet Gabriele d'Annunzio as "a petrified scream". The next door oratory, also home to the **Museo della Sanita**, houses a famous group of 14 similarly expressive terracotta statues by Alfonso Lombardi called *Death of the Virgin*.

Palazzo dell'Archiginnasio

ⓘ *piazza Galvani 1, via dell'Archiginnasio, T051-276811, www.archiginnasio.it. Mon-Fri 0930-1845, Sat 0900-1345. Free.*

This was the seat of Bologna's university from 1563 until 1803 when it and the other faculties within the city were united at via Zamboni.

The beautiful interior courtyard with its double loggia is encrusted with 7000 or so heraldic shields emblazoned under the arches where noblemen, eminent professors, students and rich people immortalized their families. Such was the rush for wall space that shields were often disfigured by competing families, leading to a law being passed to prevent such profanation.

The **Teatro Anatomico** was the third university dissection theatre in the world (Paris and Padua take the honours). Built in 1595 but bombed during the Second World War, what you now see is a replica. Its cedar wood-panelled walls and tiered benches surround a marble-topped dissection table. The *baldacchino* above the Reader (Professor's) chair

Kids might like...

Basilica di San Petronio The astronomical clock seems to enthrall the young and curious, page 18.

Specola dell'Osservatorio Astronomico and Museo di Anatomia Umana The nearest thing Bologna has to a planetarium, housing telescopes and other complicated old instruments for star-gazing, and, if your children have reached the age where they are obsessed with innards, they might be ready for the adjacent anatomy museum, page 28.

La Torre degli Asinelli Older kids might moan all the way up but tell them the view from the top will be worth it (it is), page 26.

Museo di Architettura Militare Intricately carved models of armaments and toy soldiers, page 28.

The Giardini Margherita and the Giardini della Montagnola are good places for a picnic and to run around daft on the lawns and among the trees. Bologna also has a number of swimming pools that might keep art-weary children happy; see page 48.

is help up by the écorché wood statues of skinned torsos by Giannotti. It's here that the Inquisition priest would have sat ready to intervene if proceedings threatened the participants' spirituality.

The Archiginnasio also houses the **Biblioteca Comunale** (municipal library), located here since 1838 and containing over 700,000 books and a collection of rare manuscripts that make it one of the most important libraries in Italy. If old books are your thing you can peruse the catalogue before you visit and arrange access; see the website for details. Perhaps two or three times a year, the Biblioteca holds beautifully curated if simply displayed exhibitions that are always worth seeing.

Finally, pop your head round the door of the **Aula Magna** – the former library of the Institute of Sciences now used for special events. Donizetti directed the first performance of Rossini's *Stabat Mater* here in 1842.

Just in front of the Archiginnasio, the **piazza Galvani** is named after the 19th-century Bolognese scientist, Luigi Galvani, who conducted ground-breaking experiments in electricity using frogs and from whom we get the word 'galvanize'. The statue in the square shows him peering into a book with a petrified frog on the page.

Museo Civico Archeologico

① *via dell'Archiginnasio 2, T051-2757211. Tue-Sat 0900-1830, Sun 1000-1830. €4, concessions €2, under-14s free.*

Just a few doors down from Palazzo dell'Archiginnasio, the former Ospedale di Santa Maria della Morte, a hospital for the terminally ill and for criminals sentenced to death, has become Bologna's archaeological museum. There are rows upon rows of Egyptian artefacts and bas-reliefs (second in Italy only to the collection in Turin), various Greek and Roman antiquities, including a bust of Emperor Nero, and an important collection of relics from the Etruscan civilization that made Bologna (or Felsina as they named it) the capital of northern Etruria and one of the most important economic centres from around the fifth century BC. The highlight for many is the marble stairway and its monumental statue of Neptune with oversized hands (relatively speaking).

Metropolitana di San Pietro

ⓘ *via dell'Indipendenza 7, T051-222112. Mon-Fri 0730-1845, Sat and Sun 0800-1845. Free.*
Bologna's squat cathedral sits flush with one of the city's busiest streets: it's not till you look up that you realize the scale of this beast. The two 13th-century lions in Veronese marble by Mastro Ventura that guard its entrance are magnificent but ineffectual; they have not been able to stave off the fires and earthquakes down the ages, which may explain the patchwork of renovations. Only a beautiful spiral column inside, supported by the statue of a cross-legged man, remains from its former elegance. Every year in May the image of Bolognese saint la Madonna di San Luca is brought down here from her sanctuary on the hill (see Festivals, page 51). Turning out of the church and left into via Altabella you find the remains of an arch known as the **Porta dei Laureati** (gate of the graduates) through which new graduates once passed.

Associazione Amici delle Acque e dei Sotterranei di Bologna

ⓘ *viale Pietramellara 11, T051-623 2255, www.amicidelleacque.org. Booking essential. Make sure you wear sensible shoes.*
Bologna has a hidden past as a city of underground passages and waterways. These can be explored thanks to a dedicated team of volunteers who work to preserve and educate people about them. There are five locations to visit.

The **Bagni di Mario**, via Bagni de Mario 8-10, was built in the 16th century on the site of a natural reservoir to feed the Fontana Nettuno. The **Aposa**, on piazza Minghetti, was the main single irrigation channel on which the city was first founded and which was covered over for reasons of hygiene. The **Bova** was the old port. It marked the confluence of the Canale Cavaticcio and the Canale delle Moline and the start of the Canale Navile. **Il Cavaticcio** was a tributary of the Canale Navile and wasn't used for productive purposes until 1995, when the hydroelectric power station was built. The **Remonda** was an old spring that used to provide water for the hospitals nearby, until it was connected to the Bagni dei Mario to provide water for the fountain in the piazza above.

The university quarter (the Northeast) → For listings, see pages 41-57.

This district is suffused with a lively and bohemian atmosphere in and around its 17th-and 18th-century palazzos, porticoed streets and intriguing alleys. Heralded by the city's famous Due Torri (two towers) at its head, the main artery of university life is via Zamboni, along which are the university's faculty buildings and the bars in which the students spend their time 'revising'. Halfway along, piazza Verdi is the veritable heart of studentland, and also theatreland, while at the other end, at the junction with via delle Belle Arti, is the famous Pinacoteca art museum. Tucked in, just north of via Rizzoli, are the sheer backalleys of Bologna's former Jewish ghetto, still redolent of the suspicion that reigned in the 1500s. Further north around via Piella and via Cattani are some of Bologna's less-visited streets, offering a slice of local working-class life and, in a sliver of the old underground waterway, a glimpse of the city's concealed past. Beyond them is piazza VIII Agosto and the Montagnola gardens, which come alive on Fridays and Saturdays, attracting crowds to the city's fleamarket. Returning south to piazza Maggiore along the main drag of via dell' Indipendenza is the city's cavernous cathedral.

La Torre degli Asinelli and La Torre Garisenda
ⓘ *La Torre Garisenda is closed for renovation works. La Torre degli Asinelli 0900-1800 in summer, until 1700 in winter. €3.*

Known colloquially as Le Due Torri, Bologna's twin towers have become the city's most immediately recognizable icon. Yet despite their apparent solitude on the city's skyline there used to be many more towers. Any self-respecting Bolognese noble family had a tower and Bologna's skyline boasted over one hundred of them. It was in the urban regeneration program of 1889 that the engineer Giuseppe Ceri campaigned vociferously for Bologna's "old and useless" towers to be pulled down. The aberration was approved, proving that the 20th century did not have a monopoly on the wrecking of our cities. The Due Torri are two of only a few towers of any significant height that survive. These early skyscrapers served as watchtowers to warn against an attack on the city and as a place of refuge should such an attack penetrate the walls. In the 14th century they also had a brief role as a prison. Nowadays, beyond being a tourist attraction, the Due Torri serve as reception masts, a use of which Marconi, the Bolognese inventor of radio, would surely have approved.

At a height of nearly 98 m, La Torre degli Asinelli is the taller of the two, commissioned in the early 12th century by the powerful Asinelli family from which it takes its name. There are 498 sturdy oak steps leading to the top, twisting like an Escher fantasy around the inside wall, which is otherwise hollow, and providing for many cosy trysts on the way up and down. On a clear day you can see as far as the Adriatic to the east and the Alps to the north.

Built almost simultaneously, the leaning Torre Garisenda was originally much higher than its current 47.5 m. It started to lurch through subsidence in the mid-1300s and was truncated from its original 77 m for fear that it might topple.

At the foot of the Garisenda tower you can see an inscription quoting the reference made to the tower in Canto XXXI of the Inferno of Dante's *Divina Commedia*, where the poet uses it as a simile for the looming giant, Antaeus.

Ghetto Ebraico
Hemmed in by via Goito and full of evocatively named streets such as via dell'Inferno (Hell Street) this was formerly Bologna's Jewish ghetto. Although it is thought that the Jewish community was allowed to contribute much to Bologna's cultural beginnings in

La famiglia Bentivoglio: patrons of the arts

The Bentivoglio family was one of the great warring dynasties of medieval Bologna. At the height of their power in 1460, Sante Bentivoglio commissioned the construction of an immense family palace that stretched over most of the northern side of via Zamboni. Sante's son Giovanni II, though not an artist himself, was a keen appreciator of the arts and of beauty in general and it was during his 46-year reign that the arts flourished – in particular the school of Francesco Francia. The city also gained many of its more renowned embellishments at this time, especially in the university quarter, which was the family's stronghold (see Chiesa di San Giacomo Maggiore, below). A pact between the King of France and the pope eventually led to Giovanni II's exile and overthrow. In the years that followed, all reminders of the Bentivoglio dynasty were destroyed, including their palace. The family is perhaps best evoked these days in the famous jazz club that bears their name on via Mascarella and the trendy wine-bar, called Le Stanze del Tenente located in their former family chapel.

the 12th century, in the 1500s they were, as in many cities, ghettoized and forced to live in this confined area in constant fear of persecution. Here are also to be found a number of the city's other surviving towers: the Torre degli Uguzzoni in vicolo Tubertini, the 11th-century Torre Prendiparte (59 m) in via Sant'Asolò, also known as *la coronata* (crowned one) on account of its crenellations, the Casa-torre Guidozagni, near via Albrroli which was lowered in 1487 to its current height, and the Torre degli Azzoguidi.

Chiesa di San Giacomo Maggiore
ⓘ *via Zamboni/piazza Rossini, T051-225970. Mon-Fri 0730-1230 and 1530-1830.*
Originally built in the mid-13th century, the church was appropriated in the 15th century by the Bentivoglio family, who made this area of the city their power base; see box, above. Most of the revisions to the style and structure of the church were carried out on their orders. Perhaps the most striking of these is the beautiful pink side arcade. The recurring motif on the capitals is the seashell, symbol of the traveller and pilgrim San Giacomo (St James). The apse of the church still supports the remains of the second circle of the old city wall.

Within San Giacomo's Renaissance interior is the altar by Lorenzo Costa depicting family victories over other Bolognese dynasties. In addition to building towers, it was also fashionable to show your power by buying and decorating your own chapel.

Teatro Comunale
ⓘ *via Zamboni 30/Largo Respighi 1, T051-529019, www.tcbo.it. Guided tours in Italian and English on Sun and Mon; contact the ticket office for details.*
Bologna's city theatre was built in the 18th century on the site of the stables of the magnificent Bentivoglio palace, which had been razed to the ground when that dynasty was overthrown in 1507. It was designed by Antonio Bibiena, a member of the renowned Galli family of Italian theatre designers. The colosseum-like 'boxes' and the U-shaped arena were a favoured form at the time. The theatre opened in 1763 with a performance of Gluck's *Triumph of Clelia*. These days the programme is dedicated to the highest of brows with opera, ballet and visiting national orchestras.

Conservatorio di Musica GB Martini

ⓘ *piazza Rossini 2, T051-221483, www.conservatorio-bologna.com. Mon-Sat 0900-1300. Free.*
Bologna played host to many famous Italian composers such as Verdi, Rossini and Puccini and its music conservatory was a place of study and composition for many others, among them Bellini, Gluck, Wagner and, briefly, Mozart. Just off piazza Rossini, the building is a former Augustine convent confiscated, like many, by Napoleon and put to other use. It is easy to see how the cloistered setting might have provided inspiration. The magnificent concert hall has a huge organ and a gallery of portraits of great composers, musicians and divas of bygone days. It is attached to one of the two sites of the **International Library** and **Museum of the Music of Bologna** ⓘ *www.museomusicabologna.it*, the other being Palazzo Sanguinetti in Strada Maggiore, and holds precious *incunabulums* (a pre-1501 pamphlet), autographed scripts and rare scores dating from the 16th to 18th centuries, including the original of *The Barber of Seville*.

Musei di Palazzo Poggi

ⓘ *via Zamboni 31-33, T051-209 9610, www.museopalazzopoggi.unibo.it. Tue-Fri 1000-1300 and 1400-1600, Sat and Sun 1030-1330 and 1430-1730 for all museums. €3, students, over-65s and the disabled €1.*
The seat of Europe's oldest university was originally located in the Archiginnasio (see page 23) but was moved here in 1803 by Napoleon who wanted to bring all the city's proliferating faculties together in one place to create a kind of campus. This is the thoughtland of *la dotta* (the learned), home of the university library and many of the university's main faculties and museums. The 16th-century building was the former home of the Poggi family. Although of humble origin, the family spent almost their entire wealth on the construction of the palace to signify their social ascent, following the election of Giovanni Poggi to cardinal in 1551.

The Palazzo Poggi houses a series of fascinating (if sometimes dully presented) museums reflecting the vast range of subjects that were pioneered at the university by its early pupils.

L'Accademia della Scienza is the university's science institute, whose lower rooms are decorated in frescoes representing Ulysses by Pellgrino Tibaldi. The entrance at number 33 leads into a pleasant courtyard with a statue to Hercules in its centre by Angelo Pio. The Aula Carducci has been preserved to show where Bologna's famous poet gave his lectures between 1860 and 1904.

Atop the Palazzo Poggi and accounting for its rather odd shape is **La Specola dell'Osservatorio Astronomico** and **Museo di Astronomia**, a tower that houses the university's observatory and museum of astronomy. The ancient instruments for the measuring and examination of the skies are evocative and fascinating for their rather Heath Robinson-esque appearance. There are a number of other museums, the best being the Museo di Architettura Militare, the Museo Ostretrico Giovanni Antonio Galli and the Museo di Anatomia Umana.

The **Museo di Architettura Militare** places military developments in the context of scientific and technological advancements. Exquisitely constructed models of various forms of armament and toy soldiers are on display, plus early defence diagrams carved in beautiful marquetry.

Museo Ostretrico Giovanni Antonio Galli, the university's obstetrics museum, heralds that time when men and medicine (as rudimentary as it was then) muscled in on childbirth. Don't miss the 18th-century instruments and incredible life-size models by Galli in wax and wood demonstrating the different phases of pregnancy in order to prepare 18th-century midwives for every eventuality.

So long as you're not squeamish, the **Museo di Anatomia Umana** is perhaps the highlight of Palazzo Poggi. These beautiful replicas of what lies within required bodies and parts to be procured to assist the wax pouring process. Ercole Lelli focused on the layers of life-sized men and women, some flayed so you can see through the muscle and bone. The models of Anna Morandi (a woman, in the 18th century, at the forefront of her field of science) and her husband, Giovanni Manzolini, were more interested in organs: the sense organs, the genitals and the cardiovascular system. Look out for Morandi's beautiful hands. Clemente Susini's wax model of a naked woman dead (or dying) sliced from loin to chops and with moveable internal parts is rather grisly but you can see what he clumsily was trying to do.

Museo delle Cere Anatomiche Luigi Cattaneo

ⓘ *via Irnerio 48, T051-209 1556, www.museocereanatomiche.it. Mon-Thu 0900-1230 and 1400-1630, Fri 0900-1230. Free.*

If you haven't seen enough internal organs represented in wax, Giuseppe Astorri and Cesare Bettini's models of malformations and bodies ravaged by illness are macabre and gory but fascinating.

Museo di Geologia e Paleontologia Giovanni Capellini

ⓘ *via Zamboni 63, T051-209 4555, www.museocapellini.org. Mon-Fri 0900-1300. Sat and Sun 1000-1800. Free.*

The university's other main collection of faculties and museums is across the road from Palazzo Poggi further down towards the decaying 13th-century gate of Porta San Donato. The best of these museums is Italy's largest museum of palaeontology, containing over 1000 pieces, of which the most appealing (especially to children) will be one of only four existing examples in Europe of the friendly but enormous diplodocus dinosaur, 26 m long and 4 m tall.

Orto Botanico

ⓘ *via Irnerio 42, T051-209 1325, Mon-Fri 0830-1530; Museo Botanico at L'Erbario Via Irnerio T051-209 1304, Mon-Fri 0900-1300. Free.*

The botanical gardens and herbarium make for some tranquility. Founded in 1658, it is home to over 5000 species of local and exotic plants, while the Herbarium has specimens of over 110,000 dried plants. At 2 ha, this geometrically beautiful garden of soothing lawns is a favourite for lounging students hanging out between lectures. During the summer months the grass tends to turn crispy so if you fancy a loll, be prepared for some crunch.

La Pinacoteca Nazionale

ⓘ *via delle Belle Arti 56, T051-420 9411, www.pinacotecabologna.it. Tue-Wed, 0900-1330, Thu 0900-1900, Fri-Sat 1400-1900, Sun 1400-1900. €4, €3 with museum card, concessions €2. Free for under-18s and over-60s.*

The gallery has the largest collection of canvasses by artists from the influential 17th-century Bolognese school, among them Tibaldi, Reni, the Carracci brothers and Guercino, as well as some late Titian. However, the highlights are the Byzantine works by Vitale di Bologna and the great Giotto, who has an entire room devoted to him (sadly closed at the time of writing due to damage caused by the 2012 earthquake). The gallery was founded by Napoleon as part of his programme for cultural reform and the collection was based on a set of donations to Pope Clement VII. To this Napoleon added all the art he was able to confiscate from the various churches, convents and monasteries he suppressed during his occupation. In so doing his vision was to unify the canvasses (now located in a suppressed Jesuit convent) with the Accademia delle Belle Arti next door – a logical union of the practice of art and examples of its perfection. Napoleon's reforms did not stop many of the works of art ending up in the Louvre, some of which have since been returned. Changing photographic exhibitions are housed in the basement.

Via delle Moline and Bologna's canals

Unlike most big cities Bologna was not built on a river so in the 12th century a canal was built to divert water from the westerly River Reno to the city centre. The water served not only for sanitation and refreshment but also, through the watermills after which via delle Moline is named, to power the silk and hemp industries that were Bologna's main medieval commercial activities. Up until the early 20th century the canal also served as a transportation network for the import of essential goods to the city. The canal lock at Casalecchio, west of Bologna, used to be one of the city's most picturesque spots until suburban sprawl and modern transit methods dictated that the canals fell into disuse and were covered over by roads. Although it may seem unlikely, water still flows through the foundations of old Bologna but it is visible in only a few places, most notably the bridge on via Piella opposite which is a peep-hole into the watery past, and between via Capo di Lucca and via Alessandrini.

Piazza VIII Agosto

Named after the battle in which the Bolognese repelled the invading Austrians in the First War of Italian Independence in 1848, this square looks for five days a week like an ugly and anonymous car park. But at weekends it becomes **La Piazzola** (see Markets, page 55), a huge and colourful market which draws locals and bargain hunters from the provinces in their droves. Wares on offer range from shoes, gloves and other leather goods to books, china and household items.

Giardini Pubblici della Montagnola

ⓘ *Open during daylight hours.*

The public Montagnola Gardens represent the largest green space inside the Centro Storico. They were landscaped by Giambattista Martinetti in 1806 on the mound created by the excavations and ruins of the papal castle, Castello di Galliera, of which a ruin still remains at their northern end. A grand set of steps leads up into the gardens at the foot of which is a dramatic and sensuous statue to Venus and Neptune by Diego Sarti.

Santo Stefano and around (the Southeast) → *For listings, see pages 41-57.*

This is Bologna's most picturesque, stately and tranquil district. Fed by the attractive capillaries of via Santo Stefano and via Castiglione, the beauty of this area is nowhere more evident than in the triangular piazza Santo Stefano. The important strada Maggiore, once part of the Roman via Emilia, witnessed the coming and going, the coronation and invasions of alternate patriarchs and popes.

Piazza Santo Stefano

Surrounded by intriguing and beautiful buildings, this piazza is one of Bologna's most picturesque locations. Triangular in shape, the cobbled square is paved with lines of flat, grey stones, an aesthetic device in conflict with classical ideas of symmetry but intended when coming into the piazza from the north to lead the eye towards the church at the piazza's southern end.

Chiesa di Santo Stefano

① *via Santo Stefano 24, T051-223256, www.abbaziasantostefano.it. Daily 0900-1200 and 1530-1830.*

Along with the Basilica of San Petronio and the Due Torri, this church is one of the must-sees for any visitor to Bologna. At its peak it was a Russian doll of seven interlinked churches within churches that came about after Lombards and both Benedictine and Celestine monks had their way. The complex is sometimes referred to as La Santa Gerusalemme after the seven connecting sanctuaries in the Holy City. Sadly, poor restoration between 1870 and 1930 caused some inexplicable demolition and the reduction of the number of churches to the current four.

The first and principal church is the **Chiesa del Santissimo Crocefisso**. Its beautiful crypt is composed of columns, capitals and other materials from the original Roman construction and bears a pagan inscription to Isis.

The **Basilica dei Santi Vitale e Agricola** is thought to be Bologna's oldest Christian church, again built from the original pagan construction with 11th-century Lombardic naves, and housing the sarcopoghi of the two martyrs of Bologna from which it takes its name. The tranquil **cortile di Pilato** is named after the Lombardic facsimile of Pontius Pilate's bowl in its centre (where he 'washed his hands' of Christ).

To the north is the **Chiesa del San Sepolcro** which contains the bones of Bologna's patron saint Petronius (except the skull which is in the basilica). At Easter the sepulchre is opened to allow people in to recreate the discovery of the Resurrection.

To the west is the **Chiesa della Trinità**, virtually unrecognizable as a church after the restorations, but housing a beautiful fresco of the *Adoration of the Magi* by Simone de' Crocefissi. Beyond this is the peaceful Romanesque cloister with a beautifully harmonious double loggia supported by capitals playfully decorated with sculpted animals, built by the Benedictines in the 11th century.

Chiesa di San Domenico

① *piazza San Domenico, T051-640 0411. Daily 0700-1300 and 1530-1930.*

Begun in 1221 to commemorate the life of Domingo de Guzmán, the founder of the Dominican order, this church contains one of the masterpieces of Bolognese heritage, the Fabergé-esque *arca* or canopy to Nicola Pisano's tomb of the saint in the right-hand nave, designed and carved by Niccolo de Bari; the beauty of the canopy earned him the name Niccolo dell'Arca. He died before all the statuettes had been completed, leaving the outstanding work – the figures of St Petronius and St Procolus – to no less a hand than Michelangelo. Michelangelo also carved the prominent kneeling angel on the front – a detail that has sold a lot of postcards for the city. Among the bas-reliefs on the ark is a little dog. The dog motif is also repeated on the plinth below the sarcophagus. Legend has it that before his birth, Domenico's mother had a vision that she would give birth to a dog that would spread light and happiness in the name of the Lord.

Strada Maggiore

This important street, a suburban section of the Roman via Emilia, is lined with a series of former noble residences. Outside **Palazzo Bargellini** ① *strada Maggiore 44, T051-236708, Tue-Sun 0900-1400, free*, are two enormous, sinuous and muscular statues of Atlas supporting the balcony above the door. Inside there's a fine art collection, which includes many masterpieces by both Crespis and Donato Creti. The same building also houses the **Museo d'Arte Industriale** (which, translated, would be Museum of Applied Arts) which displays furniture and decorative art from various eras and provides a window onto middle-class and noble Bolognese interiors dating from the 16th to the 18th centuries.

Around Piazza Maggiore

San Petronio

In the fifth century, during the decline of the Roman Empire, Bologna fell into ruin as all the political and administrative infrastructure disappeared. Petronius was a local bishop at the time about whom little is known, other than that he was a follower of Saint Ambrosius, the patron saint of Milan. Legend, however, has credited Petronius with rescuing Bologna from terminal decline by defining the city's boundaries and embarking upon the design and construction of a number of buildings, ensuring the city's continued protection and development. Most notable of these buildings is the complex of interlinked churches of Santo Stefano, inspired by a similar design that Petronius brought back from a pilgrimage to Palestine and the Holy City. It was not until the Middle Ages, as Bologna developed its university and resilient civic spirit, that her citizens began to seek a symbol of their origins with which they could identify. The result of their collective root-searching was to elevate their mysterious saviour-bishop to the status of patron saint.

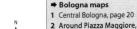

➡ **Bologna maps**
1 Central Bologna, page 20
2 Around Piazza Maggiore, page 32

100 metres
100 yards

Where to stay 🛏
Bologna nel Cuore B&B 1
Cappello Rosso 2
Cavour 11
Centrale 6
Commercianti 4
Corona d'Oro 13
Majestic Baglioni 21
Novecento 3
Orologio 5
Panorama 19
San Donato 17

Restaurants 🍴
Bricco d'Oro 15
Carracci 26
Centro Natura 31
Da Gianni a la Vecia Bulagna 3
Dell'Orsa 7
Diana 27
Franco Rossi 5
Gran Café 8
Majani 25

Pappagallo 1
Pasticceria Il Duca D'amalfi 18
Rodrigo 2
Tamburini 4
Terzi 17
Torinese 19
Trattoria Battibecco 21

Bars and clubs 🍷
Al Calice 1
Alla Corte di Bacco 15
Bottega del Vino Olindo Faccioli 7
Café De Paris 2
Caffe Commercianti 3
Caffe Sette Chiese 16
Caffe Zamboni 5
Caracol 20
Kinki Club 14
La Scuderia 11
Osteria Contavalli 9
Zanarini 4

Just off strada Maggiore, via Fondazza 37 was where the Bologna artist Giorgio Morandi lived (see box, page 37).

Casa Carducci and the Museo Civico del Risorgimento

① *piazza Carducci, T051-347592. Tue-Sun 0900-1300. €5, concessions €4.*

His earlier more humble lodgings being in via Broccaindosso, the poet Carducci was given this 16th-century residence as a new home by Queen Margherita of Savoy with whom he was head over heels in love. Carducci lived here from 1890 until his death in 1907, when his vast collection of books, letters and manuscripts was donated by the queen to the citizens of Bologna in the form of the Carducci library. Since 1990 it has been home also to the **Museo Civico del Risorgimento**, a museum celebrating the creation of the unified Italian state in 1861; there are some surprisingly good illustrations and art about war to be found here.

Around via del Pratello (the Southwest) → *For listings, see pages 41-57.*

The southwest of the Centro Storico contrasts the elegant via d'Azeglio – catwalk and hunting ground for Bologna's dedicated followers of fashion among wallet-bruising boutiques – and via del Pratello and via San Felice, famous for their concentration of years-old drinking holes. The important artery of via Saragozza leads past the Collegio di Spagna, up to the porta Saragozza, gateway to the city's great colonnaded pilgrimage site on the hill, the **Santuario di San Luca**.

Collegio di Spagna
ⓘ *via del Collegio di Spagna, T051-330408. Only the courtyard can be visited.*
This building is one of Bologna's more unusual pieces of architecture – due to the Hispanic colour – it was built to house students from Spain (known as *los Bolonios*). The Archbishop of Toledo, briefly a papal minister of the city before being overthrown by the council, bequeathed the rest of his fortune (after funding a suitably lavish funeral) to the building of a college to house 24 Spanish students from noble families. It is said that these students and their successors enjoyed impunity from the law as they were subjects of the Spanish crown.

Chiesa di San Francesco
ⓘ *piazza San Francesco, T051-221762. Daily 0630-1200 and 1500-1900.*
Completed between 1236 and 1263, this church and its convent were established as the HQ of the Franciscan order following their arrival in the city in 1211. It is a fine, towering example of Gothic architecture with a French influence; a heavy and complex forest of spidery flying buttresses. Worth looking at is the beautiful marble altarpiece conceived by the Masegne brothers in Venice in 1392, depicting scenes from the life of St Francis, and the pyramidal mausoleums to *i glossari*, the university's founding lecturers and legal scholars, in the peaceful cloister of the convent next door.

Teatro Romano
ⓘ *via de' Carbonesi 7.*
Inside the department store Coin lie the partial remains of a Roman theatre, estimated to date back to 80 BC, which are an unusual feature for any shop.

Porta Saragozza
With its three crenellated towers this is easily the most magnificent of the 10 gates of the outer city. Restored in the 19th century, a number of embellishments were added, no doubt to add to the majesty of the cloistered path to the Santuario di San Luca on the hill. For a walk through the Portico di San Luca to the Santuario, see page 39.

Around via Galliera (the Northwest) → *For listings, see pages 41-57.*

Badly damaged both by Allied bombardments and by subsequent bad taste in its reconstruction, the area to the northwest of piazza Maggiore belongs to the 20th century with all its follies and challenges. Modern concrete is dotted with a few old streets and a watery, industrial underground history. Here wider boulevards replace the winding narrow alleys and concrete, glass and shiny marble replace the ageing red stone, wooden beams and porticoes. This is urban Bologna and its post-industrial heritage has been grabbed and converted by the young and the creative, making this part of the city feel really dynamic and edgy.

Museo Civico Medievale
ⓘ *via Manzoni 4, T051-219 3930. Tue-Fri 0900-1500, Sun 1000-1830. €4, concessions €2.*
Located in the beautiful 15th-century Palazzo Ghislardi Fava, with its elegant entrance courtyard, this museum inspires even those who are not immediately interested in its rich collection of artefacts from the Middle Ages. Here, against a wallpaper of paintings by the Carracci family and their pupils, the enthusiast can admire myriad objects ranging from pieces of armour and musical instruments to ceramics and shoes that helped the wearer (a lady) wade through the slurry on the city's streets without getting her hems soiled.

Mercato delle Erbe
ⓘ *via Ugo Bassi 2.*
Bologna's covered market has occupied the elegant neoclassical building between via Ugo Bassi and via Belvedere since 1910. Inside row upon row of stalls are laden with fresh produce from fruit and vegetables to dairy produce and meat – not the herbs you'd expect from the name. In the annex is the **Mercato del Pesce** (fish market).

Chiesa della Madonna del Colombano
ⓘ *Entrance through the Casa dei Mutilato, via Parigi 1, T051-232862. Open 0830-1130 and 1530-1800. Visit to the upstairs oratory by request only.*
One of the real hidden treasures of Bologna is the oratory on the first floor of this otherwise unspectacular 16th-century church. It is arguably the most concentrated symphony of artistic endeavour and the most beautiful individual space in the whole city. The ground-floor *Virgin and Child* by Lippo di Dalmasio and other paintings by Antonio Carracci are a prelude to the stunning upstairs oratory, which seems as if it were almost a private chamber where Guido Reni, il Domenichino, Lorenzo Garbieri and other pupils of the Carracci academy could experiment with colours, forms, subjects and themes.

Teatro Arena del Sole
ⓘ *via dell'Indipendenza 44, T051-291 1910. Mon 1530-1900, Tue-Sat 1100-1900.*
In contrast to Bologna's other main theatre, the Comunale, this 19th-century arena was conceived as a return to the Greco-Roman idea of a democratic theatre in the shape of a horseshoe. The theatre seats 900 people in its six tiers and puts on popular children's shows.

Cineteca di Bologna
ⓘ *via Riva di Reno 72, T051-219 4820, www.cinetecadibologna.it. Tickets for the cinema: €6-7 (€5 Wed), €4 for students, €3.50 for over-60s.*

Giorgio Morandi (1890-1964)

Morandi was born in Bologna and spent most of his life painting there or in the village of Vergato, 40 km from the city. His landscapes have been compared to the work of Cezanne for the recurring presence of similarly angular shapes and soft hues. Painting during a period of immense social upheaval, technological innovation and artistic explosion, he was initially drawn towards the work of the Futurists and Cubists.

But ultimately he found his peace in more metaphysical painting, aligning himself with the artists Carra and De Chirico. He became the artist of simple everyday things: vases, fruit, windows, discovering them as if for the first time, revealing their hidden depths, and imbuing them with an existential significance. He once said, "Everything is a mystery, ourselves and the most simple, most infinitesimal of things."

Manifattura delle Arti (the Arts Factory) is the name give to the group of revitalized industrial buildings that are now exhibition areas and arts cinemas. Cineteca di Bologna is housed in a former tobacco factory transformed into cinemas, a film library and centre for film studies. It houses the archives of Pier Pasolini and Charlie Chaplin, accessible to the public by appointment. **Cinema Lumière**, see page 50, has two cinemas (Sala Scorsese with 175 seats and Sala Mastroianni/Officinema with 142 seats) which offer cinephiles a truly atmospheric viewing experience. Cineteca's excellent year-round programming, from Spaghetti Western specials to Vittorio de Sica retrospectives, sit alongside internationally renowned festivals such as **Biografilm**, a festival in June dedicated to biographical films, and **Il Cinema Ritrovato** in July, which shows old but restored films (see Festivals, page 51, for more details) and takes some of its shows into piazza Maggiore, an unmissable *Cinema Paradiso* experience.

MAMbo

ⓘ *via Don Minzoni 14, T051-649 6611, www.mambo-bologna.org. Tue-Fri 1200-1800, Thu-Sun 1200-2000 €6. €4 for students and over-60s.*

Bologna's answer to the Tate Modern is a former bakery, a 1917 building that played an important role feeding the city in the First World War. Now, with its hugely impressive collection of Italian contemporary art, thoughtfully put together, it feeds the soul. Its room dedicated to the political struggles of Bologna – **Arte e Ideologia**, with works by Renato Gattuso and Fabio Mauri – sounds like a turn-off but it's so powerful it makes you want to see and know more. It also curates and hosts temporary exhibitions and has a very cool, decidedly Northern European-style café with retro furniture. The shop has quirky arty objects and books. While its permanent home at Collezioni Comunali d'Art at piazza Maggiore is being done up, **Museo Morandi** is being accommodated at MAMbo. At first sight Giorgio Morandi (see box, above), Bologna's best-known and loved abstract portrait artist, seems to paint the same things over and over again. Some insist on spending time with these paintings, to reveal the subtle changes to colour, light and shape. "Nothing is more abstract than reality" Morandi once said.

Beyond the walls → *For listings, see pages 41-57.*

Parco Nord

Further along via Stalingrado (a road name that, like many others in this area, such as via Yuri Gagarin, emphasizes the city's leftist political stance) and just beyond the ring road, this park area is used for pop concerts, demonstrations and visiting circuses, and also has its own resident Luna Park where children and families can enjoy a fairground experience of the real sort.

Museo Ducati

ⓘ *via C Ducati 3, T051-641 3111/3259, www.ducati.it. Visit by prior arrangement only with 90-min tours Mon-Fri 0900-1400, Sat 1000-1200. Museum-only tours. €10. Near the airport, take the No 36 bus (25 mins) or a taxi (€15).*

A tour at the Ducati factory retraces the history of the famous marque from its origins through to the present day. Many of the original prototypes and race-winning bikes – which are now being replicated as production bikes as part of the Ducati renaissance – are on display.

Carpigiani Gelato Museum

ⓘ *via Emilia 45, Anzola Emilia, T051-650 5360, www.gelatomuseum.com.*

Prior reservation needed. The craft of ice cream making deserves a museum and now this one presents the history of the machinery, the recipes, the flavours and the cones. There are plenty of opportunities to scoop and lick.

Bologna's hills → For listings, see pages 41-57.

The foothills of the Apennines begin just outside the city walls with villas, parks and the 666 arches of the Portico di San Luca.

Portico di San Luca
① Follow the porticoes all the way from Porta Saragozza, in the southwest of the Centro Storico, up the hill to San Luca.
Stretching 3.6 km and encompassing 666 arches and 15 chapels en route, this extraordinary feat of both architectural engineering and devotion allows the people of Bologna to reach the icon of San Luca, held in the Santuario di San Luca at the hill's summit, without getting wet or sunburnt. In an uncustomary display of unity amongst the warring dynasties of Bologna, each arch of the portico was financed by a combination of noble families, religious groups, merchants and artisans. Each group or family placed plaques and offerings opposite their arch in acts of worship and also to secure their own fame and immortality. Sadly most of these have now disappeared or been badly damaged, and the best example is probably the *Madonna and Child* (known as *la Madonna grassa*, the fat Madonna) by Andrea Ferri under the 170th arch. The portico was the design of the architect, Giovanni Monti. The first stone was laid in 1674 and the summit was reached in 1739.

Santuario della Madonna di San Luca
① via di San Luca, T051-614 2339. Open 0700-1230 and 1430-1900. Free. To reach villa Spada, take bus No 20 from via dell'Indipendenza. From Porta Saragozza this walk takes 3-4 hrs there and back. The hill comes at the end and is quite steep. There are some bars and cafés for refreshment on the early part of the walk but nothing nearer the Santuario so bring water. Note the church is closed 1230-1430.
Sitting atop the Colle della Guardia hill at a height of 291 m this grandiose basilica is the home of the icon of San Luca, the religious saint of Bologna (as opposed to Petronius, the patron saint; see box, page 33). Records tell of a religious community on the hill as far back as 1193 and an image of the Madonna has been exhibited in a small chapel there since that time. Legend has it that it was discovered by a Greek monk in Constantinople, complete with a message that it should be installed on a hill somewhere called Monte della Guardia. In actual fact, modern dating techniques show the icon to be 12th century and possibly a copy of a ninth- or 10th-century Byzantine-inspired work made by a Bolognese painter.

The current building is the design of Carlo Dotti, started in 1723 and completed by his son, Gian Giacomo in 1775. From the outside, apart from the circular dome, the design looks more fit for a villa than a basilica, with its classical columns, arches and pediments and its Palladian harmonies. The famous icon is kept in the company of numerous more beautiful paintings and frescoes.

Ever since 1433, every year in May, just before Ascension Day, a copy of the icon is brought down the portico in procession to be installed and exhibited for one week in the cathedral of San Pietro before being returned to its home on the hill (see Festivals, page 51).

Colle dell'Osservanza
① To walk, head for viale Antonio Aldini and turn off at via San Mamolo but taking the southwesterly fork up via dell'Osservanza (there's a big sign). This walk takes about 2-3 hrs and even if you haven't arranged to see Villa Aldini, the Parco di Villa Ghigi is work taking a detour for. It's a steady incline up the Colle so be prepared for some exertion.

Bologna's arcades

Some enterprising person has calculated that there are 44 km of arcades in Bologna, including those leading up to San Luca but not including the modern arcades in rebuilt areas, such as via Marconi in the northwest. The longest distance you can cover without emerging from underneath an arcade is the 8 km from the Chiesa degli Alemanni near porta Maggiore up to San Luca. Arcades are the city's leitmotif, loved by all for the changing perspectives and the tranquility they afford. The first arcades are thought to have been built around the year 1000 to accommodate the city's expansion at the founding of the university and arrival of foreign students. Medieval additions sat precariously on top of houses with the support of wooden braces. Arcades were a practical solution for providing adequate support, increasing space above and providing shelter for pedestrians and merchants below. A law was passed making the minimum height seven feet so that people on horseback could pass under them. The symmetry of their design also fitted with the classical and humanist ideas of proportion and harmony that were being championed in the architecture of the time.

The Colle dell'Osservanza is named after the 'Observance' of the Franciscan Reforms that began in Bologna in the church of San Paolo in Monte. Located at the end of the road, this early 15th-century church has beautiful views in all directions. These views are supposed to have been praised in 1805 by Napoleon, whose eulogy fell on the ears of his ambassador, Antonio Aldini. Seeking to please the Emperor, Aldini got rid of the monks and, in 1811, commissioned a villa, the nearby neoclassical temple-like **Villa Aldini** ① *via dell'Osservanza 35, T051-580248, visit by arrangement only as the villa is usually closed to the public except for occasional exhibitions*, to be given as a present. Sadly the Emperor never saw the completed villa as he was soon to meet his Waterloo.

Beneath the Osservanza hill on via San Mamolo is the **Parco di Villa Ghigi** ① *daily 0900-1800*, accessible from the church of San Paolo in Monte through via di Gaibola. At 29 ha, this is one of Bologna's largest parks, a beautiful rolling combination of rampant meadows and fields, cultivated, orderly vineyards and a great variety of towering trees.

Giardini di Margherita

① *viale Gozzadini. Summer 0600-2400, Oct-Mar 0700-1800. Bus Nos 13 and 28 will get you there. Alternatively, it's an easy 20-min walk from piazza Maggiore and it takes 1-2 hrs to walk round it. The gardens border the southeast wall and can be accessed from viale Gozzadini.*
Just beyond the southern outer city wall of the Centro Storico lie the glorious Margherita gardens, inaugurated in 1879 and named after the wife of King Umberto I. The gardens were inspired by the Romantic design of the English parks of the 19th century and were designed by Ernesto di Sambuy from Piemonte.

At the centre is a lake complete with fountains reminiscent of St James' and Regent's Park in London. Majestic cedars, pines and chestnuts line the many paths and grassy areas that do their best to replicate English lawns. A number of pavilions are dotted around the park, vestiges of the Emiliana Exhibition of 1888. From the edge of the main lawn you can see an Etruscan sarcophagus, part of a necropolis that was uncovered here when the gardens were created. This is Bologna's largest public park and, apart from being a fine place to stroll, sit, think or read, it has lovely vistas into the rolling lower Apennines.

Bologna listings

For hotel and restaurant price codes and other relevant information, see pages 11-12.

● Where to stay

Centro Storico: piazza Maggiore and around *p18, maps p20 and p32*

€€ Bologna nel Cuore B&B, via C Battisti 29, T051-269442, www.bolognanelcuore.it. Maria Ketty runs this B&B from a handsome palazzo, with enthusiastic Emilian hospitality. The 2 immaculately kept whitewashed rooms have colourful touches and stylish bathrooms. Maria does bountiful breakfasts (fresh fruit, quality cold cuts, pastries and jams) and is ever-ready with top cultural and culinary tips. There are 2 similarly styled apartments ideal for families and longer stays.

€€ Cappello Rosso, via de' Fusari 9, T051-261891, www.alcappellorosso.it. A 600-year-old former hostelry near piazza Maggiore that reputedly lodged the builders of the Basilica San Petronio. Among the 33 rooms – with contemporary furnishings, TV, free Wi-Fi and silk kimono – are some quirky themed ones by artists, designers and fashionistas. Room 305 celebrates the Olivetti typewriter while 104 was given a black and red comic-art makeover in 2010 by delegates of the annual BilBOlbul comic fair. They also have 5 sleek apartments in the Falcone Borsellino gallery.

€€ Commercianti, via de' Pignattari 11, T051-745 7511, www.art-hotel-commercianti.it. Fabulous central location by the basilica of San Petronio; ask for a room on the 3rd floor with terrace overlooking the church. Once part of the town hall, the public spaces and some guest rooms retain original woodwork beams, fireplaces and stonework. Some spacious suites are suitable for families.

€€ Orologio, via IV Novembre 10, T051-745 7411, www.art-hotel-orologio.it. Another self-styled 'art hotel', just a stone's throw from the southwest corner of piazza Maggiore. It's a tall narrow building on a pedestrian street. Ask for rooms with fine views over Palazzo Comunale and the eponymous clock is on the façade (it doesn't strike at night). Throughout there's a traditional feel with modern facilities: patterned furnishings and marble bathrooms with quality bed linen and a/c. Garage, tourism services and bike hire available.

€€-€ Centrale, via della Zecca 2, T051-225114, www.albergocentralebologna.it. Between via Ugo Bassi and piazza Roosevelt. A centrally located and unpretentious hotel on the 3rd and 4th floors of an 18th-century noble's residence. Some of the spacious and functional rooms – there's nothing fancy – have good views to the Due Torri and over the terracotta rooftops. Check the website for special off-season offers.

The university quarter (the Northeast) *p26, maps p20 and p32*

€€ Corona d'Oro, via Oberdan 12, T051-745 7611, www.bolognarthotels.it. Just north of via Rizzoli is the 15th-century Palazzo Azzoguidi, a hotel since the early 1800s that retains much of its antique charm despite recent renovation. Fine architectural details include wooden porticoed façade, Venetian-style belle époque veranda and a grand light-filled atrium/hall that is a wonderful space to relax in. Many of the 30-plus rooms and suites have high-ceilings with original painted panels, spacious marble bathrooms, and simple contemporary furnishings and artworks. Excellent guest services include free Wi-Fi, garage and bicycle hire, guided tours, theatre tickets, discounts at restaurants and cookery courses.

€ Cavour, via Goito 4, T051-228111, www.cavour-hotel.com. Off via dell' Independenza north of the Cattedrale di San Pietro is this handsome yet intimate hotel with a beguiling vaulted cloister courtyard. Recent refurbishment has created serene and bright public spaces, and revamped rooms. Among the 38 guest rooms are spacious superior and deluxe rooms – the top-floor rooms have oak beams and rooftop views. Book online for great-value deals. A pricey new suite offers lots of space, extras and bathroom of red Verona marble, a huge mosaic-tiled shower.

€ Holiday, via Bertiera 13, T051-235326, www.hotelholiday-bo.com. For the budget conscious after a handy location – off via dell' Indipendenza and near Piazza Maggiore – this place is a decent option although the narrow side street is a bit shabby. The 30-odd guest rooms are uninspiring and functional and many lack quality mattresses. Upper floor rooms have decent views and it's pretty quiet. Garage available to guests.

€ Paradise, via Cattani 7, T051-231792, www.hotelparadisebologna.it. Well-run small budget hotel near via dell'Indipendenza among fascinating side streets, canals and arcades. As well as the functional 18 rooms with recently renovated white bathrooms, there are handy studio set-ups with kitchen corners for up to 4 people. Ask for spacious upper rooms with wooden beams and good views.

€ San Donato, via Zamboni 16, T051-235395, www.hotelsandonato.it. In a plum location – opposite the Palazzo Malvezzi de' Medici – under the 2 towers and on the edge of the university quarter. It may be part of the Best Western group but this hotel escapes feeling like a chain hotel through smart public spaces and personal service. The terrace bar overlooking rooftops is a fine spot for an evening aperitivo.

€ Tre Vecchi, via dell'Indipendenza 47, T051-231991, www.zanhotel.it. Lying south of piazza VIII Agosto, this elegant hotel by a leafy green has some quite grand public spaces. Decor in the 95 rooms does vary though between the recently refurbished, quite tasteful with muted colours to Venetian gold-fringed fussy. Buffet breakfast is served in an atmospheric space with brick-vaulted ceilings and cheery frescoes. It may be plain kitsch in parts but provides

a good-value backup option for groups and families especially; triples and junior suites are mighty reasonable by booking online.

Around Santo Stefano (the Southeast) *p31, maps p20 and p32*

€€ Antica Casa Zucchini, via Santo Stefano 36, T347-911 0731, www.anticacasazucchini. it. The 15th-century palazzo brimming with architectural features and quirky objects makes for a very special B&B stay near the Santo Stefano church. From the huge *portone* (door) and porticoed courtyard with Istria stone capitals to the frescoed salons, there's atmosphere, history and legend aplenty here. The 3 high-ceilinged rooms are cavernous – so plenty of room for families – and bathrooms mix original features with modern facilities. You can relax with a coffee in the grand antique-filled library. Breakfast consists of home-made breads, pastries and preserves – and the hospitality from Famiglia Zucchini is spot on. It's all very civilized: there's free Wi-Fi, DVD players and afternoon tea in the winter.

€€ Porta San Mamolo, via del Falcone 6/8, T051-583056, www.hotel-portasanmamolo. it. Between via Paglietta and via Miramonte Ruini this small romantic hotel wins many plaudits for its good-value accommodation and excellent customer service. There's a choice of well-presented and maintained guest rooms for most group sizes: it would win no design prizes for the chintz but overall clean and well thought out with a/c throughout. Public areas are pleasant especially the light-filled breakfast room, leafy garden and terrace with seating. Excellent facilities include 24-hr bar/reception, rooms for the disabled and private garage.

€€ Santo Stefano, via S. Stefano 84, T051-308458, www.bedandbreakfastsantostefano. com. Breakfast is served in a handsome room with parquet and windows overlooking the arcaded street and the Santissima Trinità church. Classic modern design pieces including the iconic Castiglione Arco lamp and Kartell chairs mixed with the odd antique and a backgammon board. The whitewashed contemporary feel with vibrant artworks and fabrics is more minimal in the guest rooms. En suite bathrooms are bright and clean, some with rain showers and a bath. Free Wi-Fi, garage 200 m away.

€ **Hotel Touring**, via Mattuiani 1, T051-584305, www.hoteltouring.it. Just off piazza dei Tribunali, the beautifully refurbished and well-equipped Touring retains an elegant atmosphere through mellow colours and touches of stucco. Classic rooms have a very modern interpretation of Stile Liberty (Art Nouveau) while Gold rooms have a little more flair: 441 has a balcony. The spacious suites have a compact kitchen. Breakfast is bountiful, with a good selection of pastries, fruit and savoury bites. Large panoramic roof terrace with a jacuzzi has stunning views of the rooftops, towers and hills.

€ **Residence Mirasole**, vicolo del Falcone 24, T051-991 7791, www.residencemirasole.it. For visitors seeking an apartment with kitchen facilities for longer stays this place is an ever-reliable choice. The owners regularly cater for those visiting the nearby hospital so are happy to deal with all sorts of queries. The studio flat is a good budget option and even has views of the Torre degli Asinelli.

Around via del Pratello (the Southwest) *p35, maps p20 and p32*
€€ **Novecento**, piazza Galileo 4, T051-754 7311, www.bolognarthotels.it.
One of Bologna's growing list of boutique hotels, the Novecento is the only upscale accommodation in the southwest centre of Bologna. The decor harks back to the clean, angular lines of the 1930s – all wood, leather and discreet lighting in a modern setting. It lacks genuine art deco character though so some may find it soulless.

€ **Panorama**, via Livraghi 1, T051-221802, www.hotelpanoramabologna.it. South off via Ugo Bassi on the 4th floor of an elegant building, this small and welcoming family hotel offers good value for money. The 9 rooms range from doubles to 4-bed rooms and can be a tad noisy due to thin walls. There are no en suites, hence the rock-bottom prices.

€ **Re Enzo**, via Santa Croce 26, T051-523322, www.hotelreenzo.it. Small, maybe a bit dated but friendly **Best Western** hotel on the fringes of the Centro Storico between via del Pratello and via San Felice. It may be geared towards the business market with its mirrored bar straight out of 1970s Italian *giallo* (thriller) TV series, but overall expect pretty good value for a short stay. Classic rooms are very tired looking but the newer deluxe rooms have a more contemporary feel. It's outside the traffic-limited zone and there's garage parking with supplement.

Around via Galliera (the Northwest) *p36, maps p20 and p32*
€€€ **Majestic Baglioni**, via dell' Indipendenza 8, T051-225445, www.grandhotelmajestic.duetorrihotels.com. On the busy southern end of via dell' Independenza towards piazza Maggiore, the revamped grand hotel Majestic attracts celebs, royalty and those after luxury and a genuinely friendly service (you can tell the staff love working here). Secreted in the sprawling yet intimate complex is a wing of the 15th-century Palazzo Ghisilardi Fava with Carracci brother masterpieces, A-lister apartments (Macca's Venetian-style suite and an art-deco rooftop bolthole made for James Bond), refined restaurant, wine-cellar dining room and spa/gym. Regular punters' rooms have ornate fabrics, marble bathrooms, 5-star standard plasma TV/minibar/safe unit. Terraces overlook the San Pietro cathedral. If you're going to splash out, do it here.

€€ **Starhotel Excelsior**, viale Pietramellara 51, T051-246178, www.starhotels.com. It's a handy spot for the train station – just off piazza delle Medaglie d'Oro – although the underwhelming feel of this self-styled 'luxury' chain Starhotel may disappoint. From the austere façade to the nondescript guest rooms it's plainly designed for business travellers. Repeat custom means the breakfasts are very good though. A minimalist bar and restaurant attracts an evening crowd. Back rooms overlook a garden.

€ **Metropolitan**, via Dell'Orso 6, T051-229393, www.hotelmetropolitan.com. Zen minimalism-influenced design, decent services and a tranquil side-street locale make Il Met a relaxing place to stay. Their Met apartments nearby continue the Oriental design theme, and add extra space and a kitchen corner – suitable for families and longer stays. Free Wi-Fi and a huge breakfast choice.

Bologna outskirts

€€ **Pozzo di Mezzo**, via del Pozzo 41, Savena, T373-702 9133, www.pozzodi mezzo.it. Located 4 km southeast of the Centro Storico is this exceptional B&B, which brings boutique living to a verdant setting amid the hills. Within the impressive brick buildings of this walled residence are 5 tasteful rooms with sleek en suites. The quality breakfast spread fills a granite slab in the large kitchen straight from a lifestyle magazine, or outside in the large garden.

Camping

Camping Hotel – Citta di Bologna, via Romita 12/4, T051-325318, www.hotel camping.com. At the northern end of via Stalingrado is this relative oasis in a verdant setting near the Fiera district. As well as camping grounds, chalets and bungalows there are good onsite facilities including a shop, swimming pool and gym. Take bus No 68 from near the train station.

Youth hostels

There are 2 youth hostels 6 km outside the city. Take bus Nos 93, 21B and 302: **San Sisto**, via Vaidagola 14, T051-519202, www.ostellodibologna.com, and **Due Torri**, via Viadagola 5, T051-501810. Expect to pay from €20 for a bed and basic facilities including a few showers, laundry, Wi-Fi, canteen and nearby shopping centre.

🍴 Restaurants

Centro Storico: piazza Maggiore and around *p18, maps p20 and p32*

€€€ **Pappagallo**, piazza Mercanzia 3, T051-231200. Closed Sun. Set in the walls of an old 14th-century palazzo right underneath the 2 towers, this historic and elegant restaurant, in a single high-ceilinged, echoing hall, is formal and refined. The menu offers a variety of Mediterranean dishes as well as Bolognese classics and a fine selection of local wines and after-dinner liqueurs.

€€€ **Rodrigo**, via della Zecca 2, T051-235536. Closed Sun. Located in the building that was formerly the National Mint, Rodrigo has been in business for 50 years. With wall-to-wall wine bottles (the wine list is accordingly varied and extensive) and chandeliers, it is well known for its white truffles, porcini and mushrooms between Sep and Dec.

€€ **Da Gianni a la Vecia Bulagna**, via Clavature 18, T051-229434. Closed Mon and also Sun evenings in summer. Small and rustic, this is another of Bologna's institutions that has remained unchanged since the 1950s. Fresh handmade pasta, excellent *bollito misto*, *polpettone* and *fritto misto*, to be washed down with a fine locally produced Sangiovese or Albana. When in season try the chestnut tortelloni.

€ **Tamburini**, via Caprarie 1, T051-234726, www.tamburini.com. Mon-Fri 1200-1430, also Sat in winter. Set in the Quadrilatero district, this simple self-service canteen offers a tailor-made selection from its hanging garden of delicacies spread out around the shop. Do as the locals and order a pitcher of draught house wine. It is usually packed at lunchtime so if you can bear to wait a little you will be able to eat in peace.

Caffès

Pasticceria Il Duca D'amalfi, piazza de' Celestini 3a, piazza Maggiore T051-265146. A corner of Campania with azure blue recalling Amalfi Coast sea and Neapolitan pastries such as *sfogliatelle* and *pastiera* cake.

Torinese, piazza re Enzo 1a, T051-236743.
Excellent hot chocolate as befits the name.

The university quarter (the Northeast) *p26, maps p20 and p32*

€€€ Franco Rossi, via Goito 3, T051-238818, www.ristorantefrancorossi.it.
Closed Sun except during trade fairs.
Feeling like an exclusive drawing room, it serves a slightly lighter and more modern take on heavy Bolognese tradition. Franco will serve and advise you while his brother Lino works magic behind the scenes.

€€ Cantina Bentivoglio, via Mascarella 4b, T051-265416, www.cantinabentivoglio.it.
Tue-Sat 2000-0200. The Ronnie Scott's of Bologna and something of an institution in the city. What you're really paying for is the music, the appropriately cool ambience and an extensive wine list of over 400 labels. It's advisable to book, especially at weekends and if you want to eat late.

€ Dell'Orsa, via Mentana 1, T051-231576, www.osteriadellorsa.com. Daily until 0100.
Popular student lunch hangout serving simple menu of regional dishes all day until 0100: great crostini, a broad range of beers, amid the verve of young Bologna.

€ Gran Cafe, via Altabella 12, T051-220498, www.grancafebologna.it. Mon-Sat 1200-1430 and 1400-2130. If you want to keep it real and cheap this self-serve canteen in a old-fashioned bar has loads of atmosphere and happy and helpful staff. The best thing: a really good cup of tea for €1.30.

€ La Mariposa, via Bertiera 12, T051-225656.
Closed Sat eve and Sun. A genuine and humble trattoria still with its rather kitsch post-war decor. Very welcoming, delicious and superb value. A taste of the real Bologna.

€ Trattoria del Rosso, via Augusto Righi 30, T051-236730, www.trattoriadelrosso.com.
A large dining room with chunky tables, a huge old mirror and a steady flow of diners enjoying its splendid *Menu di Rosso* – 2 courses with a small carafe of wine. Outside the menu, a plate of pasta with *ragù* costs €7.

Caffès

Del Museo, via Zamboni 58, T051-246620.
Early closing Sat. Welcoming and retro, with dark wood, sofas, it's great for tête-à-tête and romantic drinks served by Felix the funny barman. Popular with work-shy students and professors.

Terzi, via Oberdan 10, T051-236470.
Offering a wide selection of coffees and teas. A great place for a long, lazy breakfast.

Santo Stefano and around (the Southeast) *p31, maps p20 and p32*

€€€ Antica Osteria Romagnola, via Rialto 13, T051-263699. Closed all day Mon and Tue lunch. Rustic, welcoming and always a-buzz, with dark wood panels, musical instruments and mirrors on the walls, and a characteristic inner courtyard. Superb local and regional cuisine tailor-made to your taste. Particularly tasty *mortadella a cubetti* and lasagne.

€€€ Drogheria della Rosa, via Cartoleria 10, T051 266 864 www.drogheriadellarosa.it.
Closed Sun. This cosy restaurant run by the ebullient Emanuele Addone used to be a food store (hence its name) and still retains the original furnishings, doors and window frames. Superior dishes from all over Emilia-Romagna are served with an exceptional choice of wines.

€€ Da Fabio, via del Cestello 2, T051-220481, www.dafabio.it. Evenings only.
Closed Sun. Wonderful and plentiful regional dishes in this cosy, intimate and unprepossessing little restaurant with personal service.

€ Clorofilla, strada Maggiore 64, T051-235343. Closed Sun. One of Bologna's few healthy eating restaurants with a minimalist-naturalist decor. It mixes ingredients from all round the world complete with explanations of their healthy properties. Particularly big on salads, which might provide light relief for non-vegetarians. There is a wide selection of teas and tisanes, and even the beer and wine are organic.

Caffès and gelaterie

Bricco d'Oro, via Farini 6, T051-236231.
Very good hot chocolate topped with
mountainous cream. Also a broad selection
of bites at aperitivo time.

Gelaterias

Sorbetteria Castiglione, via Castiglioni
44, T051-233257, www.lasorbetteria.it.
Tue-Sun 1730-2345. Locals will cross
the entire town for the ice creams here,
which are just that bit creamier, subtler
and naughtier than elsewhere.

Around via del Pratello (the
Southwest) *p35, maps p20 and p32*
€€€ Trattoria Battibecco, via Battibecco 4,
T051-223 2298, www.battibecco.com.
Closed Sat lunch and all day Sun. One of
Bologna's most expensive and luxurious
restaurants, as far away from a trattoria as
can be. The decor is sophisticated with a
wooden ceiling, tiled floor and trompe
l'oeil walls with backlit recesses. Serving
traditional dishes and an array of fish dishes.
€€ Meloncello, via Saragozza 240, T051-
614 3947, www.trattoriameloncello.it.
This old trattoria has, for years, provided
sustenance for those who are about to make
the pilgrimage up the porticoes to San
Luca or restored them coming down. The
rabbit with polenta is delicious and stuffed
courgette a speciality. Essential to book
ahead during the festival of San Luca in May.
€€ Montesino, via del Pratello 74, T051-
523426. Congenial hangout for good food
and wine, with a leaning towards the
Sardinian roots of the owner. A quiet place
as the owner will not accept groups. The
poems written on the tablecloths are
reputedly published in a tri-annual collection.

Caffè and gelaterie

Gelateria Ugo, via San Felice 24, T051
263849. According to many locals the
best *gelato* in town and certainly rightfully
famous for high-quality creamy licks.

Majani, via De' Carbonesi 5, T051-234302.
A Bolognese institution and the sweet
equivalent of Tamburini: an elegant and
mouth-watering art nouveau shrine to the
city's famous chocolate-maker Signora
Majani, as it was when the shop was
founded in 1834.

Around via Galliera (the Northwest)
p36, maps p20 and p32
€€€ Carracci, via Manzoni 2, T051-225455.
Closed Mon. This famous restaurant is
located within the premises of the **Grand
Hotel Baglioni**, the luxury address for visitors
to Bologna. The restaurant itself is set in a
magnificent hall with frescoes by artists from
the Carracci school whose name it bears.
The menu covers local specialities as well
as many international dishes all beautifully
presented and served by staff who seem
genuinely happy to be there.
€€€ Diana, via dell'Indipendenza 24, T051-
231302, www.ristorantedianabologna.com.
Closed Mon. Part of the establishment since
the 1920s this elegant and sophisticated
restaurant, complete with crystal chandeliers,
is one for gourmets wanting to appreciate
the finer nuances in the local cuisine.
€€ Il Pirata del Porto, via del Porto 42,
T051-552750, www.ilpiratadelporto.com.
Closed Mon. With a wood-burning pizzeria
oven and a flaming grill for fish and meats,
this place is very popular so you may need
to book. Popular with the gay community.
€ Ex Forno, MAMbo, via Don Minzoni 14,
T051-649 3896. Closed Mon. MAMbo's
restaurant is a French bistro with retro
modernist furniture and well-executed
European dishes, such as grilled fish with
couscous, huge salads and pasta. It adjoins
the gallery's bar so you can move from
aperitivi into eating with just a few steps.

Caffès

Calderoni, via dell'Indipendenza 70, T051-
248208. A popular bar on the main drag.
Downstairs, a range of pastas, salads and
cakes are on display. In the late afternoons

the upstairs turns into a piano bar serving decent cocktails and delicious ice creams.
Centro Natura, via degli Albari 4, T051-235643. A vegetarian café selling juices, teas, coffees and healthy meals.
Impero, via dell'Indipendenza 39, T051-232337. Historic *pasticceria* with a modern facelift serving delicious sweets, pastries and cakes – like *mignon*, brioche, *cassata* and *bavarese* – plus savoury snacks including pizza. Less crowded early afternoon.

Bars and clubs

Ever since the city became a university centre, its students have needed to be distracted from their studies, inspired by the world as seen though the bottom of a glass, comforted through existential angst and cheered by the clink of a celebratory toast. The drinking traditions of Bologna's *osterie* go back almost a thousand years and are still intact now, even if the venues themselves have gone a little more upmarket. Add to that historic vibrancy a present-day openness and an ability to absorb and experiment with new influences and you have a city that is more unchained than most in Italy.

You'll note that many of these bars and clubs are also places to eat. In Italy you eat and drink at the same time: it's only northern Europeans, particularly those who live on an island, who make such a strong distinction.

Centro Storico: piazza Maggiore and around *p18, maps p20 and p32*
Bars
Al Calice, via Clavature 13, T051-264506. Closed Sun. Spilling out onto the street this bar has a friendly vibe and does good but pricey food.
Café De Paris, piazza Minghetti, T051-234980. Open daily until late. A perhaps too-chic bar but from 1900, through the rolling fug of expensive perfumes and the whoosh of incessantly tossed locks you'll see plates of pasta, *pizze*, crisps, salami

and olives. Eat them up as they offer some comfort for not being in the same league as the local clientele.
Caffe Commercianti, strada Maggiore 23/c, T051-984 4385. Despite its rather sedate hours (it closes at 2200 during the week and Sat, but 0100 on Fri) this bar, with its jugs of margheritas and its cocktail-shaking barmen, is very popular. Fri night is Friendly Party Night and it is.
Zanarini, piazza Galvani 1, T051-275 0041. Round the back of San Petronino is this modern bar. The drinks are a bit more at €8 but generous and the buffet comes with puddings so it works out as less, eh?

The university quarter (the Northeast) *p26, maps p20 and p32*
Bars
Caffe Zamboni, via Zamboni 6, T051-273102, www.caffezamboni.it. Full of *professori* and students alike, this university might win the prize for the biggest plates of salami – including mortadella – cheese, pasta, foccacia and vegetable fritters offered to drinkers.
La Stanze, via del Borgo di San Pietro, T051-228767. Closed Mon. At 1800 they start to arrive for the bounteous buffet of *pasta al forno*, grilled vegetables and *pizze*. It's very modish and hip, so much so you wonder whether the crumbling frescos in this cavernous space are real or c 2004.
Bottega del Vino Olindo Faccioli, via Altabella 15, T051-223171. Mon-Sat 1800-0200. A historic tavern still retains its 1920s interior with dark wood furnishings, stylish chairs and someone who is probably a poet or a writer in a world of his own. A characterful spot for wine and some cold cuts.
Cantina Bentivoglio, via Mascarella 4/b, T051-222119, www.cantinabentivoglio.it. Tue-Sun from 2000. This huge cavernous jazz café offers great wine, simple food and live jazz – proper jazz – every night. You can choose to book a table by the band and pay a little extra, or stick to the quieter rooms on ground level.

Aperitivo time

Buying a drink in Bologna might seem a little pricey. Bars at night can ask €6-8 for a glass of wine, prosecco or spritz (a mix of bitter Campari of sweet Aperol with white wine and soda). However, this is because they lay on free food or *stuzzichini*: pizza, salami (including the local mortadella), pasta, grilled vegetables and, in some bars, cakes. It's such fun to watch *stuzzichini* virgins hovering gingerly around the buffet and taking modest helpings while they watch to see if anyone is looking. But please feel no shame: there is often enough food to let you bypass dinner, which is handy if you're on a budget. Aperitivo time varies but it's generally 1800-2200.

Some clubs (eg Covo) are private members' clubs so you may need to apply for a *tessera* (membership card). However, you can avoid paying full membership (from €30 for a year) by registering online beforehand and asking for a visitor's pass (you will need to bring ID on the night). Clubs that don't require membership usually charge around €10-15 which includes an obligatory (alcoholic) drink (some let women in free before midnight). The club scene is pretty fluid so for up-to-date information on what's happening and where, look out for flyers and free magazines in the bars or cafés you like the look of.

Osteria Contavalli, via Belle Arte, 2, T051-268395. Closed Sun. Odd but fun little aperitivo bar with art shows and music.
L'Antica Stuzzicheria, via Mascarella 60c, www.anticastuzzicheria.it. Crammed full of interesting odds and ends and with extremely genial staff, this is a bar full of dark intimate corners for clandestine jugs of wine and plates of cheese with your *amore*.
La Scuderia, piazza Verdi 2, T051-656 9619, www.lascuderia.bo.it. This bar-club under a beautiful frescoed arch stands on the site of the former stables (*scuderia*) of the Bentivoglio family. Run by the Rosa Rose group it plays cool grooves for the young, the trendy, the gay until 0200. Occasionally hosts concerts and live music on the square outside.

Clubs

Corto Maltese, via del Borgo di San Pietro 9, T338-287 4055, www.cortomaltesediscobar. it. Daily until 0300. A free pub/club popular with Erasmus students. The buffet is served until midnight with huge free plates of pasta. The music and dancing starts at 2200 and goes on till 0300.
Covo Club, viale Zagabria 1, T051-505801, www.covoclub.it. Fri-Sat till 0300. A legendary venue for international and Italian alternative acts, from Animal Collective to Yo La Tengo. There's live music at 2230 each Fri and Sat then the DJ sets begin. You have to be a member to get in: visit the website to book in or chance your arm at the door (bring ID).
Kinki Club, via Zamboni 2, T051-266028. Close to the Due Torri, this club has been going for years, hosting art exhibitions, video projections and a Sun gay night.

Santo Stefano and around (the Southeast) *p31, maps p20 and p32*
Bars
Alla Corte di Bacco, corte Isolani 7, T051-237884, www.ristorantibologna.com. Closed Sun. In the medieval arcade just off piazza Santo Stefano this is a lovely little wine bar offering over 400 different labels.
Caffe Sette Chiese, piazza San Stefano 15, T051-656 9983. You can sit outside and look out onto the beautiful piazza and church. The *stuzzichini* are largely bread based but beautifully presented.
Chalet dei Giardini Margherita, viale Massimo Meliconi 1, T051-991 3789, www. chaletdeigiardinimargherita.it. Open every day in summer. By day it's a lakeside bar *caffè*,

Gay and lesbian Bologna

In tune with its long-standing tradition for emancipated thinking, Bologna is one of the cities in Italy most open in its attitude towards homosexuality and has become regarded almost as a gay centre internationally. The city is the seat of the national gay movement and is considered to have reached 'the European level' of tolerance and understanding. The local council was the first in Italy to permit gay couples to apply for communal housing and Bologna was the first place in Italy to have a special condomeria (a shop – now closed – dispensing prophylactics and advice on safe sex for both gays and heterosexuals). It has not always been a smooth ride, however; Pope John Paul II once condemned Emilia-Romagna as the most degenerate province in Italy, partly on account of its gay tolerance. Rather than there being a defined gay scene, much of the overall buzz of the city and its nightlife is fuelled by the gay community. To find out more about the gay scene in Bologna visit www.gaybologna.net.

by night there's a DJ playing and a relaxed but upbeat atmosphere. A good mixed crowd and popular with the gay community. **Godot Wine Bar**, via Cartoleria 12, T051-226315 (and **Godot Wine Store** on via Santo Stefano, 12, T051-226187). Mon-Sat 0800-0200. A great place to settle down with a glass of wine, a little mortadella and watch the interesting locals who stop by for the same.
Taberna dei Frati, via Arienti 25, T051-239880. Good place to watch the football. There's a broad selection of beers and panini served throughout the day and night.

Around via del Pratello (the Southwest) *p35, maps p20 and p32*
Bars
Caracol, piazza Galileo 6, T051-222610. Until 0200. Mexican bar/restaurant with pitchers of Margarita, plump fajitas and a very small dance floor. Happy hour 1930-2030.
Circolo Pavese, via del Pratello 51/3, T338-119 2900, www.circolopavese.it. Mon-Sat until 0300. Admission only with the ARCI (see page 50) pass card for sale on site. A place to drink wine and watch experimental theatre and short film projections in the company of Bologna's artists.
Riff Raff, via del Pratello 3, T051-222888. Open until the last person leaves. Closed Mon. For wine, cold meats cheeses and Sicilian puddings, not to mention a little genuine friendliness.
Sushi Café Kappa, piazza Malpighi 14, T051-221773. Going out is good for you when it's all water features, mellow lounge tunes, Japanese beer and *nigiri*.

Around via Galliera (the Northwest) *p36, maps p20 and p32*
Bars
Chet Baker, via Polese 7/a, T051-223795. Closed Sun. For serious jazzers, this bar with great wine and food has live music till 0300.
Ex Forno, MAMbo, via Don Minzoni 14, T051-649 3896. The bar of MAMbo has an interesting mix of vintage and contemporary furnishing, and an equally eclectic clientele. 1900 is aperitivo time with a decent spread of edibles to help line the stomach.
Macondo, via del Pratello 22, www.macondo bologna.com. Hosts music and literary events throughout the week. They do Puglian *pucce* rolls and selection of aperitivi and beers. Check out the website for latest listings, from sophisticated jazz and swing ensembles to blues, jam sessions and new band nights. Dancing goes on till 0100 during the week and 0300 at weekends.

Clubs

Cassero, piazza di Porta Lame, via Don MInzoni 18, T051-095 7200, www.cassero.it. The seat of the ARCI-Gay gay and lesbian organization is host to a hugely popular Sat and Wed party nights and other events. There's also a café, bookshop and beautiful roof garden.

⦿ Entertainment

Bologna *p18, maps p20 and p32*
Cinema

Whilst Rome has Cinecittà and Venice is home to Italy's most famous festival, the Bolognesi have had the enthusiasm and creativity to turn their city into a year-round cinema-goers dream. Tickets across all venues cost around €7 and details about their programmes and events can be found on their websites.

Cinema Capitol, via Milazzo 1, T051-241002, www.capitolmultisala.com. Hollywood blockbusters dubbed in Italian Wed-Mon or a film in English on Tue.

Cinema Lumière, via Azzo Gardino 65, T051-219 5311, www.cinetecadibologna.it. The cinephile's haven, this cinema is part of **Cineteca di Bologna**, see page 36. Famed for showing films in their original version – all hail the old-fashioned projectors. They also complement the archival showings with art house movies and are host to a number of film festivals throughout the year. And if you're a fan of Pasolini or Chaplin, **Cineteca** is home to their archives are accessible by appointment (check the website for more details).

Multisala Odeon (via Mascarella 3, T051-227916), Europa (via Pietralata 55/a, T051-523812) and the Roma d'Eassai (via Fondazza 4, T051-347470) are all owned by Circuito Cinema Bologna (www.circuito cinemabologna.it) and between them show a range of art house and independent films.

Theatre

Bologna has 14 theatres in total showing the whole gambit of drama, music, dance and all their variations. Throughout the year, musical and theatrical events are held in outdoor, industrial, religious and other interesting venues. These are listed at www.bolognawelcome.com and publicized at the tourist information office in piazza Maggiore.

Arena del Sole, via dell'Indipendenza 44, T051-2910910, www.arenadelsole.it. The **Arena del Sole** offers a diverse programme, ranging from the conservative to the avant garde. See also page 36.

Teatri di Vita, Parco dei Pini, via Emilia Ponente, T051-566330, www.teatridivita.it. On the road towards the airport, this theatre housed in what looks like an army barracks is well worth the trip for fans of contemporary dance. Here you will find one of the best ensembles in Europe as well as visiting dance companies from around the world. They also hold cinema and music events. Tickets cost €10-30. To get there take buses Nos 13, 54 or 79 from the Centro Storico.

Teatro Auditorium Manzoni, via De' Monari 1-2, T051-261303, www.auditoriumanzoni.it. Built as a cinema in1933 this Stile Liberty palace off via dell'Indipendenza has been beautifully and expensively restored for a city that loves its high arts. Audiences love the quality of the acoustics and the opulent setting. Expect visiting philharmonic orchestras, ballet and contemporary music so be sure to book ahead: such is the demand, they sell out very quickly. Very comfortably seats 1234.

Teatro Comunale, see page 27.

Teatro Duse, via Cartoleria 42, T051 231836, www.teatroduse.it. Showing a programme of classical drama Nov-May.

✿ Festivals

Bologna *p18, maps p20 and p32*
January
Italy's most important international contemporary art fair is **Arte Fiera**, www.artefiera.bolognafiere.it.

February
Bologna's **Carnevale** belongs to its children who usually take part in a masked parade. The **BilBolBul** (Festival of International Comics) has talks, workshops, performances and screenings, www.bilbolbul.net.

April
The first part of the internationally lauded classical music festival, **Bologna Festival**, is held in Apr; the 2nd part is in Oct. Events are held at Teatro Manzoni and other venues. Tickets cost €15-80 but sell fast so get in there quick, www.cinetecadibologna.it.

Live Arts focuses on live art performances and events in venues across the city, www.liveartsweek.it

The Future Film Festival is held in various venues and is dedicated to animation and films that use visual effects, www.futurefilmfestival.org.

May
Out on the *colli* (hills) lies the Santuario di San Luca. Every year for the **Festa di San Luca** they process with the icon of the Madonna of San Luca along the porticoed street that links the church to the city walls before going on to San Pietro in piazza Maggiore, www.bolognawelcome.com.

Today only an insipid echo of the animated and lewd 19th-century student initiation rituals, **Matricole**, remains. Whilst you can't really participate it may explain some horseplay you see on the city's streets.

The **Addobbi** ceremony, which has lost its medieval richness, takes place every Sun in May and Jun. In celebration of the arrival of the Eucharist procession the city's churches adorn themselves and the streets in colourful drapes and lights.

Angelica is an International Festival of Contemporary Music Experimental, Avant Garde, electronica and the impossible to define. It's hosted in galleries, villas, museums and purloined places, www.aaa-angelica.com.

June
Graduating is a seriously big deal in Italy and **Feste della Laurea** celebrates it. There are no city-wide graduation ceremonies, but you are sure to know about it if you find yourself in a restaurant of recent graduates, that's if you can find somewhere to eat.

Biografilm is a film festival entirely devoted to biographical films, thoughtfully combining the big budget with the independent as well as more experimental telling of life stories. It's held at the Cineteca Bologna, www.biografilm.it.

July
Il Cinema Ritrovato is a festival dedicated to film history, showcasing restorations from international archives. Attracting film enthusiasts from across Europe, it is held across 4 cinemas: Cineteca Bologna, the Lumière, the Arlecchino and newer Jolly, with a few hugely popular screenings in Piazza Maggiore, www.cinetecadibologna.it.

August
Often to the complete surprise of visitors, Italy shuts down in Aug and numerous bars, restaurants and shops close. However, if you find yourself in the city on the 15th there are some events, food tasting and live concerts in some of museums and civic spaces, as part of **Ferragosto**. Check with the tourist information office or the events section on www.bolognawelcome.com.

September
Danza Urbana is an urban dance festival celebrating all forms of contemporary dance. Venues range from the beautiful

Grand Hotel Majestic (aka the Gia Baglioni) to small alleyways to the Giardini di Cavaticcio. It's participative too, with hip hop and breakdancing competitions, so start practicing your windmill now, www.danzaurbana.it.

October

This the 2nd part of the internationally lauded classical music festival, **Bologna Festival**, the 1st part being held in Apr. It's held in various venues and tickets cost €15-80 but sell quickly, so get in there fast, www.cinetecadibologna.it.

If you love food you will love the **Bologna e le Città del Cibo** (City of Food Festival). In the main squares across the city stages are erected for gastronomic performances using local fresh Bolognese products, www.bolognawelcome.com.

Gender Bender is the Festival of International and Contemporary Issues on Gender, www.genderbender.it.

Over a weekend **Urban Trekking** aims to offer walking tours round the lesser known parts of the city and its environs. It's not just walking but very sociable too, with stops for drinks and food along the way, www.bolognawelcome.com.

December

The **Motor Show di Bologna** is for lovers of Ferrari, Maserati and all other things fast and shiny: the new, the old, the timeless, www.motorshow.it.
Natale (25th) The run-up to Christmas sees covered markets in piazza Maggiore and some of the other city centre streets and *presepe* (nativity) displays in the churches. If you are lucky enough to find yourself at a family Christmas dinner (they have this on Christmas Eve) expect a big old feast with tortellini and roast lamb.
Vecchione (31st) On New Year's Eve in piazza Maggiore they burn an effigy to welcome in the New Year. The Centro Storico has live music, street food and goodwill to all men and women. Expect lots of firecrackers.

◎ Shopping

Bologna *p18, maps p20 and p32*
Bologna has some great shopping. Whilst there are streets dominated by the Italian high street names this is a country where the votes of independent shopkeepers is still of some importance to the political parties – therefore their businesses still thrive and the city centres still have their hearts.

But it's not just down to politics. Italian shopping culture, especially for food is different, with old loyalties to the baker (*fornaio*), butcher (*macelleria*) and fruit seller (*fruttivendolo*) still strong. Whilst a lot of the West see shopping as a rather insular leisure pursuit, the Italians see it as an opportunity to be sociable. Many Italians still observe the *passeggiata*, where they take to the streets around 1800 to 1900 to see, be seen and have a drink or in the summer months, a gelato. Whilst shopping may not be at the forefront of people's minds, how can people walking past your shop not be good for business?

Bologna is the place to buy food. The Quadrilatero area behind piazza Maggiore is where most of the food shops are concentrated. As a university town, it is also well stocked with bookshops and art shops too. As for clothes, handbags, shoes, most of Italy's famous fashion designers and, of course, the local firms La Perla, Furla and MaxMara have typically stylish branches here, with prices still cheaper than outside Italy. And whilst it is a wealthy city, the large student community means it's not all Prada and Bulgari. There are some interesting alternative shops and an increasing number of vintage clothes shops too.

Shopping hours are normally 0930-1300 and 1530-2000, although some of the national stores open all day. Shoppers resident outside the EU can claim tax refunds on their purchases. For more information on how to do this, contact **Global Blue**, www.global-blue.com.

Antique and second-hand shops

You will find many, mostly quite expensive and stuffy antique shops along via San Vitale and via Santo Stefano. Finally, Italy has taken to second-hand and vintage. Bologna has a burgeoning number of places selling these items, some of which will 'pop up' in stalls at the city's markets (see page 55).

Antichità Barberia, via Barberia 8a, T051-332472, www.antichitabarberia.com. For serious collectors of glass, ceramics and those open to true finds.

Crocevia, via Santa Croce, 11, T051-649 0677, www.crocevia-santacroce.com. An interesting little shop selling vintage clothing, retro furnishings and objects d'arte. Between via del Pratello and via San Felice.

Il Labirinto Di Paola Sgarzi, via del Pratello 65, T051-524044. Vintage home ware, from old signs to tin boxes.

Memoires, via de Fusari 7/b, T051-223083. Just round the back of the Comune, this sells vintage jewellery accessories and trinkets.

Penelope Recycling, Galleria Falcone e Borsellino 3g, T051-412 1894. Very good quality and delightfully presented vintage clothing, some designer, some hand made. Near Porta Saragozza.

Zenobialand, via San Leonardo 3, T095-741938. An exciting shop run by a collector and lover of fine things. Cheap and cheerful. Just of via San Vitale.

Art supplies and stationery

Mesticheria Pietro Fossi, piazza Galvani 2, T051-225537. Oils, acrylics, brushes, pastels, varnishes, charcoal, inks, sketch pads; all things for the artists displayed and stored in delightfully old-fashioned wooden cabinets.

Barbers

Marchi, piazza Cavour 5/d. Chaps, step back to the 19th century and get a hot shave and pat down with some pomade at this historic barbershop.

Books

Libreria delle Moline, via delle Moline 3, T051-232053. New and old books, a shop favoured by students and bookworms.

Libreria di Cinema Teatro Musica, via Mentana 1, T051-237277. Specialist in performing arts books.

Libreria Feltrinelli, piazza di Porta Ravegnana 1, T051-266891, and at via dei Mille 12, T051-240302, and **Libreria Feltrinelli Internazionale**, via Zamboni 7, T051-268210, www.lafeltrinelli.it. Open late. Italy's largest bookseller and best bookstore chain. It doesn't look like it but Feltrinelli now owns Zanichelli Nicholas, Bologna's well known printer, and publisher at piazza Galvani 1/h, T051-239990, and are endeavouring to keep it in the old style. Time will tell...

Libreria Mondadori, via d'Azeglio, T051-275611, www.librimondadori.it. Bologna branch of the chain, owned by Italy's largest publishing house.

Libreria Nanni, via de' Musei 6-8, T051-221841. Under the portico this Parisian-style bookshop sells second-hand books and has a wonderful range of maps, political pamphlets and art books.

Libreria Veronese, via de' Foscherari 19, T051-236492, www.libreriaveronese.it. One of Bologna's oldest bookshops – open since 1888 – selling rare and beautiful books.

MODO infoshop, via Mascarella 24/b, T051-587 1012. Books on art, cinema and contemporary culture.

Department stores

Coin, via Rizzoli, T051-238624. Italy's favourite department store.

Fashion

The main shopping streets in Bologna for fashion are via Rizzoli, via D'Azeglio, via Farini and via Castiglione. If you have a limited budget but still want to spend, via dell'Indipendenza is your archetypal Italian high street. It's got **Calzedonia** (No 2) and **Goldenpoint** (No 8) for tights, intimate wear and the coolest mini-dresses; **Kiko** (No 8) and

Glossip (No 20) for make-up and perfume; L'Occitane (No 17) for French beauty products; Carpisa (No 23) for beautiful handbags; Sisley (No 30) and Benetton (No 34); and Bata (No 42) for shoes.

Outlet shopping is huge in Italy. For a fully list of all the outlets both inside the city walls and in the outlying areas, such as the wonderful Castel Guelfo, visit www. bolognawelcome.com. If getting your hands on super-cheap designer labels is one of the main reasons you are coming to Bologna and you are hiring a car a simple internet search will yield a very long list of the outlets beyond Bologna.

Cappelleria Barbetti, via IV Novembre 4, T051-233756. The most amazing hat shop. You'll think your life will be complete if you buy one of their hats. It just might be.

Corte Isolani, strada Maggiore. Housed in a medieval palazzo, this place has a chic collection of independent shops selling clothes you've not seen anywhere else.

Galleria Cavour, www.galleriacavour.net. This shopping mall off via Farini often seems like a catwalk, with Borbonese, Burberry, Bruno Magli, Emporio Armani, Fendi, Gucci, Luis Vuitton, Miu Miu, Prada and YSL. It's supremely shiny and clean and nice for a slink around even if you can't afford anything.

L'Inde le Palais, via de'Musei 6, www. lindelepalais.com. Edgy fashions from well and lesser-known European designers. Good spread of prices and great sales with up to a whopping 70% off.

Paris Texas Italy, via Altabella 11, T051-225741. It's a rather disagreeable name yet sells Italian designer clothing at very agreeable prices.

Food

Al Regno della Forma, via Oberdan 45, T051-233609. The wheels of cheese won't knock you off your feet but the pungency of this shop might.

La Baita, via Pescherie Vecchie 3, T051-223940. Tortellini and other pastas and quite a lot of cheese.

La Bottega del Caffè, via Orefici 6, T051-236720. A huge, 2-floored coffee and tea shop with sales of the leaf, bean and granule downstairs and cups of the hot stuff upstairs.

Le Sfogline, via Belvedere 7, T051-220558, www.sfogline.it. Classic tortellini and those filled whatever's in season, as well as other fresh pastas.

Majani, via De'Carbonesi 5, T051-969157, www.majani.com. Beautiful purse-emptying chocolates.

Paolo Atti e Figli, via Caprarie 7, T051-220425, www.paoloatti.com. If you fear bread will be the end of you, come here and realise that good bread, proper bread, is the only way to go.

Salumeria Bruno e Franco, via Oberdan 16, T051-233692, www.la-salumeria.it. For all your cured meat and sausage needs.

Tamburini, via Caprarie 1, T051-234726, www.tamburini.com. Prepared foods and pastas to take away and a jolly affordable self-serve restaurant too.

Homeware

Antica Cesteria, via Clavature 8a, T051-239285. Dating back to the early 1900s, this shop sells all sorts and sizes of basketware.

Ferramenta Castaldini, strada Maggiore 7, T051-221526. The lure of the ironmonger can be strong in Italy. This one has beautiful knobs, handles, house numbers, light pulls and every kind of tool and pot known to man.

Marzocchi, via Farini 24, T051-222575. For coffee makers, milk frothers, long spoons and sugar dispensers: all things an Italophile needs.

Soho, via Volturno 7, T051-267769. Things for your bookcase, your house, your desk, your friends.

Kids

Hoffman, via Altabella 23, T051-223066. Designed by Carlo Scarpa this shop has some very interesting architectural features and some marvellously educational toys.

Markets

DecoMela Art, via San Giuseppe. Generally the 2nd weekend Feb-Jun and Sep-Dec. See www.bolognawelcome.com for exact dates. Selling locally produced and international handicrafts and jewellery, including some vintage or recycled bijoux.

Il Mercato dei Tigli, via San Giuseppe. Various dates from Mar-Jun, Sep-Dec check www.bolognawelcome.com for details. Crafts.

La Piazzola, piazza VIII Agosto. Every Fri and Sat. Formerly called and still known as Mercato della Montagnola. Cheap clothing, soft furnishings, homeware, bric a brac. There are some excellent vintage pop-up shops here including **Lamu** (www.lamuvintage.it), selling the most amazing vintage frames for glasses and sunglasses.

Mercato, piazza Puntoni. Mar-Jun and Oct-Dec every Tue. A small collection of stalls but with some very interesting vintage clothing and accessories.

Mercato Antiquario, piazza San Stefano. Every 2nd Sat and Sun. Vintage clothing, old cinema posters, retro paraphernalia, antiques, furniture, glass, jewellery.

Mercato del collezionismo (ex Celo Celo Mamanca), piazza VIII Agosto. Thu only. Antiques, collectables and various ageing jumble.

Mercato dell'antiquariato, via Giacomo Matteotti. Sep-Jun 1st Tue and Mar-Jun and Sep-Dec also the 2nd Tue of every month. A small market with vintage and antique collectables, linen and homeware.

Mercato della Terra, cortile della Cineteca, via Azzo Gardino. Oct-Apr every Sat 0900-1400, May-Sep (although there may be a break in Aug) Mon 1730-2130. Locally produced cheeses, cured meats, bread, beer and vegetables with street food too.

Mercato di Mezzo, via Peschiere Vecchie. Every Mon-Sat 0700-1300 and 1630-1930 (closed Thu afternoon). Sells artisan foods, fruits, and vegetables and is worth visiting for the sensory experience.

Mercato de piazza San Francisco, piazza San Francesco. Sep-Jun every Tue 0800-1300. Sells plants and flowers, although it might be tricky getting these home.

Supermarkets

If the cheese shops are too pricey for you, you can still buy great Parmigiano Reggiano and Grana Padano in the supermarket, as well as Aperol, Birra Moretti and Barilla pasta Bucatini No 9.

Conad, via Angelo Finelli 8, T051-241518.
Incoop Due Torri, via San Vitale 4, T051-232243.
Pam, via Guglielmo Marconi 28, T051-520404.

Wine

Enoteca Gilberto, via Drapperie 5, T051-223925. Wine, spirits, liquori, digestivi and, er...cleaning fluid? Think of it as a mini market with a damned good offy.

Enoteca Italiana, via Marsala 2, T051-235989. A vast selection of regional and Italian wines in town. Tasting freely indulged and they've got cold cuts too.

Scaramagli, strada Maggiore 31, T051-227132, www.scaramagli.it. It can be hard handing over money for something that will be quaffed in a flash. Weirdly, it's easy here.

☉ What to do

Bologna *p18, maps p20 and p32*
Despite their love of food, the Bolognesi generally lead a fairly active life. Theirs is a city that is made to walk around (even the elderly come out most nights for a *passeggiata*) and with a strong municipal investment in sport and communities, there are good facilities for football, tennis and swimming. Being so near the Apennines, Bologna is just an hour away from green and forested mountains and rivers that host cross-country cycling, kayaking, hiking and, in winter, skiing.

Basketball

Pallacanestro (basketball) is very popular in Bologna. Its team Virtus (www.virtus.it) are among the best in Europe and have a huge following. They play at the **Unipol Arena**, via Cervia 1, Casalecchio di Reno, T051-758758, southwest of the city. You can buy tickets at the stadium just before the match or through the website at www.titcketone.it. Tickets average €30.

Cycling

With its flatness and general calmness on the roads (for Italy) there is no better city to get on your bike. The Comune di Bologna (the local council) have an excellent leaflet *Tutta mia la città* which, although in Italian, has maps of the 12 cycling tracks around the city. You can download it from their website www.comune.bologna.it or pick it up from the tourist information office in piazza Maggiore.

Astronolo, via O Regnoli 2, T051-308828, www.astronolo.net. A bike for 24 hrs cost €15 (city bike), €24 (mountain bike) or €18 (electric bike). Weekends cost €25, €45 and €30, respectively.

Veloce, www.rentalbikeitaly.com. This outfit runs cycle tours over the Bologna hills with visits to the Basilica di San Luca and Porrettana in the Apennines. They can organize routes, top-end bikes and back-up vehicles for all levels including keen peddlers wanting to test themselves on Giro d'Italia climbs. From around €60 per person. If you like your wheels chunkier and your terrain a little more rugged, **Bike Emilia-Romagna**, www.bikeemiliaromagna.com, has some itineraries around Bologna.

Football

Like everywhere else in Italy, you will know when there's a football match on. Bologna FC have been back in Serie A for a few years and whilst they don't tend to bother the big teams, they have a loyal following with an average of 20,000 fans at each home game. You'll see men – and

some women – wearing the red and blue striped scarf of Bologna FC; taxi drivers will have the radio on and be banging the steering wheel and when you walk past a bar you'll hear the intakes of breath, the cheers, the jeers and unrepeatable expressions. It's worth going to a game if just for the spectacle of the crowd.

Stadio R Dall'Ara, via A Costa 174, to the west of the Centro Storico, ticket office T051-611 1125. The ground of Bologna FC was built in 1927 as one of Italy's first modern sports stadiums. League matches are held on Sun and tickets for home games can be obtained from the ticket office (see above) or from any branch of **Carisbo**, T051-421 1342, the local bank and the current sponsor of the team. Tickets cost upwards of €20 depending on where you want to sit. You can take the No14, 20 or 21 bus or, even better, walk with the fans (it's a 25-min walk from Piazza Maggiore).

Golf

There are 2 courses within reach of central Bologna. A round of golf will cost upwards of €40 per person.

Gold Club Bologna, via Sabattini 69 in Monte San Pietro, T051-969100, www.golfclubbologna.it. Closed Mon. Just 20 km from the city centre, this 18-hole, par 72, 5949-m lakeside course with driving range and practice greens has the added bonus of an outdoor pool for the partner that doesn't want to putt. A day ticket costs €60 and booking is essential.

Golf Club Molino del Pero, via Molino del Pero 323 in Monzuno, T051-677 0506, www.golfmolinodelpero.it. Closed Mon. Just as the land south of Bologna starts to undulate, this 18-hole, par 70, 5480-m golf course – tight to start with then wider and longer for the last 9 holes – is set amongst old trees making it feel less manicured and more natural than many courses. It has a beautiful clubhouse, converted from a hayloft, and a B&B near the 3rd hole. A day ticket costs €40-50, depending on the day.

Swimming

Bologna has a number of public swimming baths. It costs around €5-7 for a swim, depending on the day and season.

Carmen Longo Stadio, Bologna FC stadium complex, via Costa 174, T051-615 2520. With beautiful tiered viewing platforms, this is like the inside of a cruise ship. Take bus No 14, 20 or 21.

Cavina, via Biancolelli 36, T051-404312. Situated in wooded gardens that you can lounge about in, there's a covered indoor pool for serious swimmers and an outside splash pool for kids or posers. Take the No 13 bus.

Sterlino, via Murri 113, T051-623 7034. This has an indoor 25-m-long pool open all year round and a 50-m outdoor pool open in the summer. Get the 13 or 38 bus.

From Jun to Sep there are some beautiful lidos outside Bologna that are easy to get to by bus. Visit www.sogese.com for more information.

Tennis

Circolo Tennis, Giardini Margherita, viale R Cristiani 2, T051-333420, www.circolotennisbologna.com. These 7 clay courts in the heart of Giardini Margherita are for serious players (or serious posers). It has an outdoor pool, gym and restaurant. It's just a short 25-min walk from piazza Maggiore but if you want to conserve energy the 13 or 28 bus will get you there.

Walking tours

There are numerous walking tours of the city – from a Gourmet Guide to the shops and eateries of the city, to the porticoes of Bologna and one focusing on its brothels and bordellos (long since closed). Information about these can be found at a tourist information office (see page 16). For those who would rather wander around themselves the size and flatness of Bologna make for easy exploring. For those who'd like a bit of green and gradient there are 3 suggested walks along the porticoes to the Santuario della Madonna di San Luca, the Colle dell'Osservanza and the Giardini di Margherita (see page 39).

ⓘ Directory

Bologna *p18, maps p20 and p32*
Accident and emergency Hospital Maggiore, largo B, Nigrisoli 2, T051-647 8111, or if it's an emergency call T118. If you need an emergency pharmacy you can call **Farmaco Pronto**, T0800-218489. There are pharmacies on most busy streets but **La Farmacia Comunale**, piazza Maggiore 6, T051-239690, is a 24-hr chemist.

Contents

Footprint features

Emilia-Romagna

Apennine villages → *For listings, see pages 73-75.*

To the north of Bologna lie the flat lands of the Po, whilst to the south are hills and mountains to which cling villages and communities who hand on to the slower, rustic Italian life we have seen in the films. This landscape – wooded, rocky in parts, with vast verdant hillsides – and the Apennine's rich flora and fauna provide fresh respite from the stifling humidity of summer in the city. If you want to get the heart racing you can trek, climb, cycle and ski, or you can simply relax at one of the area's spa towns. You will probably need your own transport to reach the deeper recesses of the region although buses do run to some of the bigger villages.

Museo Nazionale Pompeo Aria

ⓘ *via Porettana 13, Marzabotto, T051-932352, Apr-Oct Tue-Sun 0900-1300, 1500-1830; Nov-Mar Tue-Sun 0900-1300, 1400-1730, €2.50; archaeological zone Apr-Oct daily 0800-1900; Nov-Mar 0800-1730. €2. Buses once an hour from Bologna bus station, €12 return.*

Around 10 km southwest of Bologna, the village of **Marzabotto** is famous for the considerable vestiges of the Etruscan town of Misa, dated to the sixth century BC and set in the delightful wooded Monte Sole national park. Inside there are displays of beautiful pots, figurines and reconstructions; outside there are ruins of two *sepolcreti* (graveyards) which are worth seeing and experiencing, especially in the late afternoon light. Marzabotto also achieved notoriety as the place where 770 civilians – babies, children, women and the elderly – were massacred by the Nazis in the last days of occupation in 1944 as an act of reprisal against local support for the partisan and resistance movement. Five priests were also murdered, one of which, Don Fornasini – 'the angel of Marzabotto'– had helped many of his parishioners escape but returned to the scene of the execution to bury those executed when a member of the SS found him and killed him. He and two other priests are now being beatified. The names and faces of those murdered are remembered on plaques on the side of the Palazzo Comunale in Bologna.

Montefiorino

Further west, atmospheric Montefiorino, with its steep approach and austere hilltop fort often surrounded in swirling mist, is another seat of partisan resistance in the summer of 1944. Buses leave at least once an hour from Bologna bus station, €10 return.

Castle Route

ⓘ *A car is necessary to do the whole route, though buses serve individual destinations. Ask tourist information for details.*

The legacy of power and paranoia among warring factions in the area is visible in the many castles that dominate the hilltops. The following villages are connected by beautiful winding and tree-lined roads through the hills. Heading southwest of Bologna is Vignola, famous for its cherries and also for the **Rocca di Vignola** ⓘ *piazza dei Contari 4, T059-775246 www.fondazionedivignola.it, Tue-Sun 0900-1200, 1330-1800*. It is believed that an early fortification was built in the 800s to keep out the rampaging Goths; however, the castle came later, in 1178. Thereafter it was gifted from the Este family to the Contrari family who oversaw its aggrandisement, adding a family chapel, splendid living quarters and frescos galore. In the 16th century it became to property of an absentee landlord who merely maintained it before it became municipal property. Its restoration in the 1960s has seen it regain its former glory.

Beyond this is the 13th-century **Castello di Serravalle** before the route reaches the beautiful castle-town of Monteveglio, famous not only for its imposing fortress but also for the 11th-century abbey, **Abbazia di Santa Maria**, which acts as a focal point for great walks with stunning views over the countryside. At **Bazzano**, the fort is a piece of typically extravagant reconstruction work, commissioned by Giovanni II Bentivoglio in the 15th century on the remains of a 13th-century original. In the 18th century, the poet Ugo Foscolo was imprisoned in its tower. The castle now houses the **Museo Crespellani** ① *via Contessa Matilde 10, T051-836442, www.roccadeibentivoglio.it, Tue-Fri and Sun 1500-1900, Sat 0900-1300 and 1500-1900, €4*, devoted to local history and archaeology. Bazzano is equally famous for its cherries and fine local wine. Further south still, **La Rocchetta Mattei** in Grizzana Morandi is a castle of a different sort. Commissioned in 1850 by the eccentric homeopathic doctor Cesare Mattei, it is a fantastical fairy-tale hotchpotch of architectural influences from all cultures and eras, resulting in a Transylvanian rhapsody of kitsch. Located within the castle is the **Archivo Museo Cesare Mattei** ① *051-673 0329, www. cesaremattei.com, Wed 0900-1300, Thu 1400-1800, Fri 1500-1800, Sat 1000-1300*, a weird and wonderful museum dedicated to the founder of electrohomeopathy. Nearby **Riola** is the home of an innovative church, the Chiesa di Santa Maria l'Assunta, a bold and unusual 1965 papal commission by the Finnish architect, Alvar Aalto.

Spa towns
There are more than 20 thermal spa resorts in Emilia-Romagna, survivors of the 19th-century fashion for relaxing in sulphurous decadence. These are the perfect places to go in order to detox and hydromassage away the extravagances of too much rich Bolognese food. Emilia-Romagna Tourist Board, www.emiliaromagnaterme.it, is a good place to start checking out what's available and where.

Nearest to Bologna (only 23 km) is **Castel San Pietro** ① *viale Terme 1113, T051-234475, www.termedicastelsanpietro.it*, with its sulphurous waters, mud pools, warm jets and lots of steam. Some 32 km west of Parma is **Salsomaggiore Terme** ① *viale Romagnosi 4, T0524-572100/578201, www.portalesalsomaggiore.it*, a bustling resort of 41 hotels, dedicated to the twin Italian religions of health and beauty. It has magnificent art deco architecture and still retains a belle époque Death In Venice atmosphere. Just 22 km from Modena is **Salvarola Terme** ① *Sassuolo, T0536-987530, www.termesalvarola.it*. When you start to shrivel, there's yoga, pilates, the gym or a walk in the wooded grounds.

Parks around Bologna → *For listings, see pages 73-75.*

Beyond Bologna are numerous beautiful parks notable for their interesting geology and varied flora and fauna, including many birds of prey. They also contain biking trails and have bike hire facilities. Contact the tourist office for more information about the following parks.

Parco dell'Alto Appennino Modenese (also called Parco Frignano)
① *For tourist information Piazza Marconi, 1 Fanano, T0536-68696, www.parcofrignano.it.*
Southwest of Bologna, near Fanano, and covering 15,000 ha, this mountainous terrain includes the peaks of the Tosco Emiliano ridge including Monte Cimone (2165 m). Lago di Scaffailo and Lago di Pratignano are surrounded by peat lands creating a post-glacial environment that hosts several rare marshland plants, including *Drosera rotundifolia* (the round-leaved sundew), that feast on the low-flying insects of the bog. As the altitude gets higher you walk through through wild cherry, chestnut and oak trees, the habitat of roe

and fallow deer and wild boar. Higher up birds of prey swirl around the black pine, beech and birch trees: you can see kestrels, sparrow hawks and buzzards.

Walkers may be interested in some of the trekking trails. These are pitched at all levels but for nature lovers the walks from lake Santo to Mount Rondinaio (medium difficulty, approximately four hours) and from Alpicella delle Radici to the meadows of San Geminiano (easy, approximately 3½ hours) are recommended.

Parco del Delta del Po
ⓘ *www.parcodeltapo.it.*
Fans of Michelangelo Antonioni's 1964 classic *Deserto Rosso* (*Red Desert*) will be familiar with the atmospheric wetlands and waters of the River Po delta. North of Ravenna and east of Ferrara, these 54,000 ha of marshlands, forests, dunes and lagoons has been interrupted by industry and agriculture but this only adds to its allure. The great river Po washes hundreds of thousands of tonnes of nutrient-rich silt to the delta, which brings the fish that attract over 300 species of bird, such as heron, egret, curlew, making this an ornithologist – and field recorder's – dream. However, to see the beautiful spoonbills, go to **Valle Mandriole**, or for the flamingos, head for the lagoons and salt pans of **Comacchio**. This beautiful town – known as little Venice – houses a number of small museums, such as the **Manifattura dei Marinati** ⓘ *corso Giuseppe Mazzini, 200, T0533-81742*, that explain the history of living and working life on the delta. Its **Tourist Information Office** ⓘ *via Agatopisto 3, T0533-314154, www.turismocomacchio.it*, has information about boat trips on the lagoon.

Parco dei Sassi di Roccamalatina
Just half an hour west of Bologna (head for Guiglia) is this small but beautiful national park. At only 2300 ha it may not seem much of a national park but its dreamy meadows underneath dramatic sandstone crags make for very pleasing treks. Birders are sure to see some of the 80 nesting species which include peregrine falcons and the sweet-singing Ortolan bunting – a French delicacy. But if you're busy admiring winged wonders, watch where you tread: the park is home to the *Orchis tridentata* (three-toothed orchid) a rare flower indeed. The park's **information office** ⓘ *Pieve di Trebbio 1287, Rocca Malatina di Guiglia, T059-795721, www.parcosassi.it (in Italian)*, has details of the 14 walks from short rambles to more strenuous hikes.

Parco dello Stirone
Half an hour northwest from Parma is just over 2000 ha of protected river bank. Over mining of the gravel in the 1950s and 60s resulted in a dramatic changed in the nature of this small but significant river bed and revealed a whole new understanding of the geological nature of this area. The river's dramatic canyons and gullies would not look out of place in a Western. There are three walking itineraries along the wooded sides of the river where you might see stone martens or woodpeckers. The **Visitor Centre** ⓘ *Scipione Ponte 1, Salsomaggiore Terme, T0524-581139, www.parcostirone.it (in Italian)*, has a small natural history museum and details of the walks.

Parmigiano Reggiano

Made only from milk from the pastured cows of the provinces of Parma, Reggio Emilia, Modena Bologna (west of the river Reno) and Mantova (from the adjoining Lombardia region but only the area east of the river Po), this champion of cheeses (here they call it the king of cheeses) has been produced for eight centuries. Using natural fermentation the cheese is shaped into huge truckles which are stored in vast *magazzini* for at least a year (often two or more), all the while their rinds being regularly inspected, brushed and turned to make sure they achieve the grade. The best quality Parmigiano is Parmigiano delle Vacche Rosse produced from what they call a red cow.

Protected by the European DOP (Designazione d'Origine Protetta), all cheeses will have this insignia stamped on the rind in a way that every single 'cut' has part of the name Parmigiano Reggiano; if you cannot read it is probably a 'fake'.

If you want to see how parmesan cheese is made, visit one of the main dairies, the Caseificio Consorzio Produttori Latte. Tours can be arranged by Consorzio del Formaggio Parmigiano Reggiano ⓘ *www.parmigiano-reggiano. it;* call T0521-292700 *if you are in Parma,* T0522-506159 *in Reggio Emilia, or* T059-208635 *in Modena, and* T0376-327621 *in Bologna.* You'll meet the Master Cheesemaker, taste all sorts of different types of parmesan (and parma ham) and wash them down with some local wine. Be prepared for an early start. If you can't spare the time for the tour, the Caseificio ⓘ *via Puppiola 15, T0521-601313,* in Baganzolino, just 3 km from Parma, offers great truckles of parmesan at reduced prices.

The Musei del Cibo ⓘ *www.museidel cibo.it,* are three food museums – for Parmigiano, parma ham and salami – and with one planned for tomatoes. All three are located in towns on the outskirts of Parma. They may appeal to gourmands but booking is advised before you make the trek.

Parma → *For listings, see pages 73-75.*

Everyone has heard of Parma thanks to its hanging hams and wheels of cheese. The Farnese family ruled here from the mid-16th to the mid-18th century. Their wealth and enthusiasm for ancient classical sculpture lead to them being the owners of the greatest collection of Greco-Roman antiquaries (which can be see in Naples). It thrived under French rule with Napoleon's wife, with Maria Luigia, calling the city 'la petite capitale' of Italy. Today it continues to be a sensuous enclave of affluence, elegance, sophistication, fine opera and gourmet food, whose people are convinced that their city is the centre of the universe. To understand why it is so affluent, travel through its industrial belt and you will see wealth-making factory after factory including the Barilla empire that makes half the pasta in Italy. This is a city that knows how to thrive and has all the trappings and culture that makes it an excellent place to visit.

Lying northwest of Bologna (54 miles/87 km) Parma is less than an hour away by train which run twice an hour.

Duomo
① piazza Duomo, daily 0900-1200, 1500-1900.

Dating from the 11th century, Parma's Lombard-Romanesque cathedral was built on what is believed to be the ruins of an early Roman church (3-4 AD), which was consecrated in 1106. Its external frontage has three loggia floors and three large doors. Inside, under the transcript, there's a crypt and the famous frescoes and friezes by the artists Correggio (the *Assumption* in the central cupola) and his pupil, Parmigianino (in the southern transept). Whilst the Duomo has a grand beauty of its own, it's the confection of a Battistero (or baptistery) that endears visitors. It was built by Campionese artisans (known to be the finest architects, sculptors and stonecutters) and was probably finished in 1270. Made of red Veronese marble, it has more of the delicate pinkness of a well cared-for old lady. The three large doorways facing the piazza bear the elaborate carvings of Biblical scenes by the architect Benedetto Antelami. Inside, as the walls rise up to the Byzantine-style cupola, there are coloured reliefs: alongside the Christian, there's an intriguing mixture of symbolism, including tributes to the months of the year and signs of the zodiac.

Chiesa di San Giovanni Evangelista
① piazza Duomo, daily 0800-1200 and 1500-1745.

To the east of the Duomo, this church's cupola contains Correggio's famous the *Vision of St John at Patmos*. The **Spezieria di San Giovanni** *① Tue-Sun 0900-1200*, is the lesser-known pharmacy of the Benedinctine monks who ground and boiled up tinctures and ointments and the like from the 13th to 19th century.

Camera di San Paolo
① off via Melloni, Tue-Sun 0830-1400, €2.

The back room of this former convent is famous for the sensuous and rather racy collection of frescoes. Once a nunnery, its abbess Giovanna da Piacenza commissioned Correggio (aka Antonio Allegri) to add some life and interest to these rooms. The friezes, completed in 1521, are of mythological scenes and are considered to be among his most significant work.

Palazzo della Pilotta
① piazza Pilotta.

This imposing former palace of the Farnese family is now the home to a number of museums, the most important of which is the city's art gallery, the **Pinacoteca** *① Tue-Sat 0900-1400, Sun 0900-1300, €5*, where many works by Correggio and Parmigianino are on display, alongside others by the Carraccis, Tiepolo, Canaletto and Leonardo da Vinci. Also within the Palazzo della Pilotta is the **Teatro Farnese** *① entry included on gallery ticket*, entirely rebuilt in wood as it was before being bombed in 1944. Across the River Parma stands the 16th-century Palazzo Ducale, former residence of Ottaviano Farnese, among an enormous and relaxing park of 18th-century gardens.

Casa Toscanini
① borgo Rodolfo Tanzi, T0521-285499, Tue and Sat 1000-1300, 1500-1800, Wed-Fri 1000-1300, free.

The musician and conductor, Arturo Toscanini, was born in this house on 25 March,1867. He attended Parma's Royal School of Music at the age of nine and graduated at 18. Parma was also the home of the musicians and composers, Verdi and Paganini.

A city of coffee drinkers

You can say this about any Italian city but there is something about the Reggio Emilian nature that makes going for a *caffè* a very friendly experience.

Bar Caffè Tostato, Via S Pietro 1. Offering a good range of coffees, this used to be a *bar storico* of Reggio but is now owned by foreigners who bring a new, different charm.

Caffè Pietranera, via Emilia S Pietro 29. This old perfume shop has been transformed into a lovely bar and they've kept the historical name.

Libreria all'Arco, via Farini 1. The cafeteria inside the libreria sells books – especially travel books – as well as frothing coffees.

Pasticceria La Torinese, via Fornaciari 3a. An elegant 'Viennese' style *caffè* where you can enjoy excellent pastries.

Teatro Regio
① *via Garibaldi 16, T0521-039399, www.teatroregioparma.org.*
The musical tradition of the city is characterized by the opera house which attracts dance, opera and classical music. Its exacting audiences are not afraid to boo during bad performances and organize *claques* (fan clubs) in support of favourites – in tune with opera's origins. Their Verdi festival each autumn is popular and worth trying to get a ticket for; prices vary from about €30 to more than €100.

Reggio Emilia → For listings, see pages 73-75.

Just 64 km from Bologna and on the road to Parma, Reggio Emilia is a handsome town that's well worth stopping off at. Split in two by via Emilia, the south city has a Roman layout (like all the *capuloghi di provincia* of Emilia-Romagna, each at a distance of 25 km from the other), whilst the north has the ambition and boulevards of the 20th century. Each year in May there is the **European Festival of Photography** ① *www.fotografiaeuropea.it*, that draws big names, gallerists and enthusiasts.

Palazzo Magnani
① *corso Giuseppe Garibaldi, T0522-454437, www.palazzomagnani.it, Tue-Fri 1000-1300, 1530-1900, Sat and Sun 1000-1900.*
Is interesting gallery in so far as it's a chance to see the vast and varied collection of music critic and writer, Luigi Magnani who died in 1984, in his actual home. You'll see art – and the thinking behind buying it – in a very different way. It also hosts temporary exhibitions.

Museo del Tricolore
① *piazza Prampolini, T0522-456033, Mon-Sat 0900-1200, Sat 1500-1900, Sun 1000-1300, 1500-1900.*
An excellent museum for a quick and easy introduction to the history of Italy. The grand Sala is where the tricolore was first adopted as Italy's national flag.

Collezione Maramotti
① *via Fratelli Cervi 66, T0522 382484, www.collezionemaramotti.org, Mon-Fri 1430-1830, Sat and Sun 1030-1830, but it is advisable to book online before coming.*

Just 2 km from Reggio Emilia, this little known gallery is actually one of Europe's finest collections of contemporary art. Owned by the MaxMara fashion house whose HQ is here, it has two floors of stunning Italian, European and American contemporary art from the 1950s to the present day: Francis Bacon, Mark Dion and Karla Black. As sponsors of the MaxMara Art Prize for Women they know what's happening in the art world, something that you can see in this collection.

Modena → *For listings, see pages 73-75.*

Heading 38 km northwest from Bologna to Modena along the via Emilia, it's interesting to know that the enmity between these cities goes back a long way, to a centuries-old conflict over a stolen wooden bucket. The Ghibelline Modenesi were loyal to Emperor Frederick II. When in 1325 the Guelph Bolognesi kidnapped his son, Re Enzo, two Modenesi soldiers crept into Bologna and thieved the bucket from the city's well. This bucket became a symbol of the cities' rivalry and was immortalized by Alessandro Tassoni in his satirical poem *La secchia rapita* (the stolen bucket). Modern diplomacy may have been able to write this off as foolish japery but it led to bloodshed and further humiliation for Bologna who never got their bucket back: its sits in the campanile of the city's 12th-century Duomo.

The majestic Duomo and the impenetrable, huge bulk of the Palazzo Ducale dominate the grand city centre and a tight network of labyrinthine streets remind you of its medieval past.

Duomo
① *corso Duomo 6, T059-216078, www.duomodimodena.it, Mon-Sat 1030-1200, 1530-1730.*
Dominating the piazza Grande is the 12th-century cathedral to the city's patron saint, San Geminiano, recognized as one of the finest examples of Romanesque architecture in Italy. The western façade is famous for its graceful columns and two majestic lions that support the central portal. This is surrounded by bas-reliefs depicting scenes from Genesis and from the Arthurian cycle, the work of the sculptor Wiligelmo, completed around 1100. The beautiful polychrome stained-glass windows inside, in particular *The Last Supper*, are the work of Giovanni da Modena, completed around 1450. The cathedral's other salient feature is its 88-m-high half-Gothic and half-Romanesque leaning bell tower, nicknamed La Torre Ghirlandia – the garland tower. This is where you'll find the offending wooden bucket. The cathedral was named a UNESCO World Heritage Site in 1997.

Palazzo Ducale
Occupying the entire northeastern flank of piazza Roma, you will not be able to miss the vast former court of the Este dynasty (see box, page 69). This family ruled Ferrara during the Guelph and Ghibelline feuds of the 13th to 16th centuries but subsequently decamped and brought affluence to Modena following defeat by Cesare Este at the hands of the pope in 1598. This palace was built by Bartolemeo Avanzini in 1634 on the site of the former Este castle. Rather blunt and fortress-like in aspect, it is now a military academy but you can view the public gardens round the back which adjoin the peaceful and cooling **Orto Botanico** ① *viale Caduti in Guerra 127, T059-205 6011, www.ortobot.unimo.it, Mon-Fri 0900-1300*, of the University of Modena.

Balsamic vinegar

Before you learn anything about balsamic vinegar know this: the stuff we buy from our supermarkets is Condimento Aceto Balsamico or, if you've paid a bit more, Aceto Balsamico Tradizionale di Modena. The real stuff, the good stuff, is Aceto Balsamico Tradizionale. Made by reducing a mixture of pressed Trebbiano and Lambrusco grapes. This is then stored in a series of wooden casks for 12 years. In Modena a cream-coloured cap denotes it's been stored for 12 whilst a deep red cap means it's 25 or more years old. In Reggio Emilia they use a labelling system: a red label for 12 years, a silver label for 18 and a gold for 25 years or older.

In Modena balsamic vinegar is everywhere but if you want to learn a little more so you can bore your friends at home Consorzio Produttori Aceto Balsamico Tradizionale di Modena (www.balsamico.it) are an amenable bunch who can arrange a visit to one of their local producers.

Palazzo dei Musei

① *piazzale Sant'Agostino 337, T059-203 3100, Tue-Fri 0900-1200, Sat and Sun 0900-1300 and 1500-1800 (Jun-Sep until 1900).*

The Palazzo dei Musei is a complex housing the city's main museums and galleries. On the first floor is the **Biblioteca Estense**, the collected correspondence of a despotic family dynasty with its rival emperors and popes. It is also the home of the famous Bibbio Borso, the lavishly illustrated and priceless bible of Borso d'Este. On the second floor is the **Museo d'Arte Medievale e Moderne e Etnologie**, a specialist collection of archaeological relics and artefacts. The most important floor is at the top, where the fabulous art collection of the Este family is hung in the **Galleria Estense**, combining paintings from the early Renaissance and masterpieces by the Carraccis, Guercino and Guido Reni, as well as sculptures by Niccolo dell'Arca. There is also a bust of Francesco d'Este by Bernini and Venetian canvasses by Tintoretto and Veronese. Also worthy of architectural note are the clock tower of the **Palazzo Comunale** and the pretty churches of **San Francesco** (13th century) and **San Pietro** (14th century).

Galleria Ferrari

① *via Dino Ferrari 43, Galleria Ferrari, T0536-949713, www.museo.ferrari.com, May-Sep daily 0930-1900, Oct-Apr daily 0930-1800 €13. Bus from Modena railway station (every half hour) €11 return.*

Modena is the spiritual home of lovers of the fast and shiny. Enzo Ferrari (1898-1988) was a local lad. After the the First World War, Enzo was discharged from the army only to find his father and brother had died in an outbreak of flu and that the family firm had collapsed. He got a job as an engineer building the bodies of small passengers cars. He also took to the track. A new job at Alfa Romeo provided access to a better car and he began to win races. His ascent as a driver then as a maker of cars is well documented at the Galleria Ferrari just next to the factory he founded at **Maranello**, 18 km south of Modena. The exhibition, manned by men and women in full Ferrari racetrack garb, includes models from the history of the 'prancing horse' including the GT models, the single-seater F2 (1951) up to the F2011. For an extra €13 you can book the factory and track tour which cover the production and testing process.

Ferrara → *For listings, see pages 73-75.*

Ferrara owes its imperial aspect to the powerful Este dynasty who made the city their stronghold from the 13th to 16th centuries. They elevated it from its inauspicious beginnings in the middle of a fly-ridden Po Delta swamp to the strikingly attractive city it became and still is. The major artists of the day, such as Pisanello, Mantegna and Jacopo Bellini, were known as the Ferrara School and their work was sought after, winning numerous extravagant commissions and a Europe-wide reputation. Whilst it's kept its looks, Ferrara sadly lost its power in the 18th and 19th century: those visiting, such as Dickens and Hazlitt, remarked upon its beauty, yes, but also its sense of emptiness, its ghostliness. The great Italian director Michelangelo Antonioni was born here and was inspired by the often-empty streets and the rolling mists of Po Delta, something he used or replicated in many of his films. Ferrara is a little livelier today and its streets rattle with bicycles. Locals trundle around lazily on them, lending the city an air of gentle provinciality that alleviates the domineering mortar of powers past. The centre of palace-lined arcaded streets, encircled by 9 km of ancient city wall, was declared a UNESCO World Heritage Site in 1995.

Castello Estense
ⓘ *piazza Castello, T053-299233, www.castelloestense.it, Tue-Sun 0930-1730, €8.*
Dominating the main square, the brutal, prison-like castle, surrounded by a moat and entered by the drawbridge, is the former seat of the Este family. The castle was begun at the end of the 14th century, commissioned by Nicolo II d'Este who built upon the 13th-century Torre dei Leoni. An earthquake in 1570 caused near collapse of the first floor, which was rebuilt in an altogether more sumptuous style, adding state rooms. This was very much seen as a seat of power for the Estes and they held court, threw lavish banquets and hosted artists in residence, such as the poets Ariosto and Tasso. However, it wasn't all fun and frolics in the Este camp: in 1425 Niccolo III of Este threw his wife Parsina and her 'lover' Ugo – who happened to be Niccolo's illegitimate son – into the Torre dei Leoni, where they lost their heads. The tower went on to be a Nazi/Fascist prison in the Second World War, where partisans and members of the resistance were held, tortured and often shot. Inevitably more elegant inside than its exterior image of power was meant to show, much of the building is now used for offices and is inaccessible. The *saletta* and *salone dei giochi* (games room), decorated by Sebastiano Filippi, contain colourful and energetic images of sports.

Duomo
ⓘ *piazza Trento e Trieste, T053-207449, Tue-Sat 0730-1200, 1500-1830, Sun 0730-1230, 1530-1930.*
Like that of Modena, Ferrara's cathedral is a mixture of the Gothic and Romanesque. Dedicated to San Giorgio, the city's patron saint, work was initiated in 1135 by Master Niccolo – a pupil of the architect Wiligelmo who worked on Modena's cathedral. It took over 100 years to build but there is some splendid relief work on the central portal of its façade showing Saint George slaying the dragon. The inside was damaged by fire in the 18th century and has a rather opulent baroque style. Upstairs, the **museum** ⓘ *T053-220 7449, Tue-Sat 0900-1300, 1500-1800*, contains *Madonna and the pomegranate* by Jacopo della Quercia, and a beautiful collection of illuminated choir books. The bas-reliefs, not of religious scenes but of of the months of the year, are charming.

The Este dynasty

Whilst the Estes can be traced back first to Rome then near Padova, the beginning of the family's dominance in this area began in 1264 with Obizzo II, who with the support of Venice was summoned to reinforce the Guelph – or pope – sympathizers in Ferrara. The Guelphs were at odds with the Ghibellines, the imperialists who supported the Holy Roman Emperor. Their conflict dominated the Italian city states until a semi-peace pact – the Concordat of Worms – in 1075, but in effect it raged on until the 15th century. Obizzo II arrived in Ferrara in 1264. He may have found a rather dull town. However, he was to be the first of 15 Este princes to laud it over the local populace and to bring great wealth, art and prosperity to Ferrara. Whilst the men folk had the wealth and power, it's the Este women who are better known outside of Italy. Francesco II married the Mantovani Isabella d'Este who effectively (very effectively) ran Ferrara in his absence, and was hailed 'The first lady of the world' by Niccolo Correggio. Another famous Este bride was Lucretia Borgia, daughter of Pope Alexander I, who married Alfonso in 1502 and produced an heir, Ercole II. In 1597, when the last Este prince of Ferrara, Alfonso, left no legitimate heir, Ferrara was claimed by the Papal States so the family moved to Modena and took much of their prosperity with them. Today the Estes are still there, embroidered into the fading tapestry of European royalty but not with the clout they had in the past.

Palazzo Schifanoia

① *via Scandiana 23, Tue-Sun 0900-1800, €6.*
Roughly translated as 'Palace for Dispelling Boredom' this palazzo was certainly built for the amusement of the Este family. They commissioned Cosimo Tura, head of the Ferrara school of painting, to create delightful escapist frescoes of the four seasons on the walls of the Salone dei Mesi (room of months), each linked with signs of the zodiac and everyday scenes of the court. Remarkably this cycle was not discovered until 1820, having been covered up by the papacy who took control of the city in 1598. The palazzo also houses the city's museum of local history and archaeology.

Palazzo dei Diamanti

① *corso Ercole d'Este 21, T053-220 5844, Tue-Sat 0900-1400, Sun 0900-1300, €4.*
Further north, in the grand part of the city planned by Ercole I d'Este, is the 15th-century Palazzo dei Diamanti. There is some dispute as to whether it got its name from the 12,600 nail-headed marble bossages on the façade or from Ercole himself, whose character was said to be as cold and as cutting as a diamond. The palazzo houses a number of the city's museums, most notably, on the first floor, the city's main art gallery, **La Pinacoteca Nazionale** ① *Tue-Sat 0900-1400, Sun 0900-1300, €10*, where works by Cosimo Tura and other interpreters of the Ferrara school are on display. Aside from the usual local history museums, there is also a museum to the work of the Ferrara-born film director Michelangelo Antonioni, of *Blow-Up* and *Deserto Rosso* (*Red Desert*) fame.

Imola → For listings, see pages 73-75.

Imola has a Roman forum, many beautiful churches and a couple of museums, but you could be forgiven for making the only object of your visit here a trip to the world-famous Autodromo Dino Ferrari. Built in 1950 on the site of a Roman amphitheatre that would have witnessed many chariot races, the circuit hosts many racing events and also concerts throughout the year. Imola is otherwise a pleasant, quiet place to wander around, with an intact old centre and a grid of ancient, narrow pedestrian streets, opening into classic Italian piazzas, complete with attendant bars, cafés and restaurants.

Autodromo Enzo e Dino Ferrari
ⓘ *Information/tickets: via Rosselli 2, Imola, T054-265 5111, www.autodromoimola.com.*
Named after the founder of Italy's most famous car, the Autodromo Enzo Ferrari, situated in the principality of San Marino, is arguably the spiritual home of the famous prancing-horse scuderia whose fame was made by Formula One. A fixture on the F1 calendar from 1981 to 2006, San Marino was Italy's most prestigious Grand Prix. The tough and twisty circuit always produced exciting races. One of the most memorable was Nigel Mansell, on his way to his first and only World Championship, screaming down the straight, bumper to bumper with his Williams team-mate Ayrton Senna, daring the legendary Brazilian driver to brake first and concede the corner. In 1994, the circuit and its high-speed Curva Tamburello became infamous as the site where Senna lost his life during a tragic F1 weekend that also saw the death of the Austrian driver Roland Ratzenberger.

But whilst the F1 cavalcade no longer comes to town, the World Superbike Championships roar in for a weekend of revs, roars and races. Situated about 30 km from Bologna, the circuit is well signposted both from the A14 motorway and the centre of Imola. Taxis are available from the stand by Imola railway station or piazza Matteotti.

Rocca Sforzesca
ⓘ *piazzale Giovanni delle Bande Nere, T054-2223472, May-Sep Sat and Sun 0900-1200, 1500-1900, €3.50.*
The size and power of this fortress, with its four squat towers like castles from a chess set, seems incongruous in the context of modern-day Imola, but in medieval times it was the residence of the powerful Sforza family. It was built between the mid-13th and 15th centuries, designed by Gian Galeazzo Visconti. Its purpose now is considerably more humble as a museum of armoury and medieval ceramics and the setting for occasional summer concerts.

Zoo Acquario
ⓘ *via Aspramonte, T054-224180, Tue-Sun 0900-1200, 1530-1900, €6.*
Visitors looking for a day out with kids might be interested in heading for the tropical and marine fish and animals on display here.

Ravenna → *For listings, see pages 73-75.*

An early papal seat, Ravenna was coveted by invading forces, so much so that the Byzantines, arriving after the Goths, endowed it with elaborate and spectacular mosaics, which are generally considered to be the finest examples of Byzantine art anywhere in the world. The mosaics are still remarkably intact despite bombs and 20th-century industrial ravishment. The Eastern influence makes for some interesting architecture and a worldly feel. And it's still a wealthy city, with excellent shops and restaurants.

Mosaics

The mosaics are scattered in various locations around town, in the **Museo Arcivescovile and Battisteroon** ① *piazza Arcivescovile, T0544-541688, www.ravennamosaici.it, daily Oct-Mar 0930-1700, Apr-Sep 0900-1900, €4*, and in the **Basilica di Sant'Apollinaire Nuovoon** ① *via di Roma, daily Oct-Mar 0930-1700, Apr-Sep 0900-1900, €9.50*. By far the most famous and richest concentration of mosaics, however, is to be found around the **Basilica di San Vitale** ① *via Fiandrini, T054-434266, Jun-Oct 0900-1900*, itself a wonder of geometric Byzantine design, built in AD 548 and the model for the Hagia Sofia in Istanbul. Inside the basilica and across the lawn in the **Mausoleo di Galla Placidia** is a remarkable, mind-bogglingly intricate tapestry of mosaics.

Rimini → *For listings, see pages 73-75.*

Now regarded as the Italian equivalent of Ibiza, Rimini was once an important Adriatic port and has some fascinating Roman remains. The **Arco d'Augusto**, dated to 27 BC, is one of the oldest surviving Roman arches in Italy. Older still is the five-arched bridge of **Ponte di Tiberio**, built in 22 BC out of white Istrian stone. The town was also the birthplace and psychological inspiration of the film director Federico Fellini, whose film *Amarcord* records his childhood here.

Tempio Malatestiano

① *piazza San Francesco, Tue-Sat 0830-1230, 1700-1900, Sun 1600-1900, €4.*

It was not really until the 15th century that Rimini reached the apogee of its power under the extraordinary prince-inventor-scientist-strategist-humanist, Sigismondo Malatesta. It is to him and his love for his third wife, Isotta degli Atti, that the city owes the magnificent and eclectic pagan Tempio Malatestiano. Originally a Gothic church to St Francis, Malatesta had its façade transformed by Alberti to reflect the motifs of the Arco d'Augusto. The pagan theme continues inside with angels, cupids, roses and elephants by Agostino di Duccio adorning the side chapels. The crucifix in the chapel of Isotta has been attributed to Giotto and the walls of the Reliquary Chapel are adorned by a magnificent and indulgent fresco of *Sigismondo praying at the Feet of St Sigsmondo*, painted in 1451 by Piero della Francesca.

Beaches

① *Rimini's beaches are signposted from the bus and train stations.*

Riccione and Cattolica are the two main beach resorts, but the Italian concept of a beach is unlikely to coincide with that of most visitors. As elsewhere in Italy, the whole coast has been carved up into *bagni*, private beaches the size of postage stamps which attract varying degrees of snobbery according, it would seem, to the colour of the parasols and deckchairs. There are virtually no public places to enjoy. You will be sandwiched between

Fellini

Federico Fellini (1920-1993), the celebrated cinema director, is synonymous with Rimini, for it was his childhood home that influenced so much of his oeuvre. Indeed his formative years, between his birth in 1920 and his departure to Rome in 1939, became a rich seam of material in perhaps his most well-loved cinematic masterpiece *Amarcord* – meaning 'I remember' in Romagnolo dialect. The 1973 film introduces comic archetypes and dreamlike excursions from Fellini's fumbling 1930s adolescence in a pre-war Fascist-era town set to a wistful Nino Rota soundtrack. There are plenty of Fellini haunts to walk through in the town today that were reconstructed in the mind of the maestro and at the Cinecittà studios: **Piazza Cavour** is the centre of town life in the film where a peacock, the buxom Gradisca and locals come to play and display themselves; **Cinema Fulgor**, at 162 corso d'Augusto, is where Fellini sat wide-eyed on his father's lap watching his first film; the **Grand Hotel** is Fellini's place of child-like wonder and flights of fantasy (Fellini's suite is 316); and the **Borgo San Giuliano** quarter has vibrant murals dedicated to Fellini. **Fondazione Fellini** – based in the town – looks after the Fellini archive and organizes events and screenings. There have been plans to create a Museo Fellini in the town for quite a while.

other towels, quickly have sand kicked in your face by a nearby game of beach tennis, or be pestered by one of a sweltering army of watch/sponge/glasses/you-name-it vendors. That said, if you come to observe beach goers in an anthropological sense, you will have much to report.

Emilia-Romagna listings

For hotel and restaurant price codes and other relevant information, see pages 11-12.

⬤ Where to stay

Parks around Bologna *p61*
€€ Locanda La Comacina, via E Fogli 17-19, Comacchio, T0533-311547, www.lacomacina.it. Right on the Canale Maggiore, this tidy, affable hotel is in a very atmospheric part of town. Breakfast is served in the garden and is bountiful.

Parma *p63*
€€€ Palazzo della Rosa Prati, strada al Duomo 7, T0521-386429, www. palazzodellarosaprati.co.uk. Rather handsome apartments and bar right next to the Battistero.

€€ B&B Al Battistero d'Oro, strada sant'Anna 2, T0521-239369, www. albattisterodoro.it A popular B&B just a short walk from the Duomo. Understated elegance and a fresh feel with magisterial breakfasts.

€€ Hotel Relias Fontevivo, via Roma 1a, T051-610010, www.relaisfontevivo12 monaci.com. The staff of this simply designed, 17-roomed former monastery, are happy and helpful. It's just 20 km outside the city but has a really good restaurant so there's no need for back and forth.

Reggio Emilia *p65*
€€ Hotel Posta, piazza del Monte 2, T0522-432944. Right behind the city's Duomo, they offer big comfy beds, generous breakfasts and free bikes for guests.

Modena *p66*
€€€ Canalgrande, corso Calagrande 6, T059-217160 www.canalgrandehotel.it. Located in a 17th-century, neoclassical palazzo with marble column and frescoes, this hotel has an old style comfort and geniality.

€€ Hotel Cervetta, via Cervetta 5, T059 238447, www.hotelcervetta5.com. A centrally located, small but well-looked-after hotel, with decent-sized and nicely decorated bedrooms and public rooms. Staff offer great advice about Modena.

Ferrara *p68*
€€ Hotel Annunziata, piazza Repubblica 5, Ferrara, T0532-201111, www.annunziata. it. Modern hotel, bang in the middle of everything, with rooms not unlike those in Antonioni's Deserto Rosso.

Rimini *p71*
€€€€ Grand Hotel, parco Federico Fellini, T0541-56000, www.grandhotelrimini.com. For fans of the great Italian director Fellini there could be nowhere else to stay. Truly grand (and expensive) there must be nothing more romantic than to sit on the terrace and tipple as someone tinkles the ivories.

€€ Atmosphere Suite Hotel, viale Principe di Piemonte 41, T0541-478796, www. atmospheresuitehotel.it. Right on the waterfront, these clean, contemporary suits are good value for money if you are looking to stay a few nights.

⑦ Restaurants

Parma *p63*
€€€ Il Trovatore, via Affo, T0521-236905, www.iltrovatoreristorante.com. Closed Sun. Elegant and spacious, this restaurants serves up local specialities in style.

€€€ Parizzi, via della Repubblica 71, T0521-285952, www.ristoranteparizzi.it. Closed Mon. Always considered the best in town, offering a wide range of inventive and traditional dishes with impeccable service.

€ L'Antica Enoteca Osteria Fontana, strada Farini 24, T0521-286037. Closed Sun and Mon. Mythical among locals, this authentic piece of local tradition serves inexpensive dishes and sandwiches in an atmospheric setting.

Caffès
Cocconi, strada Repubblica 22, T0521-230351. An old bar still popular among Parmigiani.

Modena *p66*
€€€ Cucina del Museo, via Sant'Agostino 5, T059-217429. Closed Mon. A tiny gem in the old centre with only 6 tables but a big menu of creative traditional and experimental dishes. Book ahead.
€€€ Fini, piazzetta San Francesco, T059-223314, www.hotelfini.it. Closed Mon and Tue. For a long time the most renowned restaurant in town and still serving delicious food with impeccable service in a nice art nouveau setting.
€€ Da Enzo, via Coltellini, T059-225177. Closed Sun dinner and Mon. Modenese specialities – with generous lashings of asceto balsamico – in an old-fashioned setting.

Caffès
Caffè Concerto, piazza Grande 26, T059-222232. This brick walled and sleekly designed *caffè* is known for its coffee but they do a great, healthy buffet lunch for €15.50.
Caffetteria Drogheria Giusti, via Farini 75/vicolo Squallore 46, T059-222533. Just next to the **Hosteria Giusti** (also good) this has good bar snacks.

Ferrara *p68*
€€€ La Zanazara, via dei Tassi 25, near Volano Lido, Comacchio, T0553-355236, www.ristorantelazanzara.com. Closed Mon and Tue. You'll need to find it but when you do you'll be dining on the most inventively cooked fresh fish from the Po Delta. A delight at sunset.
€€€ Max, piazza della Repubblica 16, Ferrara, T0532-209309. Closed Mon. Popular with a young crowd. Relatively light food.
€€ Antica Osteria delle Volte, via delle Volte 37/a, T0532-762033. Closed Tue.

In the medieval heart of Ferrara, this is a rustic and reasonably priced option with a vibrant atmosphere.
€€ Don Giovanni, corso Ercole I d'Este, T0532-243363, www.ildongiovanni.com. Closed Sun dinner and Mon. They come here for the fish, the home-made bread and the wine (over 600 to choose from).

Caffès
Artelife Caffè, 1926, Piazza Repubblica 27, T0532-248641. Somewhere to keep going back to, be it for *caffè* and *cornetti* in the morning or *spritz* and *stuzzichini* at night.
Bar Ragno, via Cavour 1, Comacchio, T053381284. Even if you don't understand a word of the good-natured banter in this canal *caffè* it's a lively spot to have a break and even better come aperitivo time.

⚙ What to do

Apennines villages *p60*
Hiking
There are numerous trails mapped out in the hills with red triangles but it is best to obtain maps and the latest information from the tourist office or the CAI (Club Alpino Italiano), T051-234856 www.cai.it. The GEA (Grande Escursione Appenninica) is a 400-km trail mapped out in 1983 that traces the mountain range from Liguria to Le Marche of which you might want to walk a section. There are various mountain refuges at which to stop and eat or stay over. **Rifugio Citta di Sarzana**, T0522-431166, is on the GEA. The CAI has details of others. For information on the national parks around Bologna, see page 61.

Skiing
In places the Apennines reach heights of 2000 m, guaranteeing good snowfall in winter. For more information about skiing in Emilia-Romagna visit the **Skiing in the Apennines** pages at www.emiliaromagnaturismo.com. There are over 20 well-equipped resorts in all, of which the following are the best:

Corno alle Scale/Budiara/Val Carlina,
30 km of runs up to 1945 m altitude.
Downhill and cross-country skiing. 80 km
from Bologna, accessible by train to Porretta.
Fiumalbo/Monte Cimone, 16 km of runs,
downhill and cross-country. Take the train
to Pistoia.
Sestola, 20 km of runs, downhill and cross-
country. 67 km from Modena, accessible by
train to Porretta.

Rimini *p71*
Swimming
Acquafan, via Pistoia, Riccione, T0541-
603050 www.aquafan.it. Jun to mid-Sep
1000-1830. This is a swimming complex of
wave pools, children's pools, grassy areas
and kids' play areas. It turns into a loud
foamy, Euro disco at night. It's pricey though
(€28 for an adult). But then again, you have
to pay for the beaches at Rimini too.

Theme parks
Italia in Miniatura, via Popilia 239, Viserba
di Rimini, T0541-732004, www.italiain
miniatura.com. Check the website for
opening hours, which vary from season to
season. Adults €22 and over 1 m €16 (under
1 m go free). 16 km north of Rimini on
the SS16. This theme park shows pint-size
versions of all the famous sights of Italy from
piazza San Marco in Venice to the leaning
tower of Pisa. There are also go-karts, a
monorail and a Pinocchio ride.

Contents

Background

History

The first signs of human settlement date from around 1000 BC, when its favourable location – safe from flooding and along strategic trade routes – allowed a Villanovan civilization to thrive as food producers, potters and blacksmiths. In 650-450 BC these settlements came together to form Estruscan Felsina that excelled in visual arts, communication and commerce. The Gauls followed lending the name Bononia, before the Romans took over in 189 BC and connected the Via Emilia to its network of roads, making it a flourishing centre. In the fifth century AD, Christianity grew under Bishop Petronius, who built the first of the churches at Santo Stefano. As the Western Empire crumbled, the area was sacked by northern tribes: Visigoths, Huns, Goths and Lombards. Resisting Rome's advances, in the 11th and 12th centuries the Bolognesi seized some control over their city when a self-appointed council of nobles brought commercial and academic advances together and the university was founded, in 1088. Like many Italian cities, Bologna was ravaged by factional fighting between Guelphs (supporters of the pope) and Ghibellines (supporters of the Holy Roman Emperor).

Whilst the battles between Bologna and the papacy continued, there were power struggles within the commune as families vied for power. Yet it continued to prosper. Its remarkable waterways (long since filled up and covered over) helped it become a centre for hemp and silk production. Whilst these industries attracted great wealth, the university attracted great minds; Dante, Boccaccio and Petrarca are all alumni.

As wars and plagues raged, the city walls were built and strengthened in the hope it would keep the unwanted out. It succumbed to the Papacy in 1506 and in 1530 Charles V was crowned Holy Roman Emperor at piazza Maggiore. The city and its noble families – such as the Bentivoglio's – desire for building and adorning churches and palazzi led to Bologna's prominence in the art world. The Carracci family established a school of fine art and commissions came from all over Italy. It was these that delighted Napoleon when he rode into town in 1796.

Bologna became the capital of Napoleon's Cispadane Republic. Closing and sacking the monasteries and churches, he cut ties with the Vatican once more. But then came his Waterloo and Bologna became part of the Papal States after the Congress of Vienna in 1815. The Papacy's support of Austrian rule did not please bold Bologna; its involvement in the Risorgimento movement led by Garibaldi's red shirts and politically manipulated by Piedmont's canny statesman Cavour helped rout the Austrians out. Annexation to Turin and the Kingdom of Sardinia in 1859 followed, then, on the Unification of Italy, it was given regional capital status under King Emanuele II in 1862.

Contemporary Bologna

Innovation, liberal thought and rebellion – three characteristics linked by a common challenge to the status quo – have always characterized the spirit of Bologna and its citizens. Bologna was always a restless subject of popes, kings and ruling dynasties and its medieval history is littered with uprisings, overthrowings and general disobedience to attempted foreign authorities. The city's university, the first of its kind in Europe, was always an engine of enlightenment and discovery, from the first principles of European law and human rights to the invention of radio. And the Bolognese rejection of Mannerism, born of an innate pragmatism, founded one of the most influential schools of classical art. These three characteristics still manifest themselves today, in a different guise, running under the surface of modern life in Bologna and connecting the city to its past.

Bologna's position at the forefront of Italian technology continues to this day. Twinned with Coventry in the UK, it seems apposite that Bologna and its environs are sometimes referred to as *la terra delle moto* – the land of motorbikes – due to the concentration of car and motorbike factories located around the city. That's about as far as the comparison can stretch, however. Apart from the significant difference in architectural beauty between Bologna and its Midlands relative, the factories in question are none other than Ducati and, nearby, Ferrari, Lamborghini and Maserati.

Independent and specialist, these famous small and medium-sized companies are typical of the type of business to be found in Bologna and different from the cumbersome conglomerates further north. These industries have contributed to make Bologna and its surroundings one of the most affluent regions in the country, dubbed the 'Third Italy', between the industrial triangle in the north and the underdeveloped south.

Bologna is also known for its innovation in the field of fashion, and in particular *pronta moda*, or off-the-peg fashion. A quick glance in the clothes shops along via dell'Indipendenza will also reveal an experimental style for young and trendy Bolognese that's akin to London and a far cry from the rigidity of the V-neck jumpers, chinos and brogues that are de rigueur elsewhere in Italy. It is said that many of the designs that end up on the catwalks of Milan start out as experimental ideas in Bologna. Remember, you saw it first here.

Interestingly dressed young people need somewhere interesting to be seen. Bologna has converted many of its former industrial zones and warehouses, especially to the northwest, into some exciting new venues. Contrary to the profoundly conservative currents running through the country, Bologna has a renowned and well-organized gay scene, a further statement of its emancipated attitude. Funky bars and clubs are packed with Bologna's arty-camp population, mixing easily with straight revellers.

Many bars serve as stages for the city's abundant artists, combining eating and drinking with short film projections, exhibitions, performance art, music, theatre and dance spectacles. Bologna and Emilia-Romagna also have a long tradition of music: nearby Parma hosts opera productions to rank alongside those of La Scala or Verona, and Modena is birthplace of Luciano Pavarotti.

Nowadays the city is, by Italian standards, a centre for jazz, hosting many international line-ups in its clubs and providing a forum for newcomers. Rock music is alive and kicking in Bologna, too. Birthplace of Lucio Dalla and beloved of Italy's only real rocker, Vasco Rossi (born in Modena), the city is a stop on the tours of many international pop acts. In 2000 Bologna was nominated a European City of Culture and like a latter-day patriarch, the progressive city council is very active in its support of artistic initiatives. The lengths of via

Zamboni, the self-professed street of art, and via delle Belle Arti are plastered with posters announcing the latest events going on in the city, from raves to poetry recitals.

Named after a young rebel, via Zamboni is where so much of what's different and radical about Bologna is routed. In the first part of the 20th century Bologna began to lean heavily to the left. Despite coming from nearby Forli, Mussolini never got a grip of Bologna. In 1926 he was in Bologna seeking to show the strength of his ruling Fascist party. A 15-year-old anarchist, Anteo Zamboni, attempted to assassinate Il Duce but was lynched by watching fascists. Bologna honoured him by naming this main thoroughfare after him.

Bologna was a key focus of resistance and, after the end of the Second World War, as if in rebellion against the memory of its recent fascist occupation, Bologna became the centre of the Left in Italy. From that moment on, and particularly during Italy's dark years of terrorism in the 1970s and 80s, the city was a mouthpiece for criticism of a centre-right government that was accused by many, such as the journalist and film director Pier Paolo Pasolini, of creeping fascism. In 1977 Bologna's 70,000-strong student population took to the streets in a revolt that was their own local version of 1968. In 1980 the city became a target and received a vendetta from neo-fascist far-right terrorists in the form of a massive bomb attack on the station, which killed 80 people and wounded 200. After Perestroika and the fall of the Berlin Wall, the Communist Party lost its footing but managed to stay in office in Bologna until 1999 when a centre-left coalition ended 54 years of Communist rule in the city.

Things have changed a bit since those days of meaningful activism and anarchy. Nowadays, the long hair, the graffiti and the bicycles are still there, but Bologna's modern-day students could be accused of living the image of the artist-rebel without the belief and direction of their predecessors. Nor is the city these days considered such a bastion of protest. Today Bologna is a land of plenty and of epicurean pleasures. Despite other regions' claims, Bologna's cuisine is the best in Italy. Cultivated, prepared, served and consumed with great pride and sensual pleasure but minimum ritual, food and wine have been Bologna's real religion since the city's foundation. Over this time the Bolognese have invented a tongue-twisting delicatessen and oral orgy of pastas, meats, cheese and sauces, from lasagne, tagliatelle and tortellini to mortadella, to name just a few. And as they have invented them, so these dishes have passed into the region's tradition. Like all Italians, the Bolognesi are deeply conservative about their culinary traditions: they are sacred. Or are they? While today's chefs respect and vaunt their city's culinary heritage, they also perceive their vocation as a process of development, a moveable or at least evolving feast, ripe for innovation. We're not talking fusion of Japanese with Moroccan food here, but specialties of the house, with subtle and significant nuances on traditional themes. The famed spirit of innovation and experimentation is now expanding the territory of the city's gastronomic traditions. It may only be a rebellion in the kitchen but who knows what it may feed.

Contents

Footnotes

Language

In hotels and bigger restaurants, you'll usually find English is spoken. The further you go from the tourist centre, however, the more trouble you may have, unless you have at least a smattering of Italian.

When communicating in shops and restaurants stick to Italian. Stress in spoken Italian usually falls on the penultimate syllable. Italian has standard sounds and is the most phonetically true language: unlike English you can work out how it sounds from how it is written and vice versa.

Vowels

a like 'a' in cat
e like 'e' in vet, or slightly more open, like eh (except after c or g, see consonants below)
i like 'i' in sip (except after c or g, see below)
o like 'o' in fox
u like 'ou' in soup

Consonants

Generally consonants sound the same as in English, though 'e' and 'i' after 'c' or 'g' make them soft (a 'ch' or a 'j' sound) and are silent themselves, whereas 'h' makes them hard (a 'k' or 'g' sound), the opposite to English. So *ciao* is pronounced 'chaow', but *chiesa* (church) is pronounced 'kee-ay-sa'.

The combination 'gli' is pronounced like the 'lli' in million, and 'gn' like 'ny' in Tanya.

Basics

thank you	*grazie*	goodnight	*buonanotte*
hi/goodbye	*ciao* (informal)	goodbye	*arrivederci*
good day		please	*per favore*
(until after lunch/		I'm sorry	*mi dispiace*
mid-afternoon)	*buongiorno*	excuse me	*permesso*
good evening		yes	*si*
(after lunch)	*buonasera*	no	*no*

Numbers

1	uno	17	diciassette
2	due	18	diciotto
3	tre	19	diciannove
4	quattro	20	venti
5	cinque	21	ventuno
6	sei	22	ventidue
7	sette	30	trenta
8	otto	40	quaranta
9	nove	50	cinquanta
10	dieci	60	sessanta
11	undici	70	settanta
12	dodici	80	ottanta
13	tredici	90	novanta
14	quattordici	100	cento
15	quindici	200	due cento
16	sedici	1000	mille

Questions

how?	come?	where?	dove?
how much?	quanto?	why?	perché?
when?	quando?	what?	che cosa?

Problems

I don't understand	non capisco
I don't know	non lo so
I don't speak Italian	non parlo italiano
How do you say ... (in Italian)?	come si dice ... (in italiano)?
Is there anyone who speaks English?	c'è qualcuno che parla inglese?

Shopping

I don't understand	non capisco
I don't know	non lo so
I don't speak Italian	non parlo italiano
How do you say ... (in Italian)?	come si dice ... (in italiano)?
Is there anyone who speaks English?	c'è qualcuno che parla inglese?

Travelling

one ticket for...	un biglietto per...
single	solo andata
return	andata e ritorno
does this go to Como?	questo va a Como?
airport	aeroporto
bus stop	fermata
train	treno
car	macchina
taxi	tassi

Hotels

a double/single room	una camera doppia/singola
a double bed	un letto matrimoniale
bathroom	bagno
Is there a view?	c'è un bel panorama?
can I see the room?	posso vedere la camera?
when is breakfast?	a che ora è la colazione?
can I have the key?	posso avere la chiave?

Time

morning	mattina
afternoon	pomeriggio
evening	sera
night	notte
soon	presto/fra poco
later	più tardi
what time is it?	che ore sono?
today/tomorrow/yesterday	oggi/domani/ieri

Days

Monday	lunedi
Tuesday	martedi
Wednesday	mercoledi
Thursday	giovedi
Friday	venerdi
Saturday	sabato
Sunday	domenica

Conversation

alright	*va bene*
right then	*allora*
who knows!	*bo!/chi sa*
good luck!	*in bocca al lupo!*
	(literally, 'in the mouth of the wolf')
one moment	*un attimo*
hello (when answering a phone)	*pronto* (literally, 'ready')
let's go!	*andiamo!*
enough/stop	*basta!*
give up!	*dai!*
I like ...	*mi piace ...*
how's it going?	*come va?*
(well, thanks)	*(bene, grazie)*
how are you?	*come sta/stai?* (polite/informal)

Menu reader

General

affumicato smoked
al sangue rare
alla griglia grilled
antipasto starter/appetizer
aperto/chiuso open/closed
arrosto roasted
ben cotto well done
bollito boiled
brodo broth
caldo hot
cameriere/cameriera waiter/waitress
conto the bill
contorni side dishes
coperto cover charge
coppa/cono cone/cup
cotto cooked
cottura media medium

crudo raw
degustazione tasting menu of several dishes
dolce dessert
fatto in casa home-made
forno a legna wood-fired oven
freddo cold
fresco fresh, uncooked
fritto fried
menu turistico tourist menu
piccante spicy
prenotazione reservation
primo first course
ripieno a stuffing or something that is stuffed
secondo second course
tortelloni/tortellini pasta parcels with meat, cheese or pumpkin filling (tortellini is the smaller)

Drinks (*bevande*)

acqua naturale/gassata/frizzante
still/sparkling water
aperitivo drinks taken before dinner,
often served with free snacks
bicchiere glass
birra beer
birra alla spina draught beer
bottiglia bottle

caffè coffee (ie espresso)
caffè macchiato/ristretto espresso with a
dash of foamed milk/strong
spremuta freshly squeezed fruit juice
stuzzichini snacks served at the bar with
aperitivi
succo juice
vino bianco/rosato/rosso white/rosé/red wine

Fruit (*frutta*) and vegetables (*legumi*)

agrumi citrus fruits
amarena sour cherry
arancia orange
carciofio globe artichoke
castagne chestnuts
cipolle onions
cocomero water melon
contorno side dish, usually grilled vegetables or oven-baked potatoes
fichi figs
finocchio fennel
fragole strawberries
frutta fresca fresh fruit
funghi mushroom
lamponi raspberries
melagrana pomegranate
melanzana eggplant/aubergine

melone light coloured melon
mele apples
noci/nocciole walnuts/hazelnuts
patate potatoes, which can be *arroste* (roast), *fritte* (fried), *novelle* (new), *pure' di* (mashed)
patatine fritte chips
peperoncino chilli pepper
peperone peppers
pesche peaches
piselli peas
pomodoro tomato
rucola rocket
sciurilli or *fiorilli* tempura courgette flowers
spinaci spinach
verdure vegetables
zucca pumpkin

Meat (*carne*)

affettati misti mixed cured meat
agnello lamb
bistecca beef steak
bollito misto beef/veal stew
braciola chop, steak or slice of meat
carpaccio finely sliced raw meat (usually beef)
cinghiale boar
coda alla vaccinara oxtail
coniglio rabbit
cotechino fatty pork sausage, eaten with lentils at Christmas and New Year
involtini thinly sliced meat, rolled and stuffed
mortadella fat-studded Bolognese pork sausage
manzo beef
Parma ham dried, cured ham

pollo chicken
polpette meatballs
polpettone meat loaf
porchetta roasted whole suckling pig
prosciutto ham – *cotto* cooked, *crudo* cured
salsicce pork sausage
salumi cured meats, usually served mixed (*salumi misto*) on a wooden platter
speck a type of cured, smoked ham
spiedini meat pieces grilled on a skewer
stufato meat stew
trippa tripe
vitello veal
zampone a pork stuffed pig's trotter from Modena, eaten with lentils at Christmas or New Year

Fish (*pesce*) and seafood (*frutti di mare*)

acciughe anchovies
aragosta lobster
baccalà salt cod
bottarga mullet-roe
branzino sea bass
calamari squid
cozze mussels
frittura di mare/frittura di paranza small fish, squid and shellfish lightly covered with flour and fried
frutti di mare seafood
gamberi shrimps/prawns
grigliata mista di pesce mixed grilled fish

orata gilt-head/sea bream
ostriche oysters
pesce spada swordfish
polpo octopus
sarde, sardine sardines
seppia cuttlefish
sogliola sole
spigola bass
stoccafisso stockfish
tonno tuna
triglia red mullet
trota trout
vongole clams

Dessert (*dolce*)

cornetto sweet croissant
crema custard
dolce dessert
gelato ice cream
granita flavoured crushed ice
panettone type of fruit bread eaten at Christmas

semifreddo a partially frozen dessert
sorbetto sorbet
tiramisù rich 'pick-me-up' dessert
torta cake
zabaglione whipped egg yolks flavoured with Marsala wine
zuppa inglese English-style trifle

Other

aceto balsamico balsamic vinegar, usually from Modena
arborio type of rice used to make risotto
burro butter
calzone pizza dough rolled with the chef's choice of filling and then baked
casatiello lard bread
fagioli white beans
formaggi misti mixed cheese plate
formaggio cheese
frittata omelette
insalata salad
latte milk
lenticchie lentils

mandorla almond
miele honey
olio oil
polenta cornmeal
pane bread
pane-integrale brown bread
pinoli pine nuts
provola cheese, sometimes with a smoky flavour
ragù a meaty sauce or ragout
riso rice
salsa sauce
sugo sauce or gravy
zuppa soup

Architectural glossary

aedicule frame around a doorway or window comprised of columns or pilasters and an entablature on top, typical of Classical and Gothic architecture; could be a mini decorative structure housing a statue.

arcade row of columns that support arches.

architrave lower part of an entablature, which meets the capitals of the columns.

baldachin canopy over a tomb, supported by columns.

campanile bell tower.

capital top or 'crown' of a column, often adorned with scrolls (Ionic) or acanthus leaves (Corinthian).

cloister open covered passage around a courtyard (usually part of a church or monastery), supported by columns or arches.

columns the Greek order of columns include Doric, plain with vertical grooves called fluting; Ionic, characterized by scrolls; and Corinthian, with a bell-shaped capital, often adorned with acanthus leaves and volutes. The Roman's Tuscan order are without decoration, while the Composite order was a mishmash of the three Grecian orders.

choir chancel of a church, used by the clergy and choir, occasionally separated from the nave by a screen.

colonnade series of columns.

cornice horizontal ledge or moulding. For practical purposes it's a gutter, draining water off the building, or a decorative feature if purely aesthetic.

cupola dome on a roof.

entablature held up by columns, the entablature includes the architrave, frieze and cornice.

frieze centre of an entablature; often decorated.

loggia open ground floor gallery, recessed gallery, or corridor on the façade of a building.

nave central body of the church, between the aisles.

narthex long porch along the entrance of a church, before the nave.

pilaster rectangular column that only slightly protrudes from a wall.

pinnacle small, often ornate, turret, popular in Gothic architecture.

plinth lower part or base of a column.

portico doorway, often roofed, serving as an entrance (real or decorative) to a building.

sacristy room off the main or side altars in a church or a separate building housing sacred vessels, vestments and records.

tracery ornamental stonework that supports the glass in Gothic windows.

Index

Notes

Notes

Notes

· THE PITKIN GUIDE ·

EVACUEES
OF THE SECOND WORLD WAR

Chris McNab

Despite its first shots being fired more than 70 years ago, the Second World War continues to hold a central place in Britain's cultural memory. It is not difficult to find reasons why. Not only were millions of men pulled from their regular lives into the armed forces, to serve at home and abroad, but death also came to British shores directly, in the form of German bombing. Although the nation had experienced some aerial bombing in the previous world war, that which threatened Britain in 1939 was unprecedented, and the British government sought new means to protect its citizens, and especially its children. One of the results was the mass, voluntary evacuation of children from those cities deemed to be major targets for the Luftwaffe. In their hundreds of thousands, children left their homes, and usually their parents, to be housed with families in safer parts of the country.

The evacuation policy was intensely emotional, breeding the heartache of sudden, then prolonged, separation. Yet while some unfortunate children experienced misery – and even cruelty – in their new homes, others discovered adventures beyond their familiar streets: some went from poverty to affluence, for example, or from grimy urban conditions to rolling open countryside. Limited numbers even found themselves evacuated abroad, to destinations such as Canada and South Africa. In different ways, evacuation broadened the horizons of thousands of young people.

More than 2.5 million children, and countless families, coped both practically and emotionally with evacuation in the Second World War. The story can be unsettling, not least because any parent can sense the anxiety of being separated from his or her child. Such is why evacuation history still resonates today.

Edward Read

Between 1915 and 1918, during the First World War, Britain experienced first hand an entirely new form of warfare – strategic bombing. Here was military action directly against the British infrastructure – its towns, cities, factories and citizens – rather than against its armed forces, made possible by rapid developments in aviation. Zeppelin airships, and later fixed-wing bombers, attacked towns and cities from Dover to Edinburgh (although the main focus was on London), killing 1,413 civilians. Although the death toll was slight compared to the slaughter that unfolded on Europe's battlefields, it illustrated that in future wars civilians would be as much a target as servicemen.

Evacuation policy was born of fear. During the 1920s and 30s, bomber aircraft ranges and destructive capabilities increased, and in 1931 a government committee report predicted that in the first day of a future war Britain would suffer

▲ *A family emerges from their Anderson shelter (named after the politician John Anderson who initiated their development) to view the wreckage of their home. The actual experience of German bombing in 1940 reinforced the message of evacuation.*

60,000 dead and 120,000 wounded, and similar casualties every week thereafter. The dreadful German bombing of Spanish cities during the Spanish Civil War (1936–39) seemed to confirm the doomsayers' message.

Protecting the populace

Discussions about reducing civilian casualties by evacuating people from target areas began in earnest with the formation of the Air Raid Precautions (ARP) Committee of the British Home Office in 1924. Various ideas stirred, including wild suggestions such as evacuating the entire population of London to the country in one massive overnight exodus. More practically, a committee report in 1925 argued that evacuation could be focused on specific social groups, principally those not deemed essential to war work – women, children, the elderly and people with disabilities.

ARP debate slackened somewhat during the later 1920s, but re-ignited in the 1930s as international politics grew more tense, especially with the military threat posed by rising National Socialism in

► *Sir John Anderson (seen here outside 10 Downing Street) was in charge of air-raid preparations and evacuation policy in 1939. Anderson served as Home Secretary from 4 September 1939, and later as Chancellor of the Exchequer.*

◄ *A War Reserve policeman erects a sign to warn people of the dangers from air raids and shelling. The early weeks of the war brought considerable anxiety to the British population, who were uncertain about the possible effects of German strategic bombing.*

▼ *Families, neighbours and ARP wardens view the damage to houses after an air raid on London. As a principal target for enemy bombings, the capital, as well as many other major cities, was designated a key 'evacuation area'.*

Germany, under its leader Adolf Hitler. In 1938, with war clouds darkening the horizon, a report was issued by the so-called Anderson Committee, chaired by Sir John Anderson and charged with looking at how the country could respond to prolonged, destructive aerial bombardment. The report laid out the foundations of a wartime evacuation policy. Essentially, it recommended the evacuation to safer locales – typically rural communities – of schoolchildren, mothers with infants and the elderly. The scheme would be voluntary, but would be vigorously encouraged. Billeting, however, would be compulsory and provided by private individuals in their own homes, with financial assistance from the government.

This proposal, plus incorporation of another plan designed specifically by the London County Council (LCC), coalesced into an official government Evacuation Scheme from November 1938. It was one of the most radical works of social engineering ever conceived. In 1939, moreover, the government would get to see if it worked.

The threat from above

On 10 November 1932, the Lord President of the Council and Chairman of the Committee of Imperial Defence (and future Prime Minister), Stanley Baldwin, made an influential speech to the House of Commons that heightened the fear of aerial bombing: 'I think it is well also for the man in the street to realize that there is no power on earth that can protect him from being bombed ... The only defence is in offence, which means that you have got to kill more women and children more quickly than the enemy if you want to save yourselves. I mention that so that people may realize what is waiting for them when the next war comes.'

A Great Upheaval

The first real-life test of government evacuation policy came a full year before the outbreak of war. The 'Munich Crisis' of September 1938, in which Germany demanded its incorporation of the Sudetenland areas of Czechoslovakia, prompted fears of an imminent European war. On 26 September, emergency measures to evacuate more than 630,000 children from London and other major cities were announced on the radio. Chaos ensued as thousands of anxious parents overwhelmed the administrative system with their queries and preparations. In the end, the threat appeared to recede following British Prime Minister Neville Chamberlain's 'Munich Agreement' with Germany, and ultimately only 4,000 children were actually evacuated at that time.

Galvanized by direct evidence of the difficulties of evacuation, the government set about reorganizing the policy. The UK was divided into three types of area: 'Evacuation Areas' – principal targets for enemy bombing, such as major towns and cities and military bases; 'Neutral Areas' – places that would neither send nor receive evacuees; and

▲ *British Prime Minister Neville Chamberlain signs the Munich Agreement in September 1938 in Munich, ceding the Czech Sudetenland to Germany. The agreement did not, as hoped, bring peace – Germany invaded Czechoslovakia in March 1939, and Poland the following September.*

➤ *This evacuation notice was typical of those published during Operation 'Pied Piper' in 1939, as the British government prepared the country's children for the start of the evacuation to safer 'reception areas'.*

EVACUATION

DETAILS OF FACILITIES ARRANGED FOR

(1) OFFICIAL PARTIES
(TO BILLETS PROVIDED BY THE GOVERNMENT)

Evacuation is available for

SCHOOL CHILDREN
MOTHERS with CHILDREN of School Age or under
EXPECTANT MOTHERS

(2) ASSISTED PRIVATE EVACUATION

A free travel voucher and billeting allowance are provided for

CHILDREN OF SCHOOL AGE or under
MOTHERS with CHILDREN OF SCHOOL AGE OR UNDER
EXPECTANT MOTHERS
AGED and BLIND PEOPLE
INFIRM and INVALIDS

who have made their own arrangements with relatives or friends for accommodation in a safer area

★ FOR INFORMATION ASK AT THE NEAREST SCHOOL

MOTHERS
Send them out of London

Give them a chance of greater safety and health

◄ *Evacuation publicity was both persuasive and somewhat intimidating. The scheme was voluntary and many parents were understandably reluctant to take part, as they could not accompany their children and had little idea where they would end up.*

'Reception Areas' – supposedly safe communities, typically in rural or remote coastal regions, that would take evacuees for billeting. Evacuees themselves were split into four categories: 1) school-age children; 2) blind and disabled people; 3) pregnant women; 4) mothers with babies or pre-school children (mother and child would be evacuated together). Although the evacuation scheme remained voluntary, unnerving poster campaigns suggested that keeping the children in harm's way was moral dereliction. Furthermore, apart from in Scotland (where children would be evacuated with their mothers), children were to be evacuated in entire schools along with their teachers, thereby applying pressure to keep children with their friends.

Following a mass registration of both evacuees and billeting accommodation, Britain appeared ready for the worst.

Operation 'Pied Piper'

In the summer of 1939, British evacuation preparations gained new urgency. A leaflet explaining the practicalities of evacuation – *Evacuation: Why and How?* – was distributed in July, and the following month teachers were recalled from their summer holidays. Rehearsals took place across the country.

Then, on 31 August, the government issued an evacuation order for the next day, actually the day on which Germany would invade Poland and the Second World War would begin. Thus children began assembling in their schools early on the morning of 1 September, and Operation 'Pied Piper', as it was aptly known, began in earnest.

It was an epic logistical challenge. London alone had 1,589 assembly points, and trains ran out of the capital's main stations every nine minutes for nine hours (although most children boarded evacuation trains at their local stations). Some children in London were even evacuated by ship from the River Thames, sailing to the east-coast ports of Great Yarmouth, Lowestoft and Felixstowe. Other evacuation areas included Birmingham, Leeds, Liverpool, Rochester, Southampton and Middlesbrough.

It was a frantic experience, but between 1 and 4 September (Britain officially declared war on 3 September), up to 3.5 million children and adults were evacuated. These figures included around 2.5 million mothers, children and other adults who were evacuated privately rather than as part of the government scheme. But they also included nearly 800,000 unaccompanied school-age children, who now faced the greatest challenge of their young lives.

▲ *Ealing Broadway train station is packed with evacuees awaiting transportation during Operation 'Pied Piper', 2 September 1939. Teachers and other evacuation assistants try to order the children, and would accompany their charges to the final destination.*

5

Despite a number of inefficiencies, Operation 'Pied Piper' largely achieved what the British government had set out to do. Hundreds of thousands of children were now away from the apparent danger areas in towns and cities, although the numbers were still not as large as the government had hoped to achieve. Also the reception areas were struggling to cope, and in many cases the volume of new arrivals exceeded the availability of bed space. Allocation systems crumbled, and billeting officers had to work tirelessly to find the children accommodation, frequently against the active resistance of local people, many of whom objected to the idea of taking a child into their homes. Assistance in dealing with the children at the reception areas was often handled by Evacuation Committees, formed from members of the Women's Voluntary Service (WVS) and Women's Institutes, and with help from the Girl Guides and Boy Scouts.

New evacuations

Now the nation waited for the war to begin in earnest. Yet the rush of evacuation was followed

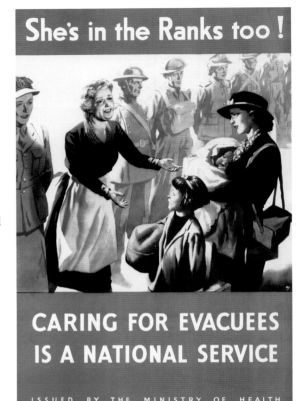

A government poster, issued by the Ministry of Health, emphasizes the fact that acting as a foster parent is a form of war service, on a par with soldiering and serving in the ATS (depicted by the woman on the left).

▲ A mother is reunited with her children in late 1939. Many evacuees had returned home by this time, as the perceived threat to Britain had not seemed to materialize during the 'Phoney War'.

by about seven months of the 'Phoney War', as it was known, in which there was actually little direct military threat to Britain. As fears diminished, therefore, many evacuees began to go home. In London, for example, some 34 per cent of evacuated schoolchildren had returned by January 1940, forcing many previously emptied schools to reopen and begin teaching again. In some places the percentage of returnees was far higher – 79 per cent in Dundee, for example. The government was not enthusiastic about the reverse migration. In February 1940 it attempted to implement a new large wave of evacuations,

Time to leave

Peter Holloway was four years old when the war began. He was evacuated in September 1939, along with his ten-year-old brother, then returned to London before the experience of the Blitz changed his parents' minds again:

'That night my father appeared as if by magic and after an earnest discussion which was incomprehensible to me, my parents made arrangements for us to join a party of evacuees to Waterloo. We were given a number and a group to join but no fixed destination. Our train was due to depart later that week, but we had to go to Waterloo in readiness for immediate departure should it be necessary. A few days later we were crammed into a compartment and locked in to avoid the possibility of children trying to leave the train.'

▲ *A Ministry of Health poster reminds parents that bringing their children back from the safety of evacuation is playing into Hitler's hands. Parents were also warned that they might have difficulty re-sending their children to safety should the need arise.*

including signed parental commitments not to bring children back until the entire school returned. The campaign was not a success, partly because by the spring of 1940 many children were still not registered for evacuation.

The situation changed from May 1940, when Hitler began his successful conquest of mainland Western Europe. By late June, France had surrendered, and Germany was only separated from Britain by the English Channel. The Royal Air Force (RAF) victory in the Battle of Britain put paid to German ambitions to invade the UK, but from the autumn of 1940 the night-bombing of British cities – 'the Blitz' – began, and ran until May 1941. Cities such as London, Coventry, Swansea, Plymouth and Sheffield were pounded mercilessly, and evacuation became a policy grounded in reality.

Unlike the mass evacuation of September 1939, those of 1940 were steadier and more controlled. Children who had been evacuated to coastal areas in southern and south-eastern England were moved again due to the threat of invasion, and during May–June an additional 160,000 children were taken out of London. The total reached about 250,000 by August.

The so-called 'trickle' evacuation continued until the end of 1941. Not all parents let their

children go, even in the most bomb-hit areas, but many now saw the sense of evacuation – some 43,000 civilians were killed in the Blitz, and approximately one in eight deaths was that of a child. It was undeniable that those away from the cities were safer.

▲ *A group of siblings undergo an evacuation rehearsal at Friar Street School in Southwark, London. During evacuation itself, it often proved difficult to billet large family units together.*

Tearful Goodbyes

Evacuation day was, for both children and parents, a day of conflicting and painful emotions. Prior to evacuation, parents already had a list of the things each child should have for the journey ahead. This list, from a Ministry of Health memo, included: 'child's gas mask, a change of underclothing, night clothes, house shoes or plimsolls, spare stockings or socks, a toothbrush, a comb, towel, soap and face cloth, handkerchiefs; and, if possible, a warm coat or mackintosh.' For many of the poorer families, paying for these items meant further financial hardship, but teachers noted that most made the sacrifice.

The days leading up to evacuation were riddled with uncertainty, as former London evacuee James Roffey remembers: 'We had to go to school every morning, ready to be evacuated. Now nobody could say when that was going to be. Parents didn't know where we were going to be taken ... they had no idea.' James went home every day with a letter saying 'No evacuation today', until 1 September 1939 'when something different happened'.

First separation

The arrival of the evacuation notice brought feverish preparations at home and school. Worried mothers scrabbled around to ensure that their children were as prepared as possible,

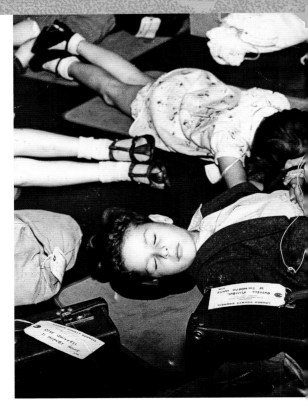

with all the required items in a bag or suitcase, plus some food for the journey (the government recommended foods such as cheese, fruit, barley sugar and sandwiches). The children were then taken down to the school, where teachers attached a luggage label to each child, on which was written the child's name, school and evacuation authority. Teachers and WVS personnel would be the children's typical travelling companions, and leaflets handed out for the teachers provided details of the specific reception areas to which they were heading, and with which children. The parents would not find out where their children had gone until several days after evacuation, notification coming via a postcard through the mail.

◄ *A typical evacuee's belongings: the small suitcase includes many of the Ministry of Health's recommendations, but also touching personal items, such as family photos and a favourite teddy bear, to comfort the child being sent away.*

◀ *Preparing for evacuation: a bird's-eye view of a group of evacuees sleeping soundly on their classroom floor amongst their travel cases and gas-mask boxes.*

▼ *A policeman oversees an evacuation of children in Fulham, London. Police officers also served the purpose of trying to keep over-emotional mothers away from their children during the evacuation process.*

Watching them go

Head teacher Judith Grunfeld remembers the evacuation of children from her school in Stoke Newington on 1 September 1939:
'Outside in the street the mothers were crowding; they shed tears, they waved and sent their loving, encouraging smiles. They did not make a scene, they just looked and prayed inwardly; they were as if stunned. But to see so many children marching together looked comforting, after all. The teachers appeared young and disciplined and many of them applied cheerful discipline with a smile.'

The initial separation was a heart-rending moment for both mothers and children. There were many tears, but the children often testified to initial excitement, as if the outing was the beginning of a school trip or similar adventure. Eventually they arrived at the bus or train station, where they began the first major journey of their evacuation.

▼ *Most of the published images of evacuees leaving home were upbeat, as the government wanted a positive image to be portrayed to the public. Many children were excited at the forthcoming 'adventure', but their parents were often devastated, staying cheerful for the sake of their children.*

The initial preparations complete, the children often then marched in crocodile fashion from the school to the transportation assembly points, typically train stations, underground stations, bus depots or even taxi ranks. (Sometimes transport was laid on to take the children to the assembly area.) It was not unknown for parents to snatch back their children at the last minute, so the police tended to keep relatives literally at a distance, the anxious adults either walking behind the children or following them from across the road. Sometimes parents simply waved goodbye from outside their own homes, and watched their children disappear from view to a destination unknown.

On the Move

◄ *Regular transport
schedules out of
London were thrown
off kilter during
times of evacuation.
Alternative transport
services were arranged
where possible,
but the enormous
amounts of traffic
meant that normal
London life was
hugely disrupted.*

▲ *Schoolchildren and their teachers wait at Hammersmith
Station in London for a train to evacuate them to the
countryside. Train carriages were often cramped and
unhygienic, and the journeys could last for many hours as
the train lines were so crowded.*

The evacuation of large numbers of children
and other citizens in September 1939
posed a huge logistical headache for road
and rail authorities. An article in *The News of
the World*, dated 3 September 1939, explained:
'The greatest exodus in human history began
soon after daybreak from most of the big cities
of the country. Virtually all public travel facilities
– trains, tubes, trams, buses and motor-coaches
– were monopolized. In London, hundreds of
thousands of children teemed into empty trains
at 72 Underground stations and all the main
line termini.'

The mainline rail network was particularly
hard-pressed, moving 1.3 million children in
just three days. Between 1 and 4 September, the
Great Western Railway alone took just under
114,000 evacuees from London to the West
Country, running 163 evacuation trains in the
process. A total of 64 trains heading out from
Birmingham on 1 and 2 September transported
22,379 evacuees to Gloucestershire and Wales.
The roads were similarly clogged with buses
and private traffic, and many workers found
it a serious issue getting into work at all. For
example, nine major roads into London were
designated as one-way only, and given over
entirely to outbound evacuation traffic. For
many city employees, the only practical solution
was to set off for work during the middle of the
night, and wait outside a factory or office until
it opened in the morning.

▲ *A group of London children board an evacuation bus. Although trains transported thousands of evacuees, buses, trams and motor-coaches were also used to cope with the sheer numbers leaving the capital.*

Anxious journeys

The journeys themselves were often an ordeal for the evacuees, particularly by rail. At the train stations, children were frequently crammed into shabby third-class carriages – 12 children in compartments designed for eight – with no toilet facilities, and on journeys lasting many hours. Evacuee James Roffey remembers: 'We got to the station and it was already packed – they were another two schools already there ... This train came in, and oh, it was a dirty, scruffy old-fashioned train ... No corridor, so therefore no toilets. They crammed us into these little compartments, slammed the door shut, and that was it.' James, along with his sister and brother, then had a four-hour journey to Pulborough in West Sussex, but given the chaos on the rail lines and the more distant locations, some journeys took as much as 12 hours.

The issue of toilet facilities became a serious one, as many children either wet themselves or were forced to urinate from train windows. (The problem was exacerbated by kindly groups of women providing the children with drinks at stops along the way.) With lesson learned,

▲ *Drinks are given to evacuees about to depart from London in 1940. Efforts were made by tens of thousands of volunteers to ensure the children were as comfortable as possible for their journey.*

during the 1940 evacuations crude on-train toilet facilities were provided in the form of buckets surrounded on three sides by canvas walls.

Eventually the evacuee's journey would come to an end at the reception area. Now, at the station or bus stop, each child would meet the local welcoming party, and the real evacuee experience would begin.

11

Finding a Home

▲ Arriving at their destinations could be an unnerving experience for the evacuees, as the uncertainty of what was to come took hold. They were usually taken to public buildings such as village halls, where a billeting officer oversaw their allocation to foster families.

The billeting of evacuees was compulsory, and those who refused to take children when they had surplus accommodation could be prosecuted, although few were. The responsibility for housing the evacuees fell to the billeting officer, who had the thankless job of imposing hundreds of children on often unwilling citizens. Sometimes the numbers of arrivals far exceeded expectations. On the Isle of Anglesey, for example, the Welsh community planned for 625 evacuees at the beginning of September; in the event, 2,468 children were deposited upon the doubtless shocked billeting officers.

For the evacuees, the arrival at their final destination was often the point when the sense of adventure wore off and anxiety set in. James Roffey remembered that on his arrival in Pulborough, the children were temporarily kept in cattle pens, so they did not get lost: 'Some of the older boys decided they had had enough. They saw a sign, "London – 52 miles", so they set off, they were going to walk home. The police had to go after them and bring them back again.' The children were eventually bussed to a nearby school, where the local women had laid on a spread of tasty food – James noted that not a single child touched anything, as nerves quashed hunger.

▲ Apprehensive children await collection by their foster families. A carefully pre-planned billeting procedure often fell apart in places where there were far too many children and far too few foster homes.

Unwelcome visitors

Although compulsory, fostering was not without recompense. For taking in one unaccompanied child, a foster carer would receive 10s 6d (53p; equivalent to £26 today) per week, or 8s 6d (43p) per week per child if more than one was taken. Additional emergency rations were also allocated to each foster household on the child's arrival.

Despite the financial compensation, many people were clearly dismayed at having to find space for a stranger. In some cases the billeting officer would already have a list of children and designated foster parents, but often the allocation process descended into a crude selection, gathered

Lined up and counted

Hazel Brown, evacuated to Kent at the age of 13 with her two sisters, remembers the process of being billeted: 'Once again we were lined up and counted and marched off through a village street to a village hall. A committee of local ladies under a billeting officer was waiting. Starting with the youngest and then with families, our names were called out and we were allocated to a household. As we left the hall to walk away we were given a tin of condensed milk and a tin of corned beef to be passed on to the foster mothers. I had never eaten corned beef before ... Elinor, Gwen and I were the last and it was dusk. Finally a voice said "I'll take them".'

◄ *A group of evacuated children arrive at their new home. Foster families received financial compensation for taking in evacuees, payments that were critical in poorer communities.*

▼ *This idyllic picture shows children being welcomed at their billet in Campsea Ash in Norfolk during late 1939. Apparently, locals here refused to call the youngsters 'evacuees' and instead chose to refer to them as 'our little holidaymakers'.*

fosterers simply pointing at a child and saying, 'I'll have that one.' In this process, many children were overlooked in favour of prettier or more respectable-looking rivals (girls were especially favoured), their sense of separation from home growing every time they were passed over. Brothers and sisters were frequently split up, sometimes having to be separated physically in a rough manner. This occurred to James Roffey, whose sister protested strongly to keep the three siblings together, but in the end 'they forcibly dragged brother John away from her. She was absolutely distraught ....'

Many adults flatly refused to take in children, despite being threatened with legal action. Nevertheless thousands of other adults did indeed open their doors to the youngsters, who then stepped into a new life a long way away from home.

Settling In

The homes in which foster children found themselves were as varied as the British people themselves. Len Townsend was evacuated at the age of nine from Bethnal Green in London to Pakenham, a village in rural Suffolk, on 1 September 1939. 'Me and my brother were waiting for someone to come and collect us. Eventually a nice car turned up, and we were told that this gentleman was going to take us to his home – he was the chauffeur for a landed estate here called Nether Hall, and we were going to stay with him and his wife.' Thus young Len and his brother moved into country opulence.

Although some people were even evacuated to Chartwell, Winston Churchill's property in Kent, it is one of the great myths that most evacuees went into homes of comfort and affluence. Rural Britain in the 1930s and 1940s had as much poverty as its urban equivalent, and thousands of the evacuees went into tough environments. James Roffey and his sister were driven out to 'a real old-fashioned, tumbledown country cottage ...', where the lady owner at first shouted that she was not going to take any evacuees and slammed

▲ *A nurse and several child evacuees explore the grounds of their new home at Tapley Park, north Devon. Some city children were plunged into a wealthy world they had never experienced, and their childhood conditions actually improved, despite the upheaval they experienced.*

Sweet duties

James Roffey, once billeted in a sweet shop, was faced with temptation all around him:
'I must have been looking rather intently at all these bars of chocolate and jars of sweets and everything. The man who was to be my foster father looked at me and put on his stern voice and said, "Well look, you must never ever help yourself. But if you are a good boy, and you do all the jobs that I give you to do, I will give you a penny worth of sweets every day." Well in those days you would probably get about 12 toffees for that, or a little bar of chocolate ... They kept chickens ... and it was my job to feed the chickens, clean out the chicken houses, carry the water to them.'

the door in their faces. Only with threats from the billeting officer did she finally relent. 'The cottage itself had no flush toilets, no piped water, no gas, no electricity, just oil lamps. They took me down the garden to a little shed – there was a bucket with a plank over it – that was the lavatory.' James and his sister spent two weeks living in these rough surroundings before being moved back into the main village to a far more conducive home – a local sweet shop and a more modern house.

Making room

Evacuees were not the only ones who had to do a lot of psychological and physical adjustment.

▲ Young schoolboys collect their mugs, which are hanging from a shed wall, before going in to dinner. Many farms had to utilize any spare space they had to house and feed the newly arrived children.

◄ Not all evacuees were lucky in their billet. Many children had to share rooms with the family's children in cramped, noisy environments. This family of seven took several evacuees into an already crowded home.

Foster carers themselves had to make significant sacrifices. Prior to the evacuation, houses in reception areas had been rigorously vetted by local billeting officers, who recorded each home's accommodation capacity. Even though the evacuees were sent to houses where there was believed to be surplus space, many families still struggled to adapt to the newcomers. Children already at the address might find themselves suddenly sharing their bedrooms with complete strangers, or having to move into their parents' bedrooms. Evacuee Len Townsend and his brother were eventually sent to live at the local vicarage, but were largely kept separate from the family, living in the maids' quarters instead.

A large number of evacuees were mothers with pre-school children. Female foster parents often resented having another woman around the house, particularly one with very different approaches to housework and childcare. Conversely, some evacuee mothers found themselves used as little more than unpaid domestic servants in large houses. Although evacuation was meant to show the best of British character, the process of billeting was not always entirely charitable.

▼ Children were often housed wherever room was found, such as this caravan in the grounds of a farm. For some it was a great adventure, especially if they were billeted with their mothers.

New Adventures

While there was undeniably a darker side to the whole evacuation experience (see pages 18–19), there was also the chance for thousands of children to encounter an entirely different way of life. The extent of urban ignorance of country ways can be exaggerated, but there was no doubt that many children found much wonder in their new environments. Peter Holloway, a four-year-old evacuee, was sent with his brother from Millwall in east London to Angmering-on-Sea in Sussex, where they were selected for billeting by 'a very pretty young woman' called Miss Grant, who drove them away in a car. 'She turned the car into a long straight road, at the end of which was a pebbly beach and my first sight of the sea ... No one ever forgets

▲ *A party of children from London get to meet a local resident of Longhope, Gloucestershire, during their evacuation – Freddie the tame fox. For many children, evacuation brought their first experience of nature outside the city.*

Witness to a final salute

'We were walking along the road to Epworth one day when three planes flew overhead, one of them crashed, and the pilot baled out, but he fell into a tree and was killed. The other planes flew on but one came back, and as he flew over the dead pilot he dipped his wings in salute.'

JEAN REED, EVACUATED WITH HER MOTHER AND BABY SISTER FROM HULL TO BELTON, LINCOLNSHIRE, WHERE THEY STAYED WITH THE VICAR, MR ROSS

their first sight of the sea – water and sky that seem to go on forever ... Half a mile away was our new home. It was an enormous private estate called "The Thatches" ... During the following weeks we grew accustomed to the grandiose style of living ....'

Learning experience

Children sent to agricultural areas often had the opportunity to learn first hand about the practicalities of country life. Not only could they go exploring through open fields, along winding streams and into sunlit woodlands – a new experience in itself if they had grown up in the inner city – but many were put to work on the land. Jobs performed by evacuees included feeding livestock, mucking out stables, assisting blacksmiths, bringing in the harvest and taking produce to market. For some the experience was transformative, and many stayed

◄ *Two young boys from London enjoy the spectacular Lake District views during their evacuation. Despite tranquil surroundings, some evacuees still witnessed air raids or dogfights, especially over the southern English countryside during the Battle of Britain in 1940.*

◄ Children help the farmer bring in the harvest. Evacuees often learned a useful set of agricultural skills, and many returned to the land to work when they grew to be adults.

in agricultural work once they reached school-leaving age at 14, at which point they were no longer classed as an evacuee. As a local government employment authority in Liverpool noted: 'Slowly, and almost solely as a natural development of the evacuation scheme, boys are beginning to see that when they reach school-leaving age, work on a farm will help the country fight its war, as well as furnishing them with healthy, interesting employment.'

Ironically, although the evacuation areas were meant to be safer than the cities, during the Battle of Britain (July–October 1940) the evacuees in rural south-eastern England witnessed aerial dogfights at close hand in the glorious summer skies above them. There was danger involved here – it was not uncommon for German fighters to strafe villages and roads

▲ Evacuees were given jobs to help their billeted families, especially from those whose own sons or farm hands had gone off to fight the war. Here we see boys from London feeding pigs on a farm in Pembrokeshire in 1940.

– and there were fatalities. For youngsters who remember these times, however, the memories are more ones of excitement than fear.

Battle of Britain memory

'We'd be setting off for school and over us would come the Messerschmitts [German Bf 109 fighter aircraft] machine gunning. And the bullets would be rattling down on the road, but none of us were hit, fortunately. Local adults told us that when this happens "Slow down and throw yourself in the ditch by the side of the road" – well every ditch that I saw was full of water and there was no way I was going in there. The aircraft were so low you could see the pilots' faces ... It was all quite exciting for a boy.'

JAMES ROFFEY, ON WITNESSING THE BATTLE OF BRITAIN FROM RURAL PULBOROUGH, SUSSEX

A Bitter Separation

Former evacuees often have entertaining stories to recount about their time away, but some will also acknowledge the mental pain of separation from parents. Homesickness was acute in most children, and James Roffey explained that most evacuees 'if they were honest ... cried themselves to sleep at night'. This was even a problem in the most pleasant of homes. Irene Weller, separated from her evacuated brothers, was billeted with a kind old couple with no children of their own. 'The woman showed me to my room and it was the first time I'd ever slept in a room of my own. But soon the pillow was wringing wet because I just sobbed and sobbed ....'

Night-time incontinence became a particular problem amongst evacuees, often brought on by sheer anxiety and fear of the unfamiliar. In the days before a real understanding of involuntary bedwetting, many children were punished harshly by their foster carers. Historian Juliet

➤ *Evacuation could be undeniably traumatic. The act of separation from families, homes and everything familiar deeply upset many evacuees, especially if they were unfortunate enough to be billeted with unwelcoming families.*

Gardiner found that punishments included 'beating them, rubbing their noses in the soiled bedding, making small children wash their wet sheets, and even in one case chaining a small Liverpool evacuee outside in a dog kennel for the night'. Incurable bedwetters could end up being sent away from their foster homes to special council hostels. There they might be housed alongside children with behavioural difficulties, or who were aggressive or disturbed.

Cruelty cases

Unfortunately, cases of evacuee children being either neglected or deliberately abused are far from uncommon, although thankfully this constituted a minority of experiences. Sometimes the evacuee was treated as little more than a source of additional income and free labour. On other occasions children could become prey to physical or sexual abuse at the hands of cruel or predatory foster parents. There were cases of children being deprived of food and kept in cages, while their 'guardian' enjoyed the child's extra rations on their own plate. David Prest, an

◄ *A nursemaid settles several evacuees on camp beds in the conservatory of a large country house in Cheltenham, Gloucestershire. Despite the best efforts of many people, conditions in billets were often cramped and uncomfortable, reinforcing the child's sense of separation from home.*

▼ *A young evacuee sits alone on a mine washed up on the beach at Deal in Kent in 1940.*

A different view

Tempered with the appalling experiences of some evacuees is this story from Nina, aged 10 when evacuated with her twin sister and elder brother from Balham, London:

'We arrived at Datchet [Kent] in the afternoon and it was such a beautiful village ... I immediately fell in love with the feel and sounds of the countryside. [Our host was] the Lady of the Manor who had sent her retired nanny to collect us ... Nanny and her sister took care of us in her farm cottage. They were lovely warm people who made us feel wanted and loved. In London we never even had a window box – just imagine how we loved the freedom to roam the green fields and help with feeding the hens, collecting eggs, pick fruit, shell peas and rake the summer hay. In the evenings we all sat in the kitchen listening to the radio, read books and played games ... our evenings were full of laughter and fun.'

In balance, it must always be remembered that many evacuees encountered kindness and gentle treatment from their new guardians. Some were welcomed almost as sons and daughters, loved and protected throughout the duration of their stay, and much missed when they finally went home.

▼ *Many foster parents were patriotic individuals, and proud to help wartime evacuees. 'Grannie' Norris, pictured here with six evacuated children, was awarded the British Empire Medal (BEM) for her care of many London evacuees.*

historian of the evacuation, interviewed 450 ex-evacuees, 12 per cent of whom reported some form of what we today classify as child abuse. The legacy of such treatment plus the sheer misery of homesickness were lasting mental problems in a significant minority of former evacuees.

Sometimes what amounted to cruelty was simply the by-product of being placed into rural poverty. One evacuee, Eleanor Smith, observed that many girls were sent to ramshackle cottages where they slept three to a bed, being bitten by bedbugs and unable to wash properly for months.

Town and Country

The evacuation brought town and country together in a way that was previously inconceivable. Literally overnight, a mass of urban children descended upon rural communities, bringing with them all the ways of city life. It was a recipe for a profound clash of cultures.

One of the immediate issues raised by the evacuation was medical in nature. In near-hysterical voices, the inhabitants of many reception areas announced that the city evacuees were riddled with transferrable medical problems. Head lice was the biggest complaint, with some medical officers reporting that up to 35 per cent of the arrivals had nits and lice, with a resulting rise in infections amongst local people. Other imports for which the evacuees were blamed included ringworm, scarlet fever, diphtheria and impetigo.

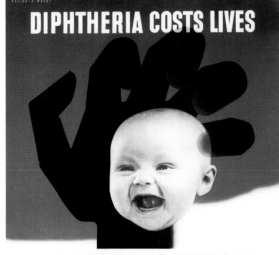

DIPHTHERIA COSTS LIVES

IMMUNISATION COSTS NOTHING

Ask at your local council offices, school or welfare centre

ISSUED BY THE MINISTRY OF HEALTH

▲ *Many Ministry of Health posters were issued during evacuation periods, as concerns about health problems and poor diets of city children were rife. Common medical worries included diphtheria, as shown in this poster.*

◄ *Evacuees were given a rudimentary health assessment on arrival at their reception area, which included head-lice checks. Lice were a big problem for children who were forced into cramped, dirty surroundings for prolonged periods of times.*

Certainly, medical assessment of evacuees was very poor in the early years of war. It often consisted of little more than a cursory comb-through with lice-killing chemicals by a nurse on arrival at the reception area. Eventually the government implemented more thorough medical assessments before the children left the evacuation areas. Yet the concern over urban illnesses was part of a more general rural shock at urban character. There were complaints that the children were dirty; that they did not know how to use a knife and fork, or a toilet; that they used terrible language; that they were thieves. A Dr Kerr published a letter in the *British Medical Journal* that stated: 'I do not think it is using language any too strong to say that in many cases the scum of the town has been poured into a clean countryside with a most callous disregard for the consequences and apparently with the most elementary safeguards for the public health.'

▲ City children evacuated to Surry line up for a dose of medicine. Doctors would try to check as many children as possible before billeting, especially if they were ill, but the sheer volume of young people in some areas made this impossible, so prevention was better than cure.

Sour grapes

The word 'scum' speaks more about snobbery than genuine concerns. There were undoubtedly clashes in culture, and many urban children could be difficult to control. Yet often those complainers with the shrillest voices were simply looking for excuses not to have children billeted on them, or to have a child removed from their home. Many of the medical problems highlighted were present in the countryside before evacuation, particularly in the poorer areas. Unfamiliar regional diets often confused evacuees, which led to accusations that they could not eat properly. Foster parent Mrs Cook, who looked after two evacuees, Iris and Betty, recalled: 'The first week one of the girls refused her Sunday dinner and when I asked what was wrong said, "I want my Sunday dinner." Questioned as to what her Sunday dinner usually comprised, the answer came, "Tatters, ham and beer!".'

➤ A Ministry of Health food chart explains the rules of a healthy diet. For evacuees, differences in urban and country diets often caused problems, resulting in clashes between the children and their new families.

A fact often overlooked was that a high percentage of children evacuated were from middle- and even upper-class homes. Being billeted in a humble rural cottage was as much a shock to the system as a poor city boy being housed in a mansion. Evacuees also had to adjust to local dialects or, in the case of children evacuated to Wales, communities speaking an entirely different language. That they could adapt well is illustrated by the fact that in 1942 two boys from Liverpool won a Welsh poetry-reading competition at the National Eisteddfod. Evacuation was a huge social shake up, and it required understanding and resilience on both sides to make it work.

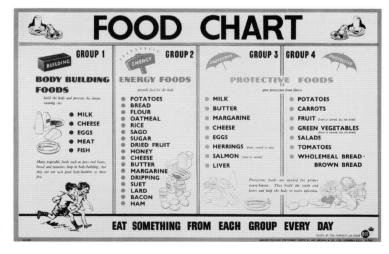

Written from the Heart

➤ *Evacuated children eagerly await the local postman for letters or parcels from home. Often, parents found it too expensive or emotionally draining to travel to see their children, so the post was the only way of communicating.*

E vacuation could be a long business. Evacuee Gordon Abbott was away from his London home for five years in total, during which time his mother visited his new north Cornwall home just once. The frequency and viability of parental visits often depended on the nature of the parents' employment, and also on where the child was billeted in the country. Rail travel was expensive for poor families, even with the introduction of concessionary tickets in November 1939, and fuel rationing limited car and bus journeys.

Another problem of parental visits was that they could re-ignite the flame of separation when the mother or father had to return home. Evacuee Irene Weller was visited by her mother and sister on one occasion, but later explained: 'It was traumatic and though I had wanted them to come so much, it was dreadful when it was time for them to go. Terrible. I had to tear my brothers away. It was awful and my Mother said, "I shall never come back again."'

Finding the words

Letter-writing was one way of handling the emotional pain. Historical and personal archives have bequeathed thousands of evacuee letters. Many are simple, poignant descriptions of a new life. Mary Adams, a 13-year-old evacuated with her sister Avril in 1941, wrote: 'I am quite well and I hope you are. We had a very nice journey here and for the first night slept in the school. Then on Wednesday we came here. The lady is quite kind to us and the house is clean. We have a room between us and sleep together in the same bed.' Others were more emotional in tone. Gordon Muer wrote to his parents about his older brother: 'Kenneth was still crying a long time after you had gone ....' Many ex-evacuees later admitted that they often kept their sorrows out of their letters, to avoid upsetting their parents unduly.

One worrying issue for parents was that of letters becoming less frequent as the evacuee settled into their new life, and home began to seem more

My Dear Mum and Dad I hope you are safe and well. We had a half-holiday on Tuesday afternoon because it was Pancake Day I like Gnosall. I came in the bus with Mrs Tagg. She says there is room for my dolls pram if you can send it for me please. I Know a lot of children in Gnosall School all in my Class from Ramsgate love from Sheila xxxxxxxxxxxxx

Infants School
Gnosall Stafford
Feb 1941

▲ *Letters from their children provided an emotional lifeline for many parents. Sheila from Ramsgate in Kent seems to have settled well at Gnosall in Staffordshire, despite missing her doll's pram.*

A letter home

'Life in the country impresses me as being very peaceful. One can sit in a field under a shady tree in complete quietness except for the singing of the birds and the rustle of the swaying boughs overhead. In the country there is not the smoky atmosphere of the city and it is much pleasanter to walk in fields with cows mooing and grazing on each side, than to walk along a grey dirty looking street, with litter thrown about the ground, and smoky houses for surroundings. It is lovely to wake up in the morning to feel the cool keen fresh air on one's face. In the autumn it is such fun to gather in the harvests and it is interesting to see the trees changing into their autumn dresses.'

FROM A LETTER WRITTEN BY ELLEN HOWARD, 13

distant. Sometimes children could be brutally blunt. Alison Sutherland was evacuated to South Africa at the age of eight, and was so enthralled with her new surroundings that in October 1940 she wrote: 'I hope you are looking after yourselves and keeping the Jerry away from our house because I almost forget about them when I am playing … I am enjoying myself very much here and we've decided that we're not going home so if you want to see us you'll have to come out here.'

▲ *A happy scene of evacuees from Deptford, London, playing in a lake in Pembrokeshire, supervised by their teacher, who was evacuated with them.*

▲ *An evacuee's self-portrait: complete with label and gas mask case, it shows clearly how traumatic the experience of evacuation could be for children, who were yet more victims of the war and its disruptive effects.*

Schooling Lively Minds

The migration of children to the countryside shook up many aspects of British society, and schooling was not spared. Being voluntary, evacuation meant that thousands of children still remained at home in the cities, despite the fact that most of their schoolmates and teachers had gone to safer places. The evacuated school would take with it many ancillary benefits, such as school meals and the healthcare provided by the school nurse.

The result was that by the spring of 1940 about 5 per cent of secondary school children and 10 per cent of primary school children in evacuation areas in England and Wales received no education at all, while only 30 per cent of primary-age children received full-time education. In Scotland, 36 per cent of children had only

▲ *In addition to regular subjects, children were drilled in wartime survival skills such as fitting their gas masks. They would sometimes study with their gas masks on to get used to wearing them.*

part-time education. There was a consequent increase in juvenile crime, as purposeless children found new ways to pass their time.

Improvised education

There was schooling for the evacuees, although the demands placed on the system meant the quality of education could be erratic. Class sizes might be enormous as evacuated schools and local schools combined. One solution was to split the school day, with local children being taught for half the day, and evacuees for the other half. Finding premises was an acute problem, with every available space being requisitioned, including village halls, barns and even open fields. An alternative was the School Camps, 31 of which were constructed between 1939 and 1941. These were large, wood-built school complexes, each housing and teaching thousands of children. The education there included an emphasis on

▲ *Schooling large numbers of evacuees could be a problem. Here the steps outside a converted hospital-school in Kent serve as an improvised classroom.*

Air-raid drills

Even in the countryside or in coastal towns, children often had to practise air-raid drills as part of their daily routine. This could be a straightforward gas-mask drill, the children donning their gas masks when given the command, and sometimes sitting at their desks and working whilst wearing their respirators. At other times the drill would involve leaving the classroom for shelters outside. Many rural schools had inadequate shelter arrangements, which might consist of trenches dug in nearby fields or, if lucky, concrete dugouts. The actual threat was very limited compared to the cities, however. One young evacuee, Dorothy King, finished a letter to her mother with these reassuring words: 'P.S. – I have not been hit by a bomb yet. P.P.S. – I have not been gassed yet.'

▲ *Temporary classrooms were often set up in spaces outdoors, even if this meant carrying large amounts of equipment outside for the duration of the lesson. Here girls from St George's Church of England School in Battersea, London, have an open-air sewing class in Pembrokeshire.*

practical skills, such as keeping livestock and managing a house.

Another problem of wartime education was finding enough teachers, and of reasonable calibre. With thousands of teachers taken out of the system by military service and war work, and country schools overloaded with children, many retired teachers were pulled back into service, or new tutors were drawn in from local women. Teacher quality could be uncertain, as evacuee John Matthews remembers: 'It was the worst school I had ever attended. The entire staff had joined up and their places were taken by a weird bunch of elderly men and women, none of whom had any experience. My teacher looked like a gipsy. He had a mass of untidy, black hair and two large gold earrings. He told us that he had worked before the war in a circus, and kept us amused with tales of lion taming and acrobats.'

There is no doubt that many wartime children had a disrupted or inadequate education, facing challenges ranging from poor-quality tutors through to a lack of pencils and exercise books. Yet in the very process of evacuation, many received a broader education, learning new skills that would serve them well after the war.

▲ *Across Britain, children had to adjust to air-raid drills as part of their daily lives. The drills for evacuees varied depending on their destination, and shelter facilities ranged from sandbagged underground shelters, like the one seen here, to crude trenches.*

To Distant Lands

Although the overwhelming majority of evacuees were distributed around the British Isles, a small but significant number ventured much farther afield. In 1940, when the threat of a German invasion seemed very real, the British government decided to take advantage of the safety offered by its dominions. Some more affluent families had already sent their children abroad privately, being able to pay the considerable fares. In June 1940, however, the government established the Children's Overseas Reception Board (CORB), to provide the means for overseas evacuation to the less well off. CORB's stated purpose was 'To consider offers from overseas to house and care for children, whether accompanied, from the European war zone, residing in Great Britain, including children orphaned by the war and to make recommendations thereon'.

▲ *The oppulent Guggenheim estate in Long Island, New York, became home to many British evacuees. These children were brought over from England on the ship* Samaria.

Seavacuees

The primary destinations for CORB evacuations were Canada, Australia, New Zealand and South Africa. When CORB opened up its service to the public, it received a flood of applications. Partly this was to do with another exercise in unnerving publicity, with press advertisements stating that overseas evacuation would guarantee children 'growing up safe from Nazi bombers'. The financial arrangements also made sense for many – the child's passage would be paid by the government (unless the child was at a fee-paying school), and maintenance payments would be the same as for British evacuees. In less than a month, CORB received 211,448 applications.

◄ *British evacuees aboard a ship in New York harbour. Wealthier families often sent their children abroad privately, but the government CORB programme opened overseas evacuation to those less well off.*

Evacuated to Britain

During the war, Britain itself received large numbers of overseas evacuees (as opposed to refugees from war-torn Europe). In June 1940, 29,000 Channel Islanders – principally children and mothers with pre-school infants – were evacuated to mainland Britain in expectation of their islands falling to the Germans. The islands were indeed occupied on 1 July, meaning that the evacuees were entirely cut off from their families for the duration of the European war, which ended in May 1945. In 1940 and 1941, Britain also took in 12,000 evacuees from Gibraltar; a further 2,000 Gibraltarians went to Jamaica and a small number to Madeira.

▲ *A memorial statue in Gibraltar commemorates the evacuation. Many of their children were sent to the safer shores of England when the war expanded into the Mediterranean in 1940.*

Ultimately only 2,664 children would actually become 'seavacuees', as they were known. They were transported to their new lives via 16 voyages between 21 July and 20 September 1940. The majority – 1,532 children – went to Canada, with Australia, South Africa and New Zealand being the other destinations, in descending order of popularity. A further 24,000 applications were approved, but on 17 September 1940 an event occurred that brought CORB's efforts to an abrupt close. A 'seavacuee' ship, the SS *City of Benares*, sailing from Liverpool to Canada, was torpedoed and sunk by a German U-boat in the Atlantic. A total of 77 of the 90 CORB children on board were killed, in addition to 181 other people (including six CORB escorts). As the U-boat war intensified, it became evident that the seas could be more dangerous than the land, and the CORB programme ceased in early October.

Those who did make it abroad faced the same challenges as all evacuees. Yet some discovered lives of great adventure. Alison Sutherland, the evacuee who found herself in South Africa (see page 23), wrote in October 1940: 'I suppose that you know that I have arrived at uncle's place and that I'm having a jolly good time. Tony the baboon died because he was overfed but there is still Jacko and Caus left. Caus is a baboon as well. I go in the lake every morning before breakfast and before dinner and another one at four in the afternoon. Yesterday we went for a walk with uncle and the monkeys.' It was evident that for some children, the war brought wider horizons.

◄ *Sadly, not all 'seavacuees' reached their destination safely. The SS* City of Benares, *pictured, was sunk on its way to Canada, resulting in the deaths of 77 children.*

Those Who Stayed

Evacuation had one overriding purpose – to get the children out of harm's way. It was not just a matter of altruism. Having experienced a lengthy world war in recent memory, the British government was all too aware that the child of the present might reach conscription or employment age with the current conflict still raging. One ex-evacuee's perhaps cynical view of evacuation is that it protected the pool of future soldiers and workers.

To judge the value of evacuation, however, it is worth looking at the experience of those children who remained with their parents in the danger zones. Children who lived through the Blitz in the cities were undoubtedly in peril. At 17 years old, Florence Rollinson remembered emerging from her London air-raid shelter after one particular raid: 'It had been three hours of continuous bombing: it all seemed totally unreal to us ... When we finally came out of the shelter the sky was red everywhere and there was an awful smell, which dad said was cordite from explosives – a smell which was to become very familiar to us. Living as we did so near to the docks, which were obviously the target, we were right in the firing line.'

Reluctant to go

For thousands of city children, many nights were spent hunkering down in various shelters, be they the London Underground system, Anderson shelters in the garden, deep cellars, or even caves and forests on the outskirts of the city, to which they would travel in the early evening. Yet despite the destruction that rained down, the numbers of children evacuated as a response to Blitz bombing decreased, many parents being unsettled by the earlier experience of evacuation. Thus while 20,500 children left London in September 1940, only 766 did so in December.

It must also be remembered that the war could visit places previously deemed safe. Brian McNab (the father of the author and a child himself during the war) received an evacuee into his house on Thornes Road, Wakefield, early in the conflict, the evacuee probably originating in Leeds. Yet on 14 March 1941, two bombs were released by a lone, lost German bomber and fell on Thornes

▲ *Four children sit outside their wrecked homes the morning after an air raid and try to take comfort from their toys. Families had to weigh up the options of risking losing their children to German bombers or sending them away.*

Life in the Underground shelters

'From the platforms to the entrance, the whole station was one incumbent mass of humanity. Even in the darkened booking hall I stumbled across huddled bodies, bodies which were no safer from bombs than if they had lain in the gutters of the silent streets outside. Little girls and boys lay across their parents' bodies because there was no room on the stairs. Hundreds of men and women were partially undressed, while small boys and girls slumbered absolutely naked. Electric lights blazed, but most of this mass of sleeping humanity slept as though they were between silken sheets.'

BRITISH NEWSPAPER ARTICLE, SEPTEMBER 1940

◄ *Firemen carry stunned children from shattered homes and shelters following a German bombing raid. Regardless of the frequent attacks and appalling risks, the number of children being evacuated out of London began to slow down in late 1940.*

➤ *A family made homeless after their house was destroyed seek refuge in a barn for the night. The baby is asleep in the manger on the wall. Despite the tragic loss of their home, they were lucky to be alive.*

▲ *Although living with the threat of bombing, these women in the maternity wing of a hospital air-raid shelter appear relaxed. Note the babies sleeping on the shelf above the women's heads.*

Road, killing six civilians, including two children. As such episodes proved, in a time of war no one's safety could be guaranteed.

By the time the Second World War ended, total casualty figures for British children under 16 were 7,736 killed and a similar number seriously injured. These are appalling figures, but they need to be put into context. The US firebombing of Tokyo on 9–10 March 1945 killed at least 100,000 civilians, including 30,000 children, in a single raid, and tens of thousands of German children also died during the Allied strategic bombing campaign. While these tragedies had their own unique conditions, we do get a sense that British evacuation saved at least hundreds, if not thousands, of young lives.

The Last Evacuees

Even after the Blitz ended in the spring of 1941, danger remained over Britain. Air attacks continued sporadically and with varying intensity through 1942 and 1943, and in the 'Little Blitz' on London in January–May 1944, bringing tragedy in their wake to seemingly safe communities. On 29 September 1942, for example, 28 children and two teachers were killed in the small town of Petworth, West Sussex, after their school was hit by three bombs from a lone German aircraft. And as if to prove that the capital was still no safer, 38 children were killed in another school bombing on 20 January 1943 in Catford, London.

In 1944, however, came an entirely new form of threat, in the form of Hitler's V-1 flying bombs and V-2 ballistic missiles, launched from bases in occupied Europe. Some 8,938 civilians were killed and 24,505 seriously injured by these weapons. Although they failed to alter the course of the war, they did cause a sharp drop in morale in southern England during the last months of the conflict.

Thus began Operation 'Rivulet', the final major evacuation of the war. It ran between July and September 1944, and was the last gasp of the evacuation era – more than a million people were moved out of the danger zones. Yet evacuation as a policy was now drawing to a close. The Allied advance through occupied Europe had, by the end of September 1944, all but removed the threat of German conventional aerial bombing, and further advances largely pushed the V-weapons out of range of the British mainland (although parts of Britain would remain classified as danger areas until the very end of the war). The rationale for evacuation was now essentially gone.

▲ A foster mother says a heartfelt goodbye to the children she had billeted. Many foster carers grew very attached to their evacuees during the course of the war and treated them as if they were their own children.

◄ A scene of devastation after a V-2 rocket fell on Smithfield Market, London, in 1945. The remote attacks from V-1 and V-2 missiles kept evacuation relevant until the very last months of the war.

▲ *Some evacuees learned a trade in their time away from home, like this young cobbler. Many older evacuees preferred to remain with their new families, perhaps apprenticed to the family businesses. Others went to war themselves.*

Coming home

Although the evacuation scheme finally ended on 31 March 1946, the programme in Britain was officially suspended on 7 September 1944. By this time, of course, hundreds of thousands of evacuees had returned home to their families, unless the war had tragically snatched those families away. Their return was a testing time for all parties. Many evacuees, some four or five years older than when they had left, found that they were more in tune with the world they left behind than with their former homes. Accents, outlooks, appearances and preferences had changed. Children who had been in affluent households had to go back to bomb-damaged terraced houses and low incomes, while those who had been sent overseas to sunnier climes suddenly found British weather appalling.

Some evacuees never went back. Older children evacuated in 1939 often reached school-leaving age before the end of the war, and found work and put down roots in the reception areas.

▼ *Parents are reunited with their children during a temporary visit to a reception area. Visits by parents to see their children in the country often became less frequent as the war went on. Some children literally did not see their parents for several years.*

▲ *Girls evacuated to the United States return home to England. They went away as school children, but returned as young ladies. Here they are seen putting on make-up before disembarking from the ship.*

Many boys even went into uniform and fought during the final months of the war. Evacuation had reshaped an entire generation of youth, and many parents scarcely recognized their sons and daughters when they returned home.

Memories

The memories that former evacuees carried with them into the post-war years varied from individual to individual. Some remembered bright summer days in the country. Others had sad mental images of anxious moments aboard an old, cramped train, heading to destinations unknown. Some went to kind, loving foster carers, who virtually became proxy parents, while others lived in fear of cruel and resentful guardians.

Ex-evacuees often have mixed emotions about their wartime experience. Many of them suffered deeply from initial homesickness, but they adapted in the rapid way only children can, and made the best of their new lives. Hence memories of sad times often sit alongside those of humorous events or half-forgotten adventures.

Evacuees, no less than any other group of society affected by the war, made a very real sacrifice. They gave up home and family for long, uncertain years, and in the process had to face mental and physical demands that would challenge many adults. They received no official acknowledgement for this sacrifice after the war, although in 1946, those who had billeted evacuees were given a certificate of recognition from The Queen. That situation is being remedied

8th June, 1946

TO-DAY, AS WE CELEBRATE VICTORY, I send this personal message to you and all other boys and girls at school. For you have shared in the hardships and dangers of a total war and you have shared no less in the triumph of the Allied Nations.

I know you will always feel proud to belong to a country which was capable of such supreme effort; proud, too, of parents and elder brothers and sisters who by their courage, endurance and enterprise brought victory. May these qualities be yours as you grow up and join in the common effort to establish among the nations of the world unity and peace.

George R.I.

▲ *This certificate from King George VI, dated 8 June 1946, thanked the children of Britain. It was issued as a memento of their hardships and sacrifices during the war, and to commemorate Britain's ultimate triumph.*

somewhat by organizations such as the Evacuees Reunion Association (ERA), and also through the study of evacuees in school education programmes. From the perspective of modern times, however, it is interesting to consider whether today's society could cope with a similar upheaval.

Acknowledgements

Written by Chris McNab. The author has asserted his moral rights.
Edited by Gill Knappett.
Designed by Jemma Cox.
Picture research by Jan Kean.

Photographs are reproduced by kind permission of: Alamy: IBC (Victor Watts), 10t 12tl 17tl 22 28tr 29cr 31cr below (Trinity Mirror/Mirrorpix), 27tr (John Norman); Getty Images: FC, 2 both, 3 both, 4tr, 5, 6bl, 7br, 9 both, 11 both, 12tr, 13 both, 15 all, 16 both, 18 both, 19 both, 21tl, 24 both, 28bl, 29bl, 30bl, 31tl & cr above; Imperial War Museum: BC, 4cr & bl, 6tr, 7tr, 14, 17cr, 20 both, 21br, 23bl, 25tr, 27bl, 30cr; Mary Evans Picture Library: 26 both (Robert Hunt Collection), 32 (Tom Gillmor);Rex Features: 8/9, 10cl, 25br.

Quotes reproduced as follows: p7 (Peter Holloway), p13 (Hazel Brown) and p18 (Irene Weller) from Juliet Gardiner's *The Children's War* (Piatkus Books, an imprint of Little, Brown Group, 2005); p9 (Judith Grunfeld) from John Welshman's *Churchill's Children: The Evacuee Experience in Wartime Britain* (Oxford University Press, 2010); p16 (Jean Reed) and p22 (Mary Adams) from www.bbc.co.uk/ww2peopleswar/stories;p19 (Nina) from http://timewitnesses.org/evacuees; p21 (Mrs Cook) by

permission of Eton Wick History Group www.etonwickhistory.co.uk/warevacuees.html; p23 (Ellen Howard) from www.nationalarchives.gov.uk; pp23 and 27 (Alison Sutherland), p25 (John Matthews) © Imperial War Museum, from www.telegraph.co.uk.

Every effort has been made to contact copyright holders; the publisher will be pleased to rectify any omissions in future editions.

Thanks to Terry Charman, Senior Historian at the Imperial War Museum, for reading the text and for his expert advice. The author would also like to acknowledge the kind help of the Evacuees Reunion Association (ERA – http://www.evacuees.org.uk/) in researching this publication. Particular thanks to Karen Follows for arranging interviews with ex-evacuees James Roffey, Len Townsend and Gordon Abbott; sincere gratitude is expressed for their fascinating memories.

Text © Pitkin Publishing.

Publication in this form © Pitkin Publishing 2012.
No part of this publication may be reproduced by any means without the permission of Pitkin Publishing and the copyright holders.

Printed in China
ISBN: 1-978-1-84165-376-1   1/12